GSG 9: FROM MUNICH TO MOGADISHU

GSG 9: FROM MUNICH TO MOGADISHU

The Birth of Germany's Counterterrorism Force

MARTIN HERZOG

CASEMATE
Pennsylvania & Yorkshire

Published in the United States of America and Great Britain in 2025 by
CASEMATE PUBLISHERS
1950 Lawrence Road, Havertown, PA 19083, USA
and
47 Church Street, Barnsley, S70 2AS, UK

This edition is based on the author's book *GSG 9: Ein deutscher Mythos*, first published by Christoph Links Verlag in 2022. It has been substantially revised, amended, and updated by the author for publication in English.

English-language edition © 2025 Martin Herzog
Martin Herzog has asserted their right to be identified as author of the work.

Hardcover Edition: ISBN 978-1-63624-572-0
Digital Edition: ISBN 978-1-63624-573-7

A CIP record for this book is available from the British Library

All rights reserved. No part of this book may be reproduced or transmitted in any form or by any means, electronic or mechanical including photocopying, recording or by any information storage and retrieval system, without permission from the publisher in writing.

Printed and bound in the United Kingdom by CPI Group (UK) Ltd, Croydon, CR0 4YY
Typeset in India by DiTech Publishing Services

For a complete list of Casemate titles, please contact:

CASEMATE PUBLISHERS (US)
Telephone (610) 853-9131
Fax (610) 853-9146
Email: casemate@casematepublishers.com
www.casematepublishers.com

CASEMATE PUBLISHERS (UK)
Telephone (0)1226 734350
Email: casemate@casemateuk.com
www.casemateuk.com

Front cover image: GSG 9 recruitment poster from the 1970s. (Bundespolizei/GSG 9)
Back cover images: GSG 9 operatives scaling a building (Bundespolizei); Fast-roping exercise onto a submarine. (Bundespolizei/GSG 9)

The Publisher's authorised representative in the EU for product safety is Authorised Rep Compliance Ltd., Ground Floor, 71 Lower Baggot Street, Dublin D02 P593, Ireland.
www.arccompliance.com

Contents

Acknowledgements — vii
Introduction — ix
Glossary — xv

1. "Merry Games" in Munich — 1
2. Troops against Terror — 17
3. Wegener in Israel — 31
4. Humble Beginnings — 43
5. Border Guard Cowboys — 57
6. Training World Champions — 73
7. A Year Full of Autumn — 87
8. The Schleyer Manhunt — 99
9. Odyssey to Africa — 115
10. Operation *Feuerzauber* — 135
11. Birth of a Legend — 159
12. Circus Wegener — 169
13. Export Hit GSG 9 — 185
14. Beyond the Legend — 195

Appendix A: Thinking the Unthinkable — 209
Appendix B: East Germany's "GSG 9" — 225
Endnotes — 233
Bibliography — 243
Index — 247

Acknowledgements

As always with projects like these, a lot of careful thought and deliberation went into this book and into all the intense research, writing and rewriting, comprehensive fact-checking, editing, and proofreading that it involved. And even though only the name of the author is to be found on this book's cover, many people have contributed massively to its inception in one way or another. Here are but a few of those without whom this book would not have been possible, or at least, would have been very different (and that is to say: certainly not better).

Greatest thanks go out to...

...all GSG 9 veterans and former commanders, as well as active operatives and their commanders, for their insights, background information, interviews, personal notes, and photographs from their private archives;

...GSG 9's executive office for their exceptional openness, which went beyond what could be expected, for their trustful cooperation, support, and patience with numerous requests;

...my friends Ray Davies and Conal Reed for working through the original translation of my script and giving valuable tips and hints on idiomatic expressions and German contexts requiring explanation in the English-speaking world;

...Steve Smith, for making sure that all is not lost in translation and for lifting the script up to a presentable level so it could be sent out to publishers;

...all the good folks at Casemate Publishers for putting all efforts into making sure this book is not only worthwhile reading, but also fun to look at and flip through, particularly publisher Ruth Sheppard, editor Lizzy Hammond, and illustrator Declan Ingram.

A special thank you, too, to memorabilia collector Philipp Meyer, police historian Frank Kawelovski, journalist and expert on the German intelligence community Erich Schmidt-Eenboom, historian and expert on the history of skyjacking Thomas Skelton-Robinson, the immensely helpful people of the Bundesarchiv in Koblenz and Berlin, the Bavarian State Archive.

Having said this, all possible errors, inaccuracies, or omissions lie with me and me alone, and I will be grateful if they are brought to my attention.

And finally, a truckload of thanks to my partner Miriam for putting up with me forcing GSG 9 dinner talks upon her for months on end and still being kind enough to read the script and give helpful advice, nonetheless.

Introduction

Meeting the legend requires taking a detour. The country road runs from the small town of Saint Augustin between meadows and bushes along the fenced-in barracks of the Federal Police. After a mile or so, just before the road seems to end in a field, it takes a sudden turn to the right, and soon the visitor is forced to stop in front of the main gate. This is one of the main installations of the 50,000-strong Bundespolizei.[*] It sure does not look like it. Security measures turn out to be ostentatiously casual: some low wire-mesh fences, a guardhouse, and a boom gate which remains open most of the time. Nothing seems to indicate that this huge police compound houses one of the world's most distinguished counterterror squads.

When formalities are complete, after registration and the exchange of a personal identity card[†] for a visitor's pass, the reporter is welcomed by the public relations manager. She is a trained officer of the Federal Police but is not dressed in their standard blue uniform. Instead, she wears the olive-green attire of the old Federal Border Guard, like most of her colleagues at GSG 9, a statement of tradition. Also, she carries a pistol in a belt holster. Yes, she nods on the way to the car, even the desk officers carry them all the time; yes, even the commander.

From the main gate, the headquarters of GSG 9 lie barely more than 100 meters dead ahead. But soon the road ends in front of massive concrete blocks. Security reasons. The street first turns right, then zigzags for a mile or so through the base, past the canteen, barracks, truck parking spaces, and workshop halls of other Federal Police units stationed on the site. Finally, the road leads back toward the exit and abruptly ends on the opposite side of the concrete blocks from earlier. We park in front of an enclosed area that is once again surrounded by a fence, but this time considerably higher than the outer one, with barbed wire on top. All other security measures are tighter, too: surveillance cameras, a massive roll-up gate in front of the barrier, another guardhouse where the visitor's pass from the main gate is exchanged for a special house pass exclusively for the stay at GSG 9 premises. We enter a barracks within the barracks.

---

[*] Bundespolizei = Federal Police. Successor of the Bundesgrenzschutz (BGS) = Federal Border Guard.
[†] Officially required by every German citizen.

The mundane-looking main administrative building, with its beige aggregate concrete façade, dates back to the early days of GSG 9 in the 1970s. A stone's throw away, a new building is soon to be erected, the PR manager explains, which is supposed to meet the requirements—and accommodate the size—of a modern special task force. When finished, GSG 9 will reside in two locations: here in Saint Augustin in the very west of Germany, and at a new facility in Berlin, some 500 kilometers away, where the recently established 4th Operational Unit has been operational for some time and, as word has it, keeps quite busy. A third permanent location for the maritime unit is currently being sought in northern Germany. Headquarters will remain here, though, between the river Rhine and the low mountain range of the Siebengebirge, close to Germany's Cold War capital, Bonn.

From above the low portal of the building hails GSG 9 insignia: the German state eagle emblazoned in gold, with sweeping oak leaves to the left and right. Inside the entrance area on the wall there are large, framed black-and-white photos: portraits of the four officers killed in action. It is essential to keep their memory alive, the PR manager explains.

The commander at the time of our visit welcomes us with a hearty handshake, coffee, and cookies. And indeed, he too wears the olive-green Border Guard uniform and carries a service pistol, always at the ready in case of alarm.

Jérôme Fuchs joined GSG 9 in 1997 and has been in charge of the special unit since 2014. Anyone expecting a grizzled warhorse will be disappointed—smart and sporty may describe him better. Weather permitting, he cycles to work every day. Put him in a turtleneck and jacket instead of a uniform and you could also picture him as a keynote speaker at international business congresses. And as a matter of fact, he is asked to talk about the management of GSG 9 on a regular basis. Leadership is a subject Fuchs is deeply invested in. He talks a lot about intrinsic motivation, trust in one's coworkers, communication and teamwork skills, a positive view of people, the right mindset—and creativity, a quality that might not necessarily spring to mind when thinking of a police unit. Sounds more like a feel-good start-up company than a scourge to terrorists. But Commander Fuchs makes it clear that these soft skills are precisely the features that guaranteed GSG 9's success over the five decades since its inception.

Within the international security community, the guys from Saint Augustin are considered one of the best counterterror squads in the world, if not the best. This reputation was forged in a single operation almost 50 years ago. In the Deutscher Herbst[*] of 1977, six of their SETs[†] stormed the Lufthansa jet *Landshut*, killed three of the four hijackers, and liberated all 86 hostages, more or less unscathed.

---

[*] German Autumn = Collective expression for the terrorist events in late 1977.

[†] SET (*Spezialeinsatztrupp*) = Special Operations Teams. Smallest operational unit within GSG 9. Originally consisted of teams of five, today of seven officers (not officially confirmed).

Since then, they have been hailed in dozens of nations as highly welcome sparring partners for their own elite units, and they have served as midwives for the creation and training of dozens of special (police) forces from the Netherlands to Indonesia to Israel to the United States, some of whom achieved international fame themselves. (For example, the US Delta Force, to name but one.) Few descriptions of the small German special intervention unit make do without the attribute "legendary."

GSG 9 knows how to capitalize on this reputation and consequently presents itself as a brand in the fight against terrorism. When the Federal Border Guard was renamed the Federal Police, only GSG 9 was allowed to keep its old name (with the addition "… of the Federal Police"). The trademark was not to be squandered.

As a brand needs a face, a legend needs a secret. Since the promotion of Commander Fuchs to deputy director of GSG 9's parent ministry in 2023, the face is currently that of Robert Hemmerling, formerly Fuchs's Number 2; the secret comes for free. Since the 1980s, house policy dictates that only the name and appearance of the current commander may be known to the public. With few exceptions, employees' full names are not to be mentioned; even the call sign that every operative is given at the start of their career is not to be printed anywhere (this book will of course abide by this guideline). The same applies to photos featuring recognizable faces. As a rule, only wives and partners know what their husbands do for a living. Even siblings and parents often can only suspect in which unit of the Federal Police their family member actually serves.

Moreover, not too much is to be made public about operational tactics, equipment, and weaponry: "*Feind liest mit*" (the enemy is peeking), as the German saying goes. And thus, during interviews, when operational unit leaders or training officers go too deep into detail, GSG 9's press officers will promptly intervene: "Sorry, we'd rather leave that bit out." Even the commander is called out when he risks revealing too much about challenges in the field of cybercrime. Without fail, this happens each time the story is about to get exciting, which is rare enough. Not because GSG 9 has no exciting stories to tell, but rather because of their self-styled image of absolute self-control, discipline, and their effort to sell what they do as unspectacular. Their job is risky, yes, but nothing more than a mere specialization. Their motto: We are ordinary police officers with extraordinary tasks. This is not entirely accurate, of course. Concealing the identity of the staff is but one example that belies the motto.

Another such example is the fact that key data about this unit remains undisclosed; even its precise number of personnel is kept secret. When GSG 9 was established in 1972, the three operational units amounted to about 120 men. Estimates today speak of some 500 in all, but there are no official figures. Nor are there for the number of operatives in the so-called SETs, nor for staff members in the technical departments, or in the medical and driving service, or even in the command staff and administration, who all make sure that these men can do their demanding jobs.

(To this day there are no women serving in the Special Operations Squads.)* Like these figures, many facts about the unit remain concealed, even those concerning its history. "Out of tactical concerns..." echoes the stereotypical statement from GSG 9 administration when asked for even the most innocent figures. This attitude fosters the legend but helps little in creating an accurate picture of this particularly sensitive tool of the executive branch of Germany's constitution.

Of course, there are files in the Bundesarchiv, Germany's national archives, but they are few. And some remain under lock and key. Many documents are still subject to archival protection periods, and a complicated release procedure that leads only to meager results, even after several months of waiting.

So no, GSG 9 is surely not an ordinary police unit. And unlike abroad, GSG 9's reputation in Germany has always oscillated between famous and infamous, between heroic glorification and trigger-happy killer squad. Derided at first as "cowboys" and "gunslingers," even among their colleagues in the Federal Border Guard, the mood towards the obscure police force turned into one of unbridled hero worship and mythological transfiguration only five years later. For a long time, the liberation of the 86 hostages from the Lufthansa aircraft *Landshut* in Mogadishu prevented the BGS unit from Saint Augustin from being viewed soberly, as did the pictures of the cool guys in jeans, trainers, and leather jackets at Cologne-Bonn Airport upon their return. Even today, the history of GSG 9 is often labeled as the story of the "Heroes of Mogadishu," the term "hero" being a rare honor awarded by the German public. Unmitigated hero worship has been strongly discouraged within German society since World War II, and even today skepticism remains strong about any kind of glamorization when it comes to the use of force, let alone weapons.

Also, it wouldn't seem appropriate to place GSG 9 on this ill-founded pedestal—and they themselves strongly oppose being elevated in this manner. Heroic stories make good copy, but "The 9ers" have little in common with the James Bond-type cliché of the lone wolf who bends the rules as he deems necessary and has no trouble breaking them if need be—all for the sake of justice, of course. This stereotype didn't even fit the moment when, in a foreign land, the legend of the "Heroes of Mogadishu" was born. They were not a bunch of trigger-happy Rambos, but 19 highly specialized, highly disciplined police officers in a collaborative operation, who ended a five-day hostage situation inside a hijacked plane in hardly more than a minute. More than 40 other specialists secured the raid from the outside: snipers,

---

* This is in contrast to other special forces, be they military or police. According to GSG 9, this is to do with the physical requirements which the special intervention unit is not ready to tone down, the benchmark being to be able to carry a wounded comrade out of the crossfire in an active firefight. In GSG 9's history, only one woman has met these demands (but later decided not to enter the unit). However, there are some female members of GSG 9, most of them serving in the medical department (see Chapter 14), and GSG 9 states they are happy to welcome women into the Special Operations Squads, should they conform to the physical demands.

paramedics, communications operators, explosives experts. While sociologists still argue about whether the concept of The Hero is outdated or not, this question has never been up for debate within GSG 9. They are not, and have never considered themselves, heroes. They were made so by others.

What is undisputed, however, is that GSG 9 has become an important part of German post-war history, due to their role in the Deutscher Herbst. Beyond the mythologizing of the task force itself, the liberation operation in the Horn of Africa turned out to be a building block for a second founding legend of the West German state. The young democracy found itself reassured of its capacity to act against its inner enemies without betraying its principles. Sixteen years later, GSG 9 once again made history, but this time with less glory. An utterly failed attempt to apprehend two top terrorists in the small town of Bad Kleinen not only resulted in the death of GSG 9 operative Michael Newrzella and a terrorist, but triggered a crisis of state, the likes of which Germany had never experienced: resignations of ministers, dismissals of high-ranking civil servants, and massive public mistrust—of the authorities, the justice system, of the media. Germany was in turmoil. GSG 9's legend crumpled.

In the three decades since, GSG 9 has largely sunk into the white noise of the modern attention economy. Only now and then does the media report arrests and raids involving the "Special Unit for Combating Terrorism and Serious Violent Crime," as reads their official description. And coming across such a headline, many German readers doubtlessly murmur, "GSG 9 … Oh, they're still around?"

Yes, they are still around. And their services are in high demand, even more so than ever. On average, they are deployed once a week, for a total of roughly 2,500 missions since their inception. This is one of the few hard figures about the force that Germany's Ministry of the Interior is willing to divulge. Most of these missions are not terribly spectacular: securing court proceedings, transferring violent criminals, arresting suspects. A little more than 50 years after its inception, the memory of GSG 9 hovers in a historical no-man's-land between faded legend and merciful oblivion. In the collective German memory, the name has become a cipher, an overarching term for any kind of "intervention force." "No need to call in GSG 9" and "call in GSG 9" have become German catchphrases. There are TV documentaries that tell of this first German special intervention unit; every now and then the odd thriller novel is published. There is a PlayStation game, and even action figures—not toys, but rather nerdy collector's items, with astonishing attention to detail, from uniforms to weapons. What remains missing, oddly enough, is an adequate portrayal of GSG 9, fleshing out its actual history on the one hand, and the creation of its legend on the other.

Even though it is not your typical hero's story, it's a good one. And like any good story, the saga of GSG 9 does not start at the beginning but somewhat earlier. In this case, three weeks before its inception, in September 1972.

Glossary

APO (Außerparlamentarische Opposition): Extra-Parliamentary Opposition. Collective term for heterogenic, mainly left-leaning or radically left oppositional groups during the late 1960s and '70s.

ATLAS: Informal association of 38 international special ops forces from the EU, United States, and Israel for the purpose of exchange, networking, and friendly competition. Founded by GSG 9's first commander, Ulrich Wegener. (In Greek mythology, Atlas is a Titan who supported the celestial vault at the westernmost point of the then-known world.)

Bewegung 2. Juni: June 2 Movement. German leftist terror organization, at times personally and operationally aligned with the RAF. Named after the lethal attack on German student Benno Ohnesorg at a protest march in Berlin on June 2, 1967, allegedly committed by West German agencies (it later turned out that the perpetrator was indeed a state agent, but sent by the East German Stasi).

BfV (Bundesamt für Verfassungsschutz): Federal Agency for the Protection of the Constitution. Secret service for and limited to the (West) German territory.

BGS (Bundesgrenzschutz): Federal Border Guard. Established in 1951 for the safeguarding the West German borders, particularly the border along the iron curtain. Precursor to the Bundeswehr, today's Bundespolizei (Federal Police), organized in *Grenzschutzgruppen* (GSGs), the GSG 9 being one of them designated for counterterrorism and heavy crime action.

BKA (Bundeskriminalamt): Federal Criminal Police Office.

BMI (Bundesministerium des Innern): Federal Ministry of the Interior.

BND (Bundesnachrichtendienst): Federal Intelligence Service. German secret service operating abroad.

Bund: Federation. Collective term for the German governmental system as a whole, as well as its individual legislative, executive, and judicial branches and agencies such as the Bundespolizei.

(Bundes-)Kanzler: (Federal) chancellor. Leader of the federal German government. The most powerful political position in (West) Germany, but not the highest state office. In terms of protocol, ranks third in line after the *Bundespräsident* (federal president) and the *Bundestagspräsident* (president of the lower parliamentary chamber, the Bundestag).

Bundesland (or Land for short, plural: Bundesländer): German provinces like Bavaria, Saxony, Hesse, and city-states like Hamburg and Berlin. The Bundesländer hold comparatively much authority and executive rights in the field of police and inner security. In general, police matters are a constitutional prerogative of the Länder, traditionally tightly protected by their respective governments. The Bundespolizei holds authority only in matters of the federal borders on land and at sea, protection of Federal buildings, international embassies, German embassies abroad, train stations, and train traffic within Germany, as well as international airports.

Bundespolizei (Federal Police): Successor of the Federal Border Guard BGS (Bundesgrenzschutz). Established in 2005.

Bundeswehr (Federal Armed Forces): West German Armed Forces, founded in 1955 (East Germany: Nationale Volksarmee, NVA, or National People's Army).

GIGN (Groupe d'intervention de la Gendarmerie nationale or National Gendarmerie Intervention Group): Elite police tactical unit of the French National Gendarmerie.

Deutscher Herbst: German Autumn. Collective expression for the terrorist events in late 1977, culminating in the skyjacking of Lufthansa Flight LH-181, ending up in Mogadishu.

Diensteinheit IX (Department IX): East Germany's version of a counterterrorism police task force, modeled after GSG 9.

DM (Deutsche Mark): Deutschmarks. Official (West) German currency from 1948–1998. When deutschmarks were replaced by the euro, two deutschmarks were worth roughly one euro.

EKO Cobra (Einsatzkommando Cobra): Mission Commando Cobra. Austrian special intervention force, counterterror unit.

FBI (Federal Bureau of Investigation): Federal Police of the United States.

FDJ (Freie Deutsche Jugend): Free German Youth. Junior staff organization of East Germany's SED party.

FRG (Federal Republic of Germany): Official name of the (West) German state (German: BRD = Bundesrepublik Deutschland).

GdP (Gewerkschaft der Polizei): Union of the Police. Largest union for police forces in Germany.

GDR (German Democratic Republic): Official name of socialist East Germany from 1949–1990 (German: DDR = Deutsche Demokratische Republik).

Gestapo (Geheime Staatspolizei): Secret State Police. Secret police force of Nazi Germany. Committed numerous atrocities in the Third Reich.

GSG 9 der Bundespolizei (Grenzschutzgruppe 9): Literally: Border Guard Group 9 of the Federal Police. Special intervention unit of the Federal Police. The only Border

Guard group allowed to keep their original name and uniforms after rebranding the Federal Border Guard as Federal Police in 2005.

IDF (Israeli Defence Force): Official name of the Israeli armed forces.

***Kripo** (Kriminalpolizei)*: Criminal Investigation Department. Detective squad within the German police force.

MEK (*Mobiles Einsatzkommando*): Literally: Mobile Task Force. Surveillance unit on the provincial level (as opposed to the GSG 9 on the federal level), mainly used for reconnaissance and manhunt missions.

MP (*Maschinenpistole*): Submachine gun.

NSDAP (Nationalsozialistische Deutsche Arbeiterpartei): Adolf Hitler's National Socialist German Workers Party, commonly known as the Nazi Party. Fascist far-right political party in Germany that existed from 1919–1945. Infamous for its instrumental role in orchestrating the Holocaust, which resulted in the systematic murder of six million Jews and millions of other victims.

OTL (*Oberstleutnant*): Lieutenant Colonel.

PFLP (Popular Front for the Liberation of Palestine): Palestinian terror organization, operating mainly in the 1970s and '80s.

PHW (*Polizei-Hauptwachtmeister*): Police Chief Sergeant.

PLO: Palestine Liberation Organization.

POW: Prisoner of war.

PVB (*Polizeivollzugsbeamter*): Literally: Law enforcement officer. Police officer.

RAF (Rote Armee Fraktion): Red Army Faction. Radical-left German terror organization, founded in the early 1970s, allegedly responsible for at least 33 killings, numerous bombings with roughly 200 persons injured, several abductions, and the hijacking of Flight LH-181 in 1977. Consisted of three so-called generations, the first being headed by Ulrike Meinhof and Andreas Baader (hence the name Baader Meinhof Gang); declared their dissolution in 1998.

RZ (Revolutionäre Zellen): Revolutionary Cells. German leftist terror organization, at times personally and operationally aligned with the RAF.

SA (*Sturmabteilung*): Storming Department. Dreaded paramilitary organization of the NSDAP.

Sajeret Matkal (Hebrew: Scouts of the General Staff): Officially General Staff reconnaissance unit. Highly secretive special task force of the Israeli military.

SAS (Special Air Service): Special task force of the British Royal Army, established in WWII.

SBS (Special Boat Service): Special task force of the British Royal Navy. The naval equivalent of the British Special Forces unit SAS.

Schupo (*Schutzpolizist*): Colloquial, short for patrol police officer (literally, protection police officer).

SED (**Sozialistische Einheitspartei Deutschlands**): Socialist Unity Party. Unchallenged ruling party throughout the history of the GDR from 1946–1989.

SEK (*Spezialeinsatzkommando*): Literally: Special Operation Commando. Special intervention unit (SIU) on the level of the provinces (as opposed to the GSG 9 on the federal level), mainly used for counterterror and heavy crime operations.

SET (*Spezialeinsatztrupp*): Special Operations Team. Smallest operational unit within GSG 9. Originally consisted of teams of five, today of seven officers (not officially confirmed). Several SETs are subsumed in a squad, several squads are subsumed in an operational unit.

SOKO (*Sonderkommission*): Special Criminal Investigation Commission. Designated commission for the investigation of one or several interconnected crime(s).

SS (*Schutzstaffel*): Protection Squadron. Major paramilitary organization in Nazi Germany, founded as a personal bodyguard squadron for Adolf Hitler. Became instrumental in fighting political enemies within Germany and in the planning and execution of the Holocaust and operating concentration camps. Its militarized arm, the Waffen-SS, committed numerous atrocities, war crimes and genocide throughout German-occupied Europe during WWII.

Stasi (*Staatssicherheit*): State Security. Short for Ministerium für Staatssicherheit (or MfS), Ministry for State Security. The infamous secret service and secret police of the GDR. It was regarded as the most important instrument of repression of the Socialist Unity Party of Germany (SED). Being the "shield and sword of the party" (the latter a self-image), it was to secure the power of the SED and suppress any opposition or deviant behavior.

SWAT (**Special Weapons and Tactics**): Special intervention unit of the US police to handle high-risk situations that regular police forces may not be equipped to manage, including hostage situations, barricaded suspects, shootouts, and terrorism threats.

Volkspolizei: People's police. Uniformed police force of the GDR from 1949–1990.

VS-NfD (*Verschlusssache—nur für den Dienstgebrauch*): Classified—only for internal use. Lowest stage of secrecy within German state agencies.

Warsaw Pact (officially: Treaty of Friendship, Cooperation, and Mutual Assistance): Political and military alliance established in 1955 in Warsaw, Poland, as a direct response to the formation of NATO. Created by the Soviet Union, Albania, Bulgaria, Czechoslovakia, East Germany, Hungary, Poland, and Romania.

YAMAM: Hebraic acronym for centralized special unit. Counterterror Task Force of the Israeli Border Police established in 1974.

CHAPTER I

"Merry Games" in Munich

Silly. Quite silly. Bright turquoise suits over white polo shirts, matching white sneakers. And boy, the outdated working men's caps they were ordered to don! French star designer André Courrèges, of miniskirt fame, believed them to be a perfect match for the high-necked jackets and stiff polyester pants he had created for the world event. Dieter Tutter and his comrades were not so sure. The young officers of the Federal Border Guard (BGS) had volunteered to come to Munich as part of the Olympic security detail. A once in a lifetime opportunity ... and all that. But this was not how they had pictured their attire. Nor their job. Dressed in their fancy uniforms, which were intentionally designed *not* to look like uniforms, they were now sitting in a small tower that served as the operations center of the Olympia Park central section. Being a designated intervention reserve, they were waiting for something to intervene. Not that they could have done a whole lot in such a case; their armament consisted of walkie-talkies, one for each officer, plus an English dictionary to facilitate communication with foreign guests and athletes.

Lieutenant Tutter of the BGS and his colleagues were not deployed as a police force but as stewards at the 1972 Olympic Games. "We had no police powers, no weapons, no nothing. We were supposed to direct streams of visitors and provide information. That was all."[1] But what about potential troublemakers? Well, they were told to unsettle them by making jokes, pelt them with sweets, or, if absolutely necessary, surround them and gently push them aside. They even had to practice these rather unorthodox tactics beforehand in exercises. But then again, these games were supposed to be light-hearted—"merry and bright," as the ubiquitous saying went. West Germany wanted to present itself at its democratic best and show its open, friendly face to the world—an Olympic celebration designed as a colorful contrast to the monumentally grim Nazi games of 1936 Berlin.

Barely three decades after the Holocaust and World War II, relations between Germany and Israel remained fragile. The two young states had dispatched their respective ambassadors only seven years prior to the games. In recent years, unsettlingly frequent incidents of violent attacks had occurred against Jewish institutions in West Germany. And yet, the Jewish state had sent the largest Olympic delegation in its history to the country of the Shoah. This was widely read as a clear sign of the international rehabilitation of the former pariah Germany, and the West German government intended to keep it that way. Droves of policemen in grey uniforms wielding submachine guns would not have suited this picture, or so went the sentiment. So they were banned from the Olympic village and the sports venues, leaving officers like Dieter Tutter with pockets full of sweets and walkie-talkies to do the job.

The fervent will to demonstrate the Federal Republic's new peacefulness did not end with the security personnel. Their colorful non-uniform and lack of armament merely underlined an ostentatious lack of concern. "The first mistake in the planning was to not secure the Olympic village properly,"[2] Ulrich Wegener (at the time the liaison officer of the Border Guard to the federal minister of the interior) later reported. On a regular basis, he accompanied his boss, Hans-Dietrich Genscher, to planning meetings of the Olympic Organizing Committee. In his function as federal minister of the interior, Genscher also served as minister of sport, and thus as vice president of the National Olympic Committee. West Germany being a federal state, however, police sovereignty in this case lay not with the national government but with both the province of the Free State of Bavaria[*] and the Munich city police. As did responsibility for the security concept with which Wegener was little impressed: "There was only one fence—it was ridiculous. People kept climbing over it… There were no security institutions for the Olympic Village that were equipped appropriately. That was the second mistake. Police regarded the whole subject more like a pastime. It was an untenable condition." Genscher had made the 40-year-old Wegener his personal liaison officer to the Federal Border Guard as soon as he was appointed minister of the interior in 1969. In the following years, Wegener rose to become Genscher's go-to adviser on all matters concerning homeland security.

Due to federal legislation, the Munich Police Chief Manfred Schreiber was appointed top security officer for the Olympic Games. Genscher, Wegener, and other federal representatives were only to advise. Accordingly, their influence on fundamental decisions was quite limited. Wegener and Horst Herold, head of the Federal Criminal Police Office BKA, both pointed out that if things went ahead as planned, Germany would "only be protecting our foreign guests with a minimum of police forces, which would never be enough—unfortunately we were not taken seriously."

The security situation at the sports venues turned out to be similarly dire. Measures were lax or non-existent. "My father got a special badge, but it simply

---

[*] Within Germany's federal system, Bavaria remained a free state by name, but with little effects otherwise.

granted free access to the VIP gallery," remembers Jörg Schleyer. He cannot recall any security checks at all, not even at the high-ranking events to which the entire family of top industrialist Hanns Martin Schleyer was often invited. "We went to the Hotel Bayerischer Hof a few times, because that's where the receptions were held for the German medal winners, and Daimler-Benz was a partner of the National Olympic Committee. For us children it was super nice. I was 18 at the time. There were no barriers or checkpoints. You would just walk in and meet the Olympic athletes."[3]

The entire Schleyer family had come to the Munich Games because mother Waltrude was brought up in the south German metropolis, and father Hanns Martin was invited as a guest of honor, being a member of the Daimler Group's Board of Management as well as a high official of the national industrial association. The Schleyers, sports enthusiasts, all of them, feverishly followed the athletic competitions day after day, along with a billion television viewers all over the world. Under the iconic curved tent roof of the Munich Olympic stadium, they watched spellbound as German athlete Heide Rosendahl won gold in the long jump, and 16-year-old Ulrike Meyfarth leapt her way to the high jump world record.

Some 4,000 journalists and 2,000 TV personnel reported live, excitedly (and for the first time in color) how American swimmer Mark Spitz ploughed through the water of the Olympic pool from gold to gold, setting new world records in the process time and again. And how, in the legendary basketball final, the Olympic champion-to-be, the United States, was doomed to watch helplessly as Russia's Alexander Belov, after an infinitely long pass from the backcourt, dunked the ball in the very last second of the match. In the ice age of the Cold War, this not only meant sporting humiliation for the home country of basketball, but a political victory for its archenemy, the USSR. "It was absolutely incredible!" enthuses the youngest Schleyer son even half a century later. "The atmosphere in the stadium was fantastic as well, the architecture outstanding. It was insanely beautiful and well done. And then there was the weather: sunshine each and every day for 10 days straight! Up to September 5, 1972—on that day, it was like someone switched the lever from sun to rain."

At dawn on September 5, eight men with sports bags wearing tracksuits climb over the poorly lit fence of the Olympic village.[4] This is nothing anybody would make a big fuss about: in the past few days, every now and then buzzed athletes could be observed choosing this unofficial route on their way to quarters after a merry party somewhere outside the village. Thus, no one even thinks of stopping these young men from climbing over the fence, let alone asking them if they belong there at all.

On their way to the Olympic village, the eight even meet a group of drunken US sportsmen. They chat animatedly with their supposed fellow athletes and help each other over the fence. This is not difficult, the obstacle being only some six feet high, having no barbed wire on top, and not being guarded in any way. Twelve of the sparse security personnel are missing that night. Several people take notice of the climbing campaign, as it later turns out, but since the unorthodox method has become established in the course of the Olympic Games, no one suspects anything. After saying their goodbyes, the eight men set off for Conollystraße 31, the accommodation for the 21 members of the Israeli delegation.

The intruders call themselves Fedayeen (Arabic for "ready to sacrifice") and are a subsection of the Black September terrorist group, which in turn is a violent offshoot of Yasser Arafat's political organization, Fatah. They know their way around, two of them having previously worked in the Olympic village. In their sports bags they carry automatic weapons and hand grenades, hidden under the tactical clothing which they change into, while being just one street corner away from their destination. When ready, they enter flat 1 of the apartment block where the Israeli athletes are now fast asleep. It's 4:30 a.m.

Rude Awakening

Ninety minutes later, Hans-Dietrich Genscher is ripped from sleep by a phone call. "The news hit me like a heavy blow. It meant that once again Jews were in peril in Germany." Genscher jumps out of bed, makes quick phone calls to Chancellor Willy Brandt, Foreign Minister Walter Scheel, and the Israeli ambassador, then alerts BGS man Wegener, who instantly tries to get more information. "I asked, 'What happened?' They couldn't really tell me. It was disastrous." Genscher and Wegener head to the Olympic village, where Police Chief Manfred Schreiber has formed an improvised crisis management group. Bavarian Minister of the Interior Bruno Merk has arrived shortly before Genscher and Wegener.[*] "He just said, 'Well, I guess we have to negotiate,'" Wegener later recalls. "I asked, 'What has happened so far in terms of operational measures?' Nothing had happened, absolutely nothing. The police just stood around.... And this was the way the whole matter went ahead. At first it was assumed that it was possible to negotiate and we would manage that way. Of course, that was a joke."

At this point, two Israeli athletes are already dead and one has managed to escape. In total, nine hostages are held by the Palestinians. But the crisis team does not yet know anything about this. How many terrorists have infiltrated the Olympic village? Unknown—and it will remain so until the very end. What is clear, however, are the demands of the terrorists, which include the release of 130 Palestinians

---

[*] By and by they were joined by the former mayor of Munich, Hans-Jochen Vogel, the chairman of the conservative regional Bavarian party, CSU Franz-Josef Strauß, the president of the West German Olympic Committee, Willi Daume, and the mayor of the Olympic village, Walter Tröger. They were later joined by the Israeli ambassador from Bonn, Ben Horin.

from Israeli prisons, plus one German inmate: "We demand of F. G. R. immediate release of: ULRIKA [*sic*] MEINHHOF," reads the text below the list of names.[5] This refers to one of the heads of the leftist terror group RAF.* Ulrike Meinhof had been arrested three months earlier after a series of deadly terrorist attacks and is now awaiting trial in a prison in Cologne. She and the Palestinians are to be released by 9:00 a.m. at the latest, as reads the ultimatum of the hostage-takers—and they leave no doubt that they are determined to immediately shoot all hostages in the case of any attempt to free them.

In the meantime, police forces have been called in from the outskirts of Munich where they were stationed out of sight. Officers with hunting rifles have taken up positions on the surrounding buildings, and the Olympic village has been cordoned off, although "cordoned off" does not reflect the actual situation. Dieter Tutter and his colleagues have formed a chain of guards enclosing a small area around the building at Conollystraße 31. "We were then tasked with keeping the spectators, tourists and the press away from the events, and did so more or less successfully. Sure enough, everybody flocked there, because everybody knew what was going on, it came live through the media." Tutter himself had learned the news via television, despite the fact that he was sitting but a few steps away in the radio room of the operations center.

The best spots are quickly taken. The gentle rises surrounding the Olympic village offer an unobstructed view of the Israeli quarters. Photographers, cameramen from the TV networks, and curious onlookers gather but a few meters from the spot where the Israeli hostages fear for their lives. In the afternoon, German TV journalist Lothar Loewe will report in a live segment that the cordoning of the area remains utterly inadequate: "Should ... the terrorists be determined to use explosives to blow themselves and the hostages up, the onlookers, journalists and also the members of the Federal Border Guard would be very much at risk."

This does not seem to concern the curious crowd, which by then will have grown to over 75,000. A semblance of a funfair atmosphere starts spreading across the premises: unhindered, children climb over the fence to the Olympic village in pursuit of autographs from athletes who are sunbathing on the surrounding meadows or preparing for their competitions, since for the time being the games go on as if nothing has happened. In the morning, the dressage competition starts in the equestrian stadium; the canoeists, the basketball players, and the boxers compete as planned; and the volleyball tournament commences regardless of the terrorist situation. It is only in the late afternoon that the Olympic Committee, under pressure from Israel, manages to interrupt the competitions.

---

* RAF (Rote Armee Fraktion) = Red Army Faction. Radical-left German terror organization, founded in the early 1970s, allegedly responsible for at least 33 killings, numerous bombings with roughly 200 people injured, abductions, and the hijacking of Flight LH-181 in 1977.

Up to this point, more than 180 international television stations have been reporting live from the Olympic Games. Now they are reporting live from the scene of a tragedy, broadcasting the pictures from Munich in real time to living rooms all over the world—and possibly also to the Israelis' Olympic quarter, because there are TV sets there, too. "About 30 cameras were pitched up opposite the building where the Palestinians were," Jörg Schleyer recalls. The events on Conollystraße 31 thus become the first act of terror in world history to be broadcast globally in real time. "We had no experience with violent crimes of this magnitude in this country. We had the Baader-Meinhof* issue—there had been the big wave of arrests in Frankfurt eight weeks before. But that was 'local terrorism.' And suddenly you have to deal with a world event."

Hectic Standstill

By the time the German authorities and government machinery got going, the first ultimatum had already passed. The second was set for 12 noon. Fundamental measures were initiated late or not at all. Even setting up a telephone line to the Palestinians took ages. And it was only in the long course of the morning that someone had the idea of calling in helicopters in case they were needed. The general disarray was not limited to technics and logistics—the ad hoc crisis team was hopelessly overwhelmed. Before the start of the games, no thought whatsoever had been put into the planning of a crisis response team. Now it had to be cobbled together on the spot, and every official was invited to join in. Consequently, representatives of all political parties and at all levels of authority were involved in the decision-making process. This was convenient for the leaders because it enabled the greatest possible consensus. But when everyone is involved, everyone wants to have a say. This "led to highly complicated decision-making structures and tended to prevent efficient reactions," as historian Matthias Dahlke notes.[6]

The terrorists categorically rejected offers of unlimited ransoms for the release of the Israeli hostages. Conversely, Israeli Prime Minister Golda Meir had made it unmistakably clear that under no circumstances would Israel give in to the terrorists' demands for a prisoner exchange: "If we budge, no Israeli in the whole world can feel safe anymore." Hectic telephone calls between German ministries and the Israeli embassy failed to make any progress—a fact that was wisely concealed from the hostage-takers. Through its ambassador in Bonn, the Israeli government let the Germans know that they could act and negotiate as they saw fit, but that the release of Palestinian prisoners was out of the question. The terrorists' threat to shoot two hostages in front of the broadcast cameras, live before the eyes of the world, did nothing to change their stance.

---

* Baader-Meinhof-Bande = Nucleus of the terrorist RAF, named after their figureheads Andreas Baader and Ulrike Meinhof.

In Bonn,* Chancellor Willy Brandt convened with his cabinet for an emergency meeting. The West German government was in a quandary, almost all out of options except for talk, negotiate, buy time. Minister of the Interior Hans-Dietrich Genscher was "authorized to do everything necessary in cooperation with the Bavarian state government to rescue the hostages." That was efficiently worded, but of little practical value. "I found myself in a situation that was unsatisfactory in every respect," Genscher later mused. "Firstly, I was not locally responsible for the protective measures in the run-up, and neither for the measures to be taken when the situation unfolded. But most important for me was witnessing the hostage-taking of Israeli athletes. After everything that happened to our Jewish fellow citizens during the Third Reich, this was an utterly terrible experience for me. It was the first time for us to be confronted with international terrorism."†

In the hours that followed, negotiating groups of varying size and composition made their way to Conollystraße 31 to talk to the terrorists, trying to persuade them to surrender, promising safe evacuation if the hostages were released, and all this while keeping in mind that Israel would never agree to an exchange. "I think we were all a little naive," Ulrich Wegener later admitted. "The ministers, too, believed that it would be helpful to talk. They actually assumed that they would succeed in convincing [the terrorists] to release the Israelis. But that was completely out of the question. Their demands were quite clear."

In painstaking talks with Police Chief Schreiber, the Palestinians agreed to a new ultimatum: 1:00 p.m. If their demands were not met by then, they again threatened to shoot two hostages. In order to gain time, Schreiber asked Minister of the Interior Genscher and his Bavarian counterpart Bruno Merk to take up direct negotiations with the Palestinians. They made their way to Conollystraße 31, where they met outside with the leader of the hostage-takers. He called himself Issa and sported a white hat, matching his white suit. Straps of hand-grenade triggers protruded from both his bulging chest pockets, one on the left, one on the right. A third grenade was clenched in his hand, ready for discharge. "He made an extraordinarily determined but also calm impression," Genscher said. "At the same time I got the feeling that he could not be dissuaded from his conditions by any argument or appeal."[7] Genscher tried anyway. He had made a decision which he had not discussed with anyone beforehand. "Shortly before [meeting with the terrorists], I called home. My wife was with me in Munich—she was waiting at the hotel. At home, my mother was on the phone. She was agitated by the events. Promising to do everything we could, I tried to calm her down. Then I asked if my then-11-year-old daughter was at home. She was playing in the garden. I asked to call her on the phone; I wanted to speak to her once more, to hear her voice, before I took a step whose outcome was completely

---

* Capital of the Federal Republic of Germany, 1949–1990.
† Interview with the author for a radio documentary in 2007.

uncertain, but which I was determined to take.... I asked Martina what she was doing. I hoped, I said, to be back in Bonn soon. After the phone call, I went to my meeting with the leader of the hostage-takers. I told him Germany was hosting these games. Germany had a special responsibility toward the Jewish people.... To enforce their demands on the Israeli government, I would be available as a hostage. [He] replied that he did not have the authority to make such a decision, then added that this was not about German hostages, but about the Israelis."[8]

The terrorists seemed quite flattered by the visit of top-tier government representatives. In retrospect, however, it was not a particularly wise tactical decision by Genscher and Merk to negotiate in person with the Palestinians. "In my view, this was another mistake, because it marked the end of the chain of command," as Ulrich Wegener later concluded. "Today, we don't do that kind of thing anymore." As a matter of principle, a lower-ranking official must always be chosen to negotiate with the kidnappers. "The latter can always say, 'I can't decide that. I have to ask my superiors first.' This can go on without end, so you win time, which is immensely important."

At least, Minister Genscher was allowed to speak briefly with the hostages. "We went up the stairs and down a long corridor until we finally reached the room, guarded by two terrorists with machine guns. They opened the door and behind it we saw an image of horror." In the middle of the room, the dead weightlifter Josef Romano lay in a pool of blood. One Israeli was tied to a chair and the other eight hostages were standing around it, hogtied to each other by the arms. "I will never forget the sight of this room for the rest of my life," Genscher confessed. "I will never be able to forget these faces—filled with fear, but also with hope." When they emerged from their short visit, Genscher again offered himself as a hostage for exchange, but without success. The only thing he and Merk managed to get out of their negotiations was to have the ultimatum extended a second time until 5:00 p.m. Upon his return, Wegener found his boss deeply moved, shell-shocked. "He was very depressed. I remember it very well ... we were talking and he said: 'They are dead serious, no question about it.' He was convinced that we were dealing with fanatics."

But even the question of how many fanatics they were dealing with was still unclear at this point. Earlier, an attempt to scout the premises in order to find out the exact number of terrorists had failed when police officers disguised as kitchen staff were sent to Conollystraße 31 with food for the hostages. Genscher now reported four, perhaps five, terrorists in the Israeli quarters. This figure was considered reliable and served as a basis for the planning of possible rescue attempts—a deadly mistake, as it would later turn out.[9]

A nonviolent solution to the deadlock seemed increasingly unlikely. Parallel to the ever more desperate attempts at negotiation, the Munich deputy police chief had been tasked with preparations for an armed hostage rescue. Since the morning, there had been deliberations about storming the building, but the conclusion was clear—too dangerous. The West German state did not have any police force at their disposal capable of dealing with such a situation (or even a military one, for that matter). Or did they?

Special Unit on Standby?

In 2012, a former agent of the West German Foreign Intelligence Service, the BND,[*] claimed in a TV documentary that BND special ops forces had been standing by for a liberation attempt during the terror attack in Munich. Allegedly, these were agents of a so-called Stay Behind unit, a secret operational group that, in the case of an invasion by forces of the Warsaw Pact,[†] was to allow the front to pass them by in order to then operate behind enemy lines. In the documentary, an alleged member of this group is quoted as saying, "We were sure we could handle the Palestinians. We were well prepared and we were keen on doing it. We could finally prove ourselves." However, these claims have not been substantiated to date, neither by government files nor by eyewitness reports. Nor does the scenario seem particularly plausible. Stay Behind agents were tasked with blowing up bridges and roads, smuggling people across borders and through the front line in case of emergency. They carried handguns solely for self-defense and were not trained as snipers or even for liberation operations. When in later years during a lecture Wegener was asked about the subject, he stated succinctly: "Not true."

Rumors about the existence of such a special group of the BND standing by started circulating in German security circles shortly after Munich. The root of these rumors might have been an offer from Israel. For one special ops unit was indeed standing by. Its name: Sajeret Matkal,[‡] at the time under the command of Ehud Barak (later head of the Israeli government). Back then, Sajeret Matkal was one of the few special forces in the world that was trained in counterterrorism and hostage rescue. When news of the Munich situation came early that day, Prime Minister Golda Meir immediately had them put on combat readiness. As early as noon, Task Force Commander Barak reported ready for departure. Barak had fought in the Six-Day War and led numerous clandestine operations. Four months earlier, his unit had stormed a hijacked Boeing 707 of the Belgian airline Sabena in Tel Aviv. One hostage was killed, but 87 were saved unharmed. From his professional point of view, he considered the German security forces completely out of their depth:

---

[*] It is still unclear which German agency is the origin of this information. This question was apparently discussed neither in the crisis team nor in the police task force.

[†] Warsaw Pact (officially: Treaty of Friendship, Cooperation, and Mutual Assistance) = Political and military alliance established in 1955 in Warsaw, Poland, as a direct response to the formation of NATO.

[‡] Sajeret Matkal (Hebraic: Scouts of the General Staff) = Officially General Staff Reconnaissance Unit. Highly secretive special task force of the Israeli military.

"There's no way the Germans can handle this, they don't even know what they've got there," he argued when talking to his superior on the telephone that very day. "The Germans have no experience whatsoever in fighting this kind of terrorist, in a matter of freeing hostages no less, and even more in a place like the Olympic village... They will make all kinds of rookie mistakes that everyone makes who is not sufficiently trained. This could cost them dearly."

That day, several dozen geared-up men waited at Tel Aviv airport, anticipating their marching orders while watching the events in Munich on live TV. The orders never came. As to why, this is not fully comprehensible to this day. In the memoirs of contemporary witnesses, statements of former Sajeret Matkal operatives are set against those of German politicians. Commander Ehud Barak was told that he could hardly be of any help in Munich, because the Israelis supposedly had already spoken to the Germans. "Oh no, it is completely out of the question to deploy foreign units ... on German soil and to carry out an operation which also goes against the Grundgesetz [West German Constitution].... The German government refused permission."[10]

Minister of the Interior Genscher, on the other hand, drew a distinctly different picture of the situation. Around noon, he wrote in his memoirs, the Israeli ambassador had announced that an Israeli security specialist would fly into Munich, but otherwise there had never been any talk of an offer to deploy the elite Israeli unit. "He denied my question whether Israel wanted to use its own forces for the liberation. To my face, he also did not criticize the measures initiated and prepared by the police crisis team."[11] The senior security official was Zvi Zamir, the head of the Israeli foreign intelligence service Mossad. Genscher's liaison officer, Wegener, picked him up at the airport. However, Israel's top intelligence official found to his dismay that his advice was not much in demand, particularly not from the Bavarian state representatives who were in the lead. Zamir later reported that at times they acted downright hostile toward him.

Was there an offer from the Israelis to carry out the liberation operation? Possibly with the participation and under the official banner of the BND, in order for Germany to save face? At any rate, this was Wegener's assumption in the follow-up to the Munich massacre in the circle of his staff. Wegener would later use the same tactics to persuade the government of Somalia to use his German task force to liberate the Lufthansa aircraft *Landshut* on Somali soil. The general idea was: We'll do the job, but under your leadership and command, at least officially. This might have worked in Munich as well. But if there was such an offer from Israel, no one took it up.

Bizarre Live TV

Thus, the German security forces were left to their own devices—and lapsed into action for action's sake. In the afternoon, police officers posted themselves in and atop the neighboring buildings of the Israeli accommodations, disguised in Olympic tracksuits, but wearing antiquated WWII helmets and openly carrying submachine guns. Under the hopeful code name of Operation *Sunshine* they were supposed to enter the building through the ventilation shafts and free the hostages. Further instructions: none. "It was all very vague and uncertain," one of the officers recalled. "All I knew was that when the signal came—'sunshine'—I had to jump up, move through the window, and hope that someone wasn't waiting on the other side with a hand grenade."[12]

But even their creep-up was broadcast live to the whole world by the omnipresent television cameras—and was also viewed in the small tower that contained the security forces' command stand just around the corner. There, Border-Guard-officer-turned-steward Dieter Tutter watched flabbergasted on a small TV set how his clueless colleagues of the Munich police force took up their positions. "I wasn't trained for a special intervention unit, since that did not yet exist. But I was quite bothered by the recognizably bungling approach in broad daylight, wearing sports gear and grandpa's steel helmet from the war. I was trained in the Federal Border Guard: off-road operations, attack on the move, exercises with machine guns and grenade launchers. We were a military-style police force. When you see policemen in half-civilian clothes staggering over the roofs, it gives you the creeps! What's all this nonsense?"

A stone's throw away, adviser Ulrich Wegener's hair stood on end as well when he saw the bizarre pictures on TV. "That was the biggest joke. Every television station was able to record it, the press was involved—you can't imagine how bad it was—there are lots of recordings of it. I was horrified. I said to Genscher: 'That goes against all tactical ground rules.' He replied, 'Well, it looks as though many of the police are completely ignorant about these things.' That's how the whole thing went down—a singular fiasco."

The helpless liberation attempt was doomed before it had even begun. Security personnel and sports fans all over the world could watch the build-up in extreme detail. There were television sets in every room of the Israeli accommodations. It remains unclear whether one of them was switched on. In any case, the police activities did not go undetected. Once again, terrorist leader Issa threatened to shoot two hostages on the spot if police forces were not withdrawn immediately. So, to the great relief of the officers involved, Police Chief Schreiber called off the kamikaze operation.

After this failure, the crisis management group had to face the impossibility of storming the building. The plans for a rescue operation now focused on the route to Fürstenfeldbruck military airfield. The Palestinians had demanded an aircraft to be flown to Cairo with the hostages. To buy time, the Germans encouraged the terrorists to believe that everything was being done to get them out of the country. In reality, the crisis team had agreed early on that this could not be allowed under any circumstances. The Israeli hostages and their kidnappers were not to leave German soil.

In the meantime, Chancellor Willy Brandt had arrived in Munich and made a stab at arranging their departure anyway. During several telephone calls with the Egyptian prime minister he tried to find a last-minute solution. Brandt informed Minister of the Interior Genscher that Cairo had flat-out refused to allow the hostage-takers into their country. "In the course of this telephone conversation … we came to the conclusion that the diplomatic efforts had to be regarded as having failed." Since the ultimatum expired at 9:00 p.m., the only chance of survival for the hostages was a liberation attempt by force, he told Genscher.[13] The question was how and where?

The terrorists and hostages were to be picked up by helicopter to then be flown to Fürstenfeldbruck military airfield. The route to the helicopter landing pad on the Olympic grounds was supposed to lead through an underground car park. There, the terrorists were to be overpowered. Or so was the plan. It collapsed when Issa, the leader of the kidnappers, inspected the location and smelled danger. It was perfectly clear to him that by moving through unclear corridors and passing unlit corners they would become easy targets. Ulrich Wegener later reported that Issa discovered several armed police officers tucked away behind parked cars, which unsurprisingly caused the Palestinian to throw a tantrum. He then demanded a bus to take them and the hostages to the helicopter, which was duly granted. All these failed attempts to catch the terrorists off guard only caused them to grow more suspicious by the minute.

Thus, the options for a successful raid were dwindling as time was relentlessly passing by. While the terrorists waited for the bus, preparations for the hostage rescue at Fürstenfeldbruck were underway. A Lufthansa Boeing 727 was waiting on the apron with engines running. A number of volunteer officers dressed as crew members were to overpower two of the terrorists in the cabin as they inspected the aircraft. At the same time, outside, the three other terrorists were to be taken out by snipers. Five officers with precision rifles were therefore posted around the helicopter landing site, four on the roofs of the control tower, an office wing and the two-story fire station, and one at ground level behind a truck.

One Big Fiasco

Shortly after 10:00 p.m., the kidnappers and their hostages exit the Israeli accommodation and are transported to two awaiting helicopters. Hans-Dietrich Genscher is watching at the window of a neighboring building. "One, two, three, four … eight!" counts the minister. Eight terrorists board the waiting bus, not five as had been assumed. A crucial piece of information! Information, though, that would never reach the operatives in Fürstenfeldbruck. Even later, no one would think of passing the total number of hostage-takers on to the operations center, since everybody falsely assumed that this had already been done.

Soon enough, the two Bell helicopters start their engines and climb over the heads of the onlookers into the night amid a flurry of flashbulbs from the photojournalists. On board: eight Palestinians and nine Israeli hostages, plus two pilots in each helicopter. A third helicopter with Ministers Genscher, Merk, other members of the crisis team, Wegener, and Israeli Intelligence Chief Zamir takes off immediately afterward but is first to land at the airport. The pilots of the other two helicopters have been instructed to fly as slowly as possible and to take detours in order to buy time for preparations for the raid.

These preparations, however, turn out to be a disaster. The 16 members of the police force which has been scheduled for the raid inside the aircraft are not volunteers by any standard, but patrol officers who have been ordered there. Their armament: one service pistol each, with 17 rounds of ammunition. Only after a heated discussion are they allowed three submachine guns between them. Subsequently, they check the plane's cabin and unanimously come to the conclusion that their chances of survival in a firefight are negligible. And there would *be* a firefight: 16 crew members assigned to a relatively small plane would necessarily arouse further suspicion among the already highly alert terrorists. On top of that, there aren't even enough Lufthansa uniforms available. Some officers have to wear their police uniform trousers instead. Unanimously, they decide that they are not available for such a "suicide mission" (in the words of one of the officers involved). They leave the aircraft—at the precise moment when the position lights of the two helicopters with the terrorists and hostages appear on the horizon.

Now it is up to the snipers, who still do not know that there are eight terrorists, not five. But for at least two of the snipers, it would have been impossible to have been informed of this essential fact anyway, because they have no radios. Allegedly, none are available. Later it will be said that there was not enough time to get one for every sniper. Well, there are plenty of walkie-talkies in the Olympic village; all the stewards like Dieter Tutter are equipped with them. Moreover, their weaponry is inadequate. The rifles are by no means precision weapons and are not suitable for long range. Riflescopes are scarce, as are infrared or night-vision devices. Bulletproof vests? Steel helmets? Zero, despite early requests by the head of operations (the official report will later describe the armament as "optimal"). Three trained snipers have also been left behind in the Olympic village. Apparently, two of them have simply been forgotten, while another one is told he is no longer needed, whereupon he goes home. But even eight snipers would barely have sufficed. Even at the time, counterterrorism experts typically reckon with at least two snipers per terrorist (today it is three). This means that even with "only" five hijackers, 10 snipers should be in position. And accordingly, at least 16 snipers to cover eight terrorists, not five.

To make matters even worse, the landing site lies in dim light. "When we arrived in Fürstenfeldbruck, it was pitch black," Zvi Zamir later reports. "I could hardly believe it. We would have floodlit the area brightly."* That had well been the plan, but the helicopters touch down some 30 yards off the intended spot and are now sitting in the dark. As another consequence, one sniper is now positioned straight in the field of fire of two others. Mossad Chief Zamir is irritated. "I thought that maybe they had additional snipers or armored cars hidden in the dark. But this was not the case. The Germans were simply out of their depth. Entirely out of their depth."

What follows next can only be described as utter chaos: When leader Issa and another terrorist inspect the cabin of the abandoned Lufthansa aircraft, they realize that this must be an ambush. Their Kalashnikovs raised, they signal as much to the others as they leave the plane. The first shots are being fired from German rifles. One of the terrorists goes down, but it is not leader Issa. This is not due to a lack of opportunity, but to a lack of resolve. In a television documentary, one of the officers will later anonymously state, "It's like you see it in crime thriller movies: there are the crosshairs with a head in the middle. But it doesn't work easy just like that. There is this kind of bite inhibition. You can't just shoot down a person who is more or less defenseless, good or evil. You have to be trained in it. And we never got that training."[14]

Some of the terrorists throw themselves under the helicopters, where they can no longer be seen by the German snipers. From under there, they fire machine-gun salvos, apparently indiscriminately, but successfully. A riot policeman, who is supposed to be backing up the snipers with his squad, is hit in the head and killed on the spot. Several projectiles penetrate the windows of the control tower where Minister Genscher and the rest of the crisis team have gathered, and where they now take cover under desks. Minutes pass without the situation changing a whole lot. The Germans cannot manage to close in on the entrenched terrorists, since some of them are in each other's line of fire. Hope now relies on armored vehicles from the Olympic village, which have been hurriedly called in. But they are stuck in a traffic jam outside the airport. And at the center of the firefight sit the helicopters with the hostages trapped inside.

In desperation, Ulrich Wegener turns to a riot police commander whose unit had been moved to the tower building and now stands at the ready, but apparently has no instructions as to what to do. "After the first shots, I spoke to the commander and asked: 'Won't you eventually intervene? Won't you go and carry out an attack to save at least a few of the hostages?'" But the officer just replies that he has not been given directives and that he needs to wait until someone gives him an order.

---

* Surprisingly, the official Bavarian investigation draws the opposite conclusion: the apron was too brightly lit and the resulting shadows irritated the snipers.

"I'm pretty sure that he was happy to not have an order," Wegener would later state sarcastically. Nothing moves forward and nothing moves back. After more than an hour, the belatedly requested armored vehicles finally arrive on the scene. As they approach, the terrorists start shooting at the hostages in the helicopters. Just before a sniper bullet takes leader Issa out, he manages to throw a hand grenade into one of the helicopters. The explosion kills all hostages inside. Those in the second helicopter are shot and killed by another terrorist.

Up in the tower, next to Genscher, Wegener is doomed to watch helplessly as the Israeli Olympic athletes are murdered. "It was one big fiasco. For me, it was the most traumatic event of my career. At that moment I swore to myself that something like that would never happen again." Even though shots are still being fired, men of the airport fire brigade try to extinguish the burning helicopter, but they are taken under fire by the terrorists. They flee from their fire truck as the wreckage, the dead, and the terrorists disappear under a carpet of foam.

"I suppose the German forces did their best, but they just didn't stand a chance," Ehud Barak says, as he analyzed the "amateurish operation" in retrospect. "I am sure that people acted to the best of their knowledge and belief. But their knowledge was very limited. It's as if you and I were in an extreme situation where we had to perform brain surgery on someone. The chances of the patient being alive at the end are very slim. But we are intelligent, capable people, we have a lot of experience in many other fields. Yes, but we don't have any experience in doing brain surgery, and it's a delicate operation based on details."

Dieter Tutter recalls, "I felt rage boiling up inside me, because on our police radios we were able to listen to all open channels: Munich police, Federal Border Guard, helicopters, all of it. It was a disaster!" Eighty-three-year-old Tutter is still agitated today when he recounts how he sat at the radios in the command post in the bell tower of the Olympic village, condemned to inactivity. "There was this unsatisfying feeling: this can't be it! After such a cruel defeat, you can't just go back to business as usual!"

At 00:30 a.m. the last shot is fired, almost two hours after the helicopters touched down. When silence finally falls on the apron, all nine hostages are dead, along with five terrorists and a German policeman, a total death toll of 17 when adding the two Israelis who have been killed in the Olympic village at the very beginning of the attack. Another policeman and a pilot are seriously injured by friendly fire, three Palestinian terrorists survive, only one of them slightly injured.

Genscher and Wegener immediately fly back to the Olympic village. A press conference has already been held there, falsely claiming success for the operation and the liberation of all hostages. It is 3:00 a.m., more than 22 hours after the Palestinian terrorists climbed over that fence in the Olympic village. Exhausted and scarred, it is now up to the minister of the interior to share the truth about the devastating outcome of the hostage crisis with the stunned reporters, and the public. "I had rarely seen Genscher as upset as on that day," adviser Wegener would later recall. "He didn't want to be spoken to anymore. He was utterly troubled that he had not been able to prevent the catastrophe. After the press conference he said to me, 'I have just sent a report to the chancellor and we must now consider what to do next.' I replied, 'We need to do one thing, minister. I have told you before, we need a special counterterrorist unit that can deal with such situations in the future.'"

Genscher saw it exactly the same way.

CHAPTER 2

Troops against Terror

The next morning, Jörg Probstmeier's secondary school schedule listed biology and German. Instead, the student listened to his visibly agitated teacher: "She told us that the liberation of the Israeli athletes had been a failure, that there had been many casualties. And she reminded us of our historical responsibility and guilt for the persecution of people of the Jewish faith in the Third Reich."[1] When she had finished, there was an embarrassed silence in the graduating class; some had tears in their eyes, as did Probstmeier. Like everyone else, he had heard about the hostage-taking, but this lesson turned out to be a key experience for the 16-year-old. Six months later, he applied for a job with the Federal Border Guard and ended up with the organization that was to be founded as a consequence of the catastrophe. "That morning, I realized that we, being the grandchildren of the Nazi generation, had a share of responsibility for ensuring that something like this would not happen again."

The "Munich massacre" sent real-time shock waves around the globe. Hundreds of millions of people on all continents had been following live how the hostage drama had unfolded in the Olympic village over the course of a whole day, and shortly after they saw the devastating footage from Fürstenfeldbruck. The image of the burnt-out helicopter wreckage on the airfield's apron would soon turn into an icon of contemporary history, a symbol of horror frozen in time. It revealed a hitherto unknown dimension of terrorism.

But almost as shocking as the act itself was the complete incompetence of state officials, politicians and security forces to cope with the situation—the reckless lack of concern in the run-up to the Olympic Games, the utter mess of responsibilities during the crisis situation, the communication chaos, and the aggregated police incapacity. The latter started with the missing barriers, equipment and armament of the officers, fundamental mistakes in the tactics of the operation, and ended with the number of snipers deployed. Many details that had led to the catastrophe would only come to light in the months and years to follow. But one thing appeared painfully clear: the German state had failed miserably.

The influential Israeli newspaper *Ha'aretz* stated with bitter overtones, "Our team went to Munich on the assumption that the host country would provide for their security.... This expectation was not fulfilled. The responsibility for this lies with the West German authorities." The Italian state radio, on the other hand, was sympathetic: "It is an exceedingly bitter price that the Germans must pay precisely for wanting to break away from the old cliché, for demilitarizing their basic attitude and perhaps handling the controls in the Olympic village a little too softly, loosely and cordially." And the London *Times* stated, "These were mistakes made by the security forces; failures of inadequacy and confusion and failure to cope with circumstances of exceptional difficulty. They were mistakes, but not crimes."

The German press was much less lenient and asked uncomfortable questions about responsibilities. "Could it have been avoided?" poked West Germany's leading news magazine, *Der Spiegel*, on its cover. Editor Rudolf Augstein commented, stunned, "I don't understand why the Israelis and the Germans, being the hosts, have provided such inadequate protection for the Israeli team. Surely it could have been assumed that a security guard disguised as a sportsman or a coach slept or, better, kept watch next to each Israeli team member."[2] In the same issue, Chancellor Brandt openly confessed that the Munich events offered "an appalling document of German incompetence."[3] International terrorism had caught the Federal Republic flat-footed.

The Decade of Terror

But the horror that had so abruptly befallen the "merry games" did not emerge out of the blue. In fact, the bloody hostage-taking was merely the sad culmination of a year of terrorist attacks, and 1972 marked the climax. For years, there had been rumblings all over Europe, be it bombs and arson attacks by the Red Brigades in Italy and the Irish Republican Army (IRA) in Northern Ireland, or aircraft hijackings by the PFLP*—international terrorism had been highly active since the late 1960s, stepping up in frequency and dimension year by year. The number of attacks worldwide increased fivefold within a decade, from just over 100 per annum in 1968 to around 500 attacks by the end of the 1970s (with the Olympic year 1972 setting a sad record with 600). The number of dead and injured also multiplied and grew from attack to attack.[4] Terrorism became more interlinked, more powerful, more professional, and more indiscriminate concerning its victims. It was not only politicians and public officials anymore who were in danger of being targeted, but business travelers, tourists—or even athletes, as had been the case in Munich.

---

* PFLP (Popular Front for the Liberation of Palestine) = Palestinian terror organization, operating mainly in the 1970s and '80s.

And what of homegrown terrorism? In the summer months before the Olympics, law enforcement had crushed what the politically interested contemporary, depending on personal political preference, used to call either the "Baader Meinhof Group" (left-leaning) or the "Baader Meinhof Gang" (conservative), which constituted the nucleus of the RAF. Within two weeks in the spring of 1972, four people were killed and over forty were injured in six bomb attacks. The RAF called it the "May Offensive," and up to this point they were the most vicious terrorist attacks the radical left group had undertaken. Now its leaders were incarcerated, awaiting trial. Many Germans breathed a sigh of relief. Prematurely, as Munich had shown. Germany's first homegrown terrorist group would turn out to be long-lived and quite dangerous, with a so-called second and third generation following the lethal footsteps of Andreas Baader, Gudrun Ensslin, Ulrike Meinhof, Horst Mahler, and Jan-Carl Raspe. Their arrests would not mark their group's end, not by a long shot. Being the figureheads of leftist German terrorism, attempts to liberate them from their alleged "political incarceration" would eventually lead to the dramatic climax of 1977 described in the later chapters of this book.

Their international ties were strong, as the incident in Munich clearly demonstrated. It was no coincidence that among the list of 130 Palestinian prisoners to be ransomed there was the demand for the release of Ulrike Meinhof, intellectual figurehead of the RAF. It was also no coincidence that in her pamphlet circulated a few weeks later, "On the Strategy of the Anti-Imperialist Struggle," Meinhof hailed the "historic mission" of the Black September terrorists as "simultaneously anti-imperialist, anti-fascist" and "avant-garde." The string-puller and contracting entity behind the Black September hostage-takers was Palestinian leader Ali Hassan Salameh, aka Abu Hassan. He was considered the most-wanted terrorist in the world. As commander in chief of the Palestinian training camps of Al Fatah, he had instructed Ulrike Meinhof in guerrilla warfare two years earlier in Jordan, along with other top RAF heads such as Andreas Baader, Horst Mahler, and Gudrun Ensslin.[5]

After Black September's first spectacular action—the hijacking of Sabena Flight 571 from Brussels to Tel Aviv in May 1972, violently terminated by Israeli commandos—the terrorist group agreed with members of the IRA, the Japanese Red Army, and representatives of the RAF in a Libyan refugee camp on mutual support for worldwide terrorist action. In addition, they planned attacks in their own countries as representatives for the other groups, as a kind of terrorist joint venture, so to speak. For example, the RAF was to carry out attacks in West Germany on behalf of the Palestinians. In return, the Middle East repeatedly offered German terrorists places of retreat. When the air in Germany became too thick, they moved to Beirut, Baghdad, or Aden, to wait and prepare for new actions.[6] This brew of German and international terrorism kept simmering in the years that followed and would reach a boiling point in the fall of 1977 when a Palestinian commando hijacked the German Lufthansa Flight LH-181 on behalf of the RAF, ending up in Mogadishu. Five years prior, few saw the extent of the web of terror that was forming, or its destructive potential. But even without this knowledge, it was clear that a situation like Munich could happen again at any time.

Back in Bonn

Hans-Dietrich Genscher returned deeply shaken from Munich to the West German capital. In his memoirs, he described the event at Fürstenfeldbruck as "the most terrible experience of my entire time in office."[7] While still in Munich, he offered his resignation to Willy Brandt. But the chancellor refused. Genscher had nothing to reproach himself for; he had done everything that could be done in his position. In meetings, the minister and his staff soon concluded that "the Munich city police and also the Bavarian state police were not at all prepared for this—but it would have been no different in any other place in Germany."[8] The analysis was as clear as it was devastating: There was no single line of defense against such ruthless terrorist attacks. For this new degree of violent confrontation, "new forms of police reaction" had to be found—or invented.

But it seemed equally clear to Genscher that the security authorities of the German provinces would not be able to do this on their own. As with the federal government, none of the provinces had specially trained police units at their disposal that could cope with such a terrorist threat. Therefore, two days after Fürstenfeldbruck, Genscher gave the order to develop "a concept for a special task force within one week."[9] The project was both urgent and delicate, because a special meeting, the Conference of Ministers of the Interior of the federal government and the Bundesländer (or federal provinces), had been called for September 13, 1972.

After World War II, the Allies came to the conclusion that Germany must never, ever again be allowed to pose a threat to its direct neighbors or the world as a whole. One measure to guarantee this was to make sure that Germany not only became a democratic state, but also one that did away with its former centrist structure, being governed from Berlin and dominated by the traditional Prussian authoritarian class. Instead, a sturdy federal system was established, handing strong legislative, executive, and judicial powers to the individual provinces—not quite as strong as that of individual states within the United States, but much stronger than in the UK, with its weak county and city councils. Starting in 1946, three years prior to the foundation of the two German states, West German provinces, or Länder, were given substantial autonomy on questions of school and university education, culture, arts and museums, local infrastructure—and, most importantly, police sovereignty. The representatives of the Länder soon took their newly acquired authority very seriously and were known to fight even the slightest hint of infringement on their autonomy in this field. Creating a special task force on the national level would of course bear the threat of doing exactly that, something the respective ministers of the interior would not take lightly.

On the eve of the conference, Chancellor Willy Brandt commented in an interview with the daily *Frankfurter Rundschau* (in consultation with the minister of the interior, as can be assumed): "For the future it is certainly true that, based on the Munich lessons, we must arrive at even more effective forms, including the existence of mobile units trained for such cases, which presumably have a higher degree of probability of success." It was one of the few occasions on which the chancellor spoke publicly on this subject. Brandt thus threw his authority into the balance and signaled support for his minister, but remained sufficiently unspecific to give him political leeway. Genscher knew how to make use of it.

The next day, the federal minister of the interior revealed his plans to his Länder colleagues: "I think we have to admit to ourselves that we have not sufficiently taken terrorist attacks of such magnitude and brutality into account in our planning.... In the security meeting with officials of my house on 9/8/1972, I therefore gave instructions to work out within this week concepts for the establishment of a special task force ... which can be called upon to solve special police tasks. I am thinking of a group of police officers of the appropriate age who would be subjected to Ranger-like* training. The most modern equipment would also have to be available. I would not hesitate, if necessary, to place the special task force at your disposal for special assignments in your area of responsibility, but would welcome it if you could also decide to set up such task forces over and above the measures taken so far."[10]

In normal times, this project would have become a delicate balancing act. In normal times, the ministers of the interior of the Länder would have defended their sovereignty over police and internal security tooth and nail, and the idea of a federal counterterrorist unit would probably have stood no chance. But times were not normal. With the images from Munich fresh in their minds, Federal Minister Genscher had an easy time with his colleagues from the provincial capitals from Kiel to Munich. In this special session, the conference of ministers of the interior unanimously agreed to his proposal, and they also decided to set up their own special police forces within their respective state police departments. In the city-state of Berlin, and in Bavaria and Hamburg, there were already rudimentary approaches for such special units. Most of the other provinces, though, did not appear to be particularly enthusiastic about revamping their departments. Police sovereignty or

---

* The Army Rangers of the US military are cited in many contemporary sources and newspaper reports as the model for GSG 9 and other Special Intervention Units. Soon-to-be commander Wegener, too, was enthusiastic about the lone wolf qualities of the Rangers. To a certain degree, this reveals the general ignorance of even supposed experts in these matters. The Rangers themselves were in no way prepared for dealing with terrorist threats at the time. Precisely to fill the gap in these capabilities, the special ops unit Delta Force was established by the US military in 1977.

not, they seemed happy to let the federal government take the lead, especially as the topic of international terrorism soon disappeared from public attention anyway.

For as big as the Olympic shock had been, it did not go deep—at least not among large parts of the public and the political class. The chancellor maintained his passive attitude, both internally and externally. Brandt did not seize the opportunity to put terrorism on the international agenda, and in discussions with his foreign policy partners the topic was left out in the following weeks and months when he met with European leaders such as British Prime Minister Edward Heath or French President Georges Pompidou. During the general election campaign for the Bundestag, the lower parliament chamber, in autumn 1972, international terrorism played no role whatsoever. The Munich attack was widely considered an isolated incident, and in its abysmal handling representatives of political parties on all levels of state had been involved. There was no political gain to be expected from any sort of campaigning. Neither the reigning center-left coalition of Social Democrats (SPD under Chancellor Brandt) and Free Democrats (FDP with Minister Genscher), nor the conservative opposition (CDU), seemed to show much hope for swaying voters with the subject of international terrorism, nor did they even seem to identify it as a serious issue at all.

Instead, the problem was put off. International terrorism was still not taken seriously, but largely perceived as a form of "foreigners' crime." Had the perpetrators not been foreigners who took foreign hostages? It appeared that Germany had rather accidentally come into the line of fire. Consequently, few regulatory measures resulted from this shrugging approach. Apart from somewhat stricter controls at German airports (which up until that time were virtually non-existent), a number of suspicious Palestinian associations were banned, a couple of Palestinian terror suspects deported, and stricter entry regulations put in place for "Arabs" and people who looked like them—a regulation which caused loud protests both at home and abroad, and otherwise turned out largely ineffective in terms of security. As historian Mathias Dahlke points out, none of the policies had any truly sustainable effect—except for one: "The initiative of founding GSG 9 is the only deliberately long-term measure that was tackled after the events in Munich and Zagreb.… The long-term orientation toward top task forces abroad as well as state-of-the-art technology and tactics created a means of fighting terror that is adequate even by today's standards."[11]

Being able to establish a counterterror police force under these circumstances was not an easy feat. Genscher knew that there was only a small window of opportunity for the inception of such a force, and it was closing fast. The constitutional question of police sovereignty in a federally organized nation was only one obstacle. Another one was the fact that anti-militarism ran strong within post-war West German society at the time. The thought of uniformed squads wearing steel helmets, bulletproof vests, and submachine guns made a lot of people feel queasy, even if it was "just" police uniforms they were wearing.

What's more, in the early 1970s the zeitgeist was moving in the exact opposite direction. There were debates about disarming the police force entirely, at least locking away the firearms of the average patrol officer, leaving him with only a truncheon and the hope of commanding authority via an impressive demeanor. This seems to have been at least part of the reason for the Bundesländer being so reluctant about creating their own task forces. Law enforcement at eye level was the motto of the day, not military-style, armed-to-the-teeth fighters.

In this case, though, Minister Hans-Dietrich Genscher found support for his plans among the public. The criticism in the national and international press about German incompetence during the hostage crisis had been loud and fierce. But it was not directed at Genscher as a person—people gave him a lot of credit for volunteering himself as a hostage, despite the fact that he was not formally responsible (the fact, however, that other politicians in Munich had offered themselves as hostages as well was somehow lost). In the weeks following the Munich massacre, Genscher's ministerial office received baskets full of mail hailing him as a hero.

The minister seized the opportunity. If the saying "to pop up out of the ground" ever applied, it was here. The legal foundations, financing, and organizational structure of the new entity were created at breakneck speed. One week after Munich, Genscher gave his speech at the special session of the Conference of the Ministers of the Interior where they unanimously agreed on establishing his special task force; again, one week later, the Budget Committee of the Bundestag unanimously approved 188 posts and 6.3 million Deutschmarks for the establishment of a task force. And only three days after that, instructions went out to the federal authority that was to set up the new unit. All in all, the whole process took barely three weeks.

By then it had also been decided which security authority was to be the new unit's parent organization. Genscher had left that open in the early days. In retrospect, it might seem rather obvious to assign such a commando unit to the Bundesgrenzschutz.[*] After all, the Federal Border Guard was the Federal Police, at least according to the law. But the letter of the law did not (yet) reflect the reality on the ground. And this reality was the fact that BGS still had a strong paramilitary inclination in their general attitude and mindset. Also, their officers did not receive regular police training, but rather a military one. BGS was still mainly used for securing the border along the Iron Curtain.

So why not locate the new anti-terrorist force within the Bundeswehr?[†] In his speech, Genscher had mentioned "Rangers," and they were a special military unit, right? But according to the minister, the option was never really envisaged: "This has not been seriously discussed."[12] And for good reason, too. What might be considered

---

[*] Bundesgrenzschutz (BGS) = Federal Border Guard.
[†] Bundeswehr = Federal Armed Forces: German Armed Forces, founded in 1955 for West Germany (East Germany: Nationale Volksarmee, NVA, or National People's Army).

unproblematic in other countries—the deployment of the military in non-military situations at home—is not covered by the Grundgesetz, West Germany's constitution. The matter was (and still is) deemed politically highly sensitive, unless it is a question of flood relief or support for vaccination campaigns. In his speech to the Conference of Ministers of the Interior, Genscher had brought up the Federal Criminal Police Office (BKA) as an alternative to the BGS. But this did not sit well with his BGS liaison officer, Wegener. "I knew how to prevent that through insistent talks with Genscher," he later reported with satisfaction. Wegener pleaded with Genscher, "We don't need more criminal investigators but a special intervention unit that can act kinetically against these terrorists." In the attempt to convince his minister, Wegener offered himself as head of the new unit to be founded (entirely selflessly, as is to be suspected). "On this, he agreed," Wegener writes in his memoir.

Was it really all down to Wegener's whispering that the new special unit was to be based at the BGS? In retrospect, the responsible minister describes the decision as the most natural thing in the world: "I thought that a Federal Police force was also the right thing to do because it could ensure a permanent presence. In addition, various BGS facilities would have had to be used anyway, starting with the helicopters, which were absolutely necessary. If you had a Federal Police force of 22,000 men at your disposal at the time, then everything spoke in favor of setting up the counterterrorist unit from this police force. After all, we didn't want to create countless new posts. The BKA would not have been able to take on the task with its personnel."[13]

It seems reasonable to assume that Genscher's initial openness to alternatives was more of a tactical consideration of the sensitivities and desires of the authorities in question; a motivating signal to avoid the appearance that the decision was cast in iron from the outset and that Wegener was already set as commander. Genscher, however, was sure that in Wegener he had hired the right man for the job: "In my opinion, he had the necessary professional and character qualifications for such a task."[14] And with that, the matter was decided. Competitors? Selection procedure? Obviously overrated. The decision to place GSG 9 directly under the Ministry of the Interior was apparently made in a similarly unpretentious manner. Only formally it stood under the regional Border Guard command, where the new unit would be located.

And so it would go on. The direct line to Genscher was worth its weight in gold for the new force, according to Wegener's aide-de-camp Hubertus Grützner: "If Genscher had not hired Wegener we would not have had the direct influence of the minister on GSG 9. The interpersonal relationship between Wegener and Genscher was characterized by trust. In this way, our ideas could be adopted undiminished. If that hadn't been the case, probably three or four people from the ministry would have gotten involved—that's just the way it is—and would have been able to inject their non-knowledge into GSG 9. This had been ruled out by the decision in favor of Wegener."[15] With Genscher's backing, Wegener pushed ahead with the founding of GSG 9 with a hands-on approach. The official federal German apparatus, not exactly known for its speed and efficiency, followed surprisingly smoothly and quickly, driven by unequivocal political will.

The first concept for the new unit was developed at a fishing pond outside the capital of Bonn, where Wegener's adjutant Grützner liked to spend his Sundays. Wegener, who had travelled there by bicycle, succinctly announced that they had been commissioned by the federal minister of the interior to deliver a draft. "We secluded ourselves and drew up this concept by hand, which we then gave to the typing service at the BMI.* Herr Genscher had the draft in his hands on Sunday and was able to present it to the cabinet the following day."[16]

And how about the name of the new unit? From the moment it became clear that it would belong to the Federal Border Guard, the files refer to it as "GSG 9," short for Grenzschutzgruppe 9 (or Border Guard Group 9). The number was due to the simple fact that so far there had been seven regular Border Guard groups in the BGS, as well as a Border Guard air wing. Wegener's concept paper soberly states that "the proposed designation adapts to this form of basic organization."[17] And that was that. One maybe wonders why neither of the two came up with a more resounding name like the ones that later became fashionable, such as Delta Force (United States), Enzian (Switzerland), or Cobra (Austria). In fact, Wegener later did call on his men to submit ideas, but anything with "Special ..." or "Counterterror ..." in its name did not fly with the German "civil servant framework," so finally they simply went along with the humble, unembellished GSG 9. But there was also a very tangible reason to keep it simple like this. The integration into the large structure of the BGS as one of their main sections came with the so-called regimental status, and thus with a far larger umbrella of personnel for the future commander than if it had been set up as a mere hundred-strong squad within one of the existing units.

Genscher's "Toy Train"

The establishment of a counterterrorism unit was a perfect fit for Genscher's overall security concept. Far from being a classical law-and-order hothead, he massively promoted the expansion of the security authorities. Since taking office in 1969, he had mainly focused on the Federal Criminal Police Office (BKA), the domestic intelligence service (BfV, or Office for the Protection of the Constitution), and finally the Federal Border Guard (BGS). "In all three areas, there was a considerable need to catch up in terms of personnel and equipment; in fact, when I took office, they were all in need of reform," Genscher writes in his memoirs. "In the preceding years, little had been done for the authorities concerned with homeland security and their staff. Violent political criminality was rampant."[18]

As early as 1969, Genscher had begun to turn the sedate federal offices upside down and transform them into modern agencies. Genscher considered terrorism

---

* BMI (Bundesministerium des Innern) = Federal Ministry of the Interior.

a challenge for creating constitutional institutions that could cope with it while safeguarding civil liberties at the same time. His biographer Hans-Dieter Heuman saw this as Genscher's greatest domestic political achievement: "The name Genscher is associated with an expansion of the Federal Criminal Police Office, the Federal Border Guard and the Office for the Protection of the Constitution that is unprecedented in the history of the Federal Republic of Germany. And yet he was at times the most popular politician in Bonn."

Policies aimed at the expansion of domestic security institutions were always met with great skepticism in West Germany. The suspicion of erecting a police super-state ran deep in German civil society. Every politician who wanted to extend existing security regulations, security agencies and personnel, or God forbid, security laws, had to face hefty headwinds by the political left inside and outside of parliament, and even from some centrist positions. The specter of the Nazi state's secret police Gestapo always loomed large, and any strengthening of law enforcement was considered proof of Germany degenerating into an authoritarian state. So Genscher knew that he was moving in a potential minefield. But he did so with the silent approval of the press and most of the public—and without stepping too much on the toes of the Länder, which always feared for their sovereign rights. "The rule of law was far from being 'exposed as a system of oppression' and rejected by the citizens, as some ideologues had hoped," Genscher's biographer summarized.[19]

Genscher's most important project was the reorganization of the Federal Criminal Police Office, BKA, under its president, the personally rather left-leaning Horst Herold. Herold's vision was to turn the BKA into some kind of German FBI, and Genscher promoted his ideas to the best of his ability. Genscher also expanded the Office for the Protection of the Constitution (BfV) by providing it with better personnel and funding. But even more than for the detectives in Wiesbaden (seat of the BKA) and the secret agents in Pulheim (seat of the BfV) near Cologne, Genscher had a soft spot for the BGS, his "toy train," as his then-Bureau Chief Klaus Kinkel later smirked. Whenever his minister was in a bad mood, he packed him in a parka and took him to the German–German border along the Iron Curtain. "He would look over with binoculars to check the locations of the barracks of the [East German] National People's Army, and in the evenings he would sing songs along with the men of the Federal Border Guard."

At the same time, the BGS had been a subject of debate since the 1960s. When Genscher took office in 1969, the BGS was even "faced with the question of its existence," according to Genscher in his political memoirs. This hybrid between police and armed forces had been founded in 1951 as a militia-like precursor to a West German army in order to secure the inner-German border. After the inception of the Bundeswehr, the military tasks were dropped by and by but were not (yet) replaced by police tasks. "When I became minister of the interior, the Federal Border Guard was a paramilitary institution intended for border security—as the name suggests. That had been rendered practically obsolete by political developments. So I found myself in the Ministry of the Interior preparing for the dissolution of the BGS. This, however, seemed to me to be a misjudgment of the internal security situation," Genscher said. Therefore, barely three weeks into office, he announced the reorganization of the BGS into a "powerful and modernly equipped police force," in a newspaper interview. One of his first official acts at that time was the appointment of a permanent BGS liaison officer: Ulrich Wegener.

Genscher followed up with action. In the course of the 1970s, the budget increased threefold, from 376 million Deutschmarks to over one billion. In addition, the minister consistently pushed for the transformation from a pure Border Guard force to a genuine Federal Police force. The proper name Bundespolizei, however, was a taboo word (and remained as such for decades), so as not to incite the Länder colleagues against the plans. Police sovereignty lay with them, so the name police was not to show up in any way on the federal level.

Genscher prepared his biggest legislative measure for 1972. In the year of the Olympics, he pushed a decisive amendment to the law through parliament regulating the BGS. This lifted the limit for the Border Guard to be deployed exclusively within a few miles of the borders and allowed for deployment deep inside the country, where it could also take on police tasks such as stopping and searching vehicles. Section 9 of the law "on the use of the Federal Border Guard to support the police of a province" had previously stated that the BGS could only be called in to maintain or restore public safety or to help in the event of natural disasters. Now the deployment was also possible "to avert an imminent danger to the existence or the free democratic basic order of the Federation or of a Bundesland."*

In national emergencies, the Federation finally had its own instrument at its disposal. Now, it could use the Federal Border Guard as a "police intervention reserve," as Genscher put it in his memoirs.[20] However, he at first found little support for the new law among the Länder. "My fatherly friend, supporter and party colleague, Willy Weyer, who as minister of the interior of North Rhine-Westphalia had a strong riot police force at his disposal, was the strongest advocate for the rights of the provinces. He had BGS-opposer Kuhlmann† breathing down his neck. In the end, however, we were able to win over everyone—the federal government and the provinces, the coalition and the opposition. And I needed them all for my plans. The new tasks of the BGS ... required a constitutional amendment and thus a two-thirds majority in the Bundestag and the Bundesrat.‡"[21] Genscher obtained this almost without any dissenting vote in July 1972, two months before the Olympic attack.

---

* Bundesland (or Land for short, plural: Bundesländer) = German provinces like Bavaria, Saxony, Hesse, and city-states like Hamburg and Berlin.
† Chairman of the police union, GdP.
‡ Bundesrat = The parliamentary upper chamber in which the provinces are represented.

The constitutional amendment also formed the legal basis on which Genscher was able to set up a counterterrorist unit like GSG 9 within a reformed BGS. There had been discussions about this within the Ministry of the Interior even before the Olympic Games. But according to Genscher, a task force on the national level would hardly have been politically feasible. "We had thought about it—very abstractly—in the few months that were available to us after the Federal Border Guard had been reclassified as a Federal Police, but the trigger moment was exclusively the Olympic Games in Munich."[22]

The minister of the interior had to contend with surprisingly little political headwind, either from the political opposition or the public. Only the aforementioned chairman of the trade union, Kuhlmann, did not hide his opinion of the BGS: "I can't see any advantages at all, but I can see serious disadvantages. I must point out once again that the BGS does not have police-trained officers. What is offered as support to the Länder are commandos that are militarily organized, trained and armed. But it must not be overlooked that officers of such special commandos must also have other qualifications than just these. Live fire can and must only be a last resort."[23] The weekly newspaper *Die Zeit* echoed the same sentiment: "Providing snipers and close combatants, however, should remain a matter for the Länder.... Nothing could have more serious consequences one day than the hasty call for a less squeamish special unit over the heads of the police officers." But apart from these two objections, there were hardly any reservations about the establishment of the new special unit at the BGS; at any rate, there were no major public debates.

Thus, the issue was settled, and the organization of the new task force was quickly established. As early as November 1972, Wegener reported to the ad hoc committee of the Conference of Ministers of the Interior on the formation of the new force as a "fully motorized airmobile unit." Specifically: "A command group ... would be attached to the commander. Below the command group, there would be 4 operational units* (= reinforced platoons) and the supply services. The 4 operational units were to be interchangeable. In the final state, they were to consist of 3 'squads' each; snipers would not be grouped in a special unit, but would belong to each of these 4 operational units, with a total of at least 18 in each case."[24] In addition, there were to be three technical groups with mechanics, technicians and explosives experts, as well as a documentation and evidence-securing squad with cameramen and sound technicians. Finally, a "helicopter chain" with pilots, caretakers, and mechanics was to provide the necessary air mobility.

Wegener promised readiness for action within three hours anywhere in the Federal Republic of Germany, taking off from Saint Augustin, the headquarters of the new unit. The nearby local airfield offered itself. It was located close to the capital, not

---

* Counter to what is stated here, GSG 9 started out with only three operational units. The fourth one would not be established until well into the 1980s.

far from the Cologne-Bonn Airport, and centrally located within West Germany. According to Wegener, there were also considerations to establish additional GSG 9 garrisons, making sure to reach any location in West Germany within 45 minutes.[25] This idea does not appear to have been pursued further, however. It certainly never materialized (not until almost 50 years later when a second location was set up in the then not-so-new capital, Berlin). Wegener promised that the deployment was to be completed on April 31, 1973.[26] Not much time, barely half a year. Recruitment had already started. On September 26, 1972, three weeks to the day after the Munich massacre, the minister of the interior had an express letter sent to the Border Guard administrations, South, Central, North and Coast:

> CONFIDENTIAL—for internal use only!
>
> Subject: Establishment of a Federal Border Guard unit for special police operations (GSG 9)
>
> 1. to combat crimes committed by gangs, e.g. aircraft hijackings, explosive attacks, hostage-taking, etc., GSG 9 will be set up drafting from all command regions.
>
> ...
>
> 3. the formation and command of GSG 9 is entrusted to OTL* Wegener of Federal Ministry of the Interior.
>
> 4. the aforementioned unit is to be composed exclusively of <u>volunteer police officers</u>. Based on voluntary reports, the commanders shall select those police enforcement officers of BGS who are
> – ready for action
> – of good character
> – professionally experienced
> – prudent
> – capable of acting independently, but are willing to subordinate themselves and have above-average mental abilities as well as physical ability.
>
> ...
>
> 9. Commander of GSG 9 will make the selection from the reported officers directly in the respective command area.[27]

This express letter was distributed to all BGS garrisons, including Kassel, where Telecommunications Officer Dieter Tutter marched to his colonel at once, the images from Munich and the feeling of utter helplessness still fresh in his mind. However, he was not prepared for the commander's reaction: "You're crazy, Tutter! I've just suggested you for the rank of captain. Man, that's nonsense; it won't work! I know this Wegener, he's a nutcase!" Tutter didn't know this Wegener person, "but for me this task force was an overdue idea. Something needed to happen! He couldn't hold me back. And I joined the special unit to fight violent crime and terrorism."

---

* OTL (*Oberstleutnant*) = Lieutenant Colonel.

When Dieter Tutter arrived in Saint Augustin shortly thereafter, he found only Wegener, as well as the designated leader of the 1st Operational Unit, Frieder Baum, and the head of the office, Manfred Kutscha. Thus, Tutter became number four of "The 9ers" as they would soon be dubbed. By mid-October, 120 men had applied to GSG 9,[28] including a dozen or so of the BGS men who, like Tutter, had been assigned to Munich. Apart from some emptied-out barracks, there was not yet much to be seen of the new special task force. No equipment, no armament, no selection procedure, no training guidelines, no operational tactics. All of that had to be procured and created. For now, there was only a commander with a lot of ideas.

CHAPTER 3

Wegener in Israel

Appointing "nutcase" Ulrich Wegener as head of the new special intervention unit seemed the obvious choice for Genscher. The minister held Wegener's pragmatic advice in high regard, and he liked his direct, hands-on approach. However, Wegener's directness did not go down well everywhere—not in the corridors of the Ministry of the Interior, which put a lot of emphasis on formal procedures, nor in the highly bureaucratic and strictly hierarchical BGS. What Genscher welcomed as unconventional was considered adventurism and just plain nonsense by many officers on the staff and commanders in the garrisons. They believed the new task force to be expensive science fiction as well as a nuisance, because it siphoned away valuable resources that could be of much better use elsewhere. Or so they believed.

Wegener, by then in his early forties, had already climbed high on the career ladder. The command of the new unit granted the minister's former liaison officer additional influence. Being classified as one of the *Grenzschutzgruppen* (Border Guard groups), GSG 9, despite barely 200 planned personnel, was at once on par with the other eight groups, each of which had several thousand Border Guard officers on duty. Formally, GSG 9 was organizationally positioned under BGS Command West, but Wegener got Genscher to place his small unit operationally straight under the ministry. This granted him unhindered access to the ear of his highest superior, allowing him to bypass annoying formalities and bureaucratic oversight by the BGS top brass. This, of course, did not exactly expand his circle of friends within the Border Guard.

Wegener's appointment was certainly meant as a signal to the BGS. At the beginning of the 1970s, the Border Guard suffered from a reform backlog which Genscher's law reform could not change overnight. In addition to all-powerful bureaucracy, the BGS still had a strong paramilitary orientation. Equipment and training, mindset and organization, were geared toward border security and national defense, but hardly toward the kind of police tasks the minister of the interior was aiming for.[1] This focus was rooted in the history of the BGS as a predecessor of the Bundeswehr. Founded in 1951, six years after the war and four years before the regular army, it was primarily intended for deployment at the eastern demarcation line of the Iron Curtain in the early years of the Cold War.

"The United Chiefs of Staff have ... agreed to recommend to the Council of Foreign Ministers that West Germany be permitted to have 5,000 Federal Police," read a joint declaration of the Allies on May 17, 1950. One year later, those 5,000 men became 10,000, then 20,000, and finally 22,000. The Federal Police's primary role was to serve as "a kind of trip wire ... toward the East," as Minister of the Interior Genscher once put it.[2] His predecessor Robert Lehr warned in the Bundestag, shortly before the establishment of the BGS in 1951: "It has certainly not escaped your attention—through the press, radio and perhaps also through your own observation—that in the last few months an ever increasing number of persons have entered illegally across our borders, namely persons whom we know, or of whom we can assume, that they are not well-disposed toward the Federal Republic of Germany, that they are determined and in some cases even expressly instructed to instigate unrest or to foment already existing unrest and to exploit it for their dark plans.... You may rest assured that, according to the information we have received, the extent of the border violations deserves the utmost attention."[3]

The Border Guard was supposed to secure a strictly defined border strip 30 kilometers deep and, in the event of war or civil unrest, fight communist insurgents and partisans. Apart from these tasks, there were but few exceptions, like guard duty outside federal buildings and the like. This changed starting from the end of the 1960s with the so-called *Notstandsgesetze*, a number of highly controversial laws. In case of national emergencies, they would partly restrict basic civil rights and allow for Border Guard forces to be dispatched inside Germany. In the event of natural disasters, accidents or danger to the existence of the democratic constitutional order it was now possible to deploy BGS units to maintain or restore public safety and order.

This formally transformed the BGS from a pure Border Guard into a versatile Federal Police force. Nevertheless, much of the original paramilitary character of the Border Guard remained intact for decades. True, military ranks were abolished from the mid-1970s onwards (against fierce resistance from conservative opposition in the Bundestag as well as from the BGS leadership). Until then, the designations ranged from *Grenzjäger* to *Generalmajor* (with the addition "i. BGS" to set them apart from Bundeswehr ranks). However, many of the older officers found it difficult to get used to police ranks such as *Polizeihauptkommissar*[*] and *Polizeihauptinspektor*[†]—and indeed, some never did. Ulrich Wegener was one of them and would not quite warm up to the new nomenclature either. During this period, the Bundesgrenzschutz also began to sort out its light and medium infantry weapons. Nevertheless, machine guns, grenade launchers and bazookas still lay dormant in BGS depots up until

---

[*] *Polizeihauptkommissar* = Chief superintendent of police.
[†] *Polizeihauptinspektor* = Chief police inspector.

the 1980s. And until 1994, according to international laws of war, BGS officers were even assigned combatant status in the case of defense. Initiated by Minister of the Interior Genscher at the end of the 1960s, the transformation into a proper Federal Police force took more than three decades until BGS was finally officially rebranded Bundespolizei in 2005.

In its early years, BGS was dependent on former members of the Wehrmacht to fill its ranks, even more so than when the Bundeswehr was founded four years later. There is a famous exchange between West Germany's first chancellor, Konrad Adenauer, and a journalist from the time of the rearmament debate. When asked, "Mr. Chancellor, will Adolf Hitler's generals also be Konrad Adenauer's generals?" he just shrugged, "I am afraid NATO will not accept 18-year-old generals from me." This was certainly even more true for the generals at the Bundesgrenzschutz. No unencumbered officers could have emerged in the few years since the war. But the Western Alliance needed West Germany as a buffer state in the confrontation with the Eastern Bloc, so the commander in chief of NATO, General Dwight D. Eisenhower, in 1951 issued a declaration of honor for former members of the Wehrmacht serving in the BGS.

In practice, the spirit within what was supposed to be a Federal Police force was military through and through. And when the Bundeswehr was founded a few years later, thousands of BGS men formed the core of the new army—one-third of the personnel was recruited from the ranks of the Border Guard. The corresponding law stipulated that one month after it came into effect, all officers would automatically become professional soldiers in the Bundeswehr. Those who did not wish to switch had to expressly object. More than half of the BGS officers, non-commissioned officers, as well as rank and file transferred to the new army, partly because immediate promotion beckoned there. For young, ambitious junior staff in the BGS on the other hand, the vacant positions meant career opportunities—including for Ulrich Wegener. His family background and early career do not indicate a particular tendency towards "nutcase-ism," but rather the opposite.

Wegener's Path to the Border Guards

Wegener was born in the final years of the Weimar Republic, Germany's first attempt at parliamentary democracy. His parents' house in the small town of Jüterbog, some 60 kilometers southwest of Berlin, sat right next to an artillery school. "The military environment had a great impact on me," Wegener later recalled. Being the son of an enthusiastic professional officer in the Reichswehr,* Ulrich Klaus Wegener grew up in a strictly conservative household. "My father was a great role model in my eyes;

---

* Reichswehr = Predecessor of the Wehrmacht in the time of the Weimar Republic and early years of the Third Reich 1921–1935.

for me, there was no other option but an officer's career."[4] Accordingly, he had no qualms identifying himself with the stereotypical Prussian values that were upheld in his family: bravery, discipline, honor, ambition, modesty, but also "courage to help others," as he writes. Young Ulrich was fascinated by Prussian military history, especially Frederick the Great, Clausewitz, and von Moltke. Their "timeless" theories on strategy and tactics shaped his thinking, Wegener claims.

On the other hand, he had no great sympathy for Adolf Hitler's National Socialists, while hardly being a resistance fighter either. At least that is how he describes it in his 2016 autobiographical account *GSG 9—Stärker als der Terror*.[5] Wegener attributes his skeptical attitude to the influence of his father, who, for all his conservatism, was a strict opponent of Hitler and his anti-Semitic ideology. When his son Ulrich felt pressured to join the Hitlerjugend (Hitler Youth), his father was not at all pleased. He advised his son to muddle through, which he did, as he freely admits, "I did not actively oppose National Socialism, but rather kept my distance. Since I wasn't an enthusiastic Hitlerjunge, I didn't take part in the celebrations where I was supposed to be present. I did not want to take part. Nevertheless, one had to apply the Nazi salute; there was no other way."

In the last days of the war, Wegener was sent to a military training camp and eventually to the Eastern Front for the final battle for Berlin. After a short spell as a POW,* he returned home, only to move on to the Western-occupied zones where he worked in agriculture and applied unsuccessfully for a college slot at the Munich School of Journalism. Back home in Jüterbog, he took his A-levels and then tried his luck again as a journalist, this time at Berlin Radio and the *Tagespost* in Potsdam. With modest ambition, he studied a little business economics and law and worked in an agricultural cooperative established by the new socialist state in Eastern Germany.

While he had had no great sympathies for Nazi ideology, his attitude toward communism and socialism was crystal clear: he hated both "like the plague." He wholeheartedly rejected the "Workers' and Farmers' Paradise" that the newly formed GDR† promised to become. He consequently founded an opposition group with a couple of friends, and distributed leaflets, not really knowing where exactly all this was heading. The Volkspolizei,‡ on the other hand, very well knew where: straight to a Potsdam prison cell of the secret agency Stasi§ and finally, after a few weeks of rather inconvenient interrogation, to a court that unceremoniously sentenced him to

---

* POW = Prisoner of war.
† GDR (German Democratic Republic) = Official name of socialist East Germany from 1949–1990 (German: DDR = Deutsche Demokratische Republik).
‡ Volkspolizei = People's police. Uniformed police force of the GDR from 1949–1990.
§ Stasi (Short for Ministerium für Staatssicherheit [or MfS]) = State Security / Ministry for State Security. The infamous secret service and secret police of the GDR. It was regarded as the most important instrument of repression of the Socialist Unity Party of Germany (SED).

18 months in jail. Three days after his release, Wegener fled to West Germany and ended up in a refugee camp. Having become seriously ill during his imprisonment and emaciated to just 60 kilograms (at a height of 1.86 meters, or 6'1"), he was sent to southern Germany for recuperation. There, various state ministries were on the lookout for personnel, including for the police service. So Wegener applied to the Baden-Württemberg riot police in 1952 and was promptly enrolled.

Six years later Wegener finally joined the Bundesgrenzschutz, the BGS. For him, it went without saying that he would eventually end up with either the Bundeswehr or the Border Guard. He took the respective entrance exams for both services on the same day. His simple reason for choosing the BGS was that their acceptance notice landed in his mailbox first. But he would not regret it. For Wegener, the BGS back then was a "top organization" and corresponded to his ideas of a military institution even more than the young Bundeswehr. He had no issue with the fact that his instructors and superiors had by and large forged their career in the Wehrmacht; on the contrary: "The military imprint meant that we all spoke the same language."

With this attitude, Wegener seemed to be cut out for the BGS and so, soon after his officer training course, he caught the eye of his superiors. He loved English literature and American swing music, and he spoke excellent English. This came in quite handy during the visits of US commanders who travelled frequently to his first duty post in Coburg, Bavaria, to inspect the US zone's border. Further promotions followed quickly. Wegener was made adjutant to the commander in Coburg, later became head of the guard at the chancellor's garden and teahouse in Bonn (during which time he met Adenauer in person) and finally took charge of the 1st Armored Unit on the eastern border in Bad Kissingen, again in Bavaria. At the time, there were almost daily reports of incidents in the region, mostly of East German refugees slipping through the still-permeable border. That is until August 1961, when GDR work crews began erecting several rows of concrete posts all along the inner-German border and strung barbed wire between them, while East Berlin started to wall itself in.

Wegener's path to the Ministry of the Interior led via the NATO exercise "Fallex 68," for which he prepared the military maneuvers for the participating BGS units. After the NATO exercise ended, his temporary assignment in Bonn turned into a permanent position. Wegener worked in intelligence evaluation and border reconnaissance and was thus among the first to learn of the Prague uprising in 1968. The following year, the new minister of the interior, Hans-Dietrich Genscher, brought him onto his staff. Genscher was impressed by Wegener's concise situation reports. He seemed to be the right kind of person to maintain direct links with the BGS, something Genscher needed to rely on if he wanted to thoroughly reform this organization.

Conversely, Wegener liked how Genscher would not delay decisions or argue them away. Wegener did not want to talk about obstacles but solutions; intellectual inertia was anathema to him. This attitude suited Genscher's plan to reform the BGS. For when he took office as minister of the interior in 1969, he was faced with the question of its existence: "Those who saw the BGS as a paramilitary organization demanded its dissolution, and in some Bundesländer there were even suspicions that the federal government—in this case the minister of the interior—wanted to ... undermine the police sovereignty of the states. In this dispute, I resolutely opposed the dissolution of the Federal Border Guard. On the contrary, I even pushed for its expansion in terms of personnel, and one of my first official acts was to appoint a liaison officer in the office of the federal minister of the interior.... That had not happened before. So Ulrich Wegener became my first liaison officer."[6]

From this time on, Genscher had Wegener brief him daily on the situation at the eastern border and regularly accompany him on troop inspections. After the horrific events in Munich, the minister's choice quickly fell on his liaison officer as the future commander of the new task force: "After working with him for almost three years, I knew him to be a man who was as determined as he was deliberate, and at the same time courageous and reliable."[7]

Israel, of All Places!

But what was Wegener's new unit supposed to look like? How would the anti-terror squad be trained, equipped and armed? There were no models, no precedent. Or almost none. The British had their SAS,* a military unit that was deemed capable of carrying out hostage rescue missions. Wegener would certainly get some useful information there if the British were willing to share it. In the United States there were the Rangers, also a military unit, but not specialized in hostage situations. In terms of police forces, the first hostage rescue teams (HRTs) and SWAT† groups were being established, but they were still in their early stages. So far, the Israelis clearly had gathered the most experience. The Sajeret Matkal of the Israeli Armed Forces had been engaged in counterterrorism since the mid-1950s, particularly in dealing with Palestinian terrorist groups. But when Wegener suggested to Genscher that he travel to the Middle East to study the inner workings of such an effective anti-terror unit, the minister reacted with complete bewilderment, "You must be crazy," he snapped, and added sarcastically, "They will certainly give you an enthusiastic welcome."[8]

Genscher knew what he was talking about: German–Israeli relations had been less than cordial even before the lethal attack at the 1972 Olympics. Embarrassingly, Munich had been merely the most spectacular event in a whole series of atrocious

---

* SAS (Special Air Service) = Special task force of the British Royal Army, established in WWII.
† SWAT (Special Weapons and Tactics) = Special Intervention Unit of the US police to handle high-risk situations that regular police forces may not be equipped to manage, including hostage situations, barricaded suspects, shootouts, and terrorism threats.

attacks on Jewish people and institutions in Germany since the end of the 1960s, blurring anti-Zionism and anti-Semitism. It started with the devastation of a number of trendy West Berlin bars owned by Jews, and a (failed) bomb attack on a Jewish commemoration of Reichsprogromnacht* in 1969. The violence continued with a failed attempt to hijack an El Al passenger plane at the Munich airport in 1970, in which one Israeli died, and several were seriously injured. It finally climaxed with the arson attack on the Jewish community in Munich a few days later, in which seven Holocaust survivors burned to death in the fire. Back then at the memorial service, Genscher had made a promise to the relatives of the victims: "The German people will never again allow violence and terror to reign on its territory. It will never again allow certain groups to be placed outside the society of people. All of you here today are witnesses to this promise."[9]

Never again. But then, two years after his solemn promise, he was doomed to watch helplessly as nine Jews were murdered on German soil in Munich. His deep, personal shock about the outcome and his determination to finally do something about these deeds seem at least in part to have been a consequence of the feeling of guilt from his broken promise. Anyway, after all that had happened in the past, Genscher probably could not imagine that the Israelis would be happy to show their arsenal and tactics to a German officer, of all people! But Wegener did not let up. He knew the head of Mossad, the Israeli intelligence service, Zvi Zamir, who had been in Munich during the Olympic Games. He had also met before with Zamir's deputy, who worked in the Israeli embassy in Bonn. Zamir agreed to advocate for him with the foreign intelligence service and with Shin Beit, the domestic intelligence service. And lo and behold! Wegener was invited to come. So Genscher gave his blessing, and the newly appointed commander set off for Israel on October 30, 1972, for a special training course of the ZAHAL† defense forces. The subject: fighting Arab terrorists with task forces.

Wegener knew this would not be an easy ride. "Of course, the Israelis were very much on the defensive at first. The murders in Munich were still right before their eyes, the Israeli special units had not been allowed to intervene, and German–Israeli relations were strained anyway."[10] And it was still getting worse. Just the day before Wegener's arrival in Israel, Palestinian terrorists hijacked a Lufthansa jet on its way from Damascus to Frankfurt and diverted it first to Munich, then to Zagreb. Their demand: release of the three surviving Olympic attackers. Otherwise, they threatened to blow up the plane with everybody inside.

---

* Reichsprogromnacht = Night of the most extensive and destructive pogroms against the German Jewish population of the Third Reich on November 9, 1938, in which the National Socialist government coordinated the looting and destroying of shops, cultural institutions, and private residences, as well as the burning down of synagogues. These acts were executed by several Nazi organizations as well as individual citizens.

† ZAHAL (Hebraic acronym for Army for the Defense of Israel, or IDF) = Israel Defense Forces.

The German government responded immediately and had the three Palestinians flown out at a moment's notice, not bothering to consult with the Israelis. Such unilateral action was not exactly conducive to a cordial relationship with Israel. The reaction in Tel Aviv was predictably violent. Prime Minister Golda Meir called back her ambassador in Bonn and declared, "We have been depressed since yesterday, aggrieved, and I would say insulted, that the human spirit, so weak and helpless, has surrendered to brutal force."[11]

One month later, the final report of the West German embassy in Tel Aviv would come to the conclusion that this was "the most serious crisis between the Federal Republic and Israel since diplomatic relations were established in 1965."[12] The temperature of German–Israeli relations dropped down to freezing. Unsurprisingly, the reception for Wegener turned out icy. Wegener found himself having fallen between two stools: On the one hand, he was sympathetic to the Israeli frustrations, particularly after what had happened in Munich. On the other hand, he was understanding of the attitude of the Bonn government not to allow any Israeli unit to operate on German soil. The fact that it ended up in an utter failure was not his personal responsibility, and after all, he was here to prevent something like this from ever happening again.

For the first few days, the Israeli officers treated him with extreme reserve. In conversations, their reproach toward the German attitude during the hostage-taking in Munich resonated time and again. After one week, Wegener was fed up with it. He reported to the commander and asked for a meeting with all the course participants. "In the evening, of course, I got to hear all sorts of things—the crimes of the National Socialists and so on. I was understanding of all of that and replied, yes, but we had to do something for the future … and create the basis for a German–Israeli friendship. This they accepted."[13] Wegener had obviously struck the right note. Participants like Ehud Barak, the then-commander of Sajeret Matkal, who had not been allowed to take action in Munich, were impressed by his sincerity and insight.

After this exchange, the atmosphere relaxed notably. It even marked the beginning of a series of lifelong friendships with Barak, Yonatan Netanyahu,* and Reuven Caspy, amongst others. Caspy, a former paratrooper, was to become founder and commander of a task force in the 1970s himself. Since the end of the 1960s, he had been involved in the development of basic tactics for hostage rescue. Wegener was to learn from him tactics for storming skyscrapers, hotels, theaters, cinemas, ships and trains. The first thing—and key—explained Caspy, was to acknowledge that a hostage situation was entirely different from classical military field or urban combat. Approach, self-protection, arming—everything needed to be rethought

---

* Brother of the future prime minister, Benjamin Netanyahu. He died in 1976 in a commando raid at Entebbe airport, Uganda, where Palestinian and German terrorists had taken Israeli and international tourists hostage.

when there was not only an armed enemy behind the door, but a hostage in need of protection. "So you can't just throw a hand grenade into the room and then shoot everything down with automatic gunfire from left-to-right and right-to-left. You have to move into the room and you need special ammunition. With a single high-velocity bullet, for example, you can shoot three, four, five people at once if they are standing behind each other. That's where you need low-velocity bullets. You also have to be better, stronger, faster than the terrorist with his Kalashnikov. And you have to make sure to only shoot him, not the hostage. Accordingly, we had to adjust the mission doctrine, because we had, unfortunately, a lot of experience with Palestinian terror, so we had to get better and better."[14]

These were exactly the things Wegener wanted to learn. Caspy describes him as an extremely hard-working, quick-learning colleague with a genuine interest in the matter, who would not stop asking questions unless he was fully satisfied with the answers. Ehud Barak, too, kept Wegener in mind as someone who was sponge-like and absorbed everything he was shown, be it theory or practice: "At first Wegener did not speak very much. He asked a lot of questions, he looked on very interested.... He understood very well that the difference between heaven and hell lies in the details and that anti-terror work is a highly professional matter.... We were ready to take it quite far with him when we realized how important it was to set up such a counterterror unit in Germany."[15]

Considering the backdrop of German–Israeli history and the delicate relations between the two states after Munich and Zagreb, it is astonishing how deeply the Israeli security authorities were willing to let Wegener see their cards. He was given access to the Israeli Ministry of Defense, Mossad, and the special ops unit Sajeret Matkal. He later wrote, "This time was highly important and valuable to me. They made no secret of how they proceeded. I gained insights into counterterrorism that were still completely unknown in Europe and which reflected the conditions in the Middle East. This was essential for us, as we knew that in the future we would also have to deal with Palestinians again and again."[16]

Much of what Wegener learned in Israel would later be reflected in the equipment and training regimen of GSG 9. The Israeli security authorities granted Wegener much more insight than others, as Reuven Caspy confirms: "I helped set up some special units in other countries, but that was always just basic training, never more. Not like GSG 9. The Israeli government was nowhere as open as it was with the Germans. We were like brothers." And to emphasize how extraordinary it was, he speaks the last word in German: "We gave him everything, we gave him '*Alles!*'" For some reason or other, the Israelis trusted him.

But why? A German, no less, and at the worst of all possible times too, right in the middle of the deepest diplomatic crisis to date between Israel and Germany. The answer is twofold: Germany had obviously become targeted by Palestinian terror. Despite the political ill-feeling, there was a growing sense among Israelis that they were on the same side. "We had the same problem, the same enemy," Caspy explains. For Israel, he says, it was important to elevate the Germans to the Israeli's level of knowledge on terrorism and antiterror strategies in order to be better prepared for a possible second Munich-type event. People like the Sajeret Matkal commander, Ehud Barak, trusted Wegener to raise up the necessary discipline, diligence, and the right mental attitude for this task. And he had the skill set to get it across to a German unit. "It was immediately clear to me that they would be extremely good once they learned," Barak later recalled. "Because they are systematic; they know that the whole thing requires a lot of practice and training, and they work extremely meticulously."[17]

The second reason for the openness toward Wegener lay in his personality. He exuded trust and credibility, according to Caspy, and "he was incredibly accessible." Wegener possessed the gift of establishing a connection with everyone right from the start, be it a minister or a journalist. His companions described him as charismatic, radiating an aura of trust, leadership (and to some degree, dominance). But there was more, says Caspy, which seemed at odds with Wegener's stereotypical Prussian appearance: tall, blue eyes, ascetic-looking, short hair with a strict side parting, concerned with form, no-nonsense attitude. "Wegener was indeed German. But he had an Israeli character." Trying to explain what exactly he means by this, Caspy suggests himself as a counterexample: "I am Israeli, but I have a rather German character. For example, I am always on time. When Wegener came to Israel, he immediately understood the Israeli way: you never stubbornly push straight ahead toward your destination, but you are always supposed to act in a flexible manner, sometimes moving to the left, sometimes to the right. That way you are never blocked."

According to the Israelis, this mental agility is essential for successful counterterrorism operations—and for Ehud Barak it was the key to trusting Wegener: "A special intervention unit in action always works with an open mind. I believe Commander Wegener understood that at first glance. When he saw the Israeli approach, he immediately realized that this was no small thing. You can't simply transfer that from one culture to another. In Israel, people are generally much less organized than in Germany. Even in the German special intervention unit, everything is much more formalistic than over here. But Wegener understood, without the need for pointing it out, the importance of a free mind and an independent spirit. You can't dictate how you have to do something. Never! From the first minute on, each and every operation of a special unit will not go according to plan."[18]

Wegener would draw fundamental conclusions from this insight for his own leadership style and operational strategy. He later adopted some Israeli tactics one-to-one, including those for negotiations as well as storming aircraft. (Caspy said, "In Mogadishu we would have done it exactly the same way.") Above all, however, he decided to abandon the rigid *Befehlstaktik* (or Command Tactics) of traditional military units. Instead, he aimed for the consistent implementation of the so-called *Auftragstaktik* (or Mission Tactics). Within this command system, the respective leader of the operational unit is not condemned to stubbornly follow orders, but is merely tasked with the mission's objectives and is free to flexibly choose means and tactics. Hence Wegener's motto: Leadership is executed at once from above and from the fore, not from a lonely commander's hill. This attitude would lead to deep consequences for the tactics of missions themselves. But first of all for the selection and training of the men who were to carry out these missions.

In mid-November 1972 Wegener returned to Germany, carrying with him in his luggage the promise of further training and equipment support from Israel, and a sack full of ideas for building up his own unit. Wegener had apparently left the impression in Israel of being an absolutely reliable partner. In the following years, this would turn out to be extremely helpful concerning joint training camps, knowledge sharing and the exchange of intelligence.* Israel became one of the closest allies of Germany in the fight against international terrorism. And it remains so to the present day.† Even more, Wegener established friendly relations with quite a few high-ranking Israeli security personnel and was invited more than once for dinner to Israeli officers' homes with their families, as he subsequently wrote in his report to the minister of the interior.

In this report, Wegener details his findings from the special course on the "training of commando units against terrorists in the case of skyjackings and against terrorist bases": "Even if some practices and methods of the Israeli security authorities cannot be transferred to the conditions in the Federal Republic, and can only be understood from Israel's special situation, other findings can certainly be used in the fight against terrorists in the FRG.‡"[19] He also reports on the "protection of endangered objects such as airfields, harbors and other vital installations." He wrote, "In conclusion, it must be stated that the German airports so far bear no comparison with the Israeli ones in terms of thoroughness and effectiveness." Some of his other comments concerned armed flight attendants on board the Israeli airline El Al, the deployment of mobile forces in the search and pursuit of terrorists, and the detection as well as defusing

---

* Five years later, according to Caspy, the Israeli secret service would even share with Wegener their rare satellite photos of Mogadishu airport in preparation for the storming of Lufthansa Flight LH-181.

† In commemoration of the 50th anniversary of GSG 9's inception in 2022, a joint group of GSG 9 and YAMAM men parachuted down over Fürstenfeldbruck airfield near Munich, the place of the fatal 1972 shootout. After their parachute canopies had opened, they unfurled huge German and Israeli flags, dragging them behind them, symbolizing the friendship between the two task forces in particular and the two nations in general.

‡ FRG = Federal Republic of Germany. Official name of the (West) German state (German: BRD = Bundesrepublik Deutschland).

of explosive devices and explosive charges, all of which were to be implemented in the following years and decades.

Psychological training had been part of the Israeli program as well. Systematically trying to get a grip on the mindset and mentality of the opponent was a technique virtually unknown in both police and military units at the time. But Wegener embraced this unconventional yet extremely useful tactical aspect from the very beginning as an indispensable building block of GSG 9's own training.

The impressions Wegener brought back from Israel deeply informed his idea of the organization, the mission, and the tactical approach of a special police force. But for the time being, it was no more than a conceptual framework. When it came to the selection of applicants, training and equipment, not to mention creating an identity and basic operational principles, GSG 9 was still in its infancy.

CHAPTER 4

Humble Beginnings

Subsection III. Tasks of the "Concept for the Establishment and Deployment of a Federal Border Guard Unit for Special Police Operations of 19 September 1972 (VS-NfD*)" lists the prospective events which "require the deployment of specialized police forces":

- liberating hostages,
- neutralize particularly dangerous and active perpetrators,
- averting danger (hijackers, etc.),
- averting terrorist attacks with firearms, explosives or incendiary devices,
- criminal procedure measures with a high degree of danger,
- other criminal attacks which require the violent elimination of perpetrators, groups of perpetrators or the excavation of hiding places ...[1]

"Schlepping furniture. Grrreat!"[2] From reading the job description, Dieter Fox had pictured his first assignment at the elite squad somewhat differently. Like everybody else in Germany, the young Border Guard officer had held his breath as he listened live to the murderous drama unfolding in Munich. He had been assigned to stand guard at the main gate of the Chancellery in Bonn at the time and followed the events on radio and television after his duty hours. He thought of his comrades, some of whom had been sent to the Olympic village as volunteer police officers. But they could help no more than Fox.

"Wearing a uniform or not, the general feeling was one of helplessness, horror and paralysis," said Fox. So when he heard that a special police force was to be set up in the fight against terrorism, he volunteered at once. At the interview in Saint Augustin, he met Ulrich Wegener, who sat opposite him next to two other *Grenzschutz* officers. Working through a list of questions, the commander of the new unit seemed to like Fox's answers and demeanor, so he was hired on the spot. No assessment procedure, no sports test, no psychological exams. They themselves would have to invent these first, but Dieter Fox didn't know that yet.

---

* VS-NfD (*Verschlusssache—nur für den Dienstgebrauch*) = Classified—only for internal use. Lowest stage of secrecy within German state agencies.

So there he was, in the barracks of the Border Guard pioneers, exactly two months to the day after the attack in Munich, heaving dozens of lockers into the empty quarters of future recruits. "'Marvellous! If it starts out like that, this is going to be great fun.' Those were my first thoughts," Fox recalls. When he arrived, there was no equipment whatsoever to work with: "We had nothing. We had no vehicles, we had no weapons, we had … our uniforms, yes. But those weren't suitable for our purposes." Fox was one of the very first volunteers to show up at the Saint Augustin Border Guard compound. The first thing they had to do was make room for the new arrivals. This was achieved "by squeezing" the resident pioneer unit, as stated in the "Report on the Status of GSG 9" in mid-October 1972.

4—Accommodation
4.1 Since the final accommodation … has yet to be built, the members of GSG 9 will initially be housed in an interim accommodation….
4.2 The intermediate accommodation for the rest of GSG 9 (two more units) to be set up on 1.2.1973 could not yet be secured, the intermediate accommodation existing until now must be refurbished. Work on this is underway, and the additional funds required for this must still be covered—probably by deferring such work elsewhere in the BGS.
4.3 The new construction of the service and accommodation building (permanent accommodation) for GSG 9 can be completed in about 1½ years if all work proceeds favorably…. According to preliminary rough estimates, the cost of the service and accommodation building will amount to DM* 4 million.
4.4 Accommodation equipment: The furnishing of general accommodation equipment (cupboards, beds, tables, chairs, cutlery, etc.) is in progress. Since it will have to be taken from various existing inventories, certain limitations in furnishings will have to be accepted initially. The furnishing of the business rooms has been initiated but is still causing difficulties. Some typewriters, the photocopier, armored cabinets, etc. must be purchased.

For the first couple of years, GSG 9 personnel and departments would be spread out across several buildings: one for the commander and his staff and a smaller one for one of the first two operational units. The other operational unit occupied a corridor in the building of a telecommunications unit across the road. The motor vehicle workshops were also scattered around the barracks. This was not to change until 1975, when the new headquarters building was completed along with lecture halls, technical workshops, fitness rooms and surrounding service buildings. For now, they had to make do with the provisional premises and make the best of it.

"We started out by providing a small cleared-out block with the essentials," explains Dieter Tutter, who arrived even before Dieter Fox. He was designated as *Einheitsführer* (operational unit leader) for the second of the three planned operational units. At 33 years old, he was already one of the seniors among the officers of the first GSG 9 generation. Since they all were drawn from Bundesgrenzschutz ranks, the new recruits had to show several years of service, but most of them were still in

---

* DM (Deutsche Mark) = Deutschmarks. Official currency for West Germany from 1948 to 2002.

their early or mid-twenties. Before their arrival, Tutter had already lugged desks and typewriters and obtained office equipment to register new volunteers. And together with Wegener and Frieder Peter Baum, the leader of the 1st Operational Unit, he had started deliberations about what exactly they wanted to do with the people once they arrived. This was not at all self-evident, for "there was no role model for us in the BGS and no one to guide us."

Hasty Inception

Wegener had announced operational readiness for May 1, 1973. This left him only six months. Half a year for the whole package: setting up a special intervention unit, including selecting, equipping, and training people, as well as developing operational concepts and tactics. He knew this to be quite a, well, ambitious undertaking. Particularly since there was not much experience to draw from elsewhere. Counterterrorist units like the one Wegener had in mind were few and far between at the beginning of the 1970s. And what he had seen with the Israelis could only be transferred so far to the German situation.

So how does that work—creating a task force from scratch, without a blueprint or instructions taken from an already existing "Counterterrorism For Dummies" textbook? The new commander had brought back a lot of ideas from his trip to Israel. But having ideas doesn't mean that you have a plan. The commanders of the operational units, such as Dieter Tutter, were responsible for developing these ideas into tangible and teachable applications and implementing them with the newly established force: "We were all novices in this respect. But that was good! Because it meant that we didn't try to improve the stuff we already knew from the BGS—which was by no means bad stuff at all—but we had to create something completely different. And that was incredibly creative. We spent nights brooding and making concepts and discarding them again and again."

They started out radically, as everything they knew from BGS was put to the test: equipment, clothing, vehicles, weapons, organization, tactics. "There was the big headline hanging resplendently over everything, asking: Do we need it? And we came to the conclusion: we don't need nothing of it!" It started, quite banally, with the uniforms: "We were dressed completely wrong." A high-necked suit with a stiff jacket and thick patch pockets, underneath the notorious "rubber shirt"* with a tie, black lace-up shoes, and a high-rising mountain cap—all well and good for parades, formations of honor or guard duty, but totally unsuitable for close combat.

---

* The rubber shirt was a fashionable but generally hated short-sleeved shirt made from synthetic fiber (Dralon). It was dreaded amongst GSG 9 operatives because those who wore it suffered from smelly sweat patches. Also, the shirt stretched unpleasantly while sticking to the skin and chafing the wearer's neck. Finally, it was too cold in the winter and too hot in summertime.

"Peaked cap? You can't fight with that. Impossible; gone! Tie? At best, they'll strangle you with it. Gone! You can't move in a formal uniform jacket! Flashy uniform buttons are complete nonsense. Away with them! And loafers as well as *Knobelbecher*, the infamous soldiers' boots, are utterly impractical. We wanted combat boots. We turned everything upside down." They also would have preferred overalls, but apparently that was too much of an innovation.

Unfortunately, their preferred attire was nowhere to be bought. So in the following weeks the future counterterror fighters took to their needles and thread to convert their old work suits according to their needs, sewing on pockets in such a way that nothing stuck out and they couldn't get stuck in the undergrowth or on a door handle. For the rest they shopped all over the world. Socks and gloves from Finland, classic winter clothing from Sweden, anoraks from Israel. However, the German parka was also put to the test (Fox says it was "good, but heavy as a bag in the rain"). "All-terrain capability" and practicality were their main decision-making criteria, supported by tear-and-wear tests lasting four to six weeks. The final decision on what to adopt was mainly made without fuss by the commander checking it off. In order to convince the commander that T-shirts were far more practical than buttoned shirts with collars, Tutter had his operational unit line up one morning wearing their standard shirts backwards. "No need for a shirt in summer, *Herr Kommandeur*." Wegener nodded briefly, "But not in white!" he growled. "Of course not, we want black T-shirts." "Sure," Wegener agreed, "go for it!" With that, the matter was decided. Step-by-step, a light linen uniform was thus created in which the men could move freely while all rank insignia disappeared.

A particular problem turned out to be the headgear, since the previous peaked cap was for the birds. It always fell off in the most unfortunate situations. It was seemingly a mere detail, but no triviality as it turned out, since it touched on traditions and symbols particularly important in military or paramilitary organizations. Commander Wegener had brought back berets from the Israeli border guard, and his internal GSG 9 fashion task force had deemed them service-worthy. Unlike today, however, berets in Germany only existed in the Bundeswehr, and there almost exclusively in tank battalions. "At the top of the Federal Border Guard they thought: now they're completely bonkers!" grins Dieter Fox, as he recalls the visit of the inspector of the Bundesgrenzschutz, Brigadier General Rudolf Grüner.[*] The old school Bavarian officer had come to Saint Augustin to approve of the new uniforms. His reaction to the presentation of the perky caps turned out as enthusiastic as could be expected: "That's idiotic, you can't walk around like that." A heated discussion ensued about the sense and nonsense of headgear in general and the suitability of the beret in particular—until one GSG 9 man

---

[*] Inspector of the Bundesgrenzschutz: highest-ranking officer of the *Grenzschutz*. Similar to chief of staff in the US Army.

interrupted the argument, put on one of the Israeli berets, and did a somersault from a standing position: "Herr General, can I do that with our high *Grenzschutz* hat?" Exasperated, the general waved it off, "Ach, wear whatever you like!" That was the end of the matter. Dark green was the color of choice.

An odd anecdote? Sure, but typical for the early days. "We got a lot our way in this manner," says Dieter Tutter. "And we were always supported by Wegener. And when it came to bigger stuff, to procurement of technical equipment, he was always backed by Minister Genscher." Such informal, pragmatic decision-making was hardly conceivable in a regular Border Guard unit. "Wegener was non-conformist. If he had been conformist, we would have become a small super-BGS, still with a high hat and tie, maybe with nicer shoulder pieces, but not a GSG 9 like that!" Wegener was certainly no revolutionary, but within the framework of an ossified quasi-military apparatus, he was already considered an odd duck by his superiors. It is hard to imagine him getting away with it had he not had direct access to Minister Genscher's ear.

Every few weeks or so, Genscher inquired with Wegener about the progress of his pet project. "If there were any problems, I told him and didn't have to take the hierarchy of the BGS into account," Wegener later told a journalist.[3] Good for him, because the equipment for GSG 9 was expensive—at least worth considerably more than the 6.3 million Deutschmarks initially approved by the Home Affairs Committee of the Bundestag. The "Report on the Status of GSG 9" of mid-October 1972 stated that the "budgetary requirements for equipping GSG 9 with motor vehicles, helicopters, weapons, telecommunications equipment, special clothing, special accommodation equipment, etc., i.e. without personal expenses and without funds for the buildings … amounted to around 16 million Marks according to a preliminary rough estimate."[4]

> 1.3 Equipment and clothing: The delivery of the newly developed steel helmet promised by the contractor for the end of April is delayed by about 2 weeks, since the helmet shell cannot be completed by him before the end of the month and will then only be forwarded to another company for assembly of the interior fittings and chin straps. The following delivery dates have been promised for the other outstanding pieces:
> Bulletproof vests w. head protection: end of April 1973
> Anoraks: June 1973
> Work and training suit: June 1973[5]

Of course, the high procurement costs had to do with the fact that little could be taken over from the Bundesgrenzschutz inventory: GSG 9 did not need heavy off-road trucks or armored vehicles with mounted guns, but helicopters for rapid deployment. And they needed fast, agile road vehicles for hot pursuit. In the spring of 1973, a number of Volkswagen Variants and Transporters were joined by a dozen Mercedes-Benz 280SEs in anthracite grey, an acquisition that did not go entirely unnoticed by the rest of the Federal Border Guard, as Dieter Fox recalls:

"A cry went up through Germany: 'What does this Django squad want with cars like these?' Well, it's quite simple: the other side doesn't steal Volkswagen Beetles, but Porsches, Alfa Romeos and similar high-engined vehicles. So we can hardly go after them with VW buses."

The counterterror fighters-to-be always got the best that money could buy. And what money could not yet buy was specifically developed for the intended purpose. Other commanders quickly realized that GSG 9 burned through a lot of funding because of its high standards. "The reactions within the Bundesgrenzschutz were accordingly not always easy to cope with," Commander Wegener later said, sighing. "But basically, Genscher knew what was at stake and supported me. We asserted ourselves everywhere, including in the choice of armament. We had certain weapons in mind, but at that time they were only in the development stage. We went to Oberndorf to see the manufacturer Heckler & Koch. I talked to the head of development: 'Call me as soon as the weapons are ready.' And he did. We picked them right off the assembly line and put them in service at once."[6]

Each officer received the brand new semi-automatic HK P9S as a handgun, a Smith & Wesson Magnum .357 revolver as sidearm, the Heckler & Koch MP5 submachine gun,* as well as the sniper rifle PSG1, again by Heckler & Koch. The PSG1 was freshly developed after the Munich hostage-taking and included an infrared night scope. "Of course, that was kind of a 'wow' experience for us," recalls Dieter Fox of the lavish initial equipment. "Whoa! What have we got here? We all only dreamed of this. Having said that, we knew that we would have to shoot with these, and not just for practice. Some of our comrades were not capable of dealing with this; they did not cope with the psychological pressure and quit the force. Others said, 'This is exactly what we need for our missions.' Me too."

In terms of weaponry, GSG 9 was state of the art, probably second to none worldwide. In addition, they got handheld radios, each with clunky earphones and a microphone, a very clumsy predecessor of what today is called a headset. But clunkiness or not—the snipers at the Fürstenfeldbruck airfield shootout would certainly have been grateful for them. In order to transport all this gear for training or in the field, along with personal luggage and two or three officers, the big Mercedes with their large luggage compartments came in quite handy.

The armament was constantly refined, the pistol holsters being one example. "This used to happen a lot," explains Dieter Tutter. "We were moving through the terrain and suddenly the weapon was gone because it got caught on a branch and pulled out of the old holsters. Here, we were able to weigh in with our own ideas to prevent such things from happening." Much of the stuff that they came up with was later adopted by other BGS units, such as the battle dress and

---

* Ironically, the Heckler & Koch MP5 submachine gun rose to questionable fame as part of the iconic Red Army Faction logo.

combat boots. Even the much-maligned beret was soon to be found on most Border Guard heads.

This kind of inventive spirit was retained by "The 9ers" in later years. For abseiling from high buildings and helicopters, only dangerous hip harnesses were available at first—so GSG 9 technicians went on to develop safe seat harnesses in cooperation with a manufacturer, as well as a handheld device with an automatic brake to prevent the rope from slipping.[7] When it came to the question of how best to recon buildings, how to penetrate them, and what tools best to use in the process, they came up with new concepts such as the so-called water rifle. The idea of a child's toy is as self-evident as it is wrong: the device was designed to open locked doors without explosives or rams, using only a high-pressure water jet. Developed by GSG 9 technicians in the 1980s, the water rifle is in use today by special military and police forces all over the world. "Moreover, we served as a testing center for the BGS procurement office and for the Ministry of Interior," says Dieter Tutter. "When we were offered night-vision devices from three different companies, for example, all the other BGS divisions were lining up."

The same type of creativity that was in high demand for equipment and armament was at least as important for ideas regarding uses for the task force. The mission statement was short and clear enough: fighting terrorism and major crime. GSG 9 was to be deployed when classical police measures ran out of options or when situations became too dangerous for regular police. This included freeing hostages from the hands of terrorists or bank robbers, arresting armed criminals, fighting gangs, transferring and guarding violent criminals. But with what means and with what objective? What procedures and tactics were they able, willing and—most importantly—legally allowed to use? Again, there were no role models in sight. The few counterterrorist forces that existed at the beginning of the 1970s were for the most part military units with different legal requirements and, depending on the country, a completely different legal understanding and tradition. GSG 9, however, was not a military unit but a police force. They were supposed to explicitly not act under military auspices, but according to police guidelines. And that meant above all: protecting, not annihilating life.

The big question for future training and future missions was therefore, in the words of Dieter Fox, "How can we reconcile this—being tough as nails and doing 'it,' and at the same time not losing our understanding of democracy, the rule of law and the police mindset?" In Germany with its loaded history, this was a highly sensitive matter. It grew even more urgent in the face of a new phenomenon in the early 1970s: bank robberies which turned into hostage situations. Until then, the German *Schupo** on patrol duty had hardly ever come in contact with violent,

---

* *Schupo* (*Schutzpolizist*) = Colloquial, short for patrol police officer (literally, protection police officer).

hostage-taking criminals, nor indeed would his colleagues from the *Kripo*[*] or the BKA. Shortly before the Munich Olympics, there had been a hostage situation in a bank, also in Munich. Things like this had never been seen before in German history. And as the Olympic attack ended in a deadly disaster, so did the so-called Rammelmayr case, one year prior.

Lethal Shots in Munich

On August 4, 1971, shortly before closing time, two masked men stormed the Deutsche Bank branch in Munich's Prinzregentenstraße. Heavily armed, Hans Georg Rammelmayr and his accomplice, Dimitri Todorov, took 18 employees and customers hostage and demanded two million Deutschmarks and a BMW as a getaway car. Throughout the day, they released 13 of the 18 hostages one by one. The negotiations dragged on until just before midnight, while thousands of rubberneckers gathered outside. Reporters later described the atmosphere as a mixture of "Chicago and Oktoberfest." A bank robbery with hostage-taking was a familiar sight, but so far exclusively in Hollywood movies—in the pedestrian zone of a major German city not so much. The Munich police were completely overwhelmed. Hastily, volunteer police officers "with hunting experience" were recruited as snipers because there was no one with any formal training in the use of precision weapons. As in Fürstenfeldbruck a year later, there was no radio communication between the snipers.

Thus, to this day it is not entirely clear who gave the command to open fire (or even if anyone did), and if so, by what means of communication. When Rammelmayr stepped outside along with a 19-year-old female bank employee as his personal surety, police waited until he had strolled the whole 12 meters or so to the waiting getaway car, had opened the door, had his hostage get in the passenger seat, had walked around to the driver's side and was almost sitting behind the wheel. Only then was the first shot fired. This appeared to be the signal for everybody else. Snipers and police armed with submachine guns riddled the BMW with bullets. Despite being fatally wounded, the bank robber managed to shoot the young woman next to him in the BMW. She later died in hospital. Rammelmayr's accomplice Todorov remained inside the bank and was only overpowered several minutes later after another exchange of gunfire in the bank.

The "Rammelmayr case" made nationwide headlines and triggered a public debate about the accumulated incompetence of the police, and the question of whether their action amounted to an "unlawful execution" of the perpetrator (as the weekly *Der Spiegel* asked). After the Munich Olympic attack ended in a bloodbath a year later as well, the discussion among lawyers and legal politicians intensified: under

---

[*] *Kripo* (*Kriminalpolizei*) = Criminal investigation department.

what circumstances was it legally justified to apply lethal force by means of an "aimed kill shot." A uniform law for the *Bund** and the *Länder*, proposed by the Conference of Ministers of the Interior in 1975, was met with fierce rejection. The arguments ranged from fear of reintroducing the death penalty through the back door to concerns that such a regulation would pave the way to a future police state. For years, there was no hope of reconciliation in this debate.

As a consequence, a number of provinces decided to introduce their own regulations for police, which would exclude an aimed shot with lethal intent from legal persecution if it happened as a last resort. Most provinces, however, hesitated to legally formalize the use of deadly force by the police. The debate remained heated throughout the decades. As a matter of fact, no police officer was ever convicted of homicide in cases like this. The legal way out was to invoke legitimate assistance in self-defense, which reliably resulted in the acquittal of the officer in question. However, there would always be a legal investigation in the aftermath of a fatal incident. This was not a mistake but quite deliberate. Politicians and governments from the political center to the left refused to let the police off the hook too easily. The idea was, first, to keep the barriers high for the employment of such a final measure and, second, not to legally authorize a killing by the state under any circumstance. This again meant that a certain amount of insecurity always remained, and so did the feeling among many police that if they acted, they would always do so standing with one foot in a prison cell.

The debate dragged on for decades under the euphemistic term "final rescue shot." North Rhine-Westphalia only adopted a respective regulation in 2010; Schleswig-Holstein, Berlin, and Mecklenburg-Vorpommern have refrained from doing so to this day, as is the case at the federal level. Up to the present day, there is no law regulating an aimed kill shot for officers of the Bundespolizei, the renamed Bundesgrenzschutz. The use of firearms against persons is regulated in the Act on Direct Coercion in the Exercise of Public Authority by Federal Law Enforcement Officials. Section 10 states that firearms may only be used "if other measures of direct coercion have been used unsuccessfully or would be obviously unsuccessful," and only to the end of "rendering the person incapable of attack or escape." There is no mention of fatal shots. So the matter remains delicate.

When back in the day Wegener and his men tried to develop tactics and rules of engagement for GSG 9, they had to take all these legal limitations into consideration and keep political sensitivities in the back of their mind. All this while trying to create an effective, hard-hitting force at the same time. So, how could failures like the ones in Munich be prevented in the future; how could such situations ideally be resolved without bloodshed, if that was possible at all?

---

* *Bund* = Collective term for the German governmental system as a whole, as well as its individual legislative, executive, and judicial branches and agencies such as the Bundespolizei.

Lessons from Terrorist Literature

In his search for a suitable organizational set-up of his task force, Wegener first studied precedents from military history. This included the darker patches of German history, like a special Wehrmacht unit that had achieved dubious fame under the name of the Brandenburgers. He read the classics from World War I—T. E. Lawrence, aka Lawrence of Arabia, and *In Stahlgewittern* (*Storm of Steel*), Ernst Jünger's war memoir from the trenches of the Western Front. All of which was not particularly productive.

But after a while he found what he was looking for, on the opposite side of the aisle, so to speak. In the early 1970s *The Minimanual of the Urban Guerrilla*, by Brazilian communist revolutionary Carlos Marighella, circulated as an underground publication on the violent left-wing scene. It soon became the go-to book on the urban guerrilla concept for would-be revolutionaries. Wegener had his people study the revolutionary primer intensively. This thin volume of only a few dozen pages served GSG 9 well, and did so in two main ways.

First with the question: How do terrorists think, how do they work, and what can we derive from this for our tactical approach? Marighella's book on urban guerrilla warfare opened up a pathway into the mindset of terrorists, but it also allowed them to adopt tangible tactics. "None of us had a clue about urban guerrilla warfare," explains Dieter Fox. "We told ourselves, okay, if they practice that, then we'll practice the same thing and see what comes of it."[8]

Second, on an even more concrete note, Wegener organized his task forces like revolutionary cells to become as flexible and effective as possible. "In order to carry out operations, the urban guerrillero must be organized in small groups," Marighella wrote. "It consists of no more than 4 or 5 men and is called a fire group." What today might seem the natural way of organizing special command forces was anything but self-evident at the time. Wegener implemented these recommendations almost without any changes. He arranged GSG 9's three existing operational units into SETs: small teams of five men each (today it's six to seven), which are able to act largely independently of other groups or higher levels of command, in which each individual knows that they can rely blindly on the others, and that in case of emergency each can replace another immediately. This was exactly as Marighella suggests: "There must be absolute trust between the members of a fire group.... If tasks are to be fulfilled that have been developed by the strategic command, these have unconditional priority. Nevertheless, there can be no fire group without its own initiative. In order to guarantee a maximum of initiative for the individual fire groups, it is necessary to avoid any rigid form of organization."[9]

The skillset Marighella demanded of his urban guerrillas sounds suspiciously similar to the personality and requirements profile for prospective GSG 9 officers: "The qualities of the urban guerrilla are initiative, resourcefulness, flexibility, versatility and presence of mind. Above all, he must possess the ability to take the initiative.... He must always keep calm and be able to hold his nerves even under unfavorable conditions and in hopeless situations."

Wegener also discovered useful information in the writings of other revolutionaries or terrorists like the RAF's Ulrike Meinhof, and in the racism theories of the French anti-colonialist Frantz Fanon. "This all contributed to the principle we had in mind from the outset: the unit had to be unconventional." This approach went so far as Wegener procuring Russian Kalashnikovs, model AK-47. He had his men train with the bread-and-butter weapon of revolutionaries and terrorists from all over the globe—a measure which presented an outrageous monstrosity for a West German police organization: A Federal Police officer does not shoot with a communist rifle! But Wegener got his way: "If terrorists shoot with it, we have to be able to handle it!"[10]

GSG 9's founders looked far and wide to find ideas for suitable training and rules of engagement, for tactics, behavior, self-defense techniques and operational theories. They picked out useful set pieces, expanded them, adapted them to German needs, and sewed these patches together piece by piece in the attempt to form a reasonably coherent tapestry. From the Israelis they adopted methods of penetrating aircraft, from the US Marines training with obstacle courses, and from the FBI combat training. Wegener also adopted a number of tactics from the Wehrmacht and army regulations during World War II: behavior and camouflage in rural terrain, urban warfare, penetrating rooms, abseiling from buildings and the like. "The pioneers and paratroopers of the time used quite good tactical procedures," admits Dieter Fox, but only to immediately emphasize that they were not at all inclined toward the ideology of the SS[*] and the Gestapo: "We did not compare ourselves with these units, not one bit; we just used their operational and physical workout tactics. And those were good."

Fox strongly disputed any idea that GSG 9 might have had anything to do with the disreputable organizations of the Third Reich apart from the adoption of isolated techniques. This defensiveness comes as no surprise. From its very inception, there were debates within GSG 9 on the question of whether they should or should not affiliate with military units, and also adopt traditions of the German armed forces. In the process, they sometimes skirted the edge of good taste, for example in the search for GSG 9's association badge: Wegener liked the old close combat brace from World War II, donated by Adolf Hitler himself in 1942. The Reich eagle and swastika were emblazoned on it. Wegener knew that they could not use the clasp as it existed. So "we took over its basic features, the oak leaves on both sides, and we

---

[*] SS (*Schutzstaffel*) = Protection Squadron. Major paramilitary organization in Nazi Germany, founded as a personal bodyguard squadron for Adolf Hitler. Became instrumental in fighting political enemies within Germany and in the planning and execution of the Holocaust and operating concentration camps. Its militarized arm, the Waffen-SS, committed numerous atrocities, war crimes and genocide throughout German-occupied Europe during WWII.

put the *Bundesadler* (federal eagle) in the middle. This was an expression of the consciousness of tradition, but based on the *Freiheitlich-Demokratische Grundordnung* (free democratic constitutional order)."

In 2006, questions came up about Wegener's grasp on tradition and liberal democracy when in the book *Geheime Krieger* (*Secret Warriors*) he admitted to the esprit de corps of the "Brandenburgers," a special unit of the Wehrmacht that demonstrably committed war crimes in World War II. All GSG 9 officers—former and current—interviewed by the author described these statements as blunders and showed themselves embarrassed by the avowals of their former commander, claiming this to be completely off his usual stance in these matters.[11]

Top Priority: Saving Human Lives

At least in terms of daily police practice, there was apparently no big question as to what could be adapted from the tactical repertoire of the old military units and what did not meet the demands of a democratic constitutional state: "We always have to use the techniques and tactics that lead to police success," Fox explains. "GSG 9 was founded with the aim of arresting opponents if possible, and bringing them to justice so that a verdict can be reached in court. So it doesn't help to adopt tactics like 10 men aiming heavy weapons at the door and shooting into the room. Everybody in there will be dead and we haven't won anything. Our premise is to move into the room and free the hostages. To do this, I first have to eliminate the perpetrator in some way or other. If I take him alive, great. If I have to take him out—well, tough luck for him. But still, saving lives was top priority."

What may sound self-evident was by no means the case at the time, and in some parts of the world still isn't, one example being the storming of the Dubrovka Theatre in Moscow. In 2004, a hostage situation by Chechen terrorists ended with the deaths of 130 hostages as well as forty to fifty hostage-takers, all of whom were shot on the spot by Russian special forces. This illustrates the main difference between the rules of engagement of military units and police units: for the latter it is not a question of victory or defeat in an armed conflict; it is about saving lives and bringing the perpetrators to justice. In consequence, though, this means saving not only the lives of hostages and bystanders that are at stake, but also those of the hostage-takers, terrorists or violent criminals.

Israeli Task Force Commander Reuven Caspy illustrated the difference between the military and the police with the situation of a hostage-taking in a small hotel he once had to deal with: "We negotiated with the kidnappers. I know how to speak to them because I know their dialect. And I promised them everything. Everything they wanted. But in the end we shot them. We went in and after five seconds all the terrorists were dead." Caspy tells this story with a matter-of-factness that renders any questioning superfluous.

This is exactly what GSG 9 was not supposed to be. Wegener therefore issued the motto that the loss of human life must never be accepted. But how about the omnipresent suspicion that in the course of an operation, when adrenalin levels are high, the finger sometimes might be fast on the trigger and a hostage-taker dies, even though he could have been incapacitated in some other way? Anyone who poses this question, be it to a GSG 9 veteran or an active officer, will always receive the same, very clear answer: this must not happen and cannot happen. The slightest insinuation of trigger-happy tendencies is taken as an insult and met with indignant rejection. Why? "Because we are police officers, not killers!"

But neither are they suicidal. Therefore, another factor played an important role: the lives of the officers themselves. Apart from the interest of simple self-preservation, this was based on cool tactical considerations, as Dieter Fox explains: "If we are taken out ourselves, we cannot save any more lives, it's as simple as that. If we enter a room and are not adequately prepared, if we have not internalized the situation and do not go in with that bit of coldness—i.e., professional serenity—then the mission will go wrong."[12] At first, this mindset of saving lives as top priority was apparently not only difficult to grasp for laymen, but sometimes even for their comrades of the Border Guard, and for politicians and representatives of federal agencies who visited the new task force. Time and again GSG 9 officers heard questions like: Up to what level of risk will you carry out such an assignment? What number of losses would still be acceptable in order to free hostages?

Dieter Tutter considers this outrageous even after all these years: "You cannot liberate the all-encompassing heights of so-and-so like Lieutenant Kottenforz* back in World War I, losing 30 percent of your men, and go on and celebrate that as a victory! We are not soldiers who go into something with predetermined loss figures. Of course, the unexpected can always happen; something can always go wrong. If a booby trap explodes, the whole team might be lost in the operation. But if you know beforehand that's likely to happen, you can't do it that way, you have to think of something else to achieve your goal."

However, other attitudes have also been handed down. Dieter Schenk, an ex-officer with the Federal Criminal Police BKA, and an author critical of the police, describes the final maneuver briefing after a joint hostage-taking exercise in the late 1970s. He claims to have heard Commander Wegener's successor, Klaus Blätte, say, "If more than half my men come out of an operation alive, I deem the operation a success."[13] Former comrades doubt the authenticity of this statement, but it cannot be ruled out that there were—and are—such opinions present in the force. In any case, the current commander is adamant that such a view of calculated losses is not held or

---

* Fictional character in an old soldier's joke: General: "Lieutenant Kottenforz, if you take the hill with 30 percent losses, the attack will be a success."—Kottenforz: "But General, I'm afraid that's not possible, I only have 20 men!"

tolerated in today's GSG 9. For one thing, it has to do with the fact that it would hardly be legally tenable for any police force in the world. But more to the point, such cannon fodder ideology would also make little sense in the internal logic of military cost-benefit calculations, considering the time, energy and money that needs to be spent on the selection, education and training of the men from the very outset of their career. Each officer of a task force is an investment.

But for the investment to pay off, it first requires finding qualified candidates. This, however, proved to be much more difficult for GSG 9 than initially thought.

CHAPTER 5

Border Guard Cowboys

On May 14, 1973, a report by the head of the BGS department on the current strength of GSG 9 read:

> Leadership group: 9;
> 1st operational unit: 27, 2nd operational unit: 30, 3rd operational unit: 32, 4th operational unit: 0;
> Supply: 20;
> Total: 118, +2 officers reporting for duty the next day.
> Recruitment for 4th operational unit underway.[1]

Ulrich Wegener was unhappy. In the first few weeks after the inception of the unit, he had personally canvassed Border Guard locations to find capable men for his new special intervention unit (no one thought of women at that time). However, the endeavor soon turned out tedious and unproductive. One-on-one interviews with up to 50 candidates at a time that lasted all day would leave only five or 10 men who made the cut, some of whom would then drop out before they even arrived in Saint Augustin. And another 25 to 30 percent of the few who actually showed up were screened out within the first few months, either because they left of their own volition or because they were sent back to their units as unsuitable for the job.

So finding the right kind of personnel turned out to be a tough business (and remains so to this day). In the course of 1973, the question of personnel developed into a serious problem for Wegener: "GSG 9 stands and falls on this. We didn't have a proper concept at the outset on how to get people out of the existing units and how to come to a sensible selection of personnel in general." Six months after the formation of GSG 9, the number of *Polizeivollzugsbeamten** lay still well below the target strength of 175.† Filling up the ranks took much too long. The reasons for this

---

* *Polizeivollzugsbeamten* (PVB) = Law enforcement officers.
† This was to change little in the next six months; in fact, the number of officers was even to fall. When the force was presented to the media at the end of September 1973, press reports spoke of 115 men.

lay not so much in a lack of suitable candidates; rather, many garrison commanders wanted to keep their best people, not lose them to some obscure new task force which many considered a waste of resources. Dieter Tutter's boss, for sure, was one of those who did not think much of Wegener's new troop as he made clear in no uncertain terms. Dieter Fox's unit leader was no less reluctant to let go of him, if somewhat more fatalistic about it. Fox could not relate to this. "One should have said: It's an honor for us to hand over these people and see them in action." Instead, the man had sighed and sent Fox to Saint Augustin shaking his head in resignation. "Well, I guess I'm rid of you."

Other commanders did not make it so easy for their men, as Werner Heimann and his comrade Klaus Hellmann learned the hard way. "In those days," said Heimann, "the hierarchies were still such that if your boss told you, 'You can't do that,' you just wouldn't do it."[2] Early in 1973, Heimann, a lathe operator by profession, served as group leader in a technical platoon* in Lüneburg, northern Germany. He already suspected that their commander would not let them leave just like that. So they filled out their GSG 9 application forms, but left them in the drawer until the time was right.

Opportunity arose when their platoon was detached to Gorleben to build jetties along the eastern border so that patrol vehicles would not sink in the swampy paths. They would be on the road for several days, enough time for the commander's anger to dissipate after he found out about their applications. "The motors of our trucks were already idling outside. We went to the office, handed in our papers—and then hopped on the truck and took off." But alas! His boss's Rover was much faster than their convoy. As soon as they got to Gorleben, Heimann's superior reared up in front of the platoon, "'Heimann and Hellmann: come here!' And then he bawled us out: 'What do you think you're doing, applying to GSG 9? I tore up your applications, now get back to work.' But I just murmured, 'The paperwork advised us to send a copy straight to GSG 9. That's what we did.' At that he was totally pissed off and took off." When Werner Heimann and his comrade subsequently passed the entrance examination, his boss in Lüneburg completely lost it: "Get out! I don't want to see you here again!"[3]

In Saint Augustin, however, Wegener was happy for every suitable candidate. "It remained difficult to find qualified men. Finally, in April 1973, we presented the first subunits to the minister of the interior in a large-scale exercise in the Siegburg/Bonn district, because he wouldn't let up. He wanted to see results as soon as possible, as he wanted to improve his political standing. We conducted an exercise in which we stormed a brickyard. That was something to show at least. I was able to report two

---

* Technical platoons correspond to the pioneer units in the army. Their task was road and wooden footbridge construction in swampy border areas at the Iron Curtain, blast preparation, the construction of pontoon bridges, etc.

trained operational units ready for action."[4] Soon after, however, the official date for operational readiness was postponed to summer, then to fall. According to the internal files of the Ministry of the Interior, the reason for this delay was problems with the delivery of equipment for the unit: bulletproof headgear, anorak jackets, radio equipment and vehicles. The main reason, though, was the sluggish pace in filling the unit with capable officers.

When the first few volunteers had completed their basic training with GSG 9 in the spring of 1973, Wegener sent them on a promotional tour of BGS garrisons to advertise the new task force. And advertise they did. Their standard entry: dashing. A convoy of five or six heavy Mercedes 280SEs would rush through the garrison gates in close pursuit, blue lights flashing, sirens blasting, tires squealing when coming to a halt in front of the officers' mess. On radio command, two officers would get out of each car, briskly slam the doors shut and remain motionless beside the car, determined but calm expressions on their faces, berets on their heads, formidable Puma hunting knives on their left hips, service revolvers on their right hips, hanging low in a Clint Eastwood-style "quick-draw holster." At the next radio command, the group would start walking as one toward the lecture hall.

The hearty show surely made an impression on their comrades in the regular Border Guard units. Though not always as desired. The Wild West holster, fastened to the thigh with a leather thong, soon earned "The 9ers" a reputation as "Border Guard Cowboys." Being an *Einheitsführer* (operational unit commander) and instructor, Dieter Tutter was part of the promotional team at the time: "We acted like bulls in a china shop. But that soon went away." For it did not take them long to realize that the gunslinger image was rather damaging. Within BGS circles they were soon mocked: GSG 9? Ah, yes, that's the guys who boot into the supermarket with their huge hunting knife, spear a cabbage and growl, "This one's mine!"

Those who felt most attracted by the martial attitude were often the very people GSG 9 did not want, says instructor Tutter. "Our psychologist, Wolfgang Salewski, would drill this into us. He said: 'Guys, with this attitude you are recruiting the wrong people. You don't want them! These are the ones I will have to remove in the exam when it comes to the mental aptitude for such a profession. I will have to say: He is not up to the task. This is a top man in sport and in everything physical. But don't accept him into the unit.' He was right."

In the first few years, a number of people slipped through the tests who did not meet the high standards Wegener had intended for his new special police force, "because we initially placed the greatest value on physical performance," he writes in his memoirs. "The most important thing about GSG 9 are the people. If the individual person doesn't match, then the whole unit won't work out…. It happened that we accepted applicants who were excellent athletes but not intelligent enough. But the latter is what's most important."[5] Thus, GSG 9 first had to painfully learn what qualities to really look for in an applicant, although the guidelines setting out what these qualities were supposed to be seemed straightforward:

> VIII Selection of personnel
> Only volunteers shall be recruited. In the selection process, special emphasis shall be placed on the following qualities:
>
> – sense of duty,
> – commitment,
> – prudence,
> – physical fitness,
> – work experience,
> – ability to act independently,
> – willingness to subordination.[6]

Physical requirements remained important: endurance, coordination, reaction speed and, of course, strength—every GSG 9 man had to be able to carry an injured comrade or a hostage out of a danger zone. The instructors came up with plenty of creative ideas on how to test the candidates' endurance under stress. After a long march, for example, they would sit the candidates in overheated rooms in full gear, where they had to solve tasks under time pressure. But Wegener and his people soon realized that strength and resilience were only part of what they needed: "For a task force, you must be able to think further than your average soldier or policeman.... The ability to work in a team is also paramount. To this end, we developed a selection process that ran over several weeks."[7]

As early as spring 1973, Wegener therefore engaged a psychological institute to develop selection procedures and training. He later switched to the Munich Institute for Conflict Research and Crisis Consulting, which still provides advice to GSG 9 today in the selection and training of suitable candidates as well as in psychological support of their careers within the unit, and in counseling before, during and after missions. Recruitment tests have been constantly developed over the years, as Günter Weber confirms. He is the current managing director of the institute. What is wanted in a candidate, he says, is above-average intelligence—at least A-level qualifications—but with a specific intelligence structure: "Intelligence tests roughly distinguish between three levels: verbal intelligence, numerical intelligence, visual intelligence. With GSG 9, the focus certainly lies on the latter two. We don't need linguistic acrobats because we're not looking for philosophers, but people who have very good deductive reasoning skills. Because they have to deal with complex problems and then have to conceptualize and structure a certain operation, and since every operation is a little different, think about how to proceed in the respective situation. Second point: excellent spatial imagination. Because the situations you find yourself in will always have something to do with moving in space. You make plans or receive plans and people need to be able to transfer something two-dimensional into three dimensions very quickly."[8]

Just as important as numerical and visual intelligence is personality, particularly emotional stability and stress resilience, according to GSG 9 adviser Weber. A task force man needs to be able to keep his cool when facing a difficult situation. This is not to say that he needs to be an emotionless badass. Quite the opposite. The most important prerequisites are authentic communication behavior and empathy. An operative needs to put himself in the shoes of others and to strike the right tone, but at the same time he needs to be able to communicate his own emotions that he is going through in the moment. Empathy is essential and lack of empathy is often underestimated as a problem, says psychological consultant Weber. Each SET consists of no more than a handful of officers who need to be perfectly attuned to each other. Each must have antennae for the others and must not just "do his own thing."

In addition, qualities are required that seem to contradict each other at first sight: the ability to work as a team and the willingness to take the lead. "More often than not you have either the loner who is good at making independent decisions. Or you have the team player who is very much trained toward others. But we need both the team player and the courageous decision-maker all cast into one person." The cliché image of the lone fighter with a knife between his teeth would be a disaster for GSG 9. But the same goes for the opposite: "We would have a big problem with someone who doesn't have a good sense of self-esteem, who needs a lot of external recognition and confirmation and seeks to get it by acting it out. Such people, who have to compensate for their lack of self-esteem, would be absolutely unsuitable."

Consequently, self-promoters, loners, hotheads, egomaniacs and know-it-alls are not in demand at GSG 9. Furthermore, the ability to admit mistakes is considered a big plus. *Fehlerkultur*, the ability to own errors and deal with them constructively, praised in this day and age in every expensive management seminar, was cultivated within GSG 9 from the outset as an essential part of the mission analysis. At the same time, people are not supposed to get in their own way because of overzealous self-criticism. Balancing out all these virtues is tricky. But there is even more.

Psychologist Weber lists two more desired qualities in the perfect GSG 9 candidate, qualities which the uninitiated would certainly not expect in such a work environment at first: improvisational talent and creativity in all things tactical. But Dieter Fox heartily agreed: "Special units all over the world live from this. What more could I do to get an edge against the opposing side? In general, we have to assume that we are always in second position. No matter where we are, no matter what mission we follow—we as a special intervention unit can only react. Acting—that's what our opponent does."

Creativity and a talent for improvisation are considered essential in order to "get ahead of the situation," as it is called in the jargon: gaining initiative, retaining the element of surprise, and holding the reins of action in one's hands, in order to not let the situation go sideways even if it develops radically different than planned. And it will. Always. Wegener had internalized this mantra since he returned from his training course in Israel: "GSG 9 had to be set up in such a way that the commander of the operational unit could independently lead into the situation and make decisions whenever a new situation arose." This meant a great challenge in the search for candidates, because the hurdle that Wegener set for himself and his men reached conceivably high: "The idea behind the concept was this: 'We can cope with any situation.' That was and is the be-all and end-all of GSG 9."[9]

With such high standards, it quickly dawned on Wegener that a radically different type of leadership would be needed from what had been the case before. It came down to his motto: "Leadership must come from the front! The commander is the one responsible eventually. But in an emergency, everyone must be able to make decisions.... We had to be able to react quickly. The leader in the middle level under the commander must be able to change the deployment of forces at any time if the situation develops in an unexpected way. He has to report this to the commander later, but first and foremost it is he who is responsible for what happens on the ground."[10]

GSG 9's operating ground rules therefore did not follow the classic military orthodoxy that is practiced in many military and para-military organizations to this day: the sometimes lemming-like *Befehlstaktik* (or Command Tactics: an order is an order and is carried out to the letter under all circumstances). Instead, Wegener introduced the so-called *Auftragstaktik* (or Mission Tactics). "This meant that in many respects we were throwing old military principles out the window."[11] The core principle of *Auftragstaktik* is to give the team leader on the ground leeway for making his own decisions in a dynamic situation. For the planning, this means that the team leader is given a mission objective, which he must achieve within a certain framework of conditions such as time frame, available forces, resources, etc. The means and tactics he chooses in order to achieve this goal are entirely left up to him. And if the situation changes significantly while carrying out the operation, the leader on the ground is not only entitled but obliged to change his course of action in such a way that the objective is still achieved. This might be the case if, for example, communication with the superior is disrupted and immediate action is of the essence, or if unforeseen obstacles arise which need to be dealt with at once, like a blocked doorway or additional defense installations.

This type of leadership was not exactly brand new. The basic idea had been introduced in the Prussian army in the 19th century, and after World War II became part of the military identity of *Innere Führung* (Internal Leadership) of the newly established Bundeswehr. But paper is patient, as the saying goes, and *Auftragstaktik* was far from being second nature for uniformed personnel in the armed forces: "In 1972, these were entirely new ideas. Our men understood this immediately and were enthusiastic about it."[12] From its earliest days, the men of GSG 9 put this idea into action, as is confirmed by the report of a police officer from Switzerland.

In the beginning of 1973, barely four months after their inception, Léon Borer of the Bern Police Command paid a visit to Saint Augustin. One year prior, Borer had founded the Enzian task force, Switzerland's first special intervention police unit. After his return, he noted in his secret field report the mindset in the unit: "The majority of GSG 9's officers are of a critical spirit and self-confident. In no way could one speak of unconditional obedience in the sense of the old legionnaire type. This creates a special human relationship between leaders and the squad. Leaders do not demand anything of the team that they do not demonstrate themselves."[13]

Wegener was intent on setting an example in this respect. He was convinced the commander was not supposed to give orders from a distant command post, from the famous field commander's hill, as was customary for military leaders in the old days. He believed instead that he himself should lead the way: "This is the only way to inspire confidence in the troops. This is one of the reasons why one can expect top performance from special units. The example of the commander is important. He must put himself in the line of danger and act as a role model."[14] Even though this leadership principle was (and is) not undisputed, Wegener did not leave it at words. In training courses he let himself be bullied just like his men. Dieter Tutter recalls a two-week-long SWAT course at the FBI in which he formed a three-man team with Wegener and an Iranian officer: "We were beaten and kicked and he took it all. He was tough and really physically fit."

In general contact, too, Wegener's people experienced their commander quite differently than they were used to in the strict military hierarchy of the Federal Border Guard. As Dieter Fox emphasizes, "He said quite clearly: 'I am standing here in front of you as commander. But this is just because my job is to push certain things through with the upper tier. Without you, I am nothing.' This was not at all common with other commanders. On the contrary, they would always keep their distance. There was the little sub-leader at the bottom and the commander at the top. Wegener was quite a different matter. Being lieutenant colonel—which is a damn high rank—he nevertheless showed that a human being can also be a tactical leader and that a tactical leader can also be a human being. This attitude impressed every one of us and led to—if I may say—the unrelenting cohesion within GSG 9 ranks."

Sometimes, this open attitude became apparent in seemingly trivial ways. At BGS there was an unwritten law at the time that officers would work alongside the rank and file, but they would spend their off-duty hours strictly separately. Werner Heimann was not the only one who was initially taken aback by the fact that his commander would talk to him after hours, informally chatting about day-to-day topics. He was also not above sitting down with his men over a beer and bratwurst when they would have a little birthday party or something to celebrate within their operational unit: "We always invited Wegener, and he would always come, squat down with us on a tree trunk by the bonfire, have a drink, and discuss things with us."

Having said this, Wegener most certainly was not your jovial type of person. The informal use of the first name and the "*du*," the German token of trust and friendship, he only offered to very few close colleagues. Also, he refrained from telling confidential stories of a private nature. Nevertheless, they always got the feeling that they could talk to him eye to eye, his men say. Even later, when Wegener was placed under personal protection and a GSG 9 detail was responsible for his personal security, they would not have to wait outside the door as would have been the rule with others. Wegener would always take them along to events and introduce each of them to everybody else—a little gesture, sure, but not a triviality for his bodyguards like Werner Heimann: "It was a sign: He takes care of us, he doesn't just leave us out." It is because of such small everyday touches that Wegener is still revered by his men today. And even more precisely because he led missions from the front. But it was to be a long time before that would be the case. First came vocational training for the future counterterror specialists.

Volunteer Applications on a Daily Basis

The list of training objectives was long, as Wegener had defined them in the "Concept for the Establishment and Deployment of a Federal Border Guard Unit for Special Police Operations":

- training of snipers as part of the unit and as lone fighters, increased skill in the handling of all types of weapons,
- weapons science, explosives and detonators,
- mastery of all types of unarmed self-defense,
- "Ranger exercises" to enable officers to operate even under the toughest conditions,
- legal training,
- basic criminological training,
- material and psychological operational tactics,
- messaging/communication techniques and operational techniques,
- training of individual officers in special branches, e.g. special blasting service, use of chemical agents,
- knowledge of contemporary [political] ideologies,
- up-to-date overview of operational practices of terrorist groups.[15]

The instruction courses were divided into two main blocks: first, a two-and-a-half-month basic training, schooling the candidates in individual combat, judo, karate, intensive shooting and close combat, both as individual fighters and as part of the SET. In addition, there was strength and fitness training for the newcomers, such as Werner Heimann. "The first four or five weeks were mainly about torture and fitness. Every morning an obstacle course—and every morning a little faster than the day before. After that we would move out to the Siebengebirge hillside to run, then to our shooting range in the moorland of Wahner Heide to practice with various weapons." In addition, there was telecommunications training, instruction in operational law, criminology and forensics, as well as on the ideology and strategies of terrorist organizations.

After completing this first block, it was decided whether the trainee was allowed to carry on with GSG 9. For 60 percent of the candidates, this marked the end. Taking into account the ones who had dropped out in the course of the first training block, only about a third of those who passed the acceptance exams would continue with the following three-month-long special training. The second block consisted, among other things, of sniper training, explosives training, the documentation and preservation of evidence, as well as special driver training in which the safe handling of GSG 9's fast, heavy vehicles was practiced. Finally, the future task force officers would routinely train special missions such as storming aircraft and banks as well as abseiling from helicopters. In addition, they specialized in parachuting and/or diving.

The training program was tight, and the future specialists found themselves more often on the road than at their home compound in Saint Augustin. From May to September 1973 alone, the responsible department in the Ministry of the Interior listed more than a dozen training courses: High-speed training to master the heavy Mercedes Sedans at the Daimler works in Stuttgart, motorbike training, psychological training, alarm exercises in the Hanover-Goslar area, training in covert operations in the city center of Bonn (subject: hostage-taking in a high-rise parliament building), and several instruction courses in explosives, including at the Dynamite Nobel fabrication plant, on the subject of "initial explosives and detonators."[16] As was the case with the question of suitable candidates, GSG 9 as an organization experienced a steep learning curve both in basic and special training. A lot of the training exercises that Wegener's operational unit leaders came up with were somewhat off-the-cuff and turned out to be less than useful. And the training methods that turned out to be useful were simply the result of learning by doing. Nowhere was it specified in detail and universally valid what should be practiced, nor how. In the early days, recruits were simply put into one of the existing operational units and joined in as best they could while the units themselves were still in the phase of cobbling together more or less practicable tactics and training techniques. They practiced their standard exercises in a continuous loop, bringing up to speed the new recruits who were gradually trickling in.

It soon became apparent that this was less than ideal, but it was not until 1981 that a regular training unit was created. For the lack of an education manual for special intervention units, each operational unit leader would train his men more or less according to his own ideas. But then again, the instructors themselves were initially not educated in what they were supposed to teach, and Commander Wegener was concerned with all kinds of things other than the in-service training of his senior officers like Dieter Tutter: "It was quite chaotic," Tutter recalls. Thus, without an order or even an official mandate, he set himself the task of gradually writing down training regulations as well as recruitment and weapons guidelines, standardizing and documenting them with illustrations and photographs. "It's all still there," he says proudly, including the photos he took for demonstration purposes. But even half a century later he is not allowed to release the documents. Parts of them still apply today, as does the basic division into two blocks of basic and specialized training. Thus, GSG 9 does not give permission to publish any of it.

Apart from the content, there was the question of the teaching methods. Tutter recalled heated disputes between him and Deputy Commander Blätte, who would later become Wegener's successor in command and who embraced old-school military drill. The notorious "razing" was common practice at the time in the Bundeswehr as well as in the Bundesgrenzschutz. Tutter had experienced more than his share of it in his own time. One exercise popular with instructors back then was push-ups over an opened jackknife that the instructor places on the floor, the tip right under the stomach of the instructor's chosen victim. "That's such a rotten trick!" Even after all these years, Tutter was still agitated about it. There was a whole series of such nasty exercises, which were either dishonoring, mean, dangerous, primitive or all of the above: "And then all of this idiotic: 'Lie down! Get up! March! About turn!' Then down again, crawling through the mud, then about turn lying on your belt buckle and crawl back again, then cleaning your uniform and repeat from the top—I refused to participate in all that crap. This has nothing to do with real training, it only breaks people. Instructors who do that kind of stuff are unfit leaders in my opinion."

Not everyone in GSG 9 was as dismissive about this kind of drill as Dieter Tutter. The prevailing opinion among the instructors was that toughness breeds toughness, and toughness needs to hurt, again and again and again, ad nauseam. Tutter had to fight quite a few battles to keep the razing drill at least out of his own operational unit. He deemed it not only undignified and humiliating, but also counterproductive, particularly with the type of highly motivated volunteers that were the recruitment stock of GSG 9. "My motto was always: 'Each morning each man who shows up for duty hands in a fresh volunteer application in doing so, if you will, otherwise he wouldn't be here. You've come here voluntarily, and if you continue, then it's of your own volition. There is nothing to be achieved with pressure. If I push him but he doesn't want to, he will run exactly as fast as I think: Well, that's all he can do. But of course he can do better. He just doesn't want to! These people are high achievers. Actually, they do want to do better. So, you have to let the horses run free and direct them, not chase them. If you chase them, they are not faster. But if you tickle their honor, if they run of their own accord, for my sake, or for the sake of the unit, or to drive home the victory in a competition, they will run much better and faster."

This does not mean that Tutter lowered standards or let his people get away with more than other operational unit leaders would. Quite the opposite. His standard program included a great number of exercises and extreme demands to push the physical and mental limits of his trainees: forced marches lasting days on end; swimming across the notoriously dangerous river Rhine unannounced in the middle of the night after intensive shooting training; claustrophobia tests in narrow sewage pipes; 100 kilometers of nonstop paddling in a rubber dinghy; football matches in full combat gear—some of it hair-raising stuff which even back then would have prompted professional associations to take legal action, admits Tutter. His men did not care. They were all in.

The goal was always to overcome one's weaker self. And to do so, it was necessary to push the candidates far beyond their own limits, as all the veterans agreed. But, says Tutter's comrade Werner Heimann with a shrug, it was all voluntary after all: "There were two possibilities: You want to stay, then you do it. Or you don't comply, then you have to leave." Most of them stayed. There was a great, almost euphoric spirit of optimism among the young officers, recalls Heimann: "Everything we knew about the Federal Border Guard was thrown overboard. We had no rules, we had no guidelines. Anyone who had an idea on how we could move forward and improve was heard and it was put into action right away, even in shooting. There was enough ammunition; there was enough equipment."

Shooting exercises were scheduled on an almost daily basis, four times a week, five hours at a time. Unlike in regular BGS units, in the police or the Bundeswehr, there were no restrictions on the ammunition allocated to each officer. They would practice until instructors like Dieter Tutter were satisfied, sometimes even until the gun barrel was too hot to touch: "We shot until the shells piled up to our ankles." Requirements were significantly different from those of regular police units, where the average officer rarely got into the tight spot of having to use their service weapon. In contrast, GSG 9 knew that each time they were called to go on a mission they might have to fire their weapon. While patrol police practiced their aim once or twice a year, usually at static targets, shooting was to become habitual routine for GSG 9. And with all types of weapons, too, in all positions: standing up, sitting, kneeling, lying down, as well as in a wide variety of situations with varying tasks: precision shooting with rifles at distant targets; instinctive shooting: firing from the hip or from other positions where it is not possible to aim accurately; reaction shooting at the shooter's own discretion at friend/foe targets; combat shooting: firing at turntables, targets appearing at short notice, shooting at photographic slides or film pictures; shooting under stress, disrupted by noise and light effects, extreme temperatures, unfavorable weather conditions, high physical and/or nervous strain right before firing; shooting under NBC* protective gear.

Dieter Fox considered this intensive shooting training indispensable. "The idea was not to become gunslingers of the Django type, but to be able to handle the firearm like a sleepwalker and to avoid any mistake. The basic principle of weapon handling is not to be afraid. If you are afraid of the gun, you make mistakes. And the gun forgives no mistake. So I have to befriend this thing somehow. I have to be able to take it apart; I have to be able to put it back together. I need to accomplish that with my eyes closed, because I have to be able to work with it in a dark room. Everything has to come together perfectly. And this took a long time."

The instructors at the time knew a thing or two about that. In sniper exercises on moving targets, for example, it was imperative for everyone to fire on radio command at the same time. But only then. "It needed to work 10 times out of 10," said Tutter. "And if someone prematurely pulled the trigger and it went off before I gave the firing order, well, he would get a hefty scolding: 'Now, this could have cost the hostages their lives. That's utterly unacceptable! You must keep yourselves absolutely under control!'"

For the goal was not to just hit someone somehow, but to use the firearm with surgical precision to minimize damage and maintain *Verhältnismäßigkeit der Mittel* (or proportionality of the means) as stated in the German police laws. The 1973 service regulations for GSG 9 exhorts: "During shooting training, it must be borne in mind at all times that the aim of the use of firearms by the police, according to the relevant legal regulations, is to render someone incapable of attack or escape." This required discipline, perfect control and full focus on the task. If it was possible to take the opponent out of action with a precise shot without killing him, then a GSG 9 man should be able to make the call for this option within a fraction of a second and be able to place the shot safely.

Moving on, only little by little did they find out what they could put to good use for their special operations, what they could not, and what was perhaps even a hindrance to their work. In the beginning, the instructors placed great emphasis on the officer's ability to draw his weapon, unlock it quickly and fire targeted shots. This was the reason why at first everyone at GSG 9 walked about Clint Eastwood-style with those quick-draw holsters tied to the thigh that had caused so much hilarity and ridicule among their BGS colleagues during their promotional tours. But it soon dawned on them that the classic high-noon duel outside the Sweetwater Saloon's dusty corral would be a rare occurrence in practice. And other opportunities for the use of their quick-draw technique seemed likely to be scarce. In daily practice the low-hanging holster was above all a nuisance, a hindrance while getting in and out of the car, as well as fastening a seat belt when driving. Moreover, in rough terrain

---

* NBC = Nuclear, Biological, Chemical.

the weapon had a nasty habit of slipping out unnoticed, as Dieter Fox personally found out. Also: "If you had to run a longer distance, the whole thing with the gun in it would flap up and down. You couldn't tie it as tightly to your thigh as needed. Some guys then fastened a strap around the top of it. Didn't help either."

Dieter Tutter agreed that the holster was an erroneous development, even one prone to accidents. Shortly before one of the frequent demonstrations in GSG 9's shooting gallery, he wanted to practice for the "El Presidente" quick-draw exercise. It goes like this: the shooter stands facing away from the target, revolver in his holster. On command, he draws the gun while swirling around and firing two shots at the target. The time counts between the command and second shot. A quick-draw holster is ideal for this exercise. Well, typically it would be. "But my new leather holster was tight and still somewhat sticky. When doing the quick draw, the gun slipped from my hand and I instinctively grabbed it tightly. I pulled the trigger and shot myself in the right groin. It didn't hurt at first, but I was escorted out at once. The guests for the shooting demonstration arrived shortly afterwards and didn't notice anything." At the hospital, the bullet was removed from the back of the knee of the would-be John Wayne. Barely eight months later, he was able to resume his duties.

This type of gunshot wound was a recurring calamity, particularly in the early days. If there was plain recklessness involved, it sometimes meant the end of a career in GSG 9. Apart from that, the doctors had to deal mainly with rib and limb fractures, all kinds of sprains, torn tendons, and similar injuries, which the men mostly suffered during exercises in rough terrain. Commander Wegener commented matter-of-factly at the time that it was just in the nature of things that they had more casualties than other commands. One area of exercise that proved to be particularly demanding and dangerous was rapid abseiling from high-rise buildings and helicopters. For one, it was not possible to simply copy existing climbing techniques from mountaineers or mountain infantry. In the field, it was important for the men to descend in a controlled manner, but at high speed and in quick succession. Like with so many other things, they had to come up with a suitable technique themselves, so injuries were an unsurprising consequence of their lighthearted trial-and-error approach.

Second, they started out with less than suitable material for the intended purpose. They manufactured their own climbing harnesses, because those available on the market that were typically attached to the hips with tie lines turned out to be quite useless. In the beginning, they would use simple nylon ropes and even hemp ropes. But these would heat up while running fast through the karabiners, so much so that they often melted. Rope brakes that prevented slipping did not yet exist, so they had to brake and stop manually. When they proudly presented their equipment to the mountain guides at the BGS training center in the Bavarian Alps, the climbing specialists there were horrified.

Time and again, accidents and near disasters occurred. During an exercise on a fire brigade tower in Bonn, Dieter Fox had to hoist his superior Tutter back onto the platform by the waistband of his trousers just as he was about to drop backwards to abseil. Tutter had forgotten to guide the rope through a karabiner. His free fall would have ended on the concrete floor 20 meters below. Luckily, that evening he was able to celebrate his "second birthday" with his rescuer.

Others were less lucky. In September 1976, during an exercise in the low mountain range of the Eifel, Jörg Probstmeier had just safely lowered himself down from a helicopter hovering at 40 meters when he was forced to watch his comrade whirl down the rope and hit the ground right next to him. The young officer was immediately flown to a hospital but succumbed to his injuries during the flight there. Probstmeier, who had only been with the task force for 10 months at the time and was still in training, remembered a very ambitious, somewhat over-motivated comrade: "You always abseil down in pairs, simultaneously one on the right and one on the left side of the helicopter. He wanted to be the fastest and the first to reach the ground but had not calculated that it was a new rope with very high elasticity and no good braking effect yet. He probably started clamping down too late and hit the ground almost without braking. We were all very pensive afterwards."

From this incident, Wegener drew the conclusion that in the future selection of applicants, greater consideration should be given to age, thus the necessary prudence and caution in order to avoid accidents due to recklessness and overconfidence. Nevertheless, in 1980 GSG 9 had to report another accident to the Ministry of the Interior when a young operative died after an abseiling accident in the Bonn University Hospital.[17] Even the accidents that "only" ended in the emergency room, i.e. those that weren't fatal, mostly occurred during abseiling from a helicopter.[18] The bitter irony is that this very abseil technique was never applied in a field mission. Today it has been replaced by so-called fast roping, in which the officers slide down a thick rope.

Deterrence Principle

Nevertheless, the Hollywood-like helicopter stunt was to become something of a GSG 9 trademark. On September 21, 1973, one year after its inception, the young task force presented the abseil technique to press reporters and a television crew for the first time. Millions of viewers watched this "self-developed rope act" on West Germany's top political TV show, *Bericht aus Bonn (Report from Bonn)*. The reporter showed himself as being impressed by the self-defense techniques, including karate chops, but even more so by the arsenal of weapons and its "depressing" necessity: precision rifles, silenced submachine guns, and the latest infrared night-vision devices, all lined up for inspection in great numbers and variations. "Is this really a mere police unit or not rather a military force?" was the concerned question he posed to Minister Hans-Dietrich Genscher, who was present at the event. The minister denied: "It is clearly a police unit that is deployed solely according to the law of proportionality of means," whose deployment hopefully was to never happen, he quickly added. But if it were, this task force would need to confront perpetrators who would be armed with machine guns, possibly using explosive devices, and who, as Munich had shown, cared little for the lives of police officers or hostages. This meant that this police unit needed to be equipped accordingly.

The show of force and martial display at this first public demonstration was a deliberate choice. Genscher relied on the deterrent effect of those images. He repeatedly emphasized the preventive value of such a task force, and tried to allay possible doubts by recalling the unbearable situation in Munich a year earlier: "If back then they had mastered the silent subduing of a man, as the border guards here demonstrate today, they might have been able to enter through the garage entrance of the building in Conollystrasse, which was only secured by one terrorist," Genscher mused.

Nevertheless, the reaction in the press was double-sided. There was fear of militarization. Fear of an uncontrollable force. Fear of a police state in the making. "Genscher's new elite killers" read the headline of the central organ of the West German communists, *Roter Morgen*, reflecting the unease of large sections of the political left about such a militaristic demonstration of state power. Barely three decades after the fall of the Nazi state, the memory of the repressive instruments of the criminal regime was still alive, and great the distrust of any expansion of the state's means of violence, no matter how much Genscher tried to placate: "Shooting the perpetrator can never be the goal of a police operation.... We don't want a James Bond-style of thinking, nor do we want dead bodies at the end of an operation. We need calm, reasonable people for this difficult task."

Still, suspicion lingered that the "elite killers" could be used not only to fight criminals but to fight political enemies. Those who believed that the West German vassal state of American imperialism had created a death squad to persecute left-wing critics of the oppressive system were not reassured by the minister's assurances. Of course not. The *Roter Morgen* continued: "It is no coincidence that the Genscher troupe were trained and introduced at the very time when the 'wildcat' strikes had given a new impetus to the struggle of the working class and further strengthened our party." There is no evidence whatsoever to be found that supports these wild claims. But the narrative was gratefully received and parroted by state propaganda in the camp of the Socialist Bloc, particularly in Eastern Germany.

In stark contrast, the bourgeois press gushed praise for Genscher's pet project. The *Frankfurter Allgemeine Zeitung* (FAZ) wrote enthusiastically that with his latest work the minister of the interior had once again proven his ability to "always find the right way between accusations from the right ('limp state') and the left ('authoritarian structures') with a feeling for the next and best step." And the *Stuttgarter Zeitung* even enthused about the "flying fire brigade," whose snipers were able to shoot through a five-Deutschmark coin from a distance of 300 meters. The few million marks it cost was money well spent: "It would have been wrong to make savings here and thus run the risk of the force being worse equipped and having to make do with slower vehicles than terrorists and bank robbers. Only with the best possible equipment can GSG 9 do justice to its task of keeping control of the situation and mastering danger in the case of particularly serious crimes and robberies by terrorists."

Exactly one year and one week after the decision was made to create a special task force, it was ready: GSG 9 was equipped, GSG 9 was trained, GSG 9 was operational and ready to go on missions. What was missing, however, were the missions.

CHAPTER 6

Training World Champions

Low over the horizon, the familiar silhouette emerges, moving straight towards the camera: a Bell UH-1D Huey, of Vietnam War fame, closing in quickly. The image exudes an air of *Apocalypse Now*, only missing Wagner's "Ride of the Valkyries" as its soundtrack. As the helicopter approaches, six men can be spotted standing on the skids, three on each side holding fast to the fuselage, dressed in combat gear and helmets, harnessed and ready to jump. Now the helicopter hovers almost vertically above the camera while the six men whir to the ground on ropes in quick succession, moving onward in attack formation.

However, the fighters do not land in the impenetrable jungle of Indochina but on the lush green meadows next to the Border Guards officers' reception building in Saint Augustin—right in front of the amazed crowd on Open House Day. The footage is shot in 1976 by an amateur filmmaker on the 25th anniversary celebration of the BGS. In other scenes, there are families strolling around the grounds in their Sunday best, and laughing children whisking around the trucks, jeeps, and tanks on display. The rope act is the highlight of the show's performances that day.

Three years after officially being announced ready for action, "The 9ers" had perfected their abseil demonstration, and they had ample opportunity to present it. Ministers of the Interior of the Bundesländer travelled to Saint Augustin to see GSG 9's skills demonstrated, and members of parliament, police chiefs, and media representatives were invited on a regular basis to marvel at the film-ready stunts. Like a wunderkind, the task force was proudly called on by the Ministry of the Interior to perform its act for an audience which applauds in polite amazement, but otherwise does not really know what to make of the presentation. Internally, they called it *"den Otto machen"* ("doing Otto," something along the lines of acting the clown). Depending on the importance of the visitors, "the Otto" was divided into three categories, recalled Dieter Fox: the small, the medium, and the large Otto. "The big Otto was a real show, primarily designed for when the press was attending."

Only they did not really consider themselves a show troupe. They were practicing for real missions, after all. It was just ... there weren't any. Not yet. Not really. Instead, they got what today would half-jokingly be called "missions of an exercise nature," a standby alert here, securing a prisoner transport there, or supporting the police on a state visit.

For a handful of GSG 9 officers their first—still unofficial—field mission order came when Soviet leader Leonid Brezhnev paid a state visit to Bonn in April 1973. This happened even before the Ministry of the Interior had approved GSG 9 for such a mission. The risk of a terrorist attack was considered low, but for the new troupe it was an opportunity to move in public for the first time, albeit undercover. So they were deployed in plainclothes for surveillance purposes. They kept watch as a sniper squad on the buildings opposite Palais Schaumburg in Bonn, the then-seat of the Chancellery. And they secured the route to the government's guesthouse on Petersberg, a hilltop close to Bonn. "It was exciting and tactically very instructive for us," Dieter Fox recalls.

One year later, they were finally allowed to officially take action at the request of the provinces of Hesse and Bavaria, during the Soccer World Cup in Germany in 1974. They were sent to matches in Frankfurt, Düsseldorf and Munich to support the local police where they monitored the spectator terraces with field glasses from the top stadium stands—in plain sight of anyone who cared to look. Compared to the Olympic Games two years earlier, the operational police tactics had done a full 180. In Munich, all police were to remain as invisible as possible at the Olympic village and the stadiums, up to the point of their complete disarmament. Now, however, they were ordered to recognizably demonstrate their presence and strength in two-man patrols with uniforms and submachine guns.

A dozen missions of similar quality can be traced over the following years: Deployment of a unit to avert danger at the funeral of Red Army Faction terrorist Holger Meins in Hamburg; flat searches in the Rhine-Main area in support of the federal and provincial criminal police in the fight against gang crime; protection of the mourning ceremonies for the victims of the RAF attack on the embassy in Stockholm in 1975 in Bonn; protection of the trial against the Stockholm terrorists in Düsseldorf; the same at the RAF trial in Stuttgart-Stammheim; providing security details for the German delegation at the Olympic Games in Montreal in 1976. All in all, not much to write home about.

In between, "The 9ers" helped the Federal Criminal Police Office (BKA) out of a pickle. Their subdivision *Sicherungsgruppe* (SG, Security Group) in the Bonn branch was responsible for the protection of high-ranking politicians and business leaders, a task that grew more and more challenging at the time. In order to expand their services, SG had initially asked for regular Border Guard officers as additional drivers. But your average Border Guard officer would not be familiar with handling the heavy, high-motorized cars that were used for the purpose, and after they had totaled almost a dozen Mercedes and BMWs within a fortnight, authorities came to the conclusion that even the BKA's financially well-endowed budget might soon be overstretched if this continued for too long.

So GSG 9 was asked whether its operatives could help out as long as their BGS colleagues were busy taking driving safety courses. It was agreed that GSG 9's three operational units would work in shifts for four weeks each. However, it soon turned out that GSG 9 could not handle such missions as long-term assignments if they did not want to become full-time drivers. Therefore, it was decided that GSG 9 "would only be used in extreme individual cases that corresponded to their special training and in emergency situations."[1] SG had to look elsewhere.

But after all, this was how in 1976 Werner Heimann came to spend a skiing vacation with the then-Minister of Justice Hans-Jochen Vogel. That is to say, the minister and his family were on vacation in Arosa, Switzerland, and Heimann became their shadow—including on the slopes, naturally. "Yes," he grins, "with my gun at the side like in a James Bond movie. But I was rather useless at skiing at the time, still learning, so all that happened was that on the first night I could count all the bruises on this side of my body and on the next night I could count them on the other side of my body." Since an accident-free journey downhill already presented a real challenge to the GSG 9 man, a James Bond-like scenario was not on the cards had the situation arisen. Luckily, the minister's alpine ski trip proved rather uneventful in this respect.

Whether it was personal protection in deep snow or the occasional apartment search, all these missions were but dry runs for a special intervention unit destined to handle the most serious violent crimes. Despite their keenness, there was nothing they could do but continue to wait, continue to practice, continue to prepare. And to do so with as much practical orientation as possible. The BGS premises in Saint Augustin offered less than ideal conditions for lifelike exercises, so from the outset the squads were forced to travel often. They were regulars at the Hammelburg military training ground for shooting exercises, as well as in Munsterlager and at other Bundeswehr locations.

For longer special tactical courses, the entire GSG 9 went to a training facility close to the town of Lydd on the southern coast of England. There, the British Army was preparing for operations in Northern Ireland, practicing urban warfare against the IRA. Under strict secrecy, a whole district of downtown Belfast had been faithfully recreated: entire streetscapes complete with pubs from which music was blaring, and rows of houses from which remote-control cardboard comrades would emerge or prams rolled across the street, and lids of rubbish bins suddenly popped up. In Germany it was only possible to train in ruins or in factories on the verge of demolition, but here they were able to simulate a wide variety of situations undisturbed and as close to real life as possible.

The Ministry of the Interior Gets Nervous

GSG 9 practiced rescuing hostages from buildings, buses and trains on a regular basis—but first and foremost they performed drills storming aircraft. There was an immense fear of "skyjacking," a quite justified fear as it would turn out. Storming an aircraft was not a distant thought experiment—not one possibility among many, but the central scenario in the counterterrorism fight for which GSG 9 had to prepare. After the Olympic attack, an endless litany of reports and rumors shows up in the files of the Bonn Ministry of the Interior, always referencing secret information ("... as conveyed by a friendly service ..."):[2] There are reports of plans for hijackings of Lufthansa flights; or the entry of suspect elements into Europe, sometimes disguised as women or priests, supposedly with the aim of carrying out attacks on planes, airports and (mostly Israeli) embassies. The intelligence services delivered information about the theft of British, American and German uniforms, expressing apprehension about their use as disguises during an attack. More than once, Magnum Chianti wine bottles that had been converted into improvised explosive devices were detected; the same went for similarly prepared packets of cakes, cigars, and cigarettes. There were reports of intimate contacts between Western stewardesses and Palestinian suspects in Beirut and Jeddah, as well as rumors of money changing hands from Western airlines to Palestinian terrorist organizations, a kind of prepaid ransom to avoid their planes being highjacked.

In 1974, the year of the World Soccer Championships, ministerial nerves were aggravated once more. In the run-up to the global event, the Bonn Ministry registered an increasing number of planned attacks on airports, according to intelligence reports. This first major German event on the world stage after the disastrous Olympic Games went off without a hitch. But even after that, there was no "all clear." In February 1975, the responsible councilor in the Ministry of the Interior noted: "According to current reports and the attacks on air traffic since the beginning of the year, it must be assumed that the tense security situation in civil air traffic will continue.... According to BND reports, the Federal Republic of Germany is deemed to be one of the most important targets of the planned terrorist actions."[3]

From today's perspective, the whole thing appears more like a guessing game than evaluations based on actual intelligence. But there were several factors that made the situation in air traffic difficult to assess, one being a lack of information due to lax security measures which were still far removed from today's standards. This can be seen from an Israeli working paper offering recommendations to the Germans on how to increase security at airports and on aircraft: it called for screening of airport employees by secret service, armed security personnel, and comparison of checked-in passengers with those actually traveling on the plane. For the most part, measures like these are taken for granted today, but at the time apparently had not yet come to the mind of German officials.[4] Germany would only introduce routine baggage screening in 1980 as a reaction to the Mogadishu incident in 1977.

It was high time to follow up on this advice, as should have been done much earlier. For the number of skyjackings skyrocketed. Up to the end of the 1960s, there had not been a single hijacking incident with a political background. In the course of the 1970s, however, this spectacular form of hostage-taking was to become fashionable in certain circles. In the aftermath of the Israeli Six-Day War of 1967, Arab and Palestinian terrorist groups in particular resorted to this type of terror PR to galvanize international attention. The blueprint for this was provided in 1968 by the hijacking of a commercial flight of the Israeli airline El Al by three members of the PFLP. For the first time in history, a large number of random people were taken hostage to blackmail a government, in this case that of Israel.

This particularly spectacular form of hijacking enabled terrorists to take entire countries hostage by indiscriminately threatening the lives of random citizens. This way, they created a worldwide media echo. Taking into consideration that terrorist acts are little more than PR with guns, this was a recipe for success that many other terrorist organizations would copy. In the following years, many Western states struggled with the inconvenient question of how to deal with such a challenge. Should they meet the skyjackers' demands and hence demonstrate their vulnerability to blackmail, inviting a further attack? Or stand firm and sacrifice the lives of their citizens for the sake of the steadfastness of the state? Governments had faced this nasty choice before, but typically with just one or two lives at stake, usually political or economic leaders, not with a whole passenger plane full of innocent bystanders. The fact that no German government had faced this unpleasant decision so far was probably due to chance. The Federal Republic eventually would have to go through a steep—and painful—learning curve.

In the decade before the Mogadishu incident, 16 airliners were hijacked, 10 of them by members of the PFLP and one by the Fatah group Black September (plus the failed hijacking of an El Al plane in Munich in 1970). Three times the target was a German aircraft: in February 1972, the Lufthansa Boeing 747 *Baden-Württemberg* on its way from Tokyo to Frankfurt; in October of the same year, the Boeing 727 *Kiel* (the one used to extort the release of the surviving Munich bombers); and finally, in December 1973, the Boeing 737 *Worms* in Rome. This last hijacking ended after one day in Kuwait with the surrender of the hostage-takers. In the hours whilst this hijacking was still ongoing, the German government had asked Ulrich Wegener whether GSG 9 would be able to storm the plane if it were to land in Germany. Wegener said "yes" at the time. Today, however, Dieter Fox expresses strong doubts as to whether such a mission would have worked out. Even though Wegener had reported them ready for action a couple of months earlier, GSG 9 was still at an early stage of its development: "We were nowhere close to the level of readiness we were later, in 1977. We would certainly have managed to accomplish a few things, and would probably have made it into the plane, but most likely there would have been many casualties."

But, of course, the next skyjacking could happen any time. Due to the special circumstances outside and inside the vehicle, cracking an aircraft was considered the ultimate challenge for any task force, the "premium class," as Dieter Fox puts it: "Taking a ship is hot alright. You have to get up out of the water or down from a helicopter. A train car is not that easy either. But aircraft? Since you don't see anything! You don't know what's going on inside. There are only small windows, and if the blinds are down, you can't see anything at all. And you can't get in. You could get to it from below, but only one team max. So instead, you have to get in at six different access points and take up the firefight at the same time to engage the hijackers as much as possible, to keep them busy as much as possible."

In order to always get in quickly through the aircraft doors and to know their way around inside the plane, they needed to know different types of aircraft like the back of their hand. To this end, GSG 9 obtained blueprints of all the common models, as well as layout plans of the interior, detailing the seating, the location of on-board washrooms, first-class apartments, galleys, etc. Time and again, Wegener and his men meticulously practiced every part of the routine—sneaking up from behind the aircraft under its belly, silently putting on the ladders and opening the locks, quickly entering through doors and emergency exits, strictly keeping to the allocated lines of fire, efficiently evacuating the hostages and getting them out of the danger zone.

This was typically done at the Cologne International Airport,[5] which is located near the Saint Augustin compound. But Wegener took every opportunity that opened up elsewhere, often at short notice: "Wherever an aircraft was parked overnight at a German airport, we went there by helicopter and practiced. It was clear to everyone that this was sometimes a huge effort. Quite often, the airlines were not at all enthusiastic about our presence. Every now and then, the aircraft was damaged by our training exercises—as sometimes happens. After each training exercise, the maintenance service had to be called in to get the aircraft operational again, but the airlines were understanding about it."[6] At times, even Russian Aeroflot made one of its Soviet-type aircraft available. In most cases, however, they practiced on Lufthansa aircraft—even once, in Nuremberg, the Boeing 737 named *Landshut*, the very aircraft whose fate was later to be so closely linked to GSG 9. In return for making those aircraft available to them, the specialists from Saint Augustin occasionally instructed Lufthansa personnel on questions of how to act in hostage-taking situations.

Some GSG 9 operatives even trained as stewards or catering staff so that it would be possible to deploy them as undercover agents wearing Lufthansa uniforms or white service overalls. Others learned in two-week courses how to handle the special vehicles used on the apron, Follow-Me-Cars, mobile passenger gangways, and the trucks for refueling the airliners. Werner Heimann was one of the latter: "In an extreme situation like this, it couldn't be expected for the ground crew to memorize any details that were of concern to us. They would just be happy to get away with their lives, after all."

Eventually, the operators became familiar with the peculiarities of all common types of aircraft during refueling, from small sports planes to jumbo jets, so that they would be able to collect information inconspicuously in the process, like the number of terrorists and their emotional state of mind, their type of weapons, or the possible existence of explosive devices. "Typically, the fueling assistant gets on board to have the relevant documents signed. In such a case, we would even have had the chance for a peek inside the plane and see things that, of course, the normal staff never would have noticed."

But despite all the enthusiasm for the job and the opportunities it offered, what was missing were "real" assignments, be it in an aircraft or elsewhere. "The 9ers" practiced, developed their skills, and had productive exchanges with domestic and foreign task forces as the months and years went by. As will be explained in a moment, in international crises, they were not called upon, neither in the occupation of the German embassy in Stockholm by RAF terrorists in 1975; nor in the hijacking of an Air France passenger plane to Entebbe in Uganda, in which two members of the German terrorist group Revolutionäre Zellen* were involved.

In the latter case, Commander Wegener had even been sent to Africa by the German government, albeit solely with the order to sound out the situation, but otherwise to keep a low profile. In Entebbe, he met a task force from the Israeli military. Some of them were old friends from his training courses in Israel. They were preparing for a rescue operation, since most of the passengers were Israeli citizens or Americans of the Jewish faith. The operation succeeded, at least in part, but it claimed many victims: all the terrorists were shot dead,† as well as three hostages and, on the Israeli side, Wegener's friend Yonathan Netanyahu. Shortly afterward, Wegener traveled to Israel, where the entire operation was reenacted in the Negev Desert. "We adopted some of the Israeli tactics for storming airplanes and later applied them in Mogadishu: opening the doors, special equipment for the assault teams, taping the weapons to avoid noise, no helmets, psychological approach to freeing the plane, clear separation between terrorists and hostages, particularly after the raid is complete."[7]

---

* Revolutionäre Zellen (RZ) = Revolutionary Cells. German leftist terror organization, at times personally and operationally aligned with RAF.

† The Palestinian terror group that would hijack Lufthansa Flight LH-181 *Landshut* would call themselves the "Commando Martyr Halima," a tribute to the German militant Brigitte Kuhlmann, who was killed during the Entebbe operation in Uganda. Kuhlmann had used the nom de guerre "Halima."

Rambos at the Discotheque

This was all very instructive, but it did little to dampen the frustration spreading among the troops four years after they had reported ready for action. Day after day the small radio alarm receiver that each operative had to wear on his belt at all times, even when off-duty, remained silent. Day by day, it dawned a little more on Werner Heimann and his comrades that the mock title bestowed on them by the regular Border Guard units was well deserved: Training World Champions. "Of course it's frustrating when you train at such an advanced level and when you are constantly kept on standby. And then nothing happens. Well, actually you should be happy if nothing happens. But when you practice as hard as we do, you want to prove yourself at some point."

For the GSG 9 leadership, this meant an ever-growing issue. Unit leaders like Dieter Tutter found it difficult to keep their troops in check, lest they apply their skills elsewhere. These were the moments when the initial mistakes in the selection process backfired: "A Rambo mentality is the worst thing that can happen. Before we arrived at the right selection criteria, these people always came out on top in training. But soon they got bored, because there was not much for them to do due to the lack of real missions. They couldn't show anyone how good they were. So at some point they might do something stupid like trashing a discotheque, which of course meant for us: send him home!"

This did not happen too often, fortunately. If necessary, however, Tutter would announce dismissals on Fridays at the weekly attendance. He would make an example of the perpetrator in front of the assembled team: "We all know what happened. You have forfeited your privilege of being a GSG 9 officer. Group leader, take over his weapons and his GSG 9 equipment. And now, I don't want to see you here in the barracks again. Marching orders are to follow." After this announcement, the excommunicated culprit would leave with his head hanging, passing in front of his embarrassed comrades.

Tutter still considers these scenes of humiliation justified, not so much because the man's display of poor conduct damaged GSG 9's reputation; more important to him was what it revealed about the man's character. "An operative simply must not lose it, he must be in control of himself at all times. Anyone who is not able to do that is even more than just useless in a difficult mission. He is dangerous. He might start the action when the others are not ready"—a behavior that would endanger the lives of the whole squad (and hostages). Which is why Tutter, after making an example of the perpetrator, would pin a piece of paper on which an old saying was written to the blackboard to serve as the unit's motto for the coming week: "Nobody is useless, they can always serve as a bad example."

One reason for the lack of missions lay with the federal system. In Germany, the *Bund* funded GSG 9 and made them available as needed. But the determination of what constituted a case of need was typically made by the province where a situation unfolded. The Länder (provinces) were supposed to call in GSG 9. But the Länder exercised strict restraint. Apparently, many provincial ministers of the interior distrusted "Genscher's gangster army" (as the weekly *Der Spiegel* smirked). The spokesman of the Rhineland-Palatinate Ministry of the Interior was quoted as saying that "if something happens, we prefer to get help from Hesse or North Rhine-Westphalia. Because we believe that we are safer with them." This statement was in no way supported by any kind of empirical evidence, since GSG 9 so far had never been given the opportunity to show the quality of its work (or lack thereof). But Heinz Schwarz, the then-minister of the interior of Rhineland-Palatinate, even went one better. At the Conference of Ministers of the Interior, he allegedly snarled about GSG 9: "If these troops are deployed, there will be a furrow of scorched earth from the Alps to the North Sea"—a statement that enraged Wegener back then and still infuriates GSG 9 veterans to this day. Apparently, however, many of the minister's colleagues in the provinces strongly agreed with him.

In hindsight, the reservations against the deployment of GSG 9 probably had less to do with the suspected quality of the BGS specialists than with the general rivalry between the provinces and the federal government in all matters concerning police sovereignty. In the years since Munich, most of the provinces had started building up their own special police forces. In the autumn of 1972, the provincial governments had not only given Hans-Dietrich Genscher their approval for the establishment of his task force but also promised to establish similar police forces of their own. A few weeks later, the German press agency DPA* reported that the plan was already put in action: "In all federal states, powerful special police units will soon be at the ready, which—according to the prime minister of Baden-Württemberg, Dr. Hans Filbinger—will be able to 'solve particularly difficult and dangerous security tasks quickly and effectively.' Where, as in Baden-Württemberg, such units already existed before the Munich terrorist attack, personnel reinforcement is being considered; elsewhere, special squads are in various stages of planning." That was put benevolently but also turned out to be rather premature.

Although rudimentary structures of special police forces existed in some federal states in 1972—in Baden-Württemberg, Hamburg, Hesse, and Berlin—other provinces proved to be far less eager in their ambitions. While Bavaria, Saarland and Rhineland-Palatinate held out the prospect of setting up special units, Schleswig-Holstein wanted to leave it at its existing BOLO unit.† Lower Saxony and Bremen also showed no inclination to set up task forces, and North Rhine-Westphalia could not quite decide whether it wanted to or not.

---

* Deutsche Presse Agentur.
† BOLO = Be on the Lookout. BOLO units were thus manhunt or investigative units, and the BOLO department specialized in manhunts.

As if to demonstrate the proverbial diversity of the federal system, the designation of existing and future units was a hopeless mess. In overviews by the Federal Ministry of the Interior of the time, there is a clutter of "special groups," "mobile task forces," "intervention units," "state investigation units," "observation groups," and "precision rifle squads," representing a plethora of differing tasks, strengths and structures. In principle, all parties involved agreed on the need to harmonize this hodgepodge, since it would always be necessary to work together across provincial borders. There was even a "Concept for the Establishment and Deployment of Special Units of the Provinces and the Federation," which provided for a uniform structure: *Mobile Einsatzkommandos*,* designed for undercover reconnaissance, observation, surveillance, manhunts, and covert access; *Spezialeinsatzkommandos*† for use against violent perpetrators and to rescue human lives applying immediate force; *Präzisionsschützenkommandos*‡ for use in hostage situations; and finally GSG 9 "in cases of special importance."[8] While the division into SEKs, MEKs and PSKs remained in place in the Länder, GSG 9 was conceived from the outset as an integrated unit in which the various tasks were combined.

Beyond a semi-uniform designation, however, there was little that matched. After the official presentation of GSG 9 in September 1973, *Der Spiegel* mockingly noted: "What they all have in common is their diversity: each group follows a different concept." Many of these new commandos were not planned as standing units. Instead, police officers were to work in their usual capacities and task forces only be cobbled together for singular operations, exercises and trainings when deemed necessary.[9] In one province, the new units were to be made up of criminal investigators; in another of police patrol officers with special training; Baden-Württemberg preferred all-rounders, Bavaria individual specialists in close combat, surveillance, or explosives. North Rhine-Westphalia, on the other hand, referred to its existing sniper unit and waited.

The Rammelmayr case in Munich as well as the Olympic attack should have made it clear that such an inconsistent attitude could end disastrously. "All in all, it was a sad example of a lack of conception," summarized Rolf Grunert, chairman of the Federal Association of German Criminal Police Officers in the *Spiegel* article. In the Federal Ministry of the Interior, fears soon arose that the Länder might put the brakes on the development of the federal special intervention unit. In a statement for Minister Genscher, the responsible department head warned: "The need for coordination [with the provinces] is to be accepted. The formation and progress of GSG 9 [however] must not be paralyzed by this. Certain developments, particularly

---

* *Mobiles Einsatzkommando* (MEK) = Literally: Mobile Task Force. Surveillance units on the level of the provinces (as opposed to GSG 9 on the federal level).
† *Spezialeinsatzkommando* (SEK) = Literally: Special Operation Commando. Special Intervention Units on the provincial level, mainly used for counterterror and heavy crime operations.
‡ *Präzisionsschützenkommandos* (PSKs) = Precision Rifle Commands.

in the technical field, will be expediently driven forward exclusively by BMI for the time being."[10]

Chakos versus Helmets

The habit of kicking the can down the road that the provinces had cultivated was not about to change any time soon, including permanent underfunding. Most Bundesländer were dragging their feet when it came to setting up their own special intervention units. And when they did, not much more happened for months and sometimes years, North Rhine-Westphalia being but one example. At the end of 1974, the provincial Ministry of the Interior had to admit at a hearing in the provincial parliament that the training of its officers would not be completed until 1975, three years after the Munich disaster, and that only then would equipment, such as tactical suits and helmets, be available for everyone within the units. Helmets in particular posed an issue for the new task forces. In order to get his hands on some modern specimens, at least for training purposes, Walter Schmitz, the first commander of the SEK Cologne, on the quiet exchanged chakos for modern protective helmets (in North Rhine-Westphalia the old Prussian headgear was still in use until the 1970s, but already highly sought after as collector's items).

"With GSG 9 there was a clear political will for its inception and it was decently funded by the Federal Ministry of the Interior. The SEKs and MEKs of the Länder, in contrast, were not wanted politically, and we were not funded," Schmitz recalls of the early days. "We started out at the same time, but when GSG 9 reported readiness for deployment in autumn 1973, we were only just beginning to set up."[11] After the government of North Rhine-Westphalia decreed the formation of SEKs, Schmitz and three colleagues from the Cologne Police Department were sent to the province police school in the nearby town of Linnich for a training course. There they met four colleagues each from Düsseldorf and Dortmund, where SEK units were to be formed as well. "The course instructor greeted the twelve of us with the memorable words: 'I don't have a clue what I'm supposed to do with you here.'"

Special police forces on the province level faced similar problems as Wegener's GSG 9: no equipment, no tactics, no training basics. But at least the special intervention unit of the *Bund* could take advantage of its international contacts to get ideas and suggestions for their work. Joint courses with units from Israel or the UK pushed the German newcomers forward. The newly founded SEKs of the provinces had nothing of the kind. "We were very much stewing in our own juices." So it made sense to obtain knowledge from GSG 9. Schmitz got in touch with Saint Augustin and arranged joint field exercises with Dieter Tutter's unit. "We were able to learn a lot and we were able to pass on a lot. At the working level, we always had a great relationship." Relations with Commander Wegener, however, remained rather cool. The head of GSG 9 always seemed keen on keeping his distance from his colleagues in the provincial police forces.

But why did the buildup happen so painstakingly slowly? After the disaster in Munich, everybody on all levels of government and across party lines seemed to have agreed emphatically on the need for specially trained units, had they not? So why the foot dragging? One reason was simply the zeitgeist. "Special forces"*—the term smacked of remilitarization in the view of many Germans, particularly the younger generation born after the war. Hence, the order of the day was quite the opposite of heavily armed special intervention units: disarmament of the police. The GdP† called for proximity to the citizen. The police officer was supposed to step down from the pedestal of the Prussian-style authoritarian state and learn how to deal with the citizen at eye level. This included disarming the officer as much as possible. The British "bobby" was regarded a role model. He knew how to command respect without a service pistol. Tonis Hunold, head of police in the city of Duisburg, in a press article, exhorted the German officer to "always be polite without appearing submissive, intervene firmly without appearing too soft, enlighten the ignorant without humiliating them, display forbearance without being offended."[12] A call for truly superhuman abilities.

"Germany's police—the nation's whipping boys" read the ambiguous headline of the weekly *Der Spiegel* in 1973. In an 11-page cover story, the magazine described overloaded officers who, in case of doubt, were a wee quick on the draw with a truncheon and a pistol, but who, on the other hand, were also quick to be scapegoated for all kinds of social problems. In the wake of the 1968 protests, social debate called into question outdated patterns of thought, training ideals and forms of deployment. From the end of the 1960s to the mid-1970s, provincial parliaments and interior ministries imposed far-reaching reforms on their police in order to create forces that were closer to the people. This happened partly due to social pressure from outside, but also partly from within. A new generation of police officers could no longer be bothered with the authoritarian attitude of their older colleagues.

So politically, setting up special intervention and surveillance units sent the wrong signal. As the zeitgeist demanded the ideal of "the police officer as a social engineer," the wild guys of the *Spezialeinsatzkommandos* with their robust demeanor must have come across like a provocation. Similar to the sneering and jeering toward GSG 9 within the Federal Border Guard, SEK people like Walter Schmitz were eyed with suspicion by their "ordinary" police colleagues. "There were always attempts to get rid of us, even from within the police. That was not easy." Thus, with a few exceptions,

---

* In the German language, there is no distinction between military and police in this respect. The term *Spezialeinheit* (Special Force) can mean both.

† GdP (Gewerkschaft der Polizei) = Union of the Police. Largest union for police forces in Germany.

the ministers of the interior of the Länder did not exactly stand up with too much enthusiasm in support of their own special units.

However, once the SEKs and MEKs of the provincial police forces had eventually been set up and were ready for action, the ministers preferred to use their own rather than ask the federal government for GSG 9 support. When even the latecomer North Rhine-Westphalia finally presented its SEKs to the public, their Ministry of the Interior proudly trumpeted in its house paper *Die Streife* (*The Patrol*): "Although there is certainly no intention of 'competing' with GSG 9 of the Federal Border Guard, what the officers of our Special Intervention Unit can do is impressive and certainly does not have to fear comparison with GSG 9." The paper proudly reported that their SEKs were used 350 times in 1977. Calling in GSG 9 for support was not considered necessary in any of the cases. This might have had to do with the high threshold required to send a request for the specialists from Saint Augustin, which was to be done only "in particularly serious cases," and probably also with the resulting costs that the requesting province had to bear. But no one at GSG 9 believed that these were the main reasons. "Cooperation with the special task forces of the Länder was not easy. On the one hand, there was competition; on the other hand, we were dependent on each other," sighed Commander Wegener later.[13]

This kind of blockade by the provinces shook the self-confidence of his unit, who so far had not had a chance for a serious mission, let alone a baptism of fire. And this would not change until 1977. "We were cut by the provincial police forces," Dieter Tutter recalls. "Even when the manhunt for Schleyer began in 1977, we were always under the impression that we were the stopgap for the Länder." During the hot weeks of that legendary Deutscher Herbst (German Autumn), the authorities received thousands of tips about the whereabouts of the abducted economic leader. For GSG 9, though, there were only crumbs: "While others were put on hot tracks, we were stalled. Each time, we were only allowed to do the manpower-intensive but unpromising searches." Tutter's boss Wegener had the same impression.

Since the beginning of 1977, RAF terrorists had been carrying out ever more brutal attacks on state representatives and business leaders. But not a single province requested the support of GSG 9. Even after the deadly attacks on Dresdner Bank boss Jürgen Ponto and federal prosecutor General Siegfried Buback, Wegener's men would sit in Saint Augustin and impatiently paw their hooves. So in the summer of 1977, the commander considered stepping down at the end of the year if nothing changed. As it turned out, he didn't have to wait much longer.

CHAPTER 7

A Year Full of Autumn

At the end of August 1977, two plainclothes policemen were waiting on the apron of the Freiburg airfield for the arrival of the small Daimler business jet. As soon as the aircraft had taxied to its parking position and the door opened, they addressed the first person getting off: "We were sent to pick up some Mr. Schleyer. Do you know him?" Yes, sure he knew him, nodded young Jörg Schleyer, and pointed to his father, the man stepping down the gangway right behind him. The Schleyers had traveled to the Black Forest in southwest Germany to attend the wedding of their son Arnd. It was the first time that the family of the president of the mighty Employers' Association had come in direct contact with bodyguards from the security services.

"Honestly? We didn't give it much thought," recalls Jörg Schleyer.[1] "We were certainly shaken by what happened in Karlsruhe or in Oberursel. But we never believed that all of it could get so close to ourselves." A few days prior, banker Jürgen Ponto had been murdered by the Red Army Faction (RAF) terrorist group in his home near Frankfurt. Earlier, in April, the RAF had shot and killed Attorney General Siegfried Buback and his two drivers in Karlsruhe on the street in broad daylight. It was the beginning of what the RAF in its pamphlets called "Offensive 77." The Deutscher Herbst (German Autumn), as it was later dubbed, had already begun in the spring of 1977.

Not long after the encounter at Freiburg airport, the Schleyers received a call at Lake Constance, where they were spending their summer vacation after their son's wedding. Horst Herold himself, president of the Federal Criminal Police Office, the BKA, was on the phone: "Mr. Schleyer, it might well be you who is next in line. We have found clues. We are not entirely certain, but we will increase security measures for you." Herold was not yet able to say exactly what these measures were supposed to look like but affirmed that they were currently working on them. However, these could only be implemented as soon as they were back at their Stuttgart home.

At first, this did not depress the family much. Son Jörg and his older brothers found their situation rather exciting: "Of course! Suddenly there are property guards and personal security details and the police are patrolling in front of our house. But we never really thought about the possibility of my father becoming a kidnapping victim himself. This seemed far away despite everything that was happening."

This lack of concern seems astonishing, since Hanns Martin Schleyer had long been considered a possible target of the RAF, particularly since they could count on the fact that few on the political left would shed a tear for him. As president of the Employers' Association, the BDA,* Schleyer enjoyed a reputation as a tough cookie, a fierce enforcer of business interests in collective bargaining disputes, including lockouts. As chairman of the Federation of German Industries (BDI),† he was widely perceived as an "economic emperor" with a typical Nazi past. He had been a member of a militant students' fraternity with a "*Schmiss*" (dueling scar) on his cheek. He was a prolific author of anti-Semitic texts, a member of the SS since 1933, and of Hitler's NSDAP‡ since 1937. In World War II he served as an *SS-Hauptsturmführer*. After being released as a prisoner of war, he was classified merely as a "camp follower" in the denazification process, not a leader. This was due to falsifications of his curriculum vitae, and it basically gave him a free pass for his future career. In the post-war period he easily rose to become Germany's most powerful economic leader until he finally reached the zenith of his power in 1977 when he became "double president" of the two most influential business associations: the BDA and BDI.

A shining career in the Third Reich followed by a shining career in the Federal Republic. From a left-wing perspective he epitomized the prototypical representative of big business's contempt for humanity, a prime example of the strong ties that still existed between the Nazi economy and the West German state, just as Buback and Ponto were prime examples of those ties in the judiciary and the world of finance. From the RAF's point of view, this made Schleyer an ideal target. And Schleyer was well aware of this. But he didn't let on to his family, says his son Jörg. "I think he didn't want to burden my mother with the fact that something could happen to him."

The warning signs rang loud and clear, though. At the beginning of August 1977, the headline of Germany's largest tabloid, *Bild*, screamed: "Schleyer was supposed to be next." Under a pretext, one RAF member had obtained information about Schleyer from the Kiel World Economic Institute. This did not go unnoticed by the authorities. But they reacted indecisively. In retrospect, the youngest Schleyer son's nonchalance seems bizarre in hindsight, even to himself, and that of the authorities surrealistic. There was not much change in this attitude, even after Minister of the Interior Maihofer had personally informed his father that security level 1 now applied to him. "I had the impression that they didn't really expect anything to happen to

---

* BDA (Bundesvereinigung der Deutschen Arbeitgeberverbände) = Confederation of German Employers' Associations. Umbrella organization of all major employers in West Germany.
† BDI (Bundesverband der deutschen Industrie) = The Federation of German Industries. Top-tier association of the West German industrial enterprises, a powerful lobby group representing tens of thousands of companies with their several million employees.
‡ NSDAP (Nationalsozialistische Deutsche Arbeiterpartei) = National Socialist German Workers Party, commonly known as the Nazi Party.

him what had happened to Ponto. It only turned out much later that Ponto was actually supposed to be kidnapped and was killed only in the process."

It is hard to comprehend the sluggish attitude of everyone involved. The security situation had come to a head in the preceding months, after escalating since the mid-1960s. It started out with violent student protests against the state visit of the Shah of Iran and the Vietnam War in 1967, reached its first climax with a number of arson attacks, and eventually the inception of terrorist groups like the RAF, Bewegung 2. Juni,* and Revolutionäre Zellen† and their attacks in the early 1970s. Escalation reached its preliminary peak with the fatal occupation of the West German embassy in Stockholm in 1975 by an RAF command, and in the same year the kidnapping of the conservative politician Peter Lorenz, who at the time was on the campaign trail to become mayor of Berlin.

The West German state, in turn, had all too willingly taken up the gauntlet of the so far rather manageable group of violent "anarchists," as they were called. Authorities reacted with uncalled-for severity to every provocation, and escalated the situation with each measure it took. The German security situation spiraled out of control. Necessary modernization measures and the conversion of outdated hierarchies into modern instruments of homeland security met with hectic, sometimes hysterical overreactions on the legislative and executive sides.

This ladder of escalation originated in the broad resistance against the so-called *Notstandsgesetze* (emergency laws). Historian Frank Biess describes the protests against these laws as the beginning of the "fear cycle of terror in the 1970s." Justified concerns about a possible undermining of democratic rights and an expansion of the security organs that many found frightening were combined with deep-seated collective fears of an authoritarian Big Brother state. It stood in stark contrast to the early days of the Federal Republic when the state had been predominately perceived as being deficient and weak. Now it appeared authoritarian and potentially encroaching. In historical retrospect, these fears seem highly exaggerated, almost pathological, because they overemphasized the connecting lines between the Third Reich and the Federal Republic—lines that were real and impossible to be overlooked—while ignoring the strong fault lines after 1945.

In the decade from the mid-1960s to the mid-1970s, opposing existential fears fueled each other: the fear of an authoritarian, fascist police state on one side and the fear of a night-watchman state unable to protect its citizens from a bunch of anarchists gone wild on the other. Fear generated violence and violence generated fear, which generated counterviolence, which generated new fear, which generated new violence and so on—the mechanism of a feedback loop. Outrage over the Vietnam War and the state's courting of criminal regimes like that of the Persian

---

* Bewegung 2. Juni = June 2 Movement.
† Revolutionäre Zellen = Revolutionary Cells.

Shah merged with protests against the emergency laws and thus formed the nucleus for the fear–violence spiral of the 1970s. So, the terrorist threat did not develop in a vacuum.

The Spiral of Fear, Hate, and Violence

First ideas for the *Notstandsgesetze* had already been drafted in the mid-1950s when the Western Allies gradually loosened their grip on the Federal Republic. As more and more sovereignty was transferred and the presence of Allied Forces was reduced by and by, it seemed necessary to make legal provision for crisis situations, for war, insurrection, natural disasters. The first drafts provided for massive restrictions on democratic freedoms in the event of an internal or external emergency, especially restrictions on freedom of the press and freedom of speech, restrictions on the rights of parliament in favor of the executive, and restrictions on the right to go on strike. This required an amendment to the Grundgesetz, the West German Constitution, and thus a majority of two-thirds of the seats in the Bundestag. It was not until the time of the Grand Coalition between Conservatives and Social Democrats in 1966 that this majority came within reach.

By then, the bills had already been considerably toned down, but major points of controversy remained, particularly allowing for deploying the military within Germany and the lack of any time limit for emergency measures. These evoked unpleasant memories of the Enabling Act, which in 1933 had sounded the bell for Nazi-dictatorship. For many on the political left inside and outside of parliament, but even for many centrists, this criticism rang especially true, since the biographies of some of the protagonists of the legislation showed clear lines to the Nazi era; Minister of the Interior Gerhard Schröder* had been a member of Hitler's NSDAP and the SA.† And Chancellor Kiesinger had held an important position in the Reich's Foreign Ministry. Right or wrong, the planned laws fostered the impression that they were a step on the way to transforming the Federal Republic into an authoritarian state that did not care much for democratic customs and procedures. Critics saw their fears confirmed when corresponding decrees surfaced which restricted constitutional rights in the event of a state of emergency, decrees which had been sent from the Federal Ministry of the Interior to authorities of the provinces and municipalities even before the law was passed. The stipulations were already waiting in the drawers.

Soon, the term "police state in waiting" became commonplace in the political debate. Memories of the collapse of the Weimar Republic and the rise of National Socialism were omnipresent, reinforced by the continuities in personnel that could

---

* Not related to the later Chancellor Gerhard Schröder.

† SA (*Sturmabteilung*) = Storming Department. Dreaded paramilitary organization of the NSDAP.

hardly be overlooked. The "Muff of a Thousand Years"* that the 1968 student movement detected under official Talars was not only festering under the gowns of deans and professors. The so-called Außerparlamentarische Opposition† also smelled it beneath the pinstripes of German business leaders (such as Schleyer and Ponto), as well as under the office robes of German judges (such as Buback), and many uniforms of top brass military and police.

And it was true, after all. Like Schleyer, countless functionaries of the Nazi state had escaped the denazification process unshorn, they had sleekly slipped into all levels of agencies, ministries, the military, politics, the judiciary and business, and were allowed to forge careers right up to the top. Particularly affected by Nazi infestation: The Federal Criminal Police Office (BKA) and the Federal Prosecutor's Office, of all things, the two very institutions that were supposed to lead the fight against enemies of the free democratic constitution. Attorney General Buback had been a member of the NSDAP, as had all his predecessors. And before the Social Democrat Horst Herold was made president of the BKA, a former *SS-Untersturmführer* held office until 1971, 26 years after the collapse of the Third Reich.

He was not the only one in the agency. For decades after World War II, the BKA was run at all levels by hordes of former SS men. But what many felt particularly threatening and intimidating was the technical advancement. The new possibilities of electronic data processing, or EDP for short, provided this obscure agency with tools that seemed to justify all the fears of an Orwellian surveillance state. Yet the main driver of this development—Horst Herold—did not see himself in this sense at all.

Herold was far from a strict law-and-order advocate. He considered himself a "left-wing social democrat" and had been active in the Socialist German Student Association (SDS), a driving force behind the 1968 student movement, with which Herold openly sympathized. As president of the Nuremberg city police, he told his officers that demonstrations were not a crime but perfectly legal (which seemed news to many). As early as the mid-1960s, Herold had ensured that the Nuremberg city police used electronic data processing to fight crime—a first in Germany, coming at a time when room-filling calculating machines were reverently called "electronic brains" and most police officers still struggled even with mastering mechanical typewriters. Herold's motto, on the other hand, was: "Fighting crime is information processing—register, store, process."[2]

Herold's ambition did not go unnoticed. "The minister of the interior is making a trip to Middle Franconia soon. May he stop by your place?" It was Genscher's security advisor at the time, BGS liaison officer Ulrich Wegener, who inquired by

---

* Protest chant: "*Unter den Talaren / der Muff von Tausend Jahren*" = Under the talars / the muff of a thousand years, referring to the Nazi promise to build a 1,000-year Reich.
† Außerparlamentarische Opposition (APO) = Opposition Outside of Parliament.

telephone on behalf of his employer. Herold agreed enthusiastically and demonstrated the file management programs of his punched tape computers to the high-ranking visitor from Bonn. When he saw how impressed Genscher was with his inventions, Herold went one better. From his office window at police headquarters, he directed two police squads on the forecourt by silent radio command. The police director had ordered the procurement of helmets with integrated headphones for his officers, and now he directed them by microphone: March! Left around! Right turn! Stop! This was never seen before in Germany and it opened up the possibility of coordinating entire police squadrons in action, for example at demonstrations.

Herold's demonstration was effective. In 1971, Genscher promoted him to head the Federal Criminal Police Office and gave him enough money to realize his vision: turning the BKA into some kind of German FBI. Herold transformed a stuffy coordination agency into a modern instrument for fighting crime. Within 10 years, the budget rose from DM 55 million to 290 million, and the number of employees tripled to more than 3,500. By the end of the 1970s, nearly five million names were stored electronically, along with extensive files containing photos, fingerprints and handwriting samples. In addition, there was a reporting system between the federal authority and the state police forces to ensure rapid search success. Half mockingly, half respectfully, Herold was called "Commissioner Computer" in the agency. Critics, on the other hand, considered him a "megalomaniac technocrat," nicknamed the "Dr. Frankenstein of forensic technology."[3] All this triggered fears.

But BKA was far from being the all-knowing data juggernaut it was portrayed. The state security apparatus was not over-inflated in the 1970s; rather, up to this point, police and intelligence services were hopelessly under-equipped, both technically and in terms of personnel. "A reinforcement of the security organs was in the air anyway," says civil rights activist Gerhart Baum, who was parliamentary state secretary in the Ministry of the Interior at the time and later became the federal minister of the interior himself. As such, he would roll back some of the most controversial measures in the fight against terrorism at the end of the 1970s and declare a period of reflection concerning the way the state dealt with the terrorist threat.

Hence, Baum is certainly not guilty of being a security policy stirrer, in fact the opposite. Concerning the state of the security agencies at the time, however, he follows the same line as his predecessor and party colleague Genscher: "The increase in personnel in the security agencies, the reinforcement of financial resources—all of it was necessary. I say this being somebody who always wonders: Is this particular measure really necessary? But the Federal Criminal Police Office was really in a sorry state, and Genscher practically rebuilt it. The same applies to the entire federal security apparatus. GSG 9 was also part of this rebuild, and an indispensable part at that. Police must be equipped for crisis situations; that was already my opinion at the time."[4]

Back then, five years after its inception, GSG 9 still operated largely under the radar of public attention. Yes, there was broad media coverage when it was introduced in 1973. But since then, it had sunken back into obscurity. If noticed at all by critics, the task force was perceived as a mosaic piece in the overall picture of a surveillance state repression apparatus that was spreading like a virus. This included the Verfassungsschutz,* which Genscher also expanded to the best of his ability, and the Bundesgrenzschutz (BGS), which had been massively upgraded in terms of personnel and funding. But the most visible sign of the state's rearmament remained the Federal Criminal Police Office, the BKA, with its dragnet method, which later became known as the "grid search." Countless uninvolved people saw themselves subjected to general suspicion and sometimes rude treatment in the course of such comprehensive and apparently unprovoked checks.

In circles that considered themselves alternative or left-wing, there was a growing impression that it was not the terror of the RAF, Bewegung 2. Juni, or Revolutionäre Zellen that was the real danger, but an encroaching state on its way to fascism aiming at controlling politically disagreeable elements and eliminating them. Particularly, the RAF was able to insert narratives in the public debate that perfectly fit this perception, namely the narrative of the state's "isolation torture" and "extermination confinement" of RAF prisoners. Incarcerated RAF members were portrayed as being entirely isolated from the outside world and as being denied basic human rights. The RAF supporter's battle cry up until the 1990s was "Pooling now!," demanding that the convicted terrorists be incarcerated in the same penitentiary block and get the opportunity to spend time together on a daily basis. Denying them the opportunity was portrayed as inhumane and against international law. This narrative was the propaganda pillar on which a lot of the support for the terrorists rested.

"They wanted to make the state look so ugly that a reason became obvious to really have to fight it," says interior politician Baum. "And unfortunately, this has been achieved in part. For example, by criticizing the conditions of detention to which Ms. Mohnhaupt[†] was subjected in Cologne. Detention, closed off from everyone else in an isolated area of the prison, has of course had considerable psychological consequences. 'Isolation torture' has then been the polemical criticism. And that's what the supporters and terrorists have used to mobilize. And the State overreacted. Instead of de-escalating, it added fuel to the fire."

---

* Verfassungsschutz = Secret service for the interior.
† Brigitte Monhaupt, leading member of the "second RAF generation" allegedly involved heavily in the planning of the events in 1977. In the historic literature, RAF is divided into three generations: the founding generation including Andreas Baader, Ulrike Meinhof, Gudrun Ensslin, and Holger Meins amongst others from 1970–1977, the second generation including Brigitte Monhaupt, Christian Klar, and Karl-Heinz Dellwo from 1975–1981, and the third generation including Wolfgang Grams, Birgit Hogefeld, and Daniela Klette from 1982–1998 when they declared their self-dissolution.

The death of RAF man Holger Meins in Stammheim Prison during his hunger strike in 1974 had already outraged large sections of the left. The martyr-like image of the emaciated, Rasputin-like bearded face became a quasi-religious icon, a symbol of a system that despised humanity. The photograph promoted radicalization like hardly any other event of that time and paved the way underground for the second RAF generation.

Karl-Heinz Dellwo is but one example. He was (and is) convinced that the hunger-striking and force-fed RAF prisoner became a victim of state murder through deliberate neglect. "The immediate experience was that power will roll over us. That these people in power will walk over every corpse in our country to make their order sacrosanct."[5] The outrage over the so-called isolation torture had an effect far beyond the circle of the RAF and its direct supporters. It resulted in expressions of solidarity from literary figures and intellectuals all the way to Jean-Paul Sartre, who philosophically ennobled the RAF prisoners with his visit to Stammheim in 1974 to talk to figurehead Andreas Baader (even though on the return trip from the prison he allegedly blurted out: "What an asshole, this Baader!"[6]). Even far into the centrist parts of the Social Democratic spectrum, there was talk of the "imprisoned comrades." One would distance oneself from the terrorist methods, of course, but make a protest against the conditions of imprisonment by donating a Deutschmark or two to organizations such as the Rote Hilfe (or Red Aid) who supported the RAF prisoners with legal aid and such.

On the opposite side, the hotheads of the law-and-order faction stirred up the mood and declared everyone a terror supporter whom they suspected of being a so-called sympathizer. The term "sympathizer" was increasingly extended to the entire left-wing scene, blurring the distinction between "terrorist," "supporter," and "sympathizer." Thus, conservative politicians declared that the mere talk of "Baader Meinhof Group" (instead of "Baader Meinhof Gang") was an indication of a sympathizer. It was useless referring to the fact that the term "sympathizer" does not exist in the law—and rightly so. In a state guided by the rule of law, mere sympathy for anyone or anything can never constitute a criminal offense. But this did not hold anybody back in their wild claims about sympathizers. Soon an ominous feeling of "They're everywhere!" put society on edge. And it put the government under pressure. Among the indelible childhood memories of the generation that grew up in 1970s West Germany are the bold, red-framed "wanted posters" with the unflattering black-and-white photos of the RAF's "anarchists" that were stuck in every post office and on every other telephone booth.

The rhetorical dissolution of boundaries culminated in 1977 in the call for the reintroduction of the death penalty. During the hot phase of the German Autumn, two-thirds of the population agreed with this stance, according to a nationwide survey. Thus, political fears swung up between their mobilization "from above" and the indignation "from below." Both sides jointly blamed an allegedly misguided liberal policy of the ruling social-liberal coalition and its representatives such as Gerhart Baum: "There were heated arguments, blaming the government. 'This is your crop. You nurtured them!' There was an almost grotesque exaggeration of the danger. For in the end, it was a manageable circle of perpetrators. The population was not affected at all, but only high representatives from society. There was talk of a state of emergency, of the democratic substance of the republic being in danger. All stupid stuff! But we were *all* driven by it! There was an agitated atmosphere: Bonn was full of armored personnel carriers. Roadblocks were set up. You had the feeling you were in a war zone." The rhetorical armament was followed by legislative armament. The social-liberal coalition passed law after law to deal with the terrorist threat, thereby continuing to turn the spiral of fear and violence.

A Non-Declared Emergency

The first such law, in 1974, restricted a number of rights of legal defense. This was followed in 1976 by the first so-called anti-terrorism bundle of legislation. It criminalized incitement to commit criminal acts and anti-constitutional advocacy of criminal acts. At its core, however, were the provisions on the formation of a terrorist organization, which became known as the "Lex RAF" and were understood by critics as a free pass for the seamless surveillance of disagreeable groups of people, and as an erosion of the rights of suspects.

By far the harshest and most controversial anti-terrorism law that the government would rush through parliament was the so-called "no-contact law" (*Kontaktsperregesetz*) during the German Autumn in 1977. This law was also tailored to fit the RAF. It prohibited any contact between the prisoners and between them and their lawyers. The reason for this drastic measure: some of the lawyers were suspected of willingly acting as messengers between the first RAF generation in prison and the second RAF generation on the outside. As it turned out later, the suspicion was well-founded. So-called Kassibers, files with RAF instructions and orders, travelled unchecked to and from the prison. Nevertheless, the contact ban represented a massive encroachment on the constitutionally guaranteed rights of prisoners and their legal advisors. For their supporters, the law was final proof of isolation torture. Gerhart Baum was one of those who approved the no-contact law as a member of the Bundestag at the time, despite it giving him stomach pains. "In my view, this clearly went beyond the limits of what was reasonable under the rule of law. But there was a mood of hysteria at the time."

This mood would also allow the federal government to set up committees during the hot autumn weeks of 1977 that were supported by politicians, the press and the population, but had no legal legitimacy whatsoever, namely the Large and Small Crisis Staffs. In his hour of need, Chancellor Helmut Schmidt assembled these committees of ministers, federal prosecutors, heads of public authorities, prime ministers, opposition leaders, and sometimes business representatives— but they were not provided for anywhere in the constitution. On the other hand, the constitutional bodies that actually did exist were more or less entirely bypassed: the Bundesrat and the Bundestag, the two chambers of parliament with their advisory and control functions. The separation of powers was thus undermined, and it was clear to the protagonists that they were moving outside the boundaries of the constitution. Eventually, when the German Autumn storm was over, Schmidt would say in a press interview: "I can only thank the German jurists retrospectively for not having examined all this constitutionally. It's impossible to want to regulate everything."

Faced with the abduction of an economic leader and the hijacking of an aircraft full of tourists, Chancellor Schmidt and the German government would find themselves in a situation worthy of a Greek tragedy. They would have to decide between alternative courses of action, each of which would have extremely painful consequences:

- Either maintaining the ability to act in violation of the constitution (crisis staff) or loyalty to the constitution and thus political paralysis (slowness of the political decision-making process and unpredictability of the outcome);
- Either sacrificing German citizens in the name of raison d'état (Schleyer/Flight LH-181 hostages) or encouraging terrorists to commit new acts of violence.

Whatever their decision, it could only be wrong. Not exactly an enviable situation. Nevertheless, there was no significant resistance to this undeclared state of emergency. The press did not oppose the muzzle imposed on them. And even the political left, otherwise eager to demonstrate against all kinds of things, did not even think of protesting loudly in the streets. This indicates that there was an overarching social consensus supporting the government's action even beyond the constitution. Where did this consensus come from?

The main factor seems to be that the general atmosphere among the population had turned by this time. Gone were the days when middle-class kids at student parties, with a pleasant shudder, would ask each other the crucial question of the sympathizer scene: What do you think of the RAF? Would you give Ulrike Meinhof shelter if she were to show up at your door tonight? In 1971, the Allensbach polling institute conducted a representative survey under the heading "Baader-Meinhof: Criminals or Heroes?" The question: "Suppose someone from this group were to ask you for protection for one night: Would you take them in for one night or would you not do that?" The result: 10 percent of 16- to 29-year-olds and 5 percent of the total population would give shelter to RAF members. Even if sympathies for the RAF were never as strong among the population as this survey suggests at first glance, the RAF exerted a powerful appeal to young people in its early years, fueled by revolutionary romanticism. This appeal reached far into centrist circles.

This favorable view started to change in 1975 after the RAF's lethal occupation of the German embassy in Stockholm and the kidnapping of the conservative politician Peter Lorenz by Bewegung 2. Juni. These two attacks marked a turning point for the German government in dealing with terrorist blackmail attempts, but particularly for Chancellor Schmidt. At the time, the chancellor decided to give in to the demands and thus save Peter Lorenz's life. Five jailed RAF and 2. Juni terrorists were released and allowed to leave the country. Schmidt, who had hesitantly agreed, soon regretted the decision: "The next morning I realized that it was a grave mistake. I decided never to get involved in such a deal again. For the terrorists would count on such a success of future hostage-takings and would therefore continue their criminal tactics of taking hostages, while the freed men would feel encouraged to commit new crimes."[7] Schmidt was spot on as was to be proved later. Decades later, in fact, when the background was finally clarified: All but one of the prisoners who had been released and flown to Yemen soon returned to Germany in secret and immediately resumed their terrorist activities, taking part in hostage-takings, abductions, and lethal shootouts with the police.

It is difficult to determine in retrospect the extent to which such activities by ransomed terrorists contributed to the change of heart among the population. But the fact remains that initial sympathy for the RAF dwindled more and more. As late as 1975, three-quarters of the respondents in a public survey run by the renowned Meinungsforschungsinstitut Allensbach polling institute[*] were in favor of meeting the terrorists' demands and releasing RAF prisoners in order to save the life of the kidnapped Peter Lorenz. In 1977, however, the mood had changed completely. During the German Autumn, 71 percent were against any concession to the kidnappers, taking the same hard line as Chancellor Schmidt's crisis team. The coolly planned and coldly executed assassination attempt on Federal Attorney General Buback in broad daylight and the failed kidnapping attempt that ended with the murder of Dresdner Bank CEO Ponto were met with unanimous opposition and rejection among the population.

From the time the founding generation was locked behind bars, the RAF had increasingly degenerated into a "liberate-the-guerrilla guerrilla," as one RAF sympathizer mocked tongue-in-cheek. Any political goals they might have had became blurred behind the demands for the release of comrades from prison. The Red Army Faction was discredited even in large parts of the leftist scene. With the targeted murder of people, its protagonists had crossed a line that isolated them in the leftist milieu, even if empathy with their prominent victims was limited. But the second RAF generation did not think of stopping now.

In any case, the RAF had achieved one thing for sure: It had become a topic of conversation, and not only among adults. In late summer of 1977, when kids

---

[*] The Meinungsforschungsinstitut Allensbach was one of the two major polling institutes in West Germany at the time.

played in the city streets and village groves, the name of the game was no longer cops and robbers, but RAF and police, with the kids bickering over who got to be Baader, who Meinhof, and who had to pose as Buback and Ponto. Soon, another name would be added to this macabre list.

Jörg and Waltrude Schleyer had just returned from a stroll through the city on a late summer's afternoon in September 1977. The 23-year-old communications student had come for a visit during the semester break. Mother and son had spent a leisurely afternoon in a café in Stuttgart's main shopping mile, the Kronprinzenstraße.

The two of them were alone at home when the phone rang at around 6:00 p.m. "The first ones were the news agency DPA. Didn't even mention a name: 'Have you heard that there's been a kidnapping in Cologne?'—Nah, we haven't. That was all. And then two minutes later it was the *BILD* newspaper. They personified it: 'Your father …' We were speechless, really speechless. Because nothing had been confirmed yet. Only when an hour later the officials came from the Provincial Criminal Police Department in Stuttgart, was there certainty. And then there was Schmidt's speech."

The chancellor appeared in front of the cameras at 9:30 p.m. The speech was broadcast live on both nationwide TV channels. Schmidt appeared moved, but calm and determined: "The news of the assassination attempt on Hanns Martin Schleyer and [the killing of] the officials and employees accompanying him has affected me deeply.… As of tonight, four dead citizens of our state have been added to the list of victims of blind terrorists who—we have always been clear about this—have not yet reached the end of their criminal energy."

It is Monday, September 5, 1977—five years to the day after the attack at the Olympic Games in Munich. The confrontation between the state and left-wing terrorism is heading for its climax. The hijackers demand the ultimate release of 10 prisoners from several detention centers throughout Germany, otherwise Hanns Martin Schleyer would die: "The prisoners are to be brought together at Frankfurt airport by 8 a.m. on Wednesday." In order to gain time, the West German government pretends to agree to the demands and sends negotiators to the prisons to discuss possible destination countries with the incarcerated RAF members.

One week after the kidnapping, bulletproof windows will be installed in the Schleyer family's house. The German Autumn has begun.

CHAPTER 8

The Schleyer Manhunt

It had been a beautiful summer. Warm, long, and quiet. Dieter Fox had spent the school vacation of 1977 camping with his wife and two sons on the Baltic Sea island of Fehmarn, close to Denmark. News about the murderous attacks of Buback and Ponto had reached GSG 9, of course, but only as a kind of a ministerial FYI. Otherwise, nothing much had happened, no requests for them to take part in the hunt for the RAF suspects while the search apparatus of police and intelligence services were running at full speed. Wegener kept his three operational units on standby anyway. To his men, the commander seemed restless. He had them exercise even more intensively than usual. In addition to shooting and the obstacle course, they trained for house-to-house combat and searching for hostages. Just in case it dawned on somebody that they might be of some use after all.

On September 5, Dieter Fox had just returned from a skeet shooting competition in neighboring Troisdorf to hand in his equipment. GSG 9 operated its own skeet club and was a member of the Rheinischer Schützenbund (Rhenish Shooters' Association). The competitions were part of marksmanship education and training. Fox was about to head home to his family when news of an attack in Cologne came in. "Right away, this meant that none of us were going to go home that night. Wegener immediately put a stop to everything. Everyone who was outside was ordered back to the premises. We were just allowed to call home and say that we had been confined to barracks. Families had to put up with this."

It was already late in the evening, but the situation was still entirely unclear. Wegener had been informed by the government's ad hoc crisis team about the attack on Schleyer and his escort. He decided to gain an impression for himself. It was only a 30-minute ride from GSG 9 headquarters to the quiet residential borough of Braunsfeld in Cologne. The crime scene lay quiet, lit by glaring police spotlights, like a still shot from a Mafia flick: a blue pram, empty. Three Mercedes wedged into each other; the middle one riddled with bullets. Countless bullet casings scattered around and inside the trashed middle car. In front of it, four corpses scantily covered with white cloths—the driver and the bodyguards of Hanns Martin Schleyer. There was no trace, though, of the president of the Employers' Association.

Wegener had just arrived at the scene when he received a call from Minister of the Interior Maihofer, who summoned him to the chancellor's office in Bonn to discuss the situation. Maihofer had convened there with Chancellor Schmidt, Foreign Minister Genscher, Justice Minister Hans-Jochen Vogel, Chancellery Minister Hans-Jürgen Wischnewski, and government spokesman Klaus Bölling. The head of the BKA, Horst Herold, was on his way from Wiesbaden to Bonn. There, Wegener was given the task of supporting the provincial police and the BKA crisis team that had just been set up in Cologne to search for the kidnapped Hanns Martin Schleyer.

Back in Saint Augustin, Wegener gathered his men and shared what little they knew a few hours after the event: On the way back from work, only a few meters away from his official residence, Schleyer's company car had been stopped, seemingly by a mother pushing her pram across the street. As soon as the car came to a halt, the woman pulled a submachine gun from the carriage and opened fire. But apparently there was more than one attacker involved, since shots had been fired at Schleyer's Mercedes from several directions. His driver and two bodyguards were killed on the spot. It remained unclear if Schleyer was hurt in the hail of bullets, but it was clear he had been abducted. Where to and by whom was unknown. However, everything pointed to an attack by the Red Army Faction. The Federal Criminal Agency, BKA, had drawn clues from planning papers they had seized some time before. "Check out H. M.," it said, the initials H and M apparently standing for Hanns Martin, Schleyer's given names. "Discuss with Marie where to stash the guy,"[1] it went on.

A letter claiming responsibility would not emerge until the next day. In typical RAF lowercase writing, it said:

> you will ensure that all public search measures are stopped or we will shoot schleyer immediately without negotiating his release.
> raf.[2]

However, the Bonn crisis team under Chancellor Schmidt agreed on that very first evening that they would not give in to any demands. Instead, they ordered a large-scale manhunt. Tens of thousands of police and criminal investigators, agents of the domestic intelligence service, and even administrative employees were to be deployed in the coming days and weeks in search of the president of the Employers' Association.

And this time, finally, it was clear that GSG 9 would also be deployed, even though for the time being it remained obscure when and where and how. But as Wegener announced the good news back at HQ, a gloomy silence spread through the room. "We took a deep breath," says Dieter Fox. "Especially because the day had been so relaxed until then, with the clay pigeon shooting competition, which was great, cheerful, relaxed. And then you return just to find out that it's now suddenly getting serious. On the one hand you have to say: sure, that's what we're here for, that's why GSG 9 was founded in the first place. Nevertheless, we are all only human. When the time comes and the commander says, 'From now on, GSG 9 will be involved in manhunts for the RAF terrorists,' then you know that the fun part is over. No more shooting range, no more tactics practice, no more skeet shooting. From this moment on, if we move into an apartment, we have to be alert to someone pointing a gun at us. We have practiced long enough for this moment, but the toughest training is something entirely different from the first real mission."

When Wegener had finished, the unit leaders gathered the SET leaders and sent them with their respective teams for a briefing to their dormitories, where their mission bags were already waiting. They had packed them while Wegener was on his reconnaissance to Cologne and Bonn. Everybody had expected something like this. Dieter Fox also withdrew with his people. "Some of them had a certain pallor on their faces. We team leaders were also somewhat uneasy. It was the first time something like this had happened, after all. But then we were team leaders; we were responsible for four other people so we didn't let it show."

There was not much time to ponder anyway. The first operation took place the same night: the search of an old villa in Cologne. Right after the news of Schleyer's kidnapping broke, BKA Chief Herold had ordered a dragnet. Cologne had been cordoned off over a wide area, and the kidnappers were suspected to still be hiding in the city with their victim. In a discussion with Minister of the Interior Maihofer, Herold expressed confidence in his BOLO units: "The perpetrators are all known to us. Sooner or later, they will get caught in the information thicket we have created. They will fall into the traps we have laid out for them or fall victim to the dragnet mesh that is falling over them."[3] It was very well possible that Schleyer's kidnappers were hiding in one of the Cologne buildings GSG 9 was ordered to search.

At this point, West German society was already well used to roadblocks and checkpoints with heavily armed police conducting thorough car searches and identity checks. Investigators were aware of the RAF's preferred types of vehicles, so owners of certain car makes had to put up with being searched and questioned at gunpoint on a regular basis. The same was true for citizens of a certain appearance resembling the mugshot photos on the red-rimmed wanted posters that were omnipresent. Police had ramped up their search for terrorists considerably in recent years, with little tangible results, but in the process creating a general feeling of unease and subliminal hysteria within the population, feeding into the fairy tale of a surveillance state on the rise. Most were understanding about the use of the rigid methods, but quite a few also felt pestered by the ubiquitous police presence which triggered in them a feeling of being under general suspicion. In any case, these measures were not liable to go away any time soon, rather the opposite.

Hot Coffee, Warm Bed

Arriving at the villa, Fox and his team go through the procedure once more: The front man opens the door and enters with the second behind him. Fox, being team leader, moves in third. Finally, the last two secure the back. Rehearsed a thousand times, worked a thousand times. "The ensemble action within the team was so perfect that I didn't have to be afraid. I knew exactly that if I gave one of the guys a hint, he would know exactly where to go. I had no worries about that at all." Nevertheless, tension is high. RAF members are not known to be hesitant with their weapons, but rather quite trigger-happy (particularly the females who made up 60 percent of the terrorists' head count). The first person to enter a room is exposed to the greatest danger. For this reason, the team leader is never allowed in first. "If I'm taken out, I can't lead. That's the way it is set in the Mission Tactics."

The silent approach to the house is textbook. The team spreads out to the left and right of the front door. One man places himself on the ground, lying directly opposite the entrance, and aiming at the door with an MP in case there is a shooter waiting on the other side. As three SET men penetrate the building, the fourth and the fifth will provide cover. The men mutually assure visual contact, then they signal readiness. Finally, Fox gives the signal: Go!

The door is unlocked, the squad advances unhindered into the corridor. Several rooms lead off to each side. One by one they are systematically secured. "And then we get in one of the rooms and see a smoking cigarette, a steaming cup of coffee and warm beds. But no one inside. Windows open …" The police had placed an outer cordon around the property even before Fox's GSG 9 squad arrived. But the people who must have been present in the villa just moments ago disappeared into thin air. "No more than 10 minutes could have passed. That's how long a bed stays warm when it's uncovered." Officers find women's high heels and men's clothing, but no restraints, blood stains or anything else that would suggest Hanns Martin Schleyer was there.

A complete washout? Not at all. For Fox's SET, it feels more like a successful test run, taking away some of the tension, providing confidence. They now know that their squad functions in a real-life situation. Fox says, "After that, I walked out of the room and back to the car a little more relaxed. We did the usual debriefing but kept the vests on because we didn't know if we were going to get called out again to another scene."

The unsuccessful apartment raid would not be the last of its kind. A few days later, they would storm an old apartment in central Cologne and again find rooms that had been abandoned not long before. The coal stove was still roaring. As it turned out, the apartment's owners were indeed wanted terrorists. Not the wanted RAF heads, but presumably "third tier terrorists" as the local newspaper put it, some kind of bycatch of the dragnet operation.

On returning to Saint Augustin, the task force needed to regroup. Over the next few days came surveillance missions and undercover patrols. Searches of suspected hideouts were carried out again and again, most of them at night and incognito under the lead of the BKA. Initially, it was not to become known that GSG 9 was involved.

Siegfried Line Bunkers and Tower Blocks

The search for the business titan developed into the largest manhunt in German history. Several tens of thousands of officers were deployed, directed by SOKO[*] 77. At their headquarters in Cologne alone, hundreds of police officers followed up thousands of leads from the public. Designated telephone lines were open and manned 24/7, as were numbers where citizens could listen to voice recordings of terrorists in order to identify them. Telephone tapes where information could be left anonymously were overflowing. It was impossible to work through all that and follow up on all the hints and clues.

Fox recalled an operation in the midrange mountainous area called the Eifel, some 80 kilometers west of Cologne: BKA chief Herold suspected the RAF might be hiding Schleyer in the so called "Westwall," aka the Siegfried Line, a system of expansive border fortifications stemming from the Nazi era and World War II, consisting of rows of concrete dragon teeth and over 18,000 subterranean bunkers and tunnels as well as countless trenches, stretching more than 630 kilometers along the Dutch, Belgian, and French borders all the way down to Switzerland. Word was that shady characters had been hanging around the dilapidated installations south of the border city of Aachen, so GSG 9 was ordered there to check things out.

A farmer led Fox's squad to a half-buried entrance where he thought he had seen someone go inside. But the old locks seemed undamaged, the doors were not broken. They found other entrances. Beyond those a vast maze of corridors and rooms opened up, some several stories deep, some blown up, some collapsed, some partially flooded. There were no site plans so reconnaissance turned out all but impossible. For one full day, they worked their way through the underground ruins, always with a queasy feeling, because they never knew what was waiting for them around the next corner. What they did know, however, was that the kidnappers were not squeamish, as the scene at the kidnapping site had shown. But eventually, they concluded that there wasn't much point in looking any further. Apart from the sheer size of the tunnel system, it also seemed unlikely that the RAF would hide its valuable bargaining chip in one of these cold, musty holes. "We were convinced that Schleyer still had to be in the greater Cologne area." But where? That area is exactly what it says it is: greater.

To not get dispersed completely, BKA chief Herold narrowed search orders down to the most promising objects. He prioritized the targeting of high-rise buildings, preferably with underground garages, on arterial roads. It was known that the RAF preferred renting apartments in large complexes. They provided anonymity, quick access and escape routes. Electricity bills, deposits and rent were always paid in advance and in cash. In the days that followed, GSG 9 checked high-rise building

---

[*] SOKO (*Sonderkommission*) = Special Criminal Investigation Commission. Designated commission for the investigation of one or several interconnected crime(s).

after building as inconspicuously as possible and searched individual apartments or entire floors if there was any suspicion. All in all, it turned out to be not very effective, as Commander Wegener stated in retrospect: "We had to wait to be called until they had determined a certain place of custody for [Schleyer], but we were always too late."[4]

As it would turn out, Herold was right in his assumption. The RAF commando Siegfried Hausner* hid Schleyer in such a high-rise building inside the greater Cologne area. They had first taken their hostage to a multi-story housing estate on the outskirts of Cologne, and then, still on the first night, to nearby Erftstadt, just off the A1 autobahn. There, less than half an hour's drive from the crime scene, a young woman had rented apartment 104 on the third floor of the high-rise building at the address Zum Renngraben 8 only two months earlier: three rooms, 78 square meters (840 square feet), with direct access to the underground garage by elevator. The real estate agent had taken notice of the single woman because she paid the deposit of 800 Deutschmarks in cash from a bundle of 50-mark bills. Immediately after the start of her lease, the woman had all the locks changed.

Two days after the kidnapping, the real estate agent told patrol officer Ferdinand Schmitt, who, like all police in the region, was tasked with keeping his eyes peeled and reporting possible hideouts. However, the telex with his report got stuck somewhere on the way from his precinct to SOKO 77 in Cologne. To this day, it is not clear why.[5] When Schmitt's superior asked the BKA about the whereabouts of the report a few days later, he was just told to hold back on inquiries in the future. For more than a week, Schleyer squatted on a mattress in this very apartment under the changing surveillance of his RAF kidnappers.

The fact that BKA could have known where Schleyer was stashed caused a veritable scandal in the aftermath of the German Autumn. An investigative report commissioned by the federal government a year later, rendered a scathing critique of the confusion of competencies between federal and state authorities, particularly the BKA and the provincial police of North Rhine-Westphalia, and of the arrogance with which the former sometimes treated the latter's representatives: "The fight against terrorism is a joint task of all security authorities. It must be ensured that everyone is always immediately informed of the situation as far as possible, necessary and permissible. Internal secrecy must be counteracted. Even the slightest appearance that deployed forces are of inferior quality, that they are of lesser value than others for the solution of the overall task, must be scrupulously avoided."[6]

Gerhart Baum recognizes this type of interagency narrow-mindedness as an old police disease. In his time as minister for the interior a few years later he had ample opportunity to encounter this mentality himself: "'We'll manage, we'll get it done,

---

* Interestingly, Commando Hausner was named after a terrorist who'd been killed in the Stockholm embassy occupation in 1975.

we don't need you.' And it's only when they see they really can't do it on their own that they start involving others."

Basically, the mantra of BKA president Herold proved to be true: fighting crime is information processing. All the information needed to put one and one together was available. Or it would have been. The female tenant of the apartment in Erftstadt had given a street address in Wuppertal as a former residency that did not exist, and the ID card registered in her name had been reported stolen months earlier by a woman who belonged to the inner circle of RAF sympathizers. To find out, Herold's officers would have only needed to enter this information into the BKA database system. But they did not. Thus, the RAF was able to hold Schleyer in the high-rise apartment in Erftstadt-Liblar unchecked for about 10 days before taking its hostage across the more or less unguarded border near Aachen to The Hague in the Netherlands, and then on to Brussels in Belgium.

Ten days was more than enough time to free him from his prison. And it seems that there actually had been plans to thoroughly search the same high-rise building at Renngraben in Erftstadt-Liblar. Two days after patrol officer Schmitt's report, a number of suspicious communities, persons from the left-wing spectrum, and some "anarchist apartments" were to be searched all at once in the Erft district under the heading "*Rollkommando*," or Raiding Party. On a list of eight "relevantly suspicious objects," "erftstadt-liblar, zum renngraben, 3rd floor, apartment 104" was fourth in line.[7]

Five days after the kidnapping of Hanns Martin Schleyer, local and criminal police had prepared the operational concept and gathered all available submachine guns and radios. Their plan: "overtaking" the suspected hideouts by task forces. Each team consisted of "one officer with local knowledge from the upper echelons of the police as the leader, nine police officers and four detectives with the appropriate vehicles, command and control equipment."[8] The head of the Erftstadt police station, Rolf Breithaupt—Sergeant Schmitt's superior—was designated as the officer with local knowledge of the property Zum Renngraben 8. He later reported that he had explored the apartment building in civilian clothes for this purpose, twice standing in front of apartment 104 on the third floor, only a few steps away from Schleyer. "That's where he's sitting," he had said to his wife as they drove past the high-rise in the days that followed.[9]

On September 11, 1977, at 6:30 p.m., the police station in Erftstadt received "Operation Order No. 2": concerted inspection and search of the properties on the list. But Breithaupt was not to participate. Instead, "we always assumed that the apartment would be searched by the BKA or GSG 9," Breithaupt said in retrospect.[10] But then nothing happened. Why? That remains a mystery. The order to carry out a "full check" never came.

For GSG 9, it would not have been a long journey. Time and again, they patrolled past the building during surveillance missions. The Rhine-Erft district was a focal point of their searches. On behalf of SOKO 77, they carried out site observations on highway ramps in the area to check vehicle models that the RAF typically used. They followed up on tips from the public about suspicious persons, most of them not very fruitful, reports Dieter Fox: "Many simply saw ghosts. But the wanted posters were hanging on every streetlight and every tree, and we were obligated by police law to follow up on all leads." In their morning briefings, Erftstadt-Liblar was mentioned again and again as the area of operation—but never the address Zum Renngraben.

"Well, if only GSG 9 had gone in there." Hanns Martin Schleyer's youngest son shrugs his shoulders. At the time, the Schleyer family was waiting for news from the kidnappers, and Jörg's older brother Hanns-Eberhard was negotiating with the federal government for the release of their father in exchange for a ransom (which was eventually sabotaged by the government). Today, Jörg Schleyer considers the episode in Erftstadt a missed opportunity to save his father's life, or at least to shorten his ordeal. "No matter how it would have turned out, it would at least have saved my father five weeks of misery. It is sad in any case, because if the opportunity had been seized, there would have been a chance for it to end well."

Despite a feverish search, despite roadblocks and tightened border controls, police did not find a single hot trace of the kidnapped president of the Employers' Association. At some point, desperation grew so much that authorities even turned to off-the-wall tips from the public: The repeated dream of a woman from Bavaria, in which Hanns Martin Schleyer was held captive in a baroque or rococo building, was taken just as seriously and was followed up with the same rigor as a local diviner who had let his rods swing over a Cologne city map, or a clairvoyant from Holland who, after all, also advised the Dutch king. Months earlier, he had allegedly helped to track down a missing child in Japan. But not Schleyer.

The government tried to buy time by stalling the kidnappers with concessions and tactical delays while the search was intensified. The alert operation immediately after the kidnapping thus developed into a permanent state of affairs. Days turned into weeks, and the tension of the early searches turned into routine missions. This was also true for GSG 9. The three units of 32 men each were deployed on a rolling schedule: one unit openly performing manhunt missions scheduled at short notice, wearing BGS uniform, some of them moving on the road in fast Mercedes, some in helicopters for aerial searches and observation. A second unit worked undercover with civilian vehicles and phony license plates. Finally, a third unit was kept on standby and practiced at GSG 9's site or in the surrounding area, so that it could switch from training to an operational status at any time.

In addition, GSG 9 operatives served as bodyguards for high-ranking persons. Supporting the plainclothes BKA bodyguards, all public officials with security level 1 clearance were now accompanied by five uniformed GSG 9 men each. And so two gray Mercedes Sedans followed in the motorcade of the respective federal ministers, the chancellor or the federal president to their public appearances.

With their submachine guns and martial appearance, GSG 9 men were meant to serve primarily as a deterrent, which stood in contrast to the image of normality the top tier politicians wanted to create. Some even insisted that their GSG 9 detail remain outside the event halls. Despite the tense situation, they tried to avoid the impression that the government was under siege.

The Fastest Locksmith Service in Cologne

After almost six weeks of searching, GSG 9 had gained a lot of experience in penetrating apartments. Commander Wegener later smirked: "My specialists from the technical department were professionals in the field afterwards. We were the 'fastest locksmith service in Cologne' at the time."[11] On October 13, 1977, however, a special objective was up for search: the Uni-Center close to the University of Cologne, one of the largest apartment buildings in Europe, with 20 to 30 apartments on each of its 45 floors, plus a ground floor level and three basement floors. Down on the parking deck, lot 135, somebody had parked an eggplant-colored Alfa Romeo Giulia 1600. Its license plate had been wanted since Schleyer's abduction because it had been spotted on another RAF vehicle. As it turned out, the RAF had a whole series of this license plate made and had at least five stolen cars fitted with it.

In addition, an apartment on the 26th floor had already been searched days earlier and been identified as a "conspiracy apartment." Among the items found were the black top cover of the pram used in the Schleyer ambush and a metal plate with the brand name of the pram on it. The tenant of the apartment turned out to be leading RAF member Adelheid Schulz, who investigators had linked to the murder of banker Jürgen Ponto earlier that year. For weeks, the rooms had served as headquarters for the planning of Schleyer's kidnapping. Finally, this was the longed-for hot lead.

BKA now suspected Schleyer to be hidden in another one of the 968 apartments. But in which one? To find out exactly, all three GSG 9 units were deployed in, on and around the premises of the extensively cordoned-off Uni-Center, starting from five o'clock in the morning on this day, October 13. In an empty store on the parking deck level, the Border Guard had set up a provisional command center and recreation rooms. Entrances and exits of the apartment complex were closely monitored so that no one could get in and no one could get out. If the terrorists were inside the building, GSG 9 would track them down. To ensure this, the units split up and systematically combed the three wings of the Uni-Center.

Part of one unit worked their way from the ground floor up on the outside of the building, using hooked ladders to get on the balconies, as another part of the unit worked their way down by abseiling from the roof. A second unit advanced from the top floor down through the stairwells. The third unit did the same, but moving from the bottom up, so that the two units would eventually meet. Floor by floor, door by door, it was a marathon search. And all of it in full gear—helmet, equipment, weapons. The protective vests alone with sewn-in lead plates weighed 15 kilograms (33 lbs). "45 floors—that's quite a workout!" Dieter Fox says. "It might as well have served as an official part of your golden sports badge."

The search always followed the same pattern: the SET was set up in front of the apartment with officers of the criminal and local police in the background. Then a "call" was made through the shut door—"This is the police! Open up!" If no one answered, they would open the door with duplicate keys or a GSG 9 technician would help with a lock pick. Only if nothing worked would they use the crowbar to break open the door. They had only a few minutes to check each apartment. "We arrived, went in, had a look around and left." Werner Heimann and his team worked through the floors from top to bottom. "Afterwards, our colleagues from the local police or the BKA went in and took care of the rest. After all, there was one or the other door that needed to be renewed …"

In those apartments where residents were not present, the police officers left an official form—as befits German correctness:

> Due to verified evidence that terrorists have been or are still present in the Uni-Center in Cologne, the public prosecutor's office in charge has ordered the search of the apartments belonging to the apartment complex in accordance with §103 of the German Code of Criminal Procedure (search of unsuspected persons).—In the course of the execution of this order it was indispensable to check your apartment as well. Unfortunately, you were not present at the time of the inspection. Should you have any questions, please contact the Cologne Police Headquarters, tel. 2751, extension 2411.—The police regret that it was necessary to invade your privacy in the manner that occurred, but ask for your understanding in view of the difficulties of the situation, in particular also the dangers for the occupants of the building. Respectfully …[12]

In order to prevent unwanted surprises, the police had made loudspeaker announcements in front of the building before the search. But the Uni-Center is huge, not all the residents had noticed the fuss, and at this early hour not all the residents were on their feet. "We looked into a couple of astonished faces, and also interrupted one or two spicy scenes," Werner Heimann grins. "Well, [it was a] student dormitory …" However, most of the people they visited in this manner took it rather coolly, some were even amused. In the end, there were few complaints, as the local press noted later with satisfaction.

Mission Command

Searching the Uni-Center lasted almost all day, from early morning to well into the afternoon. By the end, Dieter Fox and his comrades were soaked in sweat: "We were pretty exhausted. We found a lot of things, but not Hanns Martin Schleyer. We were just about to mop up the last apartments on the top floor when the unit leaders were called to Wegener."

The commander had just received a call from the Minister of the Interior Maihofer, from the crisis management team in Bonn, and had taken issue with him when his highest superior told him: "You have to fly to Rome with six men and support the Italians in a hijacking case. A Lufthansa plane was seized on its way from Palma de Majorca to Frankfurt." Wegener was stunned. "You can't be serious!" he snapped at the minister. Six people? He wouldn't be able to do anything with that few men. "I need more information to be able to assess the situation. I'm not going there with six men, Herr Maihofer, what are you thinking?"[13] Maihofer agreed to consult again with the chancellor's office and the crisis team, which was still trying to confirm the scarce information that was available at this time.

At 2:30 p.m., they had received a message from French air traffic control in Aix-en-Provence: Flight LH-181 had deviated from its planned route on its way from Palma de Majorca to Frankfurt. The Boeing 737 was called *Landshut*, named after a cozy little town in Bavaria. What happened on board was much less picturesque. Ninety-one people were traveling back from the vacation island: five crew members, 82 tourists and, as it turned out later, four terrorists sent by the PFLP. They took control of the plane at gunpoint and forced Flight Captain Jürgen Schumann to redirect the flight to Rome's Fiumicino airport. Once there, they demanded the release of "all comrades imprisoned in the Federal Republic of Germany." The document was titled "Ultimatum to the Chancellor of the Federal Republic of Germany":

> ... The lives of the passengers and crew and the life of Dr. Hanns Martin Schleyer depend on you fulfilling the following demands:
>
> 1. release of the following RAF comrades from West German prisons: Andreas Baader, Gudrun Ensslin, Jan-Carl Raspe, Verena Becker, Werner Hoppe, Karl Heinz Dellwo, Hanna Krabbe, Bernd Rössner, Ingrid Schubert, Irmgard Möller, Günter Sonnenberg. Each person is to receive DM 100,000.
> 2. release of the following [P.]F.L.P. comrades from prison in Istanbul:—Mahdi.—Hussein.
> 3. payment of 15 million U.S. dollars according to the attached instructions.
> 4. arrange with one of the following countries to receive the comrades who have been released: Democratic Republic of Vietnam, Republic of Somalia, People's Democratic Republic of Yemen.
> 5. the German prisoners are to be taken to their destination in an aircraft provided by you....
> 9. Any attempt on your part to delay or deceive will mean the immediate expiration of the ultimatum and the execution of Hanns Martin Schleyer, the passengers and the crew of the plane.
>
> 13 October 1977, Organization for the Fight against World Imperialism.[14]

This was exactly the kind of scenario the crisis team had been dreading for some time: the Schleyer kidnappers had escalated the situation. They wanted to lend weight to their demand for the release of the RAF prisoners and to thwart the government's stalling tactics. From now on, it was no longer a question of a single human life, but of 91, as Hans-Jürgen Wischnewski wrote in his memoirs. The state minister was to become instrumental in the current crisis, the "greatest challenge of the Federal

Republic of Germany in its existence."[15] And GSG 9 was last option to master this challenge when everything else failed. But would they be up for the job?

"Confidence in GSG 9 was strong," Hans-Dietrich Genscher later reported. In the years since the inception of the counterterrorism squad, he had switched his portfolios from Interior to Foreign Affairs and as such had become an integral component of the chancellor's crisis staff. Whether the other members of the crisis team were as confident about the "training world champion" GSG 9 is anyone's guess. Wegener was given only a very general assignment: "GSG 9 will track the hijacked aircraft and prepare an assault to free the hostages." The commander did not receive any other specifications such as mission contingent, armament or equipment. He calculated that he would need two tactical units for the plane rescue, a total of 60–70 men. "The selection of the right people proved difficult. Every unit was eager to participate in the operation. The decisive factor for me was that the designated units had practiced certain attack procedures on a Boeing 737 shortly beforehand. General morale within GSG 9 was high, despite the considerable workload in the hunt for the Schleyer kidnappers."

In the end, Wegener decided not to bring two full units along with him, but to select the best people from the existing ones and to put them together in new units. In the first wave, some 20 troops were to come along, led by three or four squad leaders, plus a few technicians, medics, and telecommunication specialists. The rest of the units were supposed to join them later. Being still at the foot of the Uni-Center, Wegener instructed his subleaders to select five volunteers each for their SETs. Werner Heimann summoned his people, as did Dieter Fox: "Then I asked, 'Who wants to come along?' Most hands went up at once, but some hands just stayed down in their laps. Okay, one needs to accept that."

Fox's boss Dieter Tutter, as the most experienced unit leader, was supposed to stay behind and hold the fort. After all, the search for Schleyer was still going on, and a rescue operation for him seemed far more likely at that point than the storming of a hijacked airplane who-knows-where in the world: "I would have loved to come along, of course. But Wegener wanted to bring two units along with him. Mine was the oldest, most stable unit of the three, and I was also the longest serving. He obviously trusted me with this task, so he said, 'Tutter with his 2nd Unit stays here, but your second-in-command Fox is with me.' A few of my people were a bit miffed, but I told them, 'Let it go! They're gonna pursue them now, sure. But where do you think they'll go and how it will end? Most likely, they'll just come home.'"

Soon enough, a convoy of civilian Mercedes and VW vans thundered back from the center of Cologne to Saint Augustin, sirens howling, blue lights flashing. By now it was late afternoon, and the streets were thronged with rush hour traffic, but most drivers routinely made way. After more than five weeks of a state of emergency, constant searches, and police sirens, most people in Cologne had come to terms with the situation and gave way. When the convoy roared into the Border Guard

History's first terror attack live on TV: On September 5, 1972, the overwhelmed German security forces put almost no restrictions on press and onlookers. The crowd was able to closely witness the hostage drama unfold in the Olympic village. (© SZ Photo/Max Scheler/Bridgeman Images)

Without any special forces standing by, the Munich city police tried to stage an ill-advised rescue plan. Untrained police officers in jumpsuits armed with World War II weaponry were told to somehow liberate the hostages. (© RCS/Alinari Archives Management, Florence/Bridgeman Images)

An icon of contemporary history: One of the two helicopters that carried the terrorists and the Israeli hostages to Fürstenfeldbruck airfield on the morning after the shootout. (© Picture Alliance/DPA/Bridgeman Images)

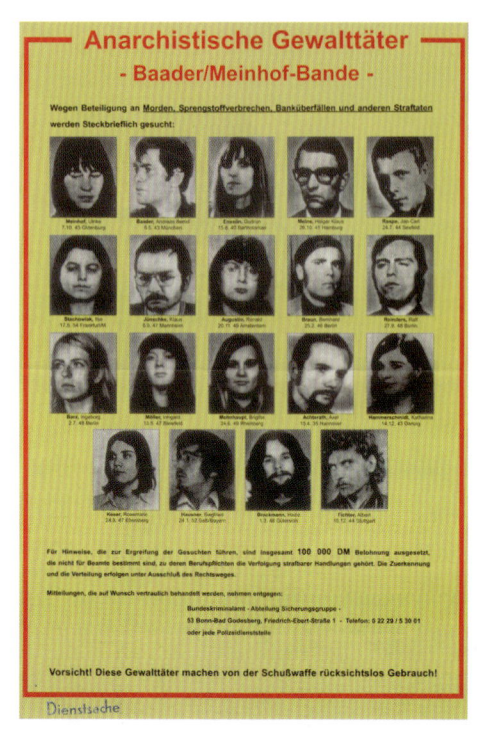

Wanted poster from the early 1970s depicting members of the terrorist group later called the RAF. At the time, they were known as the Baader Meinhof Gang, named after their figureheads Ulrike Meinhof and Andreas Baader (the first two from the left, top row). The headline reads: "Anarchist violent criminals—Baader/Meinhof gang—Wanted for involvement in murders, explosives crimes, bank robberies and other crimes," and on the bottom, "Beware! These violent criminals make ruthless use of their firearms!" A reward of 100,000 Deutschmarks is offered for information leading to the apprehension of the wanted persons. (Philipp Meyer)

On September 5, 1977, exactly five years on from the Munich Olympic Games attack, Hanns Martin Schleyer, powerful head of the West German Employer's Association, was brutally abducted by members of the RAF in Cologne, who killed Schleyer's driver and two men from his security detail in the process. This is the scene of his kidnapping. (© Picture Alliance/DPA/Bridgeman Images)

Minister of State Hans-Jürgen Wischnewski leaving the aircraft *Stuttgart* upon his return from Mogadishu. Serving as chief negotiator in a number of hostage situations and crises for the West German government, Wischnewski became known as "the nation's fireman" in the 1970s and '80s. The mission to Mogadishu, however, he considered as "the most difficult mission in my life." (© akg-images/picture-alliance/dpa)

GSG 9 Commander Ulrich Wegener (middle) with Minister of the Interior and "father of GSG 9" Hans-Dietrich Genscher, at the official presentation of the new counterterrorism force in 1973. The fact that Wegener had been Genscher's security adviser and liaison officer to the Border Guard in the late 1960s and early '70s was a considerable factor in facilitating the inception of GSG 9. (Bundespolizei/GSG 9)

Members of GSG 9 with submachine guns acting as a security detail for Federal President Walter Scheel during his stay in Hamburg in September 1977. What might seem like a standard precautionary measure today was unheard of at the time. (© akg-images/picture-alliance/dpa)

Dieter Fox with his young family playing a board game. The little box at the front of the photo is a radio alarm receiver (a pager) that GSG 9 operatives had to carry with them at all times when on standby. This image is taken from a GSG 9 recruitment brochure from the 1970s. (Bundespolizei/GSG 9)

Dieter Tutter with a banjo and Dieter Fox with a harmonica playing alongside their fellow GSG 9 comrades and posing for a GSG 9 recruitment brochure from the 1970s. (Bundespolizei/GSG 9)

Werner Heimann in front of one of GSG 9's heavy, much-envied Mercedes Sedans, mid-1970s. In their early years, their low-hanging holsters with leather straps led their comrades in other Border Guard units to nickname them "Djangos" and "cowboys." (Werner Heimann)

Werner Heimann (fourth from left) and fellow GSG 9 comrades debriefing after a so-called "alarm ride" with their heavy Mercedes Sedans from Saint Augustin to Hamburg Airport. It took them three hours and five minutes to cover the 460 kilometers, averaging 149 km/h. These alarm ride exercises were undertaken on a regular basis in the mid-1970s in order to determine the amount of time GSG 9 would need to get from Saint Augustin to anywhere in West Germany, as well as to find out whether operatives were able to participate in an operation after three or more hours of constant, highly demanding, high-speed driving on German autobahns—they were not. (Werner Heimann)

GSG 9 recruitment poster from the 1970s. The caption reads, "A task for real men." Apart from a leaflet, this is the only recruitment advertisement that GSG 9 ever produced to attract young talent from other Border Guard units. Although there was never a shortage of applicants, from its very inception GSG 9 was confronted with a shortage of suitable candidates to fill the mold of the perfect GSG 9 operative. (Bundespolizei/GSG 9)

Climbing exercise ca. 1974. Appropriate equipment for these ventures was virtually non-existent at the time, as were the respective climbing techniques. These, along with most parts of their gear, had to be invented by GSG 9 operatives and the technical department of the unit. (Dieter Tutter)

Dieter Fox testing his new service pistol and holster in the spring of 1973. The quick-draw holster was an in-house development of GSG 9; it was custom-made to suit their needs. Lacking any conventional operational clothing at the time, they used their Border Guard work suits made of so-called moleskin fabric. (Dieter Fox)

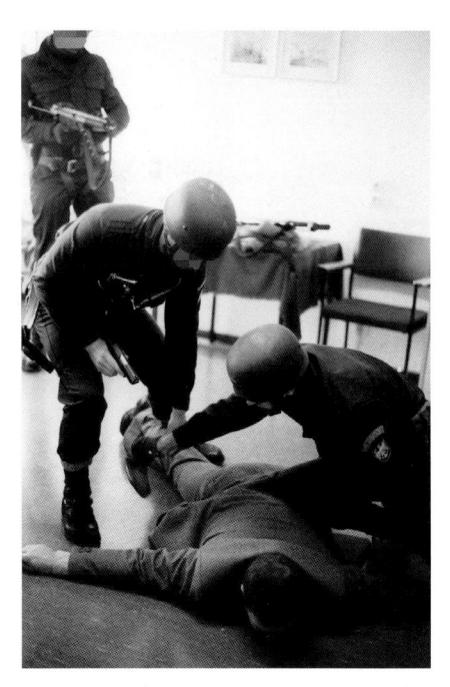

Exercise searching suspect, 1970s or early '80s. For the role of the bad guys, comrades from other GSG 9 or Border Guard units would stand in. (Bundespolizei/GSG 9)

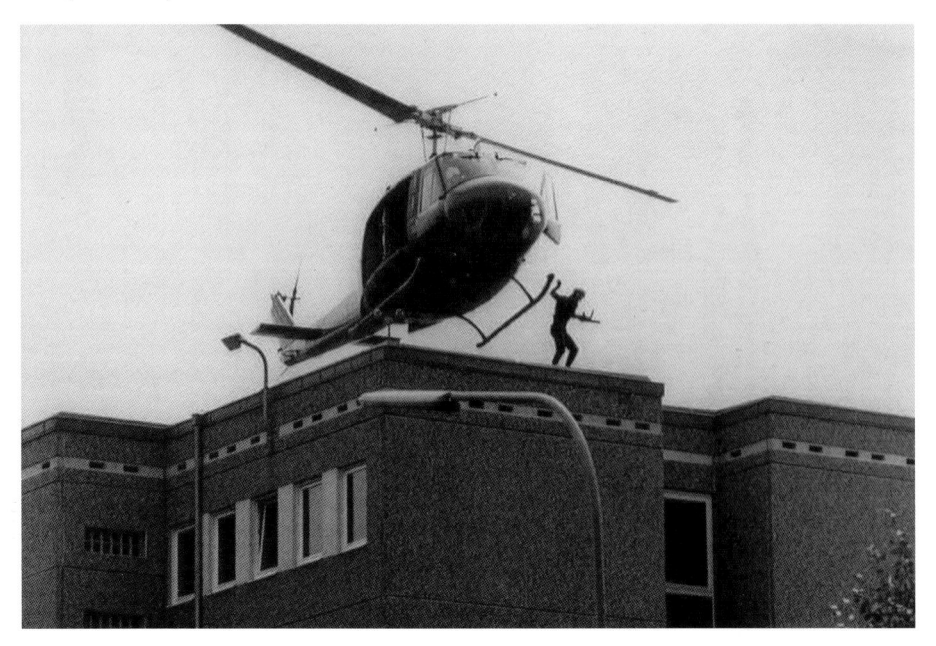

Jörg Probstmeier jumping from a Huey helicopter onto the roof of GSG 9's headquarters building in Saint Augustin as part of a tactical exercise for penetrating buildings and rooms in the 1970s. (Jörg Probstmeier)

Fun image from a photo shoot for a recruitment leaflet in a sand quarry with outdated carbine rifles from WWII, 1970s. The image was never used for the intended publication purpose. (Jörg Probstmeier)

Abseiling exercise from a Bell UH-1D Huey helicopter in the mid-1970s. Early on, abseiling became GSG 9's trademark. (Bundespolizei/GSG 9)

Another abseiling exercise in the late 1970s. Mastering the techniques for this stunt was not an easy feat to accomplish and in the first decade of their existence GSG 9 had a dismal record of several serious accidents, two of them lethal. (Jörg Probstmeier)

Werner Heimann (middle) and two of his fellow GSG 9 operatives preparing for an abseiling exercise in front of a Bell UH-1D Huey helicopter in 1975 or '76. In the early years, the demanding abseiling technique was practiced once every 10 days if helicopters were available, otherwise high-rise buildings or towers were used. For most new recruits, the challenge of pushing themselves backwards off the helicopter and jumping into the void was quite thrilling at first, but with countless repetitions the stunt soon became second nature. (Werner Heimann)

Werner Heimann abseiling from a wooden fire observation tower in a forest near Saint Augustin in 1974. In the early days of GSG 9, ropes were made of hemp, which turned out to be less than ideal. Also, there were no professional harnesses, only make-shift ones. A little later on, only hip harnesses were available. However, these were so tight that they would "pinch off everything when the rope pulled the harness upwards," as Heimann painfully remembers. "Very uncomfortable." So, GSG 9 technicians would go on to develop safe seat harnesses as well as a handheld device with an automatic brake to prevent the rope from slipping. (Werner Heimann)

Jörg Probstmeier wielding a Heckler & Koch HK MP5 submachine gun while on duty in GSG 9's command center in Saint Augustin, 1970s. (Jörg Probstmeier)

Exercise with a truck on the lawn in front of GSG 9's headquarters building, mid-1970s. (Bundespolizei/GSG 9)

Briefing for a telecommunication unit exercise in Saint Augustin, 1970s or early '80s. (Bundespolizei/GSG 9)

Jörg Probstmeier on the shooting range of the Belgian army in the Wahner Heide, close to Saint Augustin, firing the Heckler & Koch HK G3SG/1 sniper rifle, a modified G3 assault rifle. In the Mogadishu operation, Probstmeier would be part of the sniper teams safeguarding the sneaking-up approach as well as the storming of the aircraft from surrounding sand dunes. (Jörg Probstmeier)

Jörg Probstmeier at the Wahner Heide shooting range near Saint Augustin in the 1970s, wielding an HK MP5 submachine gun and sporting a second-generation protective vest. Shooting exercises with protective vests were done regularly in standing, kneeling, and lying-down positions, or on the move. (Jörg Probstmeier)

Jörg Probstmeier posing in front of a Mercedes Sedan with a G3 assault rifle at the Lydd Military Training Camp in Kent, UK, late 1970s. The G3 was used for combat shooting or for local and house-to-house combat which was intensely practiced at the Royal Army facility on the British South Coast. (Jörg Probstmeier)

Dieter Fox with the full set of equipment provided to every GSG 9 operative in the early 1970s. The sheer amount of equipment, armory, and weapons each of the men had to carry along was one of the reasons why GSG 9 used the much-envied Mercedes Sedans: three operatives complete with all their gear had to fit into each car. The second reason for the highly motorized cars was for possible pursuits, Fox says. "If the bad guys were using stolen Porsches we couldn't go after them in VW beetles." (Dieter Fox)

Team-building exercise and endurance test on the River Rhine, 1970s. This photo was taken after instructor Dieter Tutter had his men paddle their dinghy non-stop from the romantic wine-making village of Eltville all the way to Bonn, 101 kilometers in total. Starting at midnight, the men mastered the distance in 17 hours and 48 minutes, taking turns every 15 minutes or so. (Dieter Tutter)

Dieter Tutter on board a helicopter from the Bundesgrenzschutz Air Wing, mapping a flight route for a search-and-rescue exercise. Taken from a GSG 9 recruitment brochure. (Bundespolizei/GSG 9)

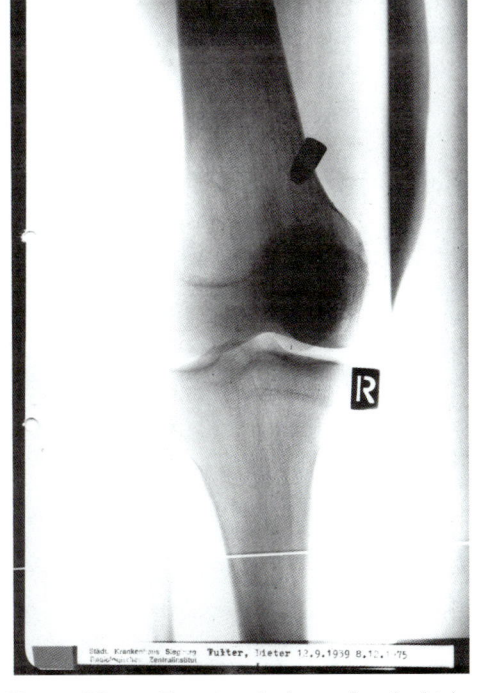

X-ray of Dieter Tutter's right knee after the high-noon-style shooting exercise "El Presidente." The gun slipped from Tutter's hand when he drew it quickly from his low-hanging hip holster. Trying to catch it, Tutter pulled the trigger. Six months later he was ready to return to duty. (Dieter Tutter)

First full GSG 9 dress uniform, in use from the 1970s to the '80s. For their first operational uniform in 1972, though, GSG 9 recruits had to take to their needle and thread themselves and rework old work suits according to their needs, making sure no shiny buttons or shoulder pieces would give them away, nothing stuck out and impeded their freedom of movement or could get stuck in the undergrowth or on a door handle. (Philipp Meyer)

Werner Heimann (back row, second from right) and seven other GSG 9 recruits during a break in the summer of 1973. For the duration of their six-month basic training, they would be grouped in squads of eight. Upon their successful completion of this first stage, each one would be assigned to their respective SET (*Spezialeinsatztrupp* or Special Operations Team) and continue with another six-month specialized training program. (Werner Heimann)

Exercise in a tight sewage pipe wearing a gas mask to test stress and claustrophobia, early 1980s. Unit leader and instructor Dieter Tutter experienced a steep learning curve with this exercise after one of his men got stuck halfway through the pipe due to anxiety at his first trial. (Dieter Tutter)

Aircraft storming theory class, taken from a recruiting brochure, late 1970s or early '80s. In order to be able to move effectively outside as well as inside passenger aircraft, GSG 9 had obtained detailed illustrations, models, and interior layout plans for the cabin and flight decks of all current commercial models, even Soviet Ilyushin and Tupolew aircraft. (Bundespolizei/GSG 9)

Werner Heimann (second from left) at a sharpshooting exercise with Heckler & Koch HK G3SG/1 in the mid-1970s. In the early years of GSG 9, sharpshooting training took place at least once a week at daytime, covering all distances between 100 and 400 meters. Additionally, night-shooting exercises were scheduled each week. (Werner Heimann)

Aircraft fueling course in the mid-1970s. GSG 9 operatives like Werner Heimann (in foreground) took special courses as "gas station attendants" to be able to approach a skyjacked aircraft inconspicuously and collect intelligence in a hostage situation. Other GSG 9 operatives would be professionally trained as drivers of baggage or gangway vehicles or even as flight attendants. (Werner Heimann)

Rare photo of GSG 9 operatives next to their aircraft on the apron in Mogadishu, sitting on their aluminum ladders and wearing civilian clothes, discussing their respective roles in their dedicated SETs, shortly before the start of Operation *Feuerzauber* (Fire Magic). (Werner Heimann)

Boeing 737, named *Landshut*, sitting on the apron at Mogadishu International Airport in the afternoon sun. After the five-day ordeal of Lufthansa Flight LH-181, the standards of hygiene on board were appalling, the cabin temperature unbearable, the toilets clogged, and the stuffy air filled with the stench of blood, sweat, feces, and fear. The hostages were forced to wet and soil their seats. (Jörg Probstmeier)

Even as the firefight inside the aircraft is still going on, GSG 9 operatives help hostages get out of their seats, and guide them through the emergency hatches and down the wing. Support teams lead the exhausted passengers to a safe space behind the nearby dunes. Of the 86 hostages, only a couple were slightly wounded, mostly by splinters and ricochets from a hand grenade thrown by a terrorist. This is the only official photo of the ongoing operation ever published by GSG 9. (Bundespolizei/GSG 9)

Interior of the *Landshut* cabin right after the aircraft storming in Mogadishu. The damage to the seats shown in this photo was caused by the detonation of a grenade one of the terrorists was able to throw during the firefight right before he was shot. A second grenade would be found the next morning unlocked, still hot, the grip squeezed in the linkage under a passenger seat. (Bundespolizei/GSG 9)

Interior of the *Landshut* cabin right after the aircraft storming in Mogadishu. View of the middle aisle from the front of the plane to the back. (Bundespolizei/GSG 9)

It is not entirely clear why the overhead panels are missing. It's probable that they have been removed by the technical search team, either just after the storming or the next morning, in search of possible hidden explosives. (Bundespolizei/GSG 9)

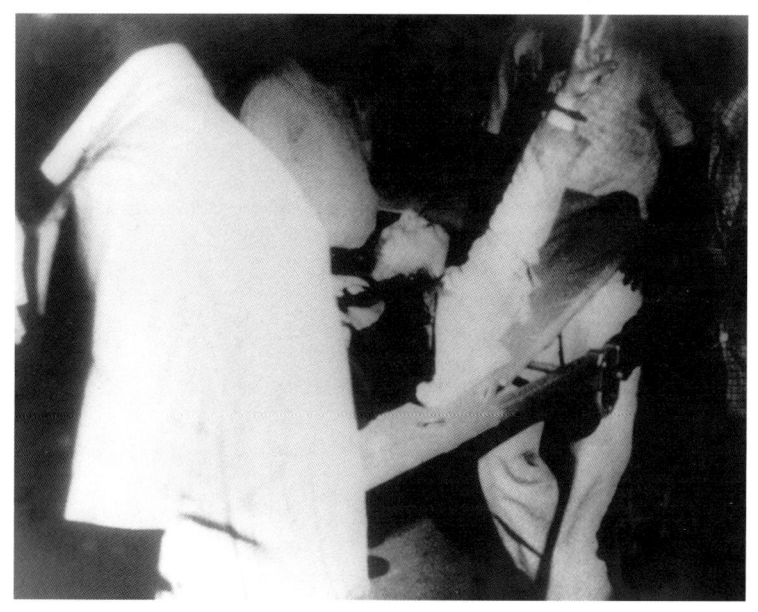

The only terrorist to survive the storming of the *Landshut* holds her hand in a "V" sign and shouts "Kill me! Kill me!" as she is carried to an ambulance. Going by the name Souhaila Andrawes, the 24-year-old was shot in the firefight and found underneath the body of another terrorist. She was sentenced to 20 years in prison, but was deported after a few months. Attempts by the German state to bring her to justice in the 1990s proved unsuccessful. (© Picture Alliance/DPA/Bridgeman Images)

The freed hostages boarding a hired passenger aircraft the morning after their rescue, seen from the Boeing 707 used by GSG 9. After the five-day odyssey with a couple of tough touchdowns, the Boeing 737 *Landshut* was in no condition to fly and would return to Germany only a few weeks later. (Werner Heimann)

Wir sind stolz auf Sie, danke!

18. Oktober 1977   Werner Maihofer
Bundesinnenminister

Minister of the Interior Werner Maihofer (left) and GSG 9 Commander Ulrich Wegener on Köln-Bonn Airport inspecting the Mogadishu returnees, who are still wearing the civilian attire they wore during the storming of the aircraft. A copy of this photo signed by both Maihofer and Wegener was sent to every participant in the Mogadishu operation. The caption reads: "We are proud of you, thank you!" (Jörg Probstmeier)

Official reception and ceremony at the Chancellery in Bonn where the GSG 9 operatives received the Bundesverdienstkreuz (Federal Cross of Merit). At first, only Wegener was supposed to receive this high honor, but he insisted that every GSG 9 operative who was part of the operation be awarded it as well. (Jörg Probstmeier)

Penetration exercise for a hostage rescue inside a building in 1978. (Bundespolizei/GSG 9)

Bus storming exercise in the 1980s. Apart from aircraft storming, GSG 9 specialized in storming trains, ships, and buses, each of them requiring special dedicated tactical approaches and techniques. (Bundespolizei/GSG 9)

Jörg Probstmeier (second from right) and his SET comrades at the Lydd Military Training Camp in Kent on the South Coast of England in the mid-1970s. (Jörg Probstmeier)

Assault exercise with GSG 9's Mercedes Sedans in the 1970s. (Bundespolizei/GSG 9)

Jörg Probstmeier in Lufthansa uniform in front of a Boeing 747 at Lima Airport in the early 1980s. Until the 1990s, many Border Guard officers were seconded to airports around the world to carry out aviation security tasks for Lufthansa flights, including checking passengers and their hand luggage and working on the apron at aircraft boarding. At any given time, at least one GSG 9 officer was deployed at each of the Lufthansa branches in Bombay, Lima, and Tel Aviv. (Jörg Probstmeier)

Members of GSG 9 and the Special Forces Detachment Berlin in front of Mercedes Sedans during a joint exercise in Saint Augustin 1978. James Stejskal (beside right Sedan, face unblurred) and his comrades were part of the first US special ops unit to cooperate with GSG 9, but they were far from the last. Intentional exchange and communal training, workshops, and exercises were an integral part of GSG 9's DNA. (James Stejskal)

Werner Heimann (11th from left) amidst his comrades of the 3rd Operational Unit in 1982. On his right, Unit leader Anselm Weygold next to SET leader "Juppes" Laux. (Werner Heimann)

GSG 9 diver. With the Baltic Sea becoming an increasingly contested region and a likely theatre for possible terrorist attacks, maritime capabilities are more important than ever. (Bundespolizei/GSG 9)

Left: Fast-roping exercise from a helicopter. The famous abseiling technique used by GSG 9 in its early years has been replaced by the technique of fast roping, which uses only the hands and feet to control the descent, instead of harnesses. It is faster and more flexible than abseiling, but also more demanding. (Bundespolizei/GSG 9). Right: Aircraft storming exercise today. (GSG 9)

GSG 9 operatives in front of a Bundespolizei helicopter. The operatives have the specialized maritime, aerial, and ground equipment of a modern-day counterterrorism unit. (Bundespolizei/GSG 9)

Fast-roping exercise onto a submarine. Compared to the classic abseiling, this technique makes the descent quicker, but also riskier. (Bundespolizei/GSG 9)

Telecommunication has changed significantly within the 50-plus years that have passed since GSG 9's inception. What basically started out as radio and landline communication has become an interwoven network of satellite, air, and ground-based communications and reconnaissance techniques, using live imagery from video and heat cameras obtained by drones and robots. (Bundespolizei/GSG 9)

Jérôme Fuchs, GSG 9 commander (2014–2023). (Bundespolizei/GSG 9)

Robert Hemmerling, GSG 9 commander (2023–time of writing). (Bundespolizei/GSG 9)

Joint para-jump of GSG 9 and YAMAM operatives over the airfield of Fürstenfeldbruck in 2022, in commemoration of the terrorist attacks in Munich in 1972. GSG 9 entertains international exchange programs and tight relations with many countries, but arguably none tighter than with the Israeli special forces. Rooted in GSG 9's inception as a consequence of the disastrous attacks at the Olympic Games leaving 11 Israelis dead in 1972, the ties between YAMAM and German GSG 9 have only grown stronger over the passing decades. (Bundespolizei/GSG 9)

premises, it was already dusk. On the lawn in front of the GSG 9 building, three Puma transport helicopters and a smaller Bell helicopter were waiting, ready to run. Their personal weapons and equipment were hurriedly loaded into the helicopters from the vehicles. Hand grenades and explosives were already stowed on board, as were foam-taped aluminum ladders to reach the aircraft doors. The men jumped in right away, no time to pack clean laundry or to freshen up after the sweaty search operation. All they brought along were a few pieces of clothing from their personal "mission bag," which they had changed into on the ride back to the headquarters. Their so-called "emergency civilian clothes"—jeans, T-shirt, sneakers. As soon as the first helicopter was loaded, it took off in the direction of Cologne Airport, no more than a quick hop. The other helicopters followed at one-minute intervals.

No more than three minutes later, they landed on the military section of the airport right next to a special Lufthansa plane, chartered by the government. A number of BKA people already sat waiting inside, as well as some employees of the Ministry of the Interior and members of the advisory staff of the German government. Weapons and equipment were not stowed in the cargo hold but were strapped to the empty seats. Once on board, Wegener and his men learned that their destination was Cyprus, not Italy, because by the time their Boeing 727 taxied toward the runway at Cologne at around 9:30 p.m., Flight LH-181 had already taken off again from Rome. Minister of the Interior Maihofer had urged the Italians not to let the plane take off under any circumstances. But his Italian counterpart was rather interested in getting rid of the problem as quickly as possible. He had the aircraft refueled and given permission to take off for Larnaca. But that, too, was only to be the first stop on a long odyssey.

A Twisted Glimmer of Hope

The Schleyer family was ignorant of all this. Like most Germans, they had learned about the skyjacking from the radio. Since the government kept to its delaying tactics, son Hanns-Eberhard tried to arrange a ransom handover independently. The RAF had named a Swiss lawyer as an intermediary, so Hanns-Eberhard tried to broker a deal to buy his father's freedom. But again, and again there were problems; again and again the money handover was postponed or aborted, and it appeared as though it was not the terrorists who caused the problem in each instance, but instead government agencies interfering with the transaction. The crisis team was biding their time, whilst for days on end the Schleyers lived in fear for the head of their family.

The kidnapping had been dragging on for over a month. Schleyer had been abducted in early September. Now, it was almost mid-October. For all that time they'd had to watch their husband and dad on the news, sitting in front of the terrorist logo featuring a star and submachine gun, wearing only his underwear, as he made desperate appeals to the German government and, with a petrified expression on his face, held up cardboard signs to the camera: "Prisoner of R.A.F. for 13 days"—"Prisoner of the R.A.F. for 20 days"—"Prisoner of the R.A.F. for 31 days." Now, on the 38th day since the kidnapping, the chances of ever getting to see him alive again were dwindling.

When news of the hijacking of Flight LH-181 reached them—as terrible as it was—son Jörg Schleyer gained new hope. "You have to look at it from the family's point of view. For us, it was almost a positive coincidence because we thought: Now it's impossible that they sacrifice 90 people, now they have to act eventually. That was our great hope." But even the BKA officials with whom they were in constant contact did not know exactly how things would continue. "They said: 'Now, we're curious as well to see what comes of this.' It was extremely nerve-racking, not only because of how long it dragged on, but also because we were completely left in the dark. The back-and-forth between Bonn and [the RAF prisoners in] Stammheim, the way they played tactical games—rightly so, probably—we only found out afterwards how it all went down. For us, the LH-181 kidnapping was the last hope that there might still be an exchange."

The German government, however, maintained the tough stance it had adopted from the outset. In his memoirs, Minister of State Wischnewski details the cabinet deliberations on the first day after the skyjacking: "The federal government could not allow itself to be blackmailed either: it could not release prisoners accused of the murder of 13 people and attempted murder of a further 43 people. On the basis of far-reaching considerations, all those involved agreed that everything possible should be done to rescue the hostages, including the exhaustion of all negotiating options and, if necessary, a police rescue operation. The cabinet took a formal decision on this. A release of the prisoners was not considered."[16] This attitude was not about to change.

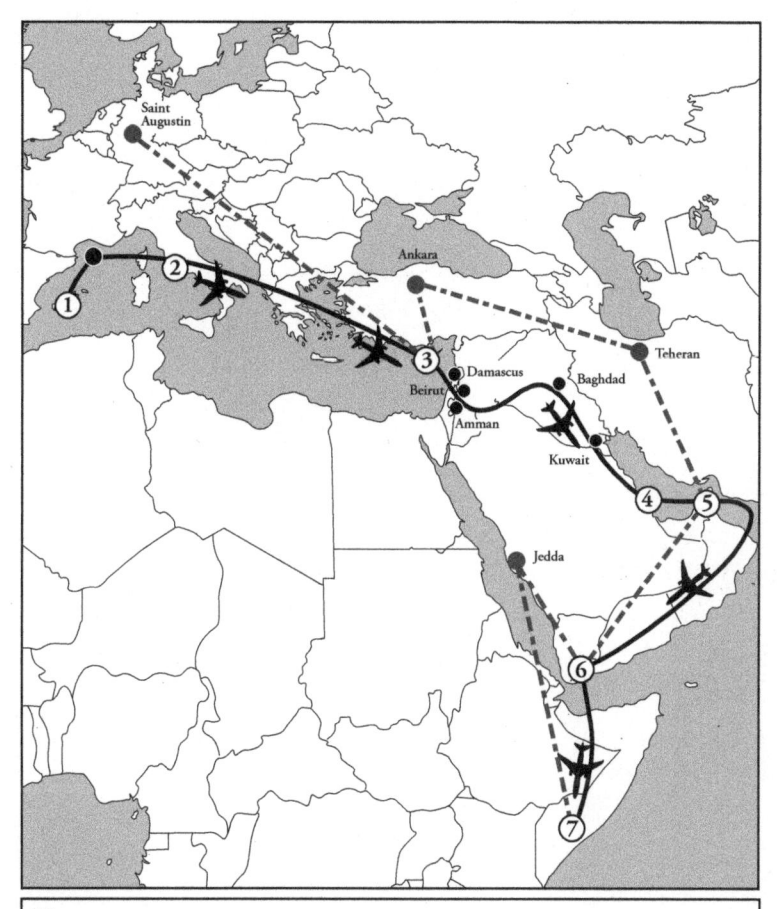

Key

(All time indications in Central European Time CET)

1. **Palma de Majorca**, Thursday, October 13, c. 1:55 p.m.: Takeoff of Lufthansa Boeing 737 *Landshut*, Flight LH-181, destination Frankfurt, with 86 passengers and 5 crew members. Around 2:30 p.m.: Air traffic control in Aix-en-Provence, France, reports that Flight LH-181 is off course.

2. **Rome**, Thursday, October 13, 3:45–5:45 p.m.: The skyjackers present their first demands—release of 11 RAF terrorists from German prisons as well as 2 Palestinain PFLP terrorists from a prison in Istanbul.

3. **Larnaka**, Cyprus, Thursday, October 13, 8:28–10:50 p.m.: Stopover.

4. **Bahrain**, Friday, October 14, 1:52–3:24 a.m.: Stopover after airports in Beirut, Damascus, Amman, Baghdad, and Kuwait refuse to give permission to land.

5. **Dubai**, Friday, October 14, 5:51 a.m.: The *Landshut* lands due to a lack of fuel, despite the airport being officially closed. Sunday, October 16, 12:19 p.m.: After lengthy negotiations and an ultimatum from the skyjackers, Flight LH-181 is refueled and allowed to continue its flight, thus nullifying preparations for a rescue attempt.

6. **Aden**, South Yemen, Sunday, October 16, 3:55 p.m.: Almost out of fuel, the *Landshut* touches down on a sandy taxiway on the edge of the airport since the runway has been blocked by armored vehicles. After a heated exchange, the captain of the *Landshut* is killed by the hijackers. Monday, October 17, 2:02 a.m.: The copilot is forced to get the plane airborne again.

7. **Mogadishu**, Monday, October 17, 4:43 a.m.: The body of the captain of the *Landshut* is handed over to the Somali authorities. The hijackers prepare to blow up the plane. Finally, the German government relents and promises to bring the imprisoned RAF members from Germany to Mogadishu. Tuesday, October 18, 00:05 a.m.: GSG 9 executes Operation *Feuerzauber* (Fire Magic).

— Flight path of Lufthansa Flight LH-181 *Landshut*
- - - Flight path of GSG 9 aircraft pursuing the *Landshut*

The *Landshut* odyssey: the route of Lufthansa Flight LH-181 and the German government aircraft that pursued it. (Declan Ingram)

CHAPTER 9

Odyssey to Africa

It was the final approach to Larnaka International Airport, just before midnight, when "Flight control suspiciously asked about who was on board." The pilot anxiously turned around to Commander Wegener on the jump seat behind him: "I told them: German experts. You guys had better pack away your violin cases."[1] In a hurry, the men threw blankets and jackets over the gun cases and ladders and pulled down the sunscreens in front of their windows. They could not count on a warm welcome. They were traveling on behalf of the German government, albeit in non-military aircraft, but few countries keep their cool when they find out that a horde of foreign police armed to the teeth is dropping into their territory without authorization. On the island of Cyprus, just divided into a Greek south and a Turkish-occupied north, they were not to expect anything different.

Not long after their plane had parked, a Cypriot officer in breeches showed up in the doorway: the chief of police of the former British part of the island, as it turned out. Wegener talked to him briefly, calmly, officer to officer. At a measured pace, the Cypriot inspected the rows of seats, tapping his officer's baton on a box here, on a ladder there, asking Wegener again and again what it was all about. Each time, Wegener explained in the most casual manner: "General logistics, equipment, just stuff one takes along." Eventually, the man took a long look at Wegener, gave him a broad grin, turned around and strolled out the door, past Dieter Fox. "He probably knew exactly what was going on. He also knew there was a police force on board. But he didn't want to lift anything up, because in the end he didn't care. We would leave anyway." He was sure of that because Flight LH-181, nicknamed the *Landshut*, had taken off again just before the German governmental aircraft landed. This time it was heading in the direction of the Persian Gulf.

What to do? The order from Bonn came in soon enough: Return to Cologne immediately. As soon as they were airborne, however, they received a new order: Ankara, Turkey. This was not the destination of Flight LH-181, but the locale of two of the prisoners the hijackers had demanded to be released. So Wegener and the employees of the Ministry of the Interior were asked to obtain information from the Turkish government about its stance on the kidnapping. In Ankara, Wegener learned that Turkey intended to stay out of the matter entirely. They also had no objection to a German rescue operation. What was to happen to the two prisoners remained an open issue, as was the GSG 9 team's next move. For the time being, their aircraft remained parked on the apron.

They waited. Wegener was dissatisfied. And they were kaput, thoroughly exhausted, like everyone else. By now it was Saturday morning, October 15. They had been on their feet for over 48 hours, had not had anything decent to eat since the mission started at the Cologne Uni-Center, and hardly any sleep. None of them knew what would happen next. As a distraction, Wegener ordered a rota of weapons checks and tactical exercises: "It was bad for my unit to just sit around and wait. That's the last thing you want to do as GSG 9 men in a situation like that. I finally gave the order to my second-in-command and my adjutant: 'Do something. Keep yourselves busy in a meaningful way.' To the unit commander I indicated, 'Schedule any on-duty subjects of your choice.' 'Ok, then we'll do a workout,' he suggested. That was a good idea."[2] Wegener talked to a Turkish commander he was in touch with, then announced, "We're playing volleyball and soccer against the Turks." Within no time, they whipped up a small tournament on the sports field of an army barracks near the airport. It served its purpose: blowing off steam. The results were fairly even: The Germans won in soccer, the Turks in volleyball.

It was already late in the year, but even now, in mid-October, the Anatolian sun was still burning down on them, which was not exactly conducive to general body hygiene. Recalling the unpleasant circumstances, Dieter Fox says, "Of course you sweat. We were then allowed into the barracks quarters to freshen up a bit. Taking a shower was out of the question, though, the washrooms were abominable. So we used some of the deodorant we had on board, somewhat tempering the intense odor."

However, hygienic conditions proved to be the least of their problems: That same evening, nine-year-old Sylvia was sitting in front of the television: "Look Mom, that's Daddy walking there!" she crowed enthusiastically. The footage showed Werner Heimann and his comrades. A television crew had tracked them down and filmed them on their way to the terminal to have lunch. In parallel, Turkish radio reported the "presence of a platoon of German soldiers."[3] Their plane was parked in the military section of the airport, but not particularly shielded from public view. So after the 8:00 p.m. "Tagesschau" news, the entire German nation knew that GSG 9 had taken up the pursuit of the *Landshut*. "That was when our families found out where we were," Heimann explains.

For the German government, this was a PR disaster. And an additional threat to the security of the hostages. The Turkish government also started to exert pressure. It decided it did not want any foreign special forces on its soil after all, be it military or police. Thus, the crisis staff in Bonn immediately ordered GSG 9 back to Germany. For the men this meant a huge disappointment, Werner Heimann says. "We didn't want to believe that at all. We only learned why we were called back well after the fact." But Wegener was not going to give up that easily. He had a telephone line established to Bonn and for the first time spoke to Helmut Schmidt personally. Then he summoned his people: "The chancellor has decided: This Boeing 727 will return to Bonn with a large part of GSG 9." However, the head of government had agreed that Wegener and a small staff of experienced people were to continue following the *Landshut* in order to be in position to plan further steps and be prepared whenever GSG 9 was needed. Who would go with him? His adjutant, Frieder Baum, of course. "And Fox," Wegener said crisply, "you're coming along, too!" At first, Dieter Fox was taken aback: "That didn't make much sense to me. But then I told myself: Okay, three is better than none. At least we will be there on the ground; we can gather intelligence and pass it on as the situation unfolds."

Soon, the government plane took off for Germany. Meanwhile, Wegener, Fox and Baum transferred to a small 12-seater business jet of the Bundesnachrichtendienst,* which had been sent to Ankara, bringing three BKA criminal investigators and four government employees of the Ministry of the Interior. Their destination: Iran. "Nobody could make any sense of that," Fox said. "But that was Wischnewski's wish: Fly to Tehran and find out what the Persians think about the whole matter." The minister of state at the Foreign Office, too, was about to travel to the region as the government's intermediary.

The reception in Iran was frosty; or rather, there was no reception at all. No government representative was present to welcome them. At least they received permission from the airport personnel to use a room in the terminal where Coca-Cola was available. There, Wegener and two German government officials spoke briefly with the airport commander, who made it clear that they would stay out of it and would certainly not let the hijacked plane land if it showed up on radar. After an hour, the delegation left without having achieved anything. In the meantime, it had become known that Flight LH-181 had arrived at Dubai airport, having been denied landing permission in Beirut, Damascus, Amman, and Kuwait.

Minister of State Wischnewski was also on his way to Dubai with further instructions from the German chancellor—and with a suitcase containing 10 million Deutschmarks just in case an opportunity opened up to buy the hostages' freedom. Obtaining this kind of money, however, had proven somewhat difficult. Everything needed to be done with due process, hostage situation or not. This was Germany, after all, wrote Wischnewski in his memoirs: "Getting 10 million Marks on a Friday afternoon in Bonn is not so easy, even in exceptional circumstances. The dutiful state secretary in the Ministry of Finance asked about the [written] cabinet resolution. There was none. But trusting cooperation led to a result after all."[4] Of course, Hans-Jürgen Wischnewski was known for delivering results.

---

* Bundesnachrichtendienst (BND) = Federal Intelligence Service.

By this time, Wischnewski had already made a name for himself as the "nation's fireman," keeping excellent contacts in the Maghreb region as well as in the entire Middle East, and playing evenly with all sides, Palestinian as well as Israeli. Chancellor Willy Brandt had therefore christened him "Ben Wisch," a nickname that stuck, even as he became part of Helmut Schmidt's "kitchen cabinet." Wischnewski had already been sent on delicate missions to Amman, Algiers, Tunis, Damascus, and Jerusalem in the past. He had also gained experience as an international crisis manager in skyjacking when in 1970 Palestinian terrorists hijacked three civilian airplanes to Amman with German hostages on board.

Just before getting on the plane to Dubai, he had returned from an extensive tour of the Middle and Far East. On behalf of the chancellor, he had combed a number of countries that the RAF prisoners had named as their preferred destinations: Algeria, Libya, Iraq, South Yemen, and finally Vietnam. His official assignment was finding out whether these countries would accept the RAF prisoners. In actual fact, Wischnewski was sent there with the exact opposite intent: persuading the respective governments not to accept them. The West German government never intended to exchange the hostages. It was all part of their strategy of buying time. Wischnewski was supposed to be the one to do the buying, a delicate and exhausting task for the diplomat. But it paled compared to the task that lay ahead of him. It was to become "probably the most difficult mission in my life," he would confess later.[5] Wischnewski took a helicopter from Bonn to Frankfurt, accompanied by a small team of advisers, and went from there by government plane to the United Arab Emirates, where he arrived just before midnight and immediately set up a landline to Bonn.

The Volunteers from the Red Cross

The Boeing 727 with GSG 9 forces on board landed in Cologne in the late afternoon of October 15, 1977. After the PR disaster in Ankara, the Ministry of the Interior had made sure that press and television were aware of their return. "Mission aborted," they were told demonstratively. However, the men already knew that they would be taking off again in a few hours, which again the press was not supposed to know.

The next morning, the posts at the main gate in Saint Augustin reported a trove of press photographers and TV crews that had set up their cameras in front of the headquarters. Thus, Dieter Tutter, as the unit leader in charge, told part of the dedicated units to scatter onto a great number of trucks. He then had them fan out from the main gate in all directions, accompanied by several emergency vehicles and empty trucks, creating as much confusion as possible among the reporters. The drivers were told to take long detours to get to the military section of Cologne Airport. Another group was flown by helicopter in a large arc to the airport. In the event that anyone approached them they were told to present their cover story: they were a Red Cross Relief Committee. The fact that this group of humanitarian aid workers consisted exclusively of young, athletic men in jeans and T-shirts meant it would not necessarily be a watertight story. But they didn't need it. Tutter's tactics worked, and the two units arrived at their plane undisclosed. They were ordered to redeploy to the Mediterranean, to be closer to the action, whenever they were needed. To this end, they had received permission to set up a base at the NATO airbase on Crete.

On their flight, Werner Heimann and his fellow SET leaders pored over the plans of the hijacked Boeing 737. For just such a case, GSG 9 kept detailed drawings of all aircraft types operated by Lufthansa. It was crucial for a successful storming that the task forces knew exactly what the aircraft looked like inside: the number and location of exits, galleys, on-board toilets, number of seats per row. Did the aircraft have one or two aisles? What was the layout of first and business class seating? If they had to get oriented once they entered, it would cost them vital seconds, and overlooked corners or hiding places could turn into deadly traps.

As they discussed the details, a steward who had been listening spoke up: "The layouts you have are the master plans. But airlines order the interior outfit of the planes according to their respective preferences, and in the *Landshut* there is a toilet on the left front." This was not shown on the blueprint Werner Heimann had brought along, so Heimann expressed that "it later turned out to be a stroke of luck that we got this information. For when we finally entered the plane, this was one of the decisive factors."

Afterwards, at cruising altitude, Heimann gave theoretical instruction on aircraft reconnaissance and aircraft assault to his men and some of the Lufthansa staff on board. Otherwise, there was not too much for them to do. At times, the atmosphere turned into something of a high school field trip. Some passed the time by playing cards, others by betting on which of them would be the ones to rescue one of the beauty queens. For word was that there was a group of young ladies on board Flight LH-181 who had taken part in a beauty pageant in a discotheque in Palma de Majorca. (This rumor would turn out to be correct.)

Others withdrew and indulged their thoughts. Jörg Probstmeier was one of them. At 21, he was the second youngest in the group and, according to his own description, somewhat of a quiet sort ("more the lemonade type of guy"). After graduating from high school, he had applied to the Border Guard, completed his training and joined GSG 9 in May 1975. Now, two years later, he looked out the window as they were crossing the Alps and wondered what destiny had in store for him. In the weeks after the Schleyer kidnapping, Probstmeier had hoped for a nonviolent solution. Even now, he would prefer not to be called to action. Not because he wanted to avoid it, but because of fundamental considerations: "Of course we are trained for this. But prevention is always preferable to a violent solution. My greatest wish was that, with negotiating skills, it would be possible to avoid this deployment of GSG 9—although in the end it was good for our reputation that it came to pass."

Dangerous Grenades

At the same time, in Saint Augustin, Acting Commander Dieter Tutter had no time for such contemplation. He had received another assignment. In several telephone conversations with Chancellor Schmidt, British Prime Minister James Callaghan had offered support to the Germans. That was gratifying, the only question being what form the support might take. Since Commander Wegener, his deputy, and most of the staff were on their way, it was up to Tutter to find out. So he took a flight to London that same night, along with the head of the foreign policy office at the Chancellery. An ad hoc staff of representatives from the foreign and defense ministries, intelligence services, Arab experts, and the ambassador of the United Arab Emirates were waiting for them at the seat of the UK government, 10 Downing Street. Prime Minister Callaghan was stuck on a visit to East Anglia due to foggy weather conditions, so the session was chaired by the undersecretary of defence. Right off the bat he offered every diplomatic, logistic and technical help the Germans would need, even support from their own task forces.[6]

The Germans were thankful, given the situation had turned out to be quite complicated. In Dubai, Flight LH-181 was sitting on the apron in the sun. The scene on board had gotten rather calamitous; the hygienic circumstances had started to get nasty. Emissary Wischnewski had arrived in the meantime and negotiations were underway, but the situation was extremely tense. The hijackers made no concessions, not even to requests that they at least release the children among the hostages. On the other end, dealing with the Dubai government was turning out to be tricky for the Germans. The assessment of the UK staff in London was that Dubai authorities would probably not object to a police operation, but would not leave it to German forces alone. They would insist on a joint execution.

In that case, they suggested two agents of the SAS might be of help, who were also present at the meeting: Major Alastair Morrison and Sergeant Barry Davies. The British traditionally maintained excellent contacts and a strong military presence in the sheikdom, so the SAS men offered maps and logistical expertise. After some thought as to how the operation might unfold, Tutter asked: "Don't you guys have those new stun grenades?" Tutter had heard about the British invention. With bright flashes and loud detonations, these so-called "flash bangs" were supposed to distract, blind and ideally incapacitate the enemy. Going by the military name G60, they basically were fireworks on steroids used to gain a tactical advantage by disorienting and stunning the opposing side long enough to take them out. The British reacted enthusiastically: "Yes, of course! You've got to have these, they're the perfect tool when entering the airplane." With this, the matter was settled. "Great! You guys give us technical support and show us how to use them."

The next day, Davies and Morrison made a stopover in Cologne on their way to Dubai. They got off the plane, each with a rucksack on their back and a small case in their hands. "What, that's all you've brought along?" an astonished Tutter asked as he welcomed them. "It's a quarter of the world's production," came the reply. "Well, let's see how they work," Tutter decreed.

In order to test the new grenades in the most realistic setting possible, he guided them into an underground nuclear bunker on the barracks grounds in Saint Augustin. In one of the corridors, he had some of his people placed in door niches. He had the lights turned off and asked his guests to detonate one of the grenades. "And then all hell broke loose. It was popping, smoking, hissing, fire everywhere, and I shouted, 'Lights on, lights on!' It was all black with smoke. Someone yelled, 'I'm on fire!'" One of the countless firecrackers that made up the grenade had exploded on one man's uniform trousers, which had caught fire and had to be put out. Tutter was not amused: "'Guys, have you ever tried this in an airplane?' No, of course not. They hadn't stormed an airplane yet, after all, and they had never been used in any other way, either."

Tutter sent the two on their way but made sure they brought along a note for Wegener: "To the commander, the two comrades from the SAS know their way around Dubai and will be of great help to you with their knowledge. Regarding what they bring along: *don't use it on the plane!*" In Dubai, Wegener would test the effect of the stun grenades again in an aircraft hangar and decide that they could only be used in the open, if at all. An entirely different matter was the new, lighter bulletproof vests, which the SAS people had thankfully also brought along in their luggage. They would come in quite handy.

Crash Course in Aircraft Storming

The small business jet with Wegener, Fox and Baum on board had landed in Dubai on the late afternoon of Sunday, October 15. Emissary Wischnewski received them, visibly annoyed: "Jeez, they don't want to play ball, they won't give GSG 9 permission to storm."[7] In its morning meeting, the large crisis staff in Bonn had determined that they should "work toward the liberation of the hostages in the hijacked Lufthansa plane—by force if necessary."[8] Since the night before, the *Landshut* had been parked at a quiet end of the airport, surrounded by armed military and medical units, where it was receiving emergency care. At first, Dubai government officials seemed open to the suggestion of a GSG 9 operation.[9] But as soon as the young defense minister of the United Arab Emirates (UAE) arrived at the scene, the official position changed considerably.

From the air traffic control tower, 29-year-old Sheikh Mohammed Bin Rashid Al Maktum conducted negotiations with the hijackers. The son of the Dubai regent was able to speak to the hijackers in their native language and he coordinated his actions "correctly" with Wischnewski, as the latter noted in his memoirs. He received Wegener, Fox and Baum in a distinctively polite and friendly manner for the briefing. In an equally friendly and polite manner he explained that he would under no circumstances allow a foreign power to carry out an operation on his soil. "Everything that happens here is done by us. I conduct the negotiations and I make the decisions on behalf of my father. If a military operation is deemed necessary, my soldiers will take over." The German delegation was horrified. "Of course, that was a blow to us," says Dieter Fox, "because we told ourselves: If this goes wrong, there will be lots of casualties. Wegener tried everything; Wischnewski also intervened. No chance."

The next morning, the Sheikh's attitude had not changed. He insisted that his own Rangers were to carry out the operation, if necessary, led by a number of British SAS and SBS[*] officers. He said to Wegener, "You can see to it that my paratroopers are trained accordingly." Wegener replied with a sigh: "Don't imagine it's that easy."[10] The Sheik's troupe had never rehearsed such a scenario before. The skills Wegener's people had practiced intensively for years, over and over, they were now supposed to teach their Arab comrades in just a few hours. Nevertheless, Wegener agreed to train the Dubaian special airborne assault unit.

At least, the external conditions in Dubai seemed better than anywhere else in the Middle East. The surrounding dunes offered visual protection, and the British were well networked and could provide support. After landing, Wegener had confidently said: "Here we could make it work." He pointed to a parked Gulf Air Boeing 737. "Fox, there's a plane over there. Show them how penetration works." Fox did as he was told. "The plane was parked outside behind a hangar, the sun beaming straight down on it. I touched the hull's skin: you could have fried eggs on it, that's how hot it was." Fox had the gangway come up and led the Dubai and British inside: "There's the lavatory, there's the checkroom, the galleys, there's the business class, then another lavatory, another checkroom ...—take a look, 10 minutes, then we'll do the first pass."

While the aircraft storm trainees were familiarizing themselves with the interior of the aircraft, Peter Heldt, head of Lufthansa's 737 fleet, joined the group. He accompanied Wischnewski as part of his entourage and pointed out a key detail to Fox, similar to what Werner Heimann and his comrades had learned on their flight: "The 737 here is a different version than the *Landshut*."—"Say what?"—"Yes, everything is reversed: where the *Landshut*'s dressing room is on the right in the direction of flight, here it is on the left and the lavatory is on the right." Fox was thunderstruck. "Oh, dear, what do we do now?"—"You'll have to explain that to them. They'll have to rethink everything if they're actually going into the *Landshut*."—"They can hardly find their way around this specimen! How am I supposed to explain to

---

[*] SBS (Special Boat Service) = Special task force of the Royal Navy. The naval equivalent of the British Special Forces unit SAS.

them that they have to flip their thinking, that everything is laterally reversed? This is going to be a disaster!"

Wegener reported the situation to the Sheik. But he stuck to his decision: "Our people will be the ones to do it. Keep going, keep training," the Sheik reiterated. Fox explained the silent approach from the back of the plane with aluminum ladders; he explained that the ladders had to be taped beforehand so they would not rattle or slip; that two men carried one ladder at a time, but only one right at the plane; that it was nevertheless put on by two; how they then had to get into position; how the door was opened quickly and silently; how two dive down under the door, then up again to slip into the plane ... "That was already too much. The approach was still okay—the whole thing of course observed by the Dubaians. The English were top fit and also hot for it. The problem was the local Rangers, they kept hesitating. Afterwards someone explained to me why. They considered the Palestinians their brothers. The hesitation was less about being able to do it than their doubts about the situation: 'I might have to kill one of my brothers.' If it had come to that, it could have nullified the operation."

Fox received the order to continue anyway—approach, positioning at all entrances, penetration. "That went completely wrong. They couldn't open the little door above the wing. They got the other doors open. But it took much too much time! The swinging of the door over the heads of the team, who have to drop that little bit when they stand on the ladder, and then the immediate entry into the plane—that's fractions of a second! It just didn't work. When they finally got inside they didn't know what positions to take. They were running all over the place, right through the lines of fire of their comrades. I just threw my hands up in horror."

Wegener ordered another attempt. Then another. And another. Fox despaired: "The more they practiced, the more insecurity got the better of them. After a while it went a little better, but I had a feeling this wasn't going to work; it was going to go wrong." Wegener reported the dismal result to the Sheik and tried again to dissuade him from the idea of sending his Rangers to the *Landshut*. Wischnewski also pleaded with him; even Helmut Schmidt had intervened in the meantime. In a lengthy telephone conversation, the chancellor had talked to the head of state of the UAE, Sheikh Zayed Bin Sultan Al Nahyan, and tried to get him to agree to a GSG 9 operation. Somewhat cloaked, he offered "that additional security experts would be sent from Germany to Dubai if he, Sheikh Zayed, agreed." Allowing the hijacked plane to take off, on the other hand, would "certainly cause the death of all passengers."[11]

The talks were in vain. Sheikh Zayed took a still harder stance. He insisted that there should be no bloodshed in his country. Defense Minister Sheikh Mohammed soon followed this line. No special force operation at all, either by GSG 9 or by the Dubaians. Wegener was frustrated: "It didn't work because they didn't want it to. They were only interested in one thing: getting rid of the *Landshut*."[12]

Who Are the Hijackers?

Meanwhile, the situation in the hijacked aircraft was becoming increasingly precarious. During the night, the auxiliary power unit (APU) supplying the onboard systems with electricity had failed. As a result, the air conditioning system also failed, and radio communications were cut off. It was not until dawn that Lufthansa employees were given permission to slide an emergency generator under the aircraft, only minutes before the fuselage would have turned into a furnace in the desert sun. But even with air conditioning, temperatures inside the *Landshut* had become intolerable, the air thick and heavy. The situation on board was abysmal. Apart from the psychological stress of being under a relentless threat of death by the terrorists, the passengers had to put up with atrocious and humiliating sanitary conditions. There were only two toilets for over 90 people, and the terrorists allowed the hostages to use them only sporadically. Nevertheless, feces piled up in the washrooms over time until the toilets could only be used standing up.

As a consequence, people were forced to wet and soil their seats. Freshening up, let alone washing, after days of being squeezed in the aircraft was out of the question. In addition, the hijackers had taken away the hostages' hand luggage and therefore their medication, in particular young women's birth control pills, which is why many of them started getting their periods on the plane. The hijackers seemed to care little. They demanded that the *Landshut* be refueled. Otherwise, they would first shoot Captain Schumann and two passengers, then another hostage every five minutes. It was only at the last minute that Dubai's defense minister ordered the tankers to be brought forward, easing the situation.

Around noon, the terrorist leader, who called himself "Captain Martyr Mahmoud," radioed: "By now, FRG had 60 hours to do something. Now the time is almost up! I point out that I and my team will have no responsibility for the victims! Helmut Schmidt has the responsibility for everything that is happening here. He has not reacted yet. Now there is not a second left. We will execute all passengers and crew. We have given you enough time, but you have not reacted! We will set a sign for later times. We will blow up the plane before we reach the next airport. This is Captain Mahmoud speaking!"[13] The threat was taken very seriously. Captain Mahmoud left no doubt about his determination. He rejected all efforts to compromise, including Wischnewski's offer to come on board himself as a hostage in exchange for the passengers. Captain Mahmoud coolly responded that they were not interested in "representatives of imperialist, fascist Germany." The leader of the hostage-takers was obviously trained and well prepared for his role. But who, exactly, was he? And who were "my team"?

Up to this point, it was still not clear who exactly the Germans were dealing with. Even the information that there were four hijackers had not been established for long beyond doubt. Early on, there had been suspicion that it was two male and two female terrorists. But it took days to actually confirm this quintessential information.[14] Captain Schumann had sent out several radio messages containing the number four, one of them talking about two different daily newspapers, the other about cigarette brands. Finally, he managed to have two cigarillos and two cigarettes smuggled out with the trash that were conspicuously tied together. That seemed to settle the matter. But who were they, what nationality, and part of what terrorist faction?

Judging by the ultimatum to the German government, Palestinians were apparently involved. At first, the government suspected that Germans were also part of the commando, as had been the case at Entebbe one year earlier. In a telephone conversation with British Prime Minister Callaghan, Chancellor Schmidt spoke of two Germans and two Arab hijackers, and a day later even of three Germans and one Palestinian.[15] Three days after the start of the hijacking, the identity of the terrorists remained unclear. But this information was of paramount importance if a rescue operation was to be successful, as Munich 1972 had dreadfully shown. Something had to be done about it. And soon, too, since Wischnewski believed he could make out clear signs of fatigue among the hijackers. Reconnaissance was vital.

Shortly after their arrival in Dubai, Wegener had said to his two companions: "See to it that we get some information about the plane." This was not without danger. Two Lufthansa employees who had approached the aircraft in a rather clumsy fashion during the night had returned shaken, their faces waxy and pale. They had been shot at from the plane. Nevertheless, Adjutant Baum, disguised in a Lufthansa uniform, managed to get close to the *Landshut* along with a supply crew and was able to take some photos of the terrorists standing in the open aircraft door. British intelligence eventually was able to tell them who they were dealing with: The leader of the hijackers, Captain Mahmoud, was identified as Zohair Youssif Akache. He was no stranger to the British, having been considered the prime suspect in the murder of the former head of the North Yemeni government, his wife and a diplomat in London six months earlier.

Captain Mahmoud seemed to be acting unpredictably. In the past few hours, he had repeatedly made radio calls, shouted incomprehensible things into his microphone, and several times threatened to blow up the plane if his demands were not fulfilled immediately. Only moments later, he would speak calmly and seemed amenable to reasoning. No one knew exactly what was happening on board, but his erratic behavior did not bode well. Not much was known about the other three at the time, apart from the fact that they were apparently also Palestinian. But it was clear that the group were doing the hijacking on behalf of their German RAF friends as part of the international terror joint venture that had been established in the years after Munich.

After their failed attempt to give untrained forces a crash course in how-to-storm-an-airplane, Frieder Baum and Dieter Fox waited outside a hangar and took a deep breath.

Inside, Britons and Dubaians were lying on planks resting or cleaning their weapons. It was around 3:00 p.m. when they heard the roaring engines of a passenger plane taking off. Moments later, they watched Flight LH-181 passing by and sailing into the sky. At first, they did not quite know whether they were supposed to be happy or sad: "I said to Frieder: 'The good thing is that the operation did not happen with these guys. The bad thing is that the *Landshut* is gone again. But at least, everyone is still alive for now.' I am still convinced that if the Dubai forces had gone in, there would have been many, many casualties. And so was Wegener. So all things considered, we were quite relieved that didn't happen."

And the Dubaians were glad to be rid of the problem. Right before the Palestinians carried out their threat and began shooting hostages, Dubai's defense minister had given in, despite the German government's insistence that "the plane be prevented from continuing its flight, even at the cost of the possible loss of individual lives."[16] So on Sunday afternoon, October 16, Flight LH-181 was on its way again, more than three days after being skyjacked. What would be the destination this time? It was guesswork among the German delegation. Wischnewski was convinced they would go for an Arab country. Wegener replied, "That may well be, but the Arab countries have all made it clear that they do not want the aircraft. They all see the difficulties that are associated with it in the Arab League. South Yemen might be a possibility, but it would be fundamentally difficult [for us], because they have a Communist government."[17] Before long, the *Landshut* appeared over the Yemeni capital Aden, after being rejected in the Sultanate of Oman. But here they were not welcome either. The government refused permission to land and blocked the runway with armored vehicles. This created an existential threat for the *Landshut*. The aircraft had not been fully refueled in Dubai; the Sheikh had only allowed a small quantity of fuel to be sent out to the plane for humanitarian reasons so that the APU could keep working—the small auxiliary engine that powered onboard systems like air conditioning, light and communications. It was not nearly enough to keep the *Landshut* in the air for a long-distance flight. Hence, the tanks were almost empty over Aden and no other airport was in range. Only a few minutes before they ran out of fuel, co-pilot Jürgen Vietor descended the aircraft in a breakneck operation onto a sandy track next to the blocked runway. There it now sat, and it was unclear whether the landing gear had survived the touchdown.

Half an hour later, the German government team also took off for Aden along with the two SAS officers whom Wischnewski had invited to come along. Wegener, Fox and Baum were glad to be able to move with their extensive gear from the cramped business plane into the spacious, almost empty Boeing 707. The long-haul aircraft usually held up to 180 passengers, but barely two dozen seats were occupied by ministry and agency staff. Here, they were at least able to wash their sweaty clothes: "We soaked our socks in the small on-board sink and then hung them somewhere to dry. But it didn't really work because the plane had no heating but only the air conditioning which was cooling the interior down. So we put the moist stuff back on, because that's all we brought along." Typically, the officers' standby bag contained clothes for a day or two: two pairs of socks, three T-shirts, one or two dress shirts, a second pair of pants, a jacket, hat and gloves. But three and a half days had already passed since they had started their shift at the Cologne Uni-Center. In Dubai, the chief stewardess had offered to shop for replacement socks, button-down shirts, and T-shirts at the airport's duty-free store. However, fresh underpants were no substitute for a decent shower. And the cologne from the aircraft's washrooms only scantily covered their odor: "The three of us smelt like baboons," Fox admits.

Death of a Pilot

After the emergency touchdown of the *Landshut* in Aden, the Yemeni government closed the entire airspace over its territory, so Wischnewski and the German delegation were not allowed to land. Relations between West Germany and the People's Democratic Republic of Yemen were not at their best anyway. Socialist East Germany and the Soviet Union were in a better position. State Secretary Wischnewski radioed Bonn to get in touch with East Berlin and Moscow in order to find out whether they were willing to intervene with their "socialist brother state." Foreign Minister Genscher himself got on the phone, although he and his GDR colleague, Oskar Fischer, otherwise were not on the best speaking terms. In the meantime, the 707 was flying holding patterns along the border of South Yemen.

After a few hours, they ran out of fuel, so they had to look for an alternative destination: Jeddah. Wischnewski chose the Kingdom of Saudi Arabia because he wanted to know how the Saudis felt about the hijacking and to enlist their support if possible. However, the communications there proved to be extremely difficult, so far removed from the events. "We always had to rely on what the Yemeni forces on the ground told us. That wasn't all that much," Commander Wegener recalled later. "Yemen was a difficult negotiating partner and we were very skeptical." The group briefly discussed flying to South Yemen in a smaller plane or even traveling by car. But the prospect of 1,500 kilometers of desert roads did not strike them as particularly tempting, and given the uncertain situation they soon abandoned these ideas. Helplessness spread within the group.

While the German delegation was still deliberating, a message arrived from Lufthansa's crisis staff in Frankfurt, which had been in permanent radio contact with Flight LH-181 since the beginning of the ordeal: There had been an altercation in Aden. Captain Schumann managed to get the hijackers' OK for stepping out and checking the landing gear. This took longer than expected.[*] Upon his return, Captain

---

[*] Up to the present day, it remains unclear why Captain Schumann took so long when he inspected the landing gear. There were rumors about him attempting to get in touch with the Yemeni forces that were positioned around the aircraft. Others suggested that he wanted to flee but then changed his mind. None of these possibilities have been supported by any solid evidence.

Mahmoud accused him of having broken his promise, made him kneel in the aisle, punched him several times in the face, and finally killed him with a shot in the head in front of all the passengers. The hijackers then forced co-pilot Jürgen Vietor to take off again after the *Landshut* had been refueled. It was October 17, 2:00 a.m.

The murder of Captain Schumann changed the situation dramatically. So far, the hijackers had acted ruthlessly and brutally at times, but nobody had been killed. The shooting of the aircraft's pilot was a vivid demonstration of their deadly determination and a strong message that they were not willing to play any games. The stakes got higher as time progressed, but the question remained: Where to next? Somalia, Wegener surmised, considering the range of the aircraft. He recalled the Israeli operation in Entebbe he witnessed a year earlier. There they had learned that Palestinian extremists were running training camps in Somalia and that the PLO* operated an office in Mogadishu staffed with 60 people. At the time, it was even suspected that the East African country had a hand in the hijacking of the Air France plane to Entebbe.

As a matter of fact, two and a half hours later, Flight LH-181 touched down at Mogadishu international Airport. Wischnewski contacted Bonn and came back with the order to follow the *Landshut* once again, one last time. As the Boeing 707 carrying the German delegation took off from Jeddah, Wischnewski muttered, "If nothing happens in Mogadishu we'll fly back; then the issue is done for us."

Somalia did not come as a great surprise to the German government. The destitute state on the Horn of Africa had already been mentioned in the terrorists' first communication as a possible host country for the RAF prisoners. Bonn had immediately contacted Mogadishu, and the Somali government had declared that it would not accept either the RAF prisoners or the *Landshut* hijackers. This was a good sign. But Somalia was also a major war zone, ruled by President Siad Barre, a former army officer who had swept to power and now was head of what is commonly known as a dictatorship. Ethnic conflicts had been smoldering in the country for decades, as well as border disputes with Kenya, Djibouti, and Ethiopia. Since the summer of 1977, violence had flared up again—a fire on which the superpowers in the East–West conflict poured kindling. The situation was therefore, again, complicated.

For many years, the country had been hanging on the drip-feed of the Soviet Union. Just recently, however, the government had made a turn toward the West. At least, it more than hinted at this a few weeks earlier during a "fact-finding mission" by Genscher's Chief of Planning Staff Klaus Kinkel. Somalia's departure from the Eastern Bloc was "more advanced than we would have thought possible," Kinkel reported at home.[18] However, the uniformed head of state was primarily interested in the supply of weapons for his various skirmishes. Neither the Federal Republic of

---

★ PLO = Palestine Liberation Organization.

Germany nor any other Western state was eager to support him. But the German government could not afford to be picky in its choice for help in this situation.

In a special session, the cabinet decided to free the hostages in Mogadishu in agreement with the Somali government, if possible by GSG 9 forces. Chancellor Schmidt had suggested as much to the Somali ambassador in Bonn, albeit in diplomatically cloaked terms. He asked "to convey to the Somali government his urgent request that the hijacked plane be prevented from taking off from Mogadishu airport. The Somali government could count on help from the German side if it requested it. A plane with German police specialists could be in Mogadishu in about six hours if the Somali government so desired. But it could also proceed on its own.... The ambassador was then told that the police specialists on their way to Djibouti were specially trained to free hijacked aircraft."[19]

The detour via Djibouti was necessary because it was initially unclear whether they would be given permission to land in Mogadishu. Schmidt sweetened the request for help with the prospect that this would "determine our behavior toward Somalia in the long term. Somalia could then count on all help from the German side." The Somali ambassador got the hint and promised to pass on the German request immediately.

"Mr. Wegener's Friends"

The welcome for the German delegation was nonetheless something between frosty and outright hostile as it arrived in Mogadishu. On approach, Wegener asked the pilot if he could touch down behind the *Landshut*, which was parked a little off to the side. He wanted to get a good look at the plane as they taxied past. However, there was not much to see: the 737 was gleaming in the sun, all the blinds were pulled down, not much else was happening. As soon as they came to a halt at their parking position, Somali officers boarded and collected all their passports. Dieter Fox felt uneasy about this. He knew from previous incidents that it could end badly if your passport is taken away in a country that is not well-disposed towards you: "It meant that they took away our identity. We left our weapons on the plane. Wegener said that if we got off the plane armed, it could get dangerous. Somalia was at war with Ethiopia at the time. This was a highly explosive matter, causing a nervousness which we were yet to experience."[20]

At first, only Minister of State Wischnewski was allowed to leave the plane. The dire atmosphere did not go unnoticed by him: "Tension and distrust were palpable." He was immediately driven to the president's house. "There I tried to use all my powers of persuasion to convey the chancellor's message." State Secretary Heinz Ruhnau had force-fed it to him on the phone, but for fear of foreign ears on the unsecured line, he had encrypted the message: Wischnewski was authorized to offer the Somalis "help in other fields as well. With the exception of the threshold we can't overstep." Wischnewski understood. "Yes, the threshold being that we are not allowed to sell certain things. They are most interested in those things, of course, given their situation. But the means by which you transport such things, we can give them." Eventually, the chancellor himself got on the line, speaking in the same semi-encoded fashion: "Mr. Wegener's friends will soon be reaching the airspace over Djibouti. If your interlocutor decides to invite them, we will let them fly through, otherwise we will let them fly holding patterns. If he does not decide, we will have to let them land in Djibouti."[21]

Thus, Wischnewski did what the Somali president expected him to do: he combined the request for Somali support with the prospect of aid and money if only Barre would let "Mr. Wegener's friends" do their job. To convince the president that Somali sovereignty would be respected, Wischnewski assured him: "Mr. President, if we take prisoners in GSG 9 operation, then of course they are your prisoners." The president asked back in amazement, "You even want to take prisoners on top of things?"[22]

Even though Wischnewski did not receive permission in this conversation to deploy GSG 9, he was able to dismantle some of the lingering mistrust. At least Barre agreed to allow Wegener to speak with the Somali chief of staff, officer to officer. Wegener found him in his airport office, chain-smoking, in front of a blueprint of the Boeing 737. He was visibly overwhelmed by the situation. Asked what his plans were, the general replied in an agitated voice, "I received orders from my president to prepare for the liberation of the aircraft. We are going to storm the aircraft." Wegener tried to keep his composure. "That's really very good and reassuring. Have you ever done anything like this before?"—"No, but we're already practicing on it."—"That is very nice, can you show me?"[23]

The general led Wegener and his two men into a hangar where the presidential plane was parked, a Boeing 720, a variant of the 707. Next to it there waited a squad of army specialists called Somali Rangers. Wegener asked the General: "Now, please demonstrate how you get into the plane with your men. That's the most important thing, after all. You have to get to the hostage takers." So the Rangers got to work. Fox experienced a feeling of déjà vu. Hadn't they been through this very game two days before? But this was no déjà vu; it was worse. "They brought a wooden ladder and two iron ladders, but they were crap, the rungs were rusted through ... They put them in place—and they couldn't get the door open. Not even of their own bird! Wegener said let's try again. So they did. And again, it didn't work, one of them fell off the ladder ...—it was a disaster."

Then Wegener sent out his two people, Baum and Fox. "We took the ladders, these pieces of scrap metal, and went up to the aircraft. I opened the door, we slipped in, wham bang, done." That's when the Somali officer said to Wegener, "Okay, I accept, this is something we can't do. You do it." But of course, the three Germans would not be able to do it alone, the general added. "No, no," said Wegener, "for one, my unit is already on its way here. But also, you can count on us requiring a joint venture with you."

"Joint venture"—the phrase worked wonders. "Try to convince your president that we are doing this together. After all, it must be in his interest to save lives, too." The general nodded and took off to talk to Siad Barre. This was now getting urgent.

Too Young to Die

The situation in the *Landshut* was getting worse by the minute. Right after landing on Monday morning, October 17, Captain Mahmoud had announced by radio to the representative of the "fascist German government" that "at 2 p.m. GMT, 5 p.m. local time, we will blow up the aircraft with all its occupants if our comrades have not arrived here by that time."[24] After this message, the body of murdered Captain Schumann was demonstratively pushed out of the plane via the rear emergency slide. The representative of the "fascist German government" was Michael Libal, the chargé d'affaires of the German embassy in Mogadishu, which otherwise had long been orphaned (German-Somali relations were not at their best indeed). Libal was tasked with maintaining steady radio contact with the hijackers, together with psychologist Wolfgang Salewski. Captain Mahmoud showed no sign of slackening resolve whatsoever. Not toward the Germans, not toward anybody. From Rome, Pope Paul VI proposed himself as an exchange hostage. In a message to the family of the late Captain Schumann, he wrote: "If it is useful, we would offer our own person for the liberation of the hostages. We appeal to the conscience of the hijackers, that they should refrain from this cruel undertaking."[25] The answer from Captain Mahmoud, though, was thundering silence.

Then, one hour before the expiration of the ultimatum, the voice of a German stewardess poured out of the radio speakers. In Wischnewski's 707, Rüdiger von Lutzau sat in his co-pilot's seat and manually recorded the radio traffic as he had been instructed: "We know now that this is the end; we know that we must die. It will be very hard for us, but we will die as bravely as we can. We are all too young to die, even the old among us are too young to die. We only hope one thing: that it will be quick, that there will not be too much pain. But perhaps it is better to die than to live in a world where human lives count for so little, in a world where something like this is possible. Where it is more important to keep nine people in prison than to save the lives of 91 people. Please tell my family that it wasn't that bad. And please tell my friend, his name is Rüdiger von Lutzau, that I loved him very much."

Von Lutzau abruptly stopped writing. It was his fiancée, Gaby Dillmann, who dictated this dramatic appeal to him. He forced himself to continue writing: "I did not know that there were people like this in the German government who are responsible for our death. I hope they can live with this guilt on their conscience."[26] After his fiancée's voice fell silent, von Lutzau got up, staggered out of the cockpit, and had to be given sedative pills by paramedics. Of course, he had been aware that Gaby was on the plane, but this was just too much.

Only much later would he learn what was happening inside the *Landshut* at the same time: the hands of the passengers and crew were being tied behind their backs with ladies' stockings. The hijackers then doused them with high-proof alcohol from the duty-free stock on board, for them to "burn better" when the explosives went off, or so they said. To this end, they planted TNT in several places on the plane and wired it to detonators, including inside the doors. Ten minutes before the deadline, the *Landshut* was set to be blown up, and Captain Mahmoud radioed again, this time in a calm, almost solemn voice: "We, Halime Command, are fighting together with the Somali people against the fascist governments of the world. We are fighting shoulder to shoulder with the Somali people against fascist Ethiopia. We do not want Somali blood to be shed on Somali soil. Please withdraw all soldiers and vehicles because we are about to ignite."[27]

Panic broke out in the Somali government. They could not withdraw their soldiers that quickly. A few seconds before the ultimatum expired, the Somali transport minister persuaded the hijackers to extend the ultimatum by half an hour. Wischnewski had his hands full trying to stay on course: "I had to prevent a Somali officer from giving the order to deploy tanks. That could have led to a terrible bloodbath."[28] Wischnewski instructed the tower to tell the kidnappers that the representative of the German government would shortly make an important announcement. Then Wischnewski talked again to President Barre. He finally gave the go-ahead for the storm by GSG 9. Chancellor Helmut Schmidt had wrung it out of him in another telephone call, barely 10 minutes before the previous ultimatum expired.[29] Wischnewski instructed the German chargé d'affaires, Libal, and the psychologist Salewski in the tower. Their plan was a combination of stall tactics and disinformation.

Captain Mahmoud's voice on the radio sounded demonstratively disinterested. "What is this about? I have already said that I am not negotiating. I am only interested in whether our comrades have been released," he said. The German chargé d'affaires replied, "We have agreed to your demands. The prisoners can be released now and should assemble at Frankfurt airport shortly."—"At last, then. Finally. Have you finally understood? But it's almost too late."—"We are ready to give in to your demands. But it's a long way from here to Germany. We need more time." Libal and Captain Mahmoud agreed to extend the deadline by 10 hours to gather the exchange prisoners and fly them to Mogadishu.

This gave Wegener time to get the aircraft with his men to Mogadishu and prepare for the assault. The command radioed the order to the GSG 9 Boeing 707 over Djibouti: "Okay, so no holding patterns anymore. Fly a little economically, it's no longer most crucial if you arrive 10 minutes earlier, instead the important thing is arriving smoothly in the darkness."—"Okay, understood."—"Land as discreetly as possible. Repeat: land as discreetly as possible."[30] This radio message was about to cause trouble at home. It was intercepted by an Israeli amateur radio operator. Soon enough, Israeli media reported on the plans to storm Flight LH-181, and the French press agency AFP broadcast a message from its Tel Aviv office in its news ticker: "The situation in Mogadishu is very tense. There is a feeling that the situation could change during the night. This was reported on Monday evening by Israeli television. The television also confirms that a West German counterterrorist commando is at the airport in the Somali capital, said to have arrived at around 4:30 p.m. on Monday."[31]

Chancellor Schmidt learned the news from the paper. The daily newspaper *Die Welt* reported the imminent attack in its lead story on the front page the next day. Schmidt raged. Government spokesman Klaus Bölling immediately picked up the phone and lashed out at the paper's editor in chief: "Guys, are you bonkers? Just imagine if some Arab buys your paper at the train station and informs the kidnappers. Even the gentlemen from the opposition here in the crisis team are outraged!" Then Schmidt himself took over the phone and threatened the man with "dire consequences if he did not immediately collect all the newspapers."[32] Which he promptly did.

The editor had his distributors spread out and pick up the copies that had already been delivered at all available sales points in the capital. This was an unprecedented act of state pressure on the press, and of course did not align with the constitution. But at the time, no one was bothered by it. In Bonn, armored personnel carriers were deployed in front of the chancellor's office, and Border Guard forces patrolled ministries and embassies with their semi-automatics at the ready. The hostage crisis was approaching its climax. Something was about to happen, that much was clear. But no one was supposed to know too soon what it was.

Meanwhile, in Mogadishu, the German delegation had its hands full. Wischnewski had his staff draw up a checklist for all the measures that now had to be taken: The fire department and ambulances had to be on standby, beds had to be kept free in the hospital, and an emergency infirmary had to be set up at the airport. They also needed additional doctors. Finally, the numerous international journalists who had gathered had to be moved from their vantage points and accommodated inside the terminal so that they no longer had a direct view of the tarmac. There was to be no live coverage of the raid on the *Landshut*. Reporters, naturally, had gotten wind of something going on at the airport. A German television journalist had heard from someone at air traffic control that a Lufthansa plane was expected. Rumor had it that GSG 9 might be on board. More and more international doctors had been spotted, preparing in the hastily set up facility in the terminal building.

Mogadishu International Airport consisted of a runway, a small, plain terminal building and not much else. No one there was prepared for such a situation. But since the president's decision, the Somalis had been highly cooperative. The Somali cabinet convened continually at the airport, which had been completely sealed off by the military. Wischnewski had problems with the telephone connection between Mogadishu and Bonn: "The dedicated line broke down again and again. Sound quality was also extremely poor. So we often had to make decisions without being able to first coordinate with Bonn."[33]

Meanwhile, Commander Wegener was looking for a quiet place where GSG 9 could prepare for the mission, out of sight of the hijacked plane. He had proposed to carry out the operation on the night of October 17 at 2:00 a.m. local time, i.e. midnight German time. The rationale was that the worn-out hijackers would be most inattentive at that time of night, that they would hopefully not notice the approach, and would react slowly in the moment of attack. Until then, the hijackers had to be kept busy and lulled into safety.

The GSG 9 plane was scheduled to land at 7:30 p.m. Until midnight, there would be time to rig up their equipment and perhaps rehearse the assault once again. Wegener arranged for the plane to land unnoticed by the terrorists. Takeoff and landing operations had come to a standstill, so a single landing aircraft would arouse suspicion. Wegener asked the chief of the Air Force for assistance. He had some MIG fighter planes take off from the neighboring air base to provide some acoustic camouflage while the incoming Boeing 707 from Djibouti touched down in the darkness—with a tailwind, parallel to the parked *Landshut*, all headlights extinguished except for position lights, wing tanks almost depleted.

CHAPTER 10

Operation *Feuerzauber*

Confidential Information—officially kept secret
Saint Augustin, February 2, 1978

To the Inspector BGS ...
Subject: Operation "Landshut" of GSG 9 on 18/10/1977
here: Mission report

I. The following forces of GSG 9 were involved in the operation "Landshut":
Commander GSG 9 and command group
   2 operational units (1st and 3rd /GSG 9)
   1 technical group (explosives specialists) parts of the telecommunications and documentation unit
   3 paramedics
   1 administrative officer
Total strength of the operational forces: 62 men[1]

While waiting for their GSG 9 comrades to arrive, Commander Wegener, Adjutant Baum and Dieter Fox were accommodated at the Hotel Curuba just outside the airport, where they were able to have a decent meal and quench their thirst. Resting, however, was out of the question. The fact that the hotel was surrounded by Somali soldiers did not contribute to their general feeling of security. At least they got their passports back when they set off at dusk in the direction of the airport. They met with a Somali officer in front of the hotel. He explained in fractured English that they would take a shortcut, right across the airport grounds, so as not to have to use the long trip around the perimeter.

After a short ride they arrived at a Somali army checkpoint: roadblocks, sandbags, a barrier and a guard with a Kalashnikov at the ready. As the jeep approached, the guard raised his weapon and peered skeptically into the car. "Password," he demanded curtly. The driver looked perplexed. "No password."—"Yes, password!" the officer insisted, taking a step back, returning his rifle to the ready position and loading it. The officer in the passenger seat appeared perfectly calm. But when he moved to get out of the car, the guard, visibly nervous, ordered him to remain seated. A second guard stepped in, elbow on his hip with the rifle in his hands and asked what was going on. After a brief exchange in Somali, he also pointed his gun at the three GSG 9 men in the back and shouted "Password!" Now the officer in the passenger seat was getting nervous, too. Somalia was at war with Ethiopia, and apparently it had not been reported from the hotel that a jeep not belonging to the airport was on its way with an unknown officer and three Germans. What would happen next, Fox wondered? After all, he said, "They were just ordinary soldiers. They had the order: if in doubt, shoot. That was the third time they demanded the password. They wouldn't ask again. I was rather fatalistic about the whole situation. We couldn't have done anything back there, anyway. I said to myself, 'In a moment, they'll pull the trigger and that'll be that.'"

At that moment, a Somali officer stepped out of a small building a few meters above the checkpoint, and called out inquiring what the commotion was about. The two guards immediately snapped to attention and reported the situation. The officer descended the stairs, scowling first at the Germans, then at the escort officer, and suddenly his countenance brightened. He ordered the guards to lower their weapons, asked the escort officer to get out, and embraced him warmly. As it turned out, the two knew each other from a joint training course. After a short palaver, the strangers were allowed to continue their journey to meet with the rest of their GSG 9 team. "Otherwise," Fox is convinced "the operation would never have been carried out. Thank God we had several guardian angels circling over us."

> Mission Report
> IV. Mission preparation and command output
> At 19:30, B 707 lands with GSG 9 forces and taxis to the reconnoitered staging area at the Mogadishu airbase (about 2,000 meters from the hijacked B 737 *Landshut*). The aircraft is immediately hermetically shielded by Som. Forces.
>
> On the order of Comm. GSG 9, weapons and equipment are unloaded and a functional check is carried out.

As soon as the Boeing 707 was in parking position Wegener, Baum, Fox and Wischnewski hurried on board. Wischnewski announced that the crisis staff in Bonn had given the final "Go" on the operation. While he didn't say so explicitly, the minister of state let it be known to anyone who could read between the lines that not only were the lives of the hostages now in their hands, but also the political future of the chancellor and the German government. When Wischnewski disembarked, Fox briefed the SETs on the situation while Wegener informed the unit leaders. Then he instructed his deputy, Blätte, to take up position on the dunes surrounding the apron with the snipers and to keep reporting what was happening on and in the *Landshut*.

In the afternoon, Wegener himself had been able to sneak up on the hijacked aircraft; the sand dunes between the runway and the sea offered good protection.

The small blinds on the passenger windows were all closed, the plane's air conditioning was humming, but otherwise it was quiet all around—good conditions for an unnoticed approach. Wegener turned to the two unit leaders: "The first priority is to rescue the 86 hostages. To do this, all the terrorists must be incapacitated. I leave it to each one of you to decide how to go about this."[2]

"The 9ers" were happy to get off the plane. They had lived on board for three days—some, like Werner Heimann, who had been on the first flight, had been on aircraft for five days with only a brief interruption. During this time, the Boeing 707 had been not only their mode of transportation but flying bedroom, living room, workroom, conference room and waiting room all at once. On Crete, they had not been allowed to leave the plane. The only exception: smokers for the length of a cigarette.

The atmosphere on the plane had oscillated in these days of uncertainty: in the first few hours the men's spirit was rather low and insecure, as they did not know what to expect, Werner Heimann recalls: "As the time went on and people had enough time to come to grips with it, they relaxed and the mood leaned toward: 'Let's hope we get into action soon.' So when Wegener got on the plane after landing and said, 'Ok guys, we're doing this tonight,' the mood was pretty good. Really good. But then again, when the assignments were handed out and everyone knew exactly what they were supposed to do, that's when everyone started wondering whether this is going to go well or not."

Thus, Dieter Fox looked into quite a few pale faces. "We've never before dealt with terrorists up close like this before. And it was clear to us that they would do anything to get their demands." And that they would not hesitate to use their weapons, as the killing of Captain Schumann had shown. After the long days of inactivity and waiting, some of them still couldn't quite believe that the operation was going ahead. For Jörg Probstmeier, however, it had been certain the moment they heard the news of Captain Schumann's murder: "As long as there were no fatalities, it was up to the negotiating team to bring this to an end without bloodshed. But since the captain had been killed in Aden, worse was to be expected. From that moment on it was clear: there's no turning back now."

After the briefing, one of the men got cold feet and confided in his squad leader. He did not consider himself able to take up his designated position to enter the aircraft. The squad leader took note without saying much. "However, it was suggested that he pack his things on our return, and so he did," nods Werner Heimann. "I think you have to accept that. Each of us can picture the situation, imagine what it will be like. But you only learn how you actually deal with it when the time comes. I'm glad he made the decision he did. It would have been much worse if he had not stood behind the mission four-square. It might well have been jeopardized by him not playing his part. A squad consisted of five men at that time. Each man means 20 percent. And if an operation requires 100 percent, and I only have 80, then I'm 20 percent short of success."

> 21.00. Issue of the preliminary order by the commander of GSG 9 to the deputy and unit commander: preliminary operational plan, division of the forces, provision of forces for emergency measures.

Each squad was assigned an aircraft door and was given a section to clear. Along with that they received penetration limits and points to secure in the aircraft as well as a firing line limit so that the squads did not get into each other's way and accidentally shoot a comrade. The operational plan called for the two operational units, divided into six assault squads, to enter all six aircraft doors simultaneously—one unit on the left side of the aircraft with three squads, the other on the right with three squads. However, Werner Heimann and the other SET leaders protested: "We said we wouldn't subscribe to that. Because I want to know who is penetrating the opposite door. With that, we SET leaders asserted ourselves. My best friend People Scholz was then assigned the front door on the right and I got the front door on the left. We were perfectly attuned to each other, and that would pay off later."

After the briefing, a unit commander took Dieter Fox aside: "Mr. Fox, you'd better get some rest. It's been five days now." Five days? Had it really only been five days? Fox was exhausted, dead beat. But after the wild ride they had been on, he couldn't imagine twiddling his thumbs while the others stormed the *Landshut*, particularly since Wegener had already agreed to him taking over the leadership of a squad. Wegener himself would even lead the assault. "I told him, 'I'm certainly not going to hang around here and wait for our Dear God to make the sun come up.'"

Fox was assigned a squad. While the others slipped into their combat suits and turned their jackets inside out so rank insignia and national emblems wouldn't show, he had to scramble to find some halfway-fitted gear: He had brought nothing, no uniform, no suit, and his comrades had not bothered to pack something for him during their short stay in Bonn. So he squeezed into a pair of overalls that a Lufthansa engineer had lent him. It was a somewhat tight fit here and there, but he could manage. Then he did like the others and burned old newspapers in the lavatory sink, ran water over the ashes, and blackened his face with the soot. It was all the camouflage they had.

There were still some hours left until the mission, so the individual squads were given time slots to rehearse their tactics on their 707 parked on the apron well outside the line of sight from the *Landshut*. Wegener observed the work of each squad. When he was finally satisfied he said, "OK, guys. Lie down, review your tasks with each other, or just relax if you can. In one and a half hours, we're on our way."[3]

In these hours before the storm, Wischnewski told Wegener that the chancellor wanted to speak with him. Wegener took a jeep to the makeshift situation room at the terminal building, where a shaky dedicated line to Bonn had been set up. Time and again it would break down and had to be painstakingly reestablished via several relay stations. But even then, communication remained difficult. In the chancellor's office, the crisis team had been conferring nonstop. It was clear to all involved that it would be a long night, but also that there was not much they could do at the moment. They would have to sit idly for the next few hours, waiting for the sparse news coming in from Africa, be it good or bad.

Helmut Schmidt asked for Wegener's assessment of the situation. "Quite normal," the commander cryptically answered. "What does that mean?" inquired Schmidt.—"We've done this sort of thing very often, chancellor—no worries." The chancellor insisted: Was Wegener really convinced of this?—"If I tell you so, then I am 100 percent convinced. It will work out, I can completely rely on my boys. The prerequisite is that you give me the order to go into action now."—"OK, we'll do it now. There is no other solution. This is your part, I have done mine."[4]

In giving this order, the chancellor was taking an enormous risk: "I reckoned there would be a number of casualties. I considered the risk of the plane being blown up at 50 percent. The whole thing was a highly risky enterprise."[5] In the event of failure, Helmut Schmidt was determined to assume political responsibility, as he writes in his memoirs: "If our risky attempt to free the people in Mogadishu with the help of a special police unit of the Border Guard (today known by the abbreviation GSG 9) had failed, and we had suffered many deaths as a result, I would have resigned the next day."[6] He had already finished the draft for his letter of resignation. All that remained for him was to wait. As with the rest of the politicians on the crisis team, the ministry officials, state secretaries, agency heads and advisors.

Each of the three dozen or so men and each of the few women tried to deal with the tension in their own way. Schmidt played chess against Hamburg's mayor, Hans-Ulrich Klose. Schmidt won. At some point, the dedicated line to Mogadishu went dead. In Rome, where the switchboard was located, they had apparently called it a day. In the situation room at Mogadishu airport, they were almost relieved. One of Wischnewski's advisors sighed: "Hopefully they don't fix it too soon, so that [Minister of the Interior] Maihofer, the old sailor, can't go on asking about the wind direction every 10 minutes."[7]

> 22.45 Issue of the mission order by Comm. GSG 9 in person to assembled unit commanders and other members of the unit.
> 23.30 Convening of the final briefing by Minister of State Wischnewski. Participants: Dept. President Boeden, BKA, representative of the Foreign Office, Representative of Deutsche Lufthansa, Som.[ali] Chief of Protocol, Commander GSG 9.
> State Minister Wischnewski confirms the German Chancellor's order to deploy GSG 9. In a subsequent conversation with State Minister Wischnewski, GSG 9 commander points out that hostages and his own forces could be injured or killed during the assault on the aircraft by GSG 9 forces. Minister of State Wischnewski responds that the German government has no other choice, and that this is the only solution. For reasons of secrecy, GSG 9's operational

plan is not disclosed during the meeting. Also, Som. security forces are not informed about the details of the plan. Towards the end of the briefing, final arrangements are discussed with the psychologist, Mr. Salewski, on diversionary measures (radio conversation between tower and terrorists) immediately before the attack.

Since the afternoon, psychologist Salewski and Michael Libal, the German envoy to Mogadishu, had been in constant contact with the kidnappers and tried to create as relaxed an atmosphere as possible under the given circumstances. Wegener instructed his radio operators to send constant updates about the alleged position of the plane with the prisoners from Germany: "Make sure that you keep the terrorists on the plane constantly informed; that is, that the people who talk to you are permanently busy there, and in such a way that we are also aware of what is happening on board."[8] This stalling tactic was meant to buy them more time. They needed a calm situation. And under no circumstances were the terrorists to suspect what would happen next.

The key to success was the unnoticed approach of the assault teams to the back of the aircraft. A delicate matter which was to happen in the middle of the night when everything around was silent. The floodlights on the apron also posed a problem. The approaching units would cast long shadows which might be seen from the aircraft doors if the terrorists decided to take a look outside. Turning off the lights, however, would have been too conspicuous. They would need to advance with utmost caution. As a distraction, the Somalis had agreed to light a bonfire within sight of the cockpit. Would it work?

Hans-Jürgen Wischnewski had been on a number of tricky missions in his long career as the German government's all-purpose fireman. But deciding the fate of ninety people pushed even him to his limits: "I've never been in a comparable situation in my life. The passengers and crew of Flight LH-181 and, of course, the men of GSG 9 were in extreme danger of their lives during the attack." When all measures had been taken, when all preparations were completed, Wischnewski sought a quiet place outside the airport building where no one could see him—and prayed. "I asked for God's help.... Despite all the careful and decisive preparations, despite all the international solidarity, but above all despite all the courage, all the prudence and the outstanding precision of our men from GSG 9, there remained a residue of imponderables."[9] In the event of the operation's failure, he decided to resign as minister of state, even if he was not personally to blame. No one was more aware of the uncertainties than the men assigned to the assault teams.

No one talked about it, but the thought that not everyone might return from the operation alive preoccupied most of them. Dieter Fox tried to channel the feelings by forcing himself to make cool tactical calculations. He mentally prepared for four to six casualties on their side: the first to enter through the front doors and in the center area. "We knew from our reconnaissance that the terrorists lingered there. If they were expecting us, they would sit by the door and shoot down the first four—even at the risk of being killed themselves afterwards. That would have been disastrous. But it was entirely possible."

Deputy Commander Blätte also expected several dead in his own ranks and even the commander himself believed this grim scenario to be realistic. At the final briefing with his men, however, he spoke only in general terms about the possibility of casualties. "He was referring primarily to the terrorists, of course, to crew members and hostages," Fox says. "But we knew we were meant as well." Then Wegener decided, "OK, I'll take command at the plane. Boys, get ready for action!"[10] Leading from the front. Wegener took his principle quite literally. Many police and military commanders still shake their heads over this attitude, half in admiration, half in lack of comprehension. For his men, however, it meant a morale boost, giving them a feeling of security for the task ahead. So Wegener geared up as well. He noticed that bulletproof vests were missing so he took his off and gave it to one of his men. Then he ordered all the forces to assume their starting and staging points.

> V. Beginning of operations
> 23.45 Dispatch of a liaison officer with radio and night observation equipment to mission control in the tower. Mission: Maintaining communications between mission control and GSG 9 leadership, observation of the aircraft and reporting of changes.
> Tuesday, 18/10/1977
> 00.10 Deployment of reconnaissance and sniper teams.
> – Determination of the location of the terrorists in the "Landshut"
> – Detection of changes in and around the aircraft
> – Eliminating terrorists in the final approach phase of the attack forces in the event of unpredictable actions by the terrorists undertaken from inside the plane.

Deputy Klaus Blätte has relocated with eight snipers in the dunes on the aircraft's side facing away from the airport building, 200 meters away from the *Landshut*. Before the storm, they are to secure the approach of the SETs and eliminate terrorists who might open fire from the aircraft doors. During the assault, their task is to ensure that no terrorist can escape through a door that may be poorly secured. Their order: eliminate the threat. The long distance does not pose a problem. For experienced shooters like Jörg Probstmeier, more than twice that distance would be feasible.

Probstmeier is disappointed that Wegener has assigned him to the reconnaissance and sniper team. He would have preferred to be in the assault squad to help penetrate the aircraft, despite the considerable risk. "As a sniper, I'm in a comfortable position: there's little chance that we'll be hit by a stray bullet and breathe our last. But of course, while you're at it, you want to help save people and use your own life as a pawn." But being only 21, Probstmeier is one of the youngest of the task force, all of whom have been assigned to the reconnaissance squad by the unit leaders. "This caused a little bit of injured vanity, of course. But you had to suck it up."

Through the scope of his safety-locked precision rifle, Probstmeier clearly recognizes the two male terrorists. They are spending extended periods of time in the cockpit, along with a man in a white pilot's shirt. He assumes it is the co-pilot. Nothing more can be seen of the interior; the blinds on all the passenger windows have been pulled down. By radio, the deputy commander reports movements in the cockpit to Wegener. Otherwise, everything remains quiet.

> 01.00 Departure of the assault forces in the following tactical order:
> – lead group
> – 1ST / GSG 9
> – 3RD / GSG 9
> – technical group
> – reserve (parts 1./ a. 3./)

The men are sweating. It is well past midnight, but the temperature is still around 30° Celsius (86° F) and the air is uncomfortably humid. Commander Wegener has lined up behind the lead group: "Our clothes were sticking to our bodies, and we had to keep a lot of things on because we were carrying all kinds of equipment."[11] At first in single file, then in double file, they approach the plane from behind, exactly in line with the rear of the plane, coming out of the blind spot where they cannot be seen from the plane's windows. Two of each assault team carry two aluminum ladders taped together at the rungs.

Their path leads over a taxiway. High grass grows to the right and left of it as well as ground scrub in which one or another poisonous creepy-crawly animal is hiding. It takes them three quarters of an hour to cover the 1,500 meters (nearly a mile) in the darkness. Time and again they need to stop, set down, reorient themselves, and intensely listen into the night: Was there a noise? No? Ok, move!

They are about 80 meters away when a huge flock of birds flutters up right next to them and soars into the night cawing. All halt! Did anyone in the aircraft hear that? "They were making such a racket, we were convinced that it couldn't have gone unnoticed," says Dieter Fox shaking his head, "but we were told afterwards they didn't hear it. However, our nerves were far, far overstretched, so that we thought that every noise is being heard, even a needle falling to the ground."

Right before they get to the plane, a shooting star lights up the night sky. As big as the star of Bethlehem, it traces a bright path through the heavens from east to west. Fox does not believe in the superstitious, but he taps the man in front of him on the shoulder and whispers, "Now we get it done." Then, finally, they reach the *Landshut* and regroup under the belly of the plane. In this position, however, they run the additional risk not only of being discovered from suspicious noises, but also of being seen: From the right, the 737 is illuminated by the apron lights, so to the left falls the long shadow of the aircraft—and the shadows of the men underneath it. Werner Heimann has a bad feeling: "If they looked out the window now, it could end badly." Fortunately for them, all the screens in front of the passenger windows are still closed; no passenger or terrorist can see out to the sides.

> 01.30 Briefing of the unit leaders on the plane on the starting positions for the assault troops. The boundaries between the 1st and 3rd units are defined once again.

As all of them are gathered under the aircraft's belly, Wegener uses tactical hand signals to once more indicate the assigned positions of the individual teams. Specialists of the technical squad silently attach highly sensitive listening devices to the outer skin of the fuselage and listen to what is going on inside: everything seems quiet. All the doors are closed, but a beastly stench seeps out of the vents. The on-board toilets of the Boeing 737 have been clogged since Dubai. The plane exhales a ghastly mixture of stale air, fear, sweat, urine, feces and blood. "Awful!" For a moment, Dieter Fox and his comrades are breathless: "For us on the outside, it was a very brief indication of what the people up in the aircraft must have been going through."

> 01.48 Start of diversion measures
> Bonfire is set by Som. Forces. Psychologist Salewski initiates the negotiation phase by informing the terrorists that the plane with the prisoners to be exchanged has already passed through the airspace around Cairo.
> 01.59 Report from reconnaissance troops: 2 terrorists in the cockpit, 1 of them a woman.
> 02.05 Arrival at assault positions by all forces (6 assault squads 1/4)

In the tower, the German Chargé d'affaires Michael Libal and psychologist Salewski talk nonstop with Captain Mahmoud in order to keep the terrorists busy, but above all to keep them in the cockpit. Because now the most delicate phase begins: attaching the storm ladders to the aircraft. Not a scratch, not a squeak, not even the slightest sound of something rubbing against the metal skin of the fuselage must be allowed to betray them. The men move in slow motion. Then, at each of the two front doors as well as the two back doors, three men per squad climb up while two secure the ladders below. Werner Heimann's head is level with the lower edge of the door at the front left: "This phase took a very long time. And the plane mustn't move; it only sits on three landing gear legs and it's pretty tippy." Finally, at the trailing end of the wings and tightly close to the aircraft's body in order not to be spotted from inside, two teams creep up to the emergency exits.

Meanwhile, Wegener remains under the plane waiting, and asks over the radio whether all positions have been taken, ready for entry. At that moment, the radios fail. All but one. As it turns out later, the immense temperature fluctuations in the cargo hold of the GSG 9 Boeing have taken their toll on the sensitive equipment. Condensation has formed and crept into the electronic circuit boards. During the equipment test right before the mission, the radios and intercom sets worked fine. Now they give up the ghost at the worst possible moment. Wegener immediately switches communication to guidance by signal—that is, hand, finger and head signals.

The wiretap technicians signal that everything remains quiet inside the *Landshut*. Except in the cockpit where Captain Mahmoud negotiates with the tower about the allegedly imminent prisoner exchange.

Since news broke in the afternoon that the German government was ready to fly out the RAF prisoners, the situation on board has eased considerably. The prospect of a nonviolent solution to the drama has enabled the hostages to endure the last hours of their ordeal. Their restraints have been released and the tone of the terrorists has become much less hostile, even friendly at times. Co-pilot Vietor has lain down in one of the two empty rows of seats in First Class to get some rest. At the very beginning of the hijacking, all passengers had to move to the back rows, leaving the front ones empty. "It was all peaceful," he recalls.[12]

While being half asleep, Vietor hears a slight scratching sound. "I thought, 'Now you're losing it! You haven't slept for five days and you hear noises that can't exist.' It must have been one of the ladders being attached to the fuselage." Vietor gets up again, steps into the cockpit, drops into the co-pilot's seat and listens briefly to the radio traffic. "And then I sat there, and I have to say this very carefully: I suddenly wanted to get out of the cockpit. Without suspecting what would happen in the next few minutes of course. Mahmoud was sitting there, it was a calm night atmosphere, but I wanted to get out." Vietor goes back and sits down with the passengers. Later, Commander Wegener would tell him that he was seen in the cockpit, the only one with a white shirt: "We would have stormed a few minutes later, whether you were sitting there or not." Vietor still owns an artificial horizon from the instrument panel directly in front of his co-pilot seat. The dent from the ricochet is clearly visible.

02.09 Reports from all deployed assault teams: Ready!

In the front left of the aircraft, Werner Heimann reports readiness. As squad leader, he stands below the aircraft door in the third position on the ladder. The one on top will open the doors, the one below will enter first, then the SET leader, then the door opener. In the silent seconds before the command to attack, Heimann forces himself to think tactically. "There's only one thought going through your head, but you have to block it out or you will not be able to do it, and that is: Hopefully the doors are not rigged, i.e. secured with detonators and explosives," he says and adds with a short laugh: "That is what we would have done if we had been the terrorists. It would have been the easiest way to secure ourselves against outside intrusion."

They had even trained for such fatal booby traps with real explosive devices, the aim being to experience their numbing effect, to feel the shock wave and to get a feeling for what it's like when shrapnel of wood and metal and glass come flying around their heads. "Getting used to this helps to relieve the psychological pressure and keep your skill and tactics at the fore," says Dieter Fox. After nearly six days of odyssey and sleep deprivation, he is now standing at the top of the ladder by the aft right boarding door of the *Landshut*. As SET leader, it is not really his job, but he is tall and can easily reach the door handle to pull it out safely to quickly open the door. "When you're at the door, just before you get in, you don't think in standard civilian categories anymore, but you think rationally-operationally. The only thing that matters is what happens right at that moment. If I make a single mistake now, then I have a problem. You can't allow any other thoughts to distract you. That's why you practice the whole procedure ad nauseam. After that, when you're inside, it's a different situation. You can think again, you can look: Am I under attack? Do I need to return fire? Is there something else that needs to be taken care of? But in the last moments before entering, you think nothing at all."

From the cockpit, Captain Mahmoud can see the beach fire that the Somalis have started. He doesn't have much time to think about it. Over the radio, the leader of the terrorists dictates the handover modalities to the German envoy. The envoy drags out the conversation, asking for repetitions:

Tower: "Captain Martyr Mahmoud, this is Michael Libal speaking, representative of the Federal Republic of Germany. Do you copy? Captain Mahmoud, I have a message for you. The aircraft will leave Cairo at 13:15 GMT. Now I would like to ask you if you have specific suggestions for the exchange of the hostages as discussed earlier. Over."

[...]

Landshut: "First, we do not want any press or TV cameras during the exchange. Second, what about the comrades coming in from Germany? Third, we wish to have a representative of the Somali government to examine the aircraft which is now parked on the apron in Mogadishu to make sure that nobody is on board."

Tower: "Which aircraft, please?"

Landshut: "The one that brought the delegation yesterday. Furthermore, we demand that Somali forces encircle the Lufthansa aircraft."

Tower: "The aircraft you just talked about?"

Landshut: "No, I'm talking about the one arriving just now. Third, nobody is to leave any of the two planes."

Tower: "Understood, understood."

Landshut: "Nobody is to approach the aircraft which is under the control of the 'Halimeh' unit, unless with explicit prior permission."

Tower: "Understood."

Landshut: "When the Germans, second, land to bring our comrades, you need to inform us beforehand."

Tower: "Yes, understood."

Landshut: They are to approach the aircraft individually. They are to be searched by Somali representatives.

Tower: "Understood."

Landshut: "Furthermore, the aircraft carrying the comrades will leave the airport immediately after we demand it to. The commander of the 'Martyr Halimeh' unit will ask one of the comrades to come to our plane for identification, in order to ensure the safety of the other comrades."

Tower: "Understood."

Landshut: "After this investigation, the comrade will return to the Somali authorities at the airport."

Tower: "Understood."

Landshut: "We will make further arrangements with the comrades coming from Turkey."

"Tower: "Repeat that."

Landshut: "We will make further arrangements with the comrades coming from Turkey."

Tower: "Understood. When they come ..."[13]

> 02.10 Storming of the plane on code word "Fire magic—GO!" through all entrances including emergency entrances of the B 737. Simultaneous ignition of 3 flash bombs (2 right fuselage side; 1 cockpit height, 1 behind right wing, 1 third behind left wing).

All hell breaks loose. Around the plane are bangs and flashes like inside a thunderstorm. The two British SAS men have run out from under the fuselage and thrown their stun grenades high above the cockpit. This is the signal for the assault troops. All six squads open the airplane doors in the same second. In Werner Heimann's squad it happens so jerkily that the door opener falls backwards from the ladder. Heimann expresses that "we were glad that it was not a Jumbo, he would have crashed down from eight meters above ground." But the man immediately gets back on his feet and follows Heimann into the plane. Fortunately for them, none of the charges on the inside of the boarding doors go off. The terrorists had removed the detonators from the explosives just moments before. But there is no time to be relieved. Heimann sees that People Scholz and his team on the opposite side are struggling with opening the right front door. It is blocked by luggage and trash. Boeing 737 doors don't just open outward but have to be pushed in first. So their door only opens to the width of a crack. At least radio communication has been re-established. "People, other door!" Heimann radios to his comrade, who immediately changes from right to the left side with his men and enters the plane behind Heimann, pushing forward to the rear in accordance with his mission, while Heimann and his squad advance to the cockpit, where, according to the reconnaissance team, two terrorists must be situated.

> VI. Fight in the plane:
> As they enter the plane, all assault squad leaders call out to the hostages: "Lie down, heads down!" ... The hostages immediately follow this instruction. All the hostages—except for one elderly gentleman—are lying between or under the seats.

There is a bang. The doors fly open. Jürgen Vietor is ripped from his doze. He has been sitting there for barely more than a minute or two. "Suddenly, out of this quiet, there was noise and shots. I was a soldier. But I've never experienced gunfire in a room. And then there was the cry: '*Köpfe runter! Köpfe runter, wo sind die Schweine?*'" This comes from Dieter Fox. He is the second of his squad to enter the *Landshut*. Through the cracking shots he yells in German, "Heads down! Heads down! Where are the pigs?" again and again. The repeated call is not off the cuff but planned. "I wanted to tell the people, on the one hand: Here are Germans and we are here to help you. And on the other hand, of course: Put your heads down when shots are being fired, so that you don't get hit and we have a clear view ahead. And it worked. The people, despite their lethargy and their miserable situation, put their heads down as best they could." Other GSG 9 men now also shout "Heads down!" in English as well as in German. Wegener had given this order—a lesson he had learned from the Entebbe hijacking case the year before when he had witnessed hostages dying because they did not understand the commands of the Israeli special forces.

> When the bow doors are opened by the two GSG 9 assault troops deployed in front, the terrorists immediately open fire. The members of the assault team determine that there are 2 terrorists (1 male and 1 female). The male terrorist—the leader Zuheir Yousef Akkacha, alias Mahmoud,...—shoots with a Tokarev 7.62mm at the intruding forces of GSG 9 and is himself hit by shots from the assault squad, but is still able to escape into the cockpit. While trying to throw a hand grenade from the cockpit against the invading members of assault troops 1 and 2, he is finally shot incapacitated in the cockpit. Earlier, one of his [Mahmoud's] shots had hit PHW* Losert, who was standing at the foot of a ladder as the safety man of a deployed assault squad, in the neck.

Before the squad with the blocked door could switch sides, the terrorist leader has fired a shot blindly through this narrowly open door and hit an officer across the neck behind the larynx. A lucky strike for the terrorist. But in some macabre way also for the man who was hit: Although the bullet went through his throat, neither the trachea nor the esophagus nor the vocal cords nor any arteries are hit. The injured man is immediately treated by the paramedics of the reserve unit. The gunman flees into the cockpit, shooting, and is shot by an officer. "It all happened incredibly quickly," Werner Heimann recalls. "There is no time to think at all, you just act, it's lightning fast."

> The female terrorist ... is also hit by several shots during the exchange of fire and falls to the ground.

Wegener enters the plane following Fox on the right and works his way forward through the center aisle. As he is moving, he listens to the reports of his men over the radio: "First terrorist down! Second one down!"

★ PHW (*Polizeihauptwachtmeister*) = Police chief sergeant.

> Another male terrorist in 1st class … shoots during the exchange of fire at storm troopers deployed in the cockpit with a 9mm Makarov pistol and is hit by several shots from the storm troopers. A shot from the Makarov hits a GSG 9 member in the left side (hip height), but it remains stuck in the armored vest without causing injuries. The terrorist falls between the rows of seats in 1st class, but is still able to throw a hand grenade between the hostages in the direction of economy class. A stewardess of the B 737 crew (Fräulein Dillmann) is injured in the legs.

Three terrorists are now incapacitated. But there were four. When Heimann's squad enters the cockpit, they know that right next to the entrance there is an on-board toilet not shown on the layout plans.

> During the firefight with the 2nd male terrorist, the bow lavatory door had opened and was immediately closed again. As was later determined, members of assault squad 1 and 2 had assumed from bullet holes in the bow door that the female terrorist … located in the toilet had shot through the [toilet] door. Several members of the two assault teams[*] then fired through the side panel and door. After the door is torn open again by a GSG 9 member, the female terrorist, who has been hit by several shots, is found to be incapacitated.

She dies on the spot. Then, all at once, there is silence in the aircraft. The firefight lasted barely more than a minute. Two terrorists are dead, another will die later, on the way to the airport terminal. The fourth terrorist is also initially considered to be fatally shot. But she will survive seriously injured. Later, lying on the stretcher on her way to the airport building, she will raise her hand and gesture the Victory Sign to the waiting cameras.[†]

> 02.14 Evacuation of the hostages
> After the 1st/GSG 9 has safely occupied the rear of the aircraft and thus the corresponding accesses, the evacuation of the hostages via the left rear door and left emergency exit is begun 4 minutes after the start of the attack. Protection of the hostages by reserve forces.[‡]

Jürgen Vietor is crouching between the seats in the wing area. "There was shooting, shooting, shooting. Finally, it calmed down a bit, and I heard from the back of the plane: 'Out this way, out this way!' I then climbed through the emergency window above the wings."

---

[*] According to the eyewitnesses, only one operative fired through the side panel and door, not both.

[†] The terrorist by the name of Souhaila Andrawes was later sentenced to 20 years in prison in April 1978 but was deported after a few months. She went on to study in Beirut, lived in Syria, and was granted political asylum in Norway in 1991, where she was tracked down by German investigators in 1994. In 1996, a Hamburg court sentenced her to 12 years for murder, kidnapping, hostage-taking, and airplane hijacking. She was later allowed to serve her sentence in Norway, where she was released early. The reason: long-term effects of her gunshot wounds in Mogadishu impeding her general health. Today she lives in Oslo with her husband and daughter. She was not available for an interview for this book.

[‡] This is according to Wegener's official report. According to GSG 9 operatives involved and Wegener's own statements given later, the evacuation began immediately after the intrusion.

> Despite repeated requests by Comm. GSG 9 and the deployed forces to leave the plane, the hostages are initially reluctant to follow this request. Only after several repetitions of this request in German and English do the hostages quickly evacuate the plane.

While the last shots are still being fired in the front of the plane, Fox and the emergency crews in the rear area begin leading the first passengers to the exits while ducking down. Even with the terrorists neutralized, hidden explosive devices might still detonate. The evacuation proves difficult at first. "The hostages reacted in a lethargic, animalistic way, just letting everything happen to them," says Fox, "Then all of a sudden the instinct kicked in: Just get out of the plane! Some fell down the ladder, we couldn't hold on to them, they just wanted to get away from the plane." The rescue forces outside, however, need to take care that the frightened, dehydrated, and often disoriented hostages don't simply run away into the open. The sniper teams have orders to shoot any person who moves toward the beach—in case they are terrorists who have escaped from a poorly secured door.

The plane quickly empties, except for a few passengers who are frozen with fear. An old gentleman insists he will not get off without his shoes. Wegener explains to him patiently that he will get new shoes outside. Another elderly man remains apathetic in his seat, slightly injured by shell splinters on his face and hands. "He didn't know what was going on, he was completely lost," Fox recalls. "We spoke to him, but he didn't react, just stared. Then we helped him get up, very slowly, and led him outside. And when he was outside, he understood bit by bit: Yes, it's over."

> All the hostages are gathered behind a hill about 50 meters away from the *Landshut* by reserve forces and checked. The snipers and reconnaissance troops take over the protection of the hostages on site.

In a small hollow behind a sand dune, the rescued are treated by medics and the reserve troops before being transported onto waiting trucks and vans. After 108 hours of terror and fear of death, the nightmare is finally over. It is unlikely that any of them know by whom they were freed. Co-pilot Vietor, like everyone else, is just glad to get out of the plane. "GSG 9? Of course, I followed that after 1972, the Munich massacre, a police force had been set up, but that they were the ones who did it, that came much later to me."

> 02.17 It is declared by GSG 9 command: All terrorists incapacitated!

Wegener instructs second-in-command Blätte to gather the task forces under the plane and check the weapons of the terrorists once again. Satisfied, Wegener notes that there have been no casualties in his own ranks. "That was a tremendous relief," he said later.[14]

> 02.17 The code word "Springtime" (end of mission) is passed on to the deployed forces and Minister of State Wischnewski, and a message is sent to command center:

90 hostages* freed,
3 hostages slightly injured,
3 terrorists killed,
1 terrorist seriously injured,
1 member of GSG 9 slightly injured by a bullet through the neck, mission accomplished.

Wischnewski immediately tries to get Chancellor Helmut Schmidt on the phone. The line to the crisis team in Bonn has been re-established but remains shaky.

Schmidt: "Schmidt here! I'm listening!"
Wischnewski: "Hello!"
Schmidt: "Speak slowly and loudly, please!"
Wischnewski: "… the plane has been cracked open!"
Schmidt: "Not understood."
Wischnewski: "The job …"
Schmidt: "The job is done."
Wischnewski: "Three dead terrorists."
Schmidt: "Three dead terrorists."
Wischnewski: "One GSG 9 man wounded."
Schmidt: "Not understood."
Wischnewski: "One GSG 9 man wounded."
Schmidt: "One."
Wischnewski: "One …"
Schmidt: "One GSG 9 man wounded."
Wischnewski: "Otherwise, no further intelligence yet."
Schmidt: "No further intelligence."
Wischnewski: "Wait a few more minutes. Now the trucks are moving."
Schmidt: "Yes, now the trucks are driving."
[State Secretary] Ruhnau: "Yes, now the cars are moving towards the plane."
Wischnewski: "And then the people will be brought out of it."
Schmidt: "I am handing back, Hans-Jürgen. I can hardly understand you."[15]

When Wegener and his aide report to Wischnewski in the tower, the minister initially cannot believe that the operation ended without any casualties among the hostages or liberators. Helmut Schmidt feels the same way when Wegener speaks to him just a few moments later. The line has been stabilized in the meantime: "How many dead, how many injured?" the chancellor wants to know.—"We have no casualties. One of my people is slightly injured, that's all. Among the terrorists, one survived seriously injured and three are dead. It all worked out very well." Schmidt is stunned and addresses Wegener as *"Herr Oberst"* (colonel). Wegener, somewhat embarrassed, replies: "I understand that you are saying that

---

* The report erroneously mentions the figure of 90 hostages. In fact, there were 86 hostages. In addition, there were the four hostage-takers.

to me now. But I am a lieutenant colonel."—"That will change," Schmidt answers with a firm voice.[16]

Later, Schmidt will state in his typical matter-of-fact way, "Wegener and GSG 9 did a good job."[17] At that moment, however, tears form in the chancellor's eyes as Wischnewski once again confirms that there have been no casualties among the hostages nor the emergency forces. Schmidt—not exactly known for his emotional outbursts—leaves the room in an attempt to conceal his true feelings. "Probably the most dramatic moment of my life" was over, as Schmidt described it later.[18] For the first time since the crisis team had been set up six weeks earlier after the kidnapping of Hanns Martin Schleyer, the mood is relaxed, almost euphoric.

> VIII. Other Measures
> 02.18 Buses for transporting hostages, fire engines and ambulances arrive at the scene. Wegener's deputy, Blätte, organizes the care and transport of the freed hostages in the direction of the airport terminal.

After his phone call with Schmidt, Wegener walks over to the *Landshut* once more to inspect the weapons and explosives that have been seized. On his way to the plane, co-pilot Vietor meets him. When Wegener asks him what he was still doing there, he hems and haws at first, then mutters: "You have to understand, I wanted to get my toupee out of the plane."

> 2.25 GSG 9 forces march back to the staging area. Report from the deployed technical group:
> 4 hand grenades in the cockpit,
> 1 in the first-class compartment,
> plus plastic explosives in several bags in the first-class compartment.

Are there more weapons hidden somewhere? The entire aircraft is searched for firearms and explosives. The technical unit seizes a total of 1.5 kilograms (3.3 lbs) of TNT. What they don't find, however, will leave a Lufthansa technician pale faced the next morning. There is another grenade jammed under a seat, armed and unlocked, with the safety pin missing. Albeit fatally wounded, one of the terrorists had been able to throw a second grenade. The first exploded and slightly injured stewardess Gaby Dillmann's leg. She was lucky because the grenade did not have a splinter casing, but "only" the explosive device. The second grenade of the same type rolled between the rows of seats and got jammed in the linkage with the pressed trigger guard. If it had also exploded, it could have caused considerable damage, even without a fragmentation casing.

> 03.00 Checking of equipment and loading of weapons and equipment in B 707 of the command.

After all squads have collected their equipment and checked their weapons, they gather in their Boeing 707. When everybody is back on board, Wischnewski barges in, soaking wet with sweat: "Guys, do you have a drink for me? I'll return the favor in Bonn." Slowly, tension is easing. But no one is really in the mood for cheering, not yet, because for the moment nobody knows for certain how their comrade Werner Losert, who'd been shot through the neck, has fared. People Scholz, his squad leader, shrugs. "Yes, Werner has been shot, we don't know how he's doing." Moments later a paramedic appears in the doorway, supporting Losert by the arm. The injured officer is wearing a thick white neck brace but is able to walk on his own. Still, Werner Heimann breathes a sigh of relief. "It was clear then that nothing serious had happened to any of us."

With Losert having joined them, the men are overcome with exuberance. Smirking, Werner Heimann says, "We didn't have any alcohol for five days and the on-board bar was full of it. And since we are who we are, we were quick to reduce the supply." A bottle of champagne is found swiftly and uncorked, and the neck of the shot comrade is subjected to a leak test: "We opened Werner's mouth and poured down some champagne. Here, see: there's not a single drop of blood dripping from his wound. It can't be that bad! He was taken care of, [and he] lay down in the back." The young men in front, however, celebrate their success with lots of pats on the back, hugs and considerably more champagne, of course. The joy over the successful operation is mixed with a ton of relief. All they had trained for across five long years, they have now proven in action.

Dieter Fox was particularly proud of having put all those critics in their place who would have expected nothing but carnage from GSG 9. "In this moment, we were aware that we had achieved something very big. This was an emotional high for me, a great deal of satisfaction, there's no way to describe that feeling." But most of all, Fox was glad the five days were over—the odyssey, the tension, the sleep deprivation, the operation. And he was glad that he survived. In a quiet minute, just before the operation commenced, he had snuck out and watched the sun sinking fiery red behind the dunes, and he had wondered whether he would see her rise again. Now, not only was he alive, but all his comrades were well and all the hostages had been saved. "It can't get any better than this," he said.

05.13 Return flight of GSG 9 commando to the Federal Republic of Germany.

Minister of State Wischnewski had promised Somali President Siad Barre that GSG 9 and the freed hostages would be gone before daybreak. A government plane with the freed hostages on board took off at 4:50 a.m. local time; the Boeing 707 with Wischnewski and GSG 9 followed a few minutes later. Before they left, Wischnewski paid Siad Barre a visit once more to thank him for his cooperation. The Somali president presented the German with a press release. It said that Somali security forces had carried out the liberation with the participation of "some German experts." It was a matter of saving face. Wischnewski did not hesitate for a moment. "I signed that. I would have done everything humanly possible to help him. We would fly home, but for him, the problems would remain."[19]

Epilogue to *Feuerzauber*

Readers familiar with the story of Operation *Feuerzauber*, particularly in the UK, might be surprised at the comparatively small portion of the narration dedicated to the two SAS operatives, Davies and Morrison. Were they not greeted as national heroes upon their return? Did they not receive the highest acclaim and honors of the highest degree? And rightfully so. After all, they devised the plan for the assault. They led GSG 9 troops to the *Landshut*. They threw the grenades that stunned the terrorists. And finally, they led the charge inside the aircraft. Or so it has been reported by the British media for decades, first immediately after the feat, then again in the mid-1990s when there was a court trial against the surviving terrorist, and finally in the obituaries of the by-then highly decorated veterans. "He threw a stun grenade and engaged the hijackers in a gunfight,"[20] wrote *The Times* in 2016 on Davies's death. He was awarded the British Empire Medal for his heroic achievements, and Morrison was made an OBE (Order of the British Empire). So why are their contributions not appropriately appreciated in the above account?

The answer is simple: because these claims are not entirely accurate (to put it in polite terms). Whether the claims align with historic facts is more than questionable. At least, they do not align with the recollections of any of GSG 9 eyewitnesses interviewed for this book. They also do not align with late Ulrich Wegener's remarks on this matter, nor with the tactics and procedures for aircraft assault GSG 9 had adopted at the time. But maybe even more importantly, these claims do not even align with Davies's own detailed account of the events.

Davies and Morrison did not lead the charge. Moreover, at no point during the hot phase of the operation were they inside the aircraft, which means they did not engage with the terrorists in the gunfight and could never have done so. And they certainly were not the masterminds of the assault plan, since tactical key decisions for penetrating the plane ran directly contrary to their suggestions. When Ulrich Wegener was confronted with their claims many years after the events, his response did not leave any desire for clarity: "Complete nonsense. The SAS men brought a completely different tactic into play than the one we preferred. We had a different concept, namely penetration of all entrances and exits on the aircraft at once."[21]

That is not to say that their contribution was unimportant or negligible. When Davies and Morrison first arrived in Dubai, Dieter Fox had an excellent first impression: "I had the feeling that these are people who know their stuff. They were professionals, calm, reasonable, approachable. They wanted to help, to support us, they wanted to provide advice and assistance, and they made a very good, professional and sober impression."

Their approach to the aircraft assault, though, was military in style (as in, to use whatever means necessary) and thus was a far cry from the type of police tactics GSG 9 intended to apply. They insisted on using stun grenades inside the aircraft, but most importantly, they were intent on using their own tactics for getting into the aircraft first. When attempting to train the makeshift assault team of Emiratis in Dubai, Fox recalls intense discussions about the matter. "They suggested that we go in through one, but certainly no more than two doors. Two doors max. That was completely contrary to our tactics. We followed the Israelis' standard tactic, which is still in use today and which we had modified for our purposes. We had specialized in going through all doors at once and had done so all the years prior in our training. We had practiced it again and again. So we told the British that we would go in through all openings that were available, all openings that the 737 offered, meaning front right door, front left, rear right, rear left and over the wings. SAS always took the position—I don't know how they do it today, but at the time they took the position—a maximum of two. Why? Don't ask me. We couldn't understand their approach and, frankly, we didn't want to understand. Wegener didn't want to either. And in terms of tactics, from what we heard from the negotiations, that would very probably have gone wrong."

The objective in entering through all available doors at once was to create the maximum of surprise, stress and disorientation for the terrorists, a feeling of being overpowered and not knowing which intruder to fight first. These split seconds of indecision were supposed to give the SETs the edge they needed to keep the upper hand. It seemed pretty straightforward. So why would the SAS handle things differently?

Davies suggested they intrude exclusively through the middle of the aircraft, via the over-wing emergency hatches, since the terrorists in Dubai threatened the execution of hostages: "My thoughts were that if the terrorists began to carry out their threatened shootings, they would naturally take the precaution of covering the main doors. It seemed less likely that they would cover the two emergency hatches. Another important factor is that the wing emergency exits are designed to be opened easily from the outside, which is why I favored this method of entry."[22] Davies then claimed that opening the other four doors at the front and the rear from the outside would have required considerable manhandling and too much time for it to be a surprise factor.

The Germans, however, would have nothing of it. Too risky. "Imagine going only through two doors," Dieter Fox argues. "Let's do the math. If something goes wrong at one door—which is what happened in Mogadishu at the front right door—then you've got only one door left. That will mean a disaster since only one man can enter at a time. You will have to send 12 people through a single door. All the other guys have to do is point their guns at this one door and that's the end of the tale."

Of course, the Germans could not argue for this out of experience, since they had never stormed an aircraft for real. But neither had the British. The only ones with real-life experience in this field at that time were the Israelis. And they had been successful. So the Germans stood by their original plan of going through all the doors simultaneously. That is how they had trained it for years on end, and how Fox practiced it with the makeshift assault team in Dubai. And that is how the operation was conducted in Mogadishu: Israeli style, not British style.

But what about the actual firefight? The British media reported that Davies and Morrison went inside the *Landshut*, leading the charge. This is peculiar, as no GSG 9 officer interviewed for this book remembers having seen either Morrison or Davies inside the aircraft or getting into it. Neither Werner Heimann nor Dieter Fox, who led their respective squads into the firefight, nor Jörg Probstmeier, who was observing the scene from his vantage position outside. As a quick survey conducted by Heimann for this book revealed, no one among the Mogadishu veterans remembers either of the SAS men inside the *Landshut*.

But then, it would have been truly odd if they actually had been inside, because this was not where they were supposed to be. Davies and Morrison were tasked with throwing the stun grenades in front of the cockpit as an important diversion measure. But that was that, says Fox. "This was Wegener's order, they had to keep their position in front as observers, they were not supposed to intrude with us." Like everybody else involved, they were given a designated task at a designated time and place, just like the snipers, the technicians, the communications officers, the paramedics, the members of the SETs who were securing the ladders, and they were to stay outside the aircraft. Not everyone was to go inside and be part of the actual fighting. In fact, more than two-thirds of the 60-strong GSG 9 team remained outside, assuming their assigned roles and tasks—as is necessary in a highly coordinated operation like this. Things spiral out of control fast if everybody just runs about the scene when their job is done.

In 1994, Barry Davies published *Fire Magic*, a juicy, first-person account of the events in Dubai and Mogadishu told from the perspective of the SAS officer who was awarded a British Empire Medal (BEM) for his heroic deeds, as the cover proudly states. The book's jacket includes the text: "On day six German GSG 9 troops, together with Davies and Morrison, entered the plane with stun grenades."[23] However, that is not how Davies describes the events in the book. So, let's have a look at Davies's account and examine what he details in his own words, starting with the beginning of the assault:

> The last thing I heard Ulrich Wegener say was "Three, two, one, GO!"
> Instinctively, I stepped away from the aircraft,* having already pulled the pins from the two stun grenades which I was clutching. I tossed the first one casually in an arc over the starboard wing. It exploded about three feet above the two GSG 9 soldiers waiting there, causing them great surprise! Just as it exploded, they punched in the panel which released the small hatchway into the aircraft. Taking a better swing, I threw the second grenade high over the cockpit. It actually exploded about two feet above the flight deck, to dramatic effect.

---

* Odd choice of words. Stepping away from the aircraft was necessary in order to throw the stun grenades. This was the plan, not an act of instinct.

After throwing the second grenade, I whipped round to see the GSG 9 soldier on my left turn the handle of the rear starboard door and with a kick throw his body clear of the ladder, still hanging on to the handle and pulling the door open on its hydraulics.* The moment he did this the internal lights of the aircraft revealed one of the female terrorists standing there in a Che Guevara tee-shirt, wearing an expression of utter astonishment. At that instant the soldier on the right rung of the ladder fired a burst and stitched her with at least six rounds. She fell to the floor, dead, and the soldier disappeared into the aircraft.†

Returning my attention to the starboard wing, I ran forward and scaled the small ladders, positioning myself by the open hatchway where the two GSG 9 had already entered. As I looked into the aircraft I saw that the hatchway had fallen on the laps of the two passengers sitting there. They sat frozen, their eyes closed tightly. Continuous gunfire rattled up and down the aircraft for what seemed a lifetime. I can remember saying to myself, "Come on, do it, do it—get it done!" Then came a couple of low thuds‡ as two of the terrorists' grenades exploded.[24]

Davies continues to describe the firefight within the aircraft's cabin and on the flight deck, the injury of stewardess Dillmann by the grenade, co-pilot Vietor's reaction, GSG 9 men's shouting of "get down!," the female terrorist in the toilet being shot. However, Davies does not tell it as a first-person account. And at no point does he claim to be witnessing the fight from inside the aircraft.§ Reading the whole segment superficially, one might be forgiven for believing that Davies made his way into the cabin through the hatch and became part of the shootout, particularly after telling himself "Come on, do it—get it done!"

But he never did. This becomes perfectly clear when he continues his account with the beginning of the evacuation of the aircraft: "Then, out of the rear starboard door, I saw figures start to appear and descend the assault ladders. One of the GSG 9 soldiers pulled the hatchway off the laps of the couple who had been trapped and at last they opened their eyes; I reached in to help them out of the aircraft."[25] So, from Davies's own account it seems obvious that he remained outside the aircraft on the wing all along while the fighting was going on inside. However, from an operational point of view, it even seems doubtful that Davies actually went up to the emergency hatch during the assault to look into the aircraft and help people get

---

* As described earlier, this incident happened at the front left door where Werner Heimann's SET was entering the aircraft. From Davies' claimed position on the other side of the plane's body, it would have been virtually impossible to observe this incident. The door on "his" side, however, was blocked and could not be opened as described above.

† The female terrorist that Davies refers to was not killed at the right rear door, but in the front of the cabin inside the washroom on the left side where she was hiding and shooting from inside. The other female terrorist was also shot inside in the front but survived. Also, there could have been no fire burst from an automatic gun since no long-barreled weapons were used by the SETs, but only by the snipers, who never fired a single shot.

‡ Davies would not have heard the sound of two grenades exploding, since only one of them exploded. As mentioned previously, the second grenade was found the next day by technical personnel. It was jammed under a passenger seat, still hot.

§ He claims to have checked the cabin for explosives afterwards, which was not confirmed by any of the interviewed GSG 9 officers, but which still might be possible.

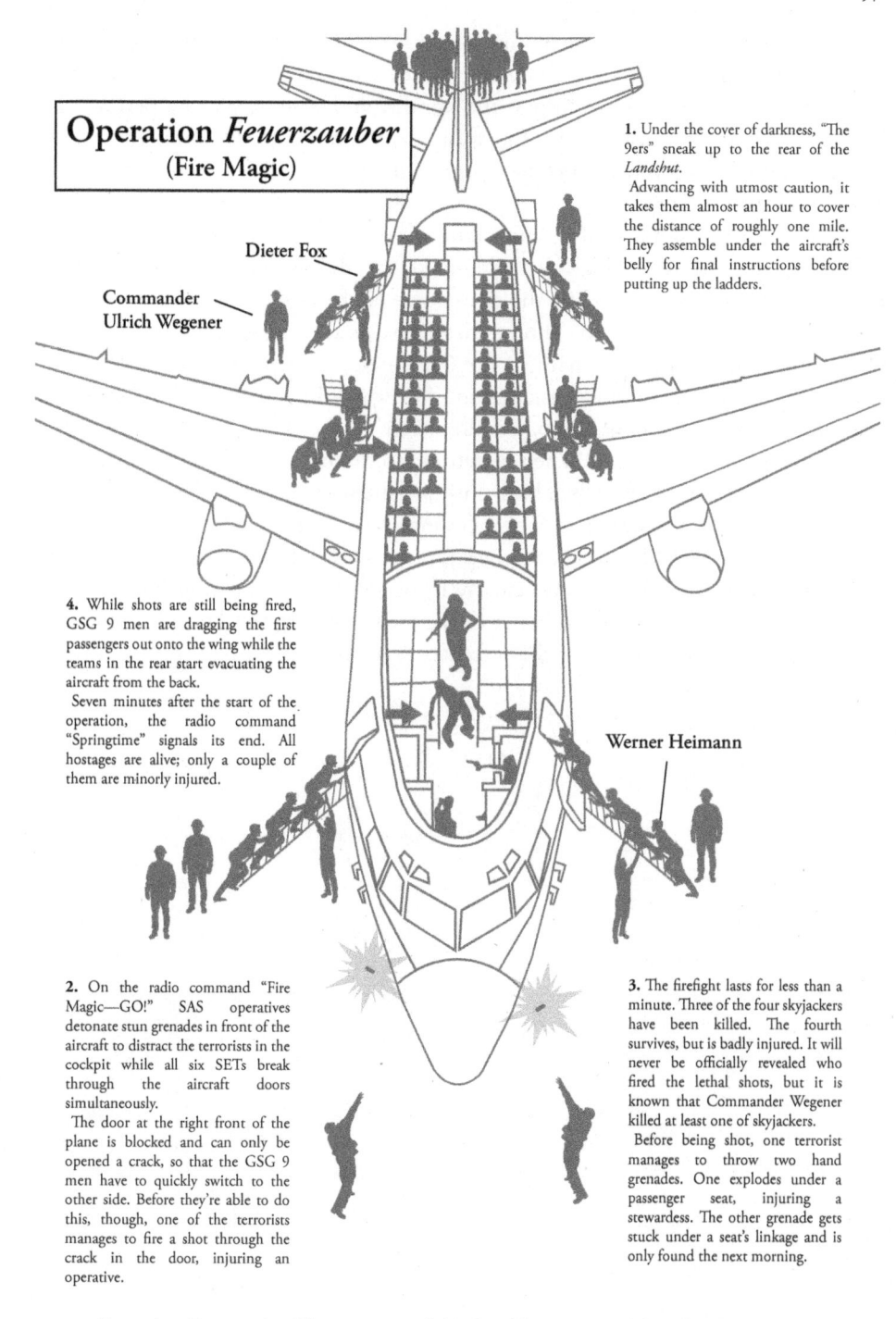

OPERATION *FEUERZAUBER* • 157

Operation *Feuerzauber*
(Fire Magic)

Dieter Fox

Commander
Ulrich Wegener

Werner Heimann

1. Under the cover of darkness, "The 9ers" sneak up to the rear of the *Landshut*.

Advancing with utmost caution, it takes them almost an hour to cover the distance of roughly one mile. They assemble under the aircraft's belly for final instructions before putting up the ladders.

4. While shots are still being fired, GSG 9 men are dragging the first passengers out onto the wing while the teams in the rear start evacuating the aircraft from the back.

Seven minutes after the start of the operation, the radio command "Springtime" signals its end. All hostages are alive; only a couple of them are minorly injured.

2. On the radio command "Fire Magic—GO!" SAS operatives detonate stun grenades in front of the aircraft to distract the terrorists in the cockpit while all six SETs break through the aircraft doors simultaneously.

The door at the right front of the plane is blocked and can only be opened a crack, so that the GSG 9 men have to quickly switch to the other side. Before they're able to do this, though, one of the terrorists manages to fire a shot through the crack in the door, injuring an operative.

3. The firefight lasts for less than a minute. Three of the four skyjackers have been killed. The fourth survives, but is badly injured. It will never be officially revealed who fired the lethal shots, but it is known that Commander Wegener killed at least one of skyjackers.

Before being shot, one terrorist manages to throw two hand grenades. One explodes under a passenger seat, injuring a stewardess. The other grenade gets stuck under a seat's linkage and is only found the next morning.

Operation *Feuerzauber*: The storming of the *Landshut* in Mogadishu. (Declan Ingram) out of the plane. On his way there, he would have had to bypass three people of the designated SET who remained outside on the wing securing the exit, and even before that he would have had to pass the standby and cover team who performed safety and evacuation tasks under the wing. It is more than doubtful that they would have let Davies move onto the wing, because Davies had no business being there whatsoever.

Davies and Morrison played an important role in the storming of Flight LH-181. It was just not the part they were celebrated for. But it appears that once the narrative of British heroes leading the charge was established, nobody in the media bothered to check again. What's more, Dieter Fox recalls an interview for a British TV documentary in the aftermath of the 9/11 attacks. After he told his story he was approached by the producer asking him if he was willing to adjust his narration to accommodate the supposedly outstanding role of the two SAS men who were considered irrevocable heroes. When he refused to do so, he was informed a couple of days later that his interview had been entirely edited out of the documentary. The same thing happened with Ulrich Wegener's interview for the same documentary. It appears as though the old bon mot amongst journalists still stands: Never let the truth get in the way of a good story. Particularly if the story features national treasures.

Apparently, patriotism got the better of the media coverage and people preferred to celebrate their two heroes for the role they wanted them to have played rather than the role they actually did play.

CHAPTER 11

Birth of a Legend

"Thirty-eight minutes past midnight, this is Deutschlandfunk* with an important news update: The 86 hostages kidnapped by terrorists in a Lufthansa Boeing have all been freed safely."[1] There was a knock on the parlor door: "Herr Tutter, telephone for you!" The officer on duty had the unit commander called down to the operations center. Bonn was on the line, the state secretary in the Ministry of the Interior. But was it good news or bad news?

"Herr Chief Inspector, let me start by telling you that the operation in Mogadishu was successful."

"Successful? How about losses?"

"Yes, one injured."

"Terrorists or hostages?"

"The hostages have all been freed. Terrorists: Well, three are dead, and one—we don't know for sure yet."

"What else?"

"Um, not much. Everything went just fine."

"Now, that's crazy!"

Tutter hung up, shook his head in disbelief, and had the entire GSG 9 rounded up from their beds to gather in the courtyard in front of the main building. "SETs, motor vehicle technicians, armorers—down to the last man. And then I announced it. There was an unbelievable cheering and happiness, we danced in a merry-go-round, hopping up and down—just like the handball players do when they have won a match."

In that moment, a ministerial motorcade rushed around the corner, fresh from the crisis team of the government. For several days, Foreign Minister Hans-Dietrich Genscher, his wife, mother, and family had been housed on the premises of the Border Guard in Saint Augustin, as had his secretary of state, Klaus Kinkel, and several other high-ranking political figures from Bonn. In view of the tense situation

---

* Deutschlandfunk = National public radio broadcasting service for Germany.

and the fact that the German capital was in a state of emergency, BKA's security service could not guarantee their safety in private apartments. Genscher was housed in the GSG 9 barracks block. "They arrived, got out of their cars, and Genscher was taken into our circle. We all linked arms with each other and then jumped and danced round and around," Dieter Tutter fondly recalls. "Nobody asked Genscher if he wanted to be included, we just made him do it, but he didn't seem to mind at all and he happily danced along."

At the same time, only a few miles away in Bonn, government spokesman Klaus Bölling appeared before the public. The tension of the past few hours was still carved into his face, but he was beaming a smile of great relief. In a flurry of flashbulbs from the capital's press, he dropped into his chair, puffing. He straightened his tie, ran both hands over his face, and took a deep breath before reading out the crisis staff's statement: "The hostages in Mogadishu are free. We are grateful that people of several nations and citizens of our country survived this brutal kidnapping. We owe a debt of gratitude to the brave men of Group 9 of the Federal Border Guard, who dared to risk their lives for the hostages, for the crew of the Lufthansa aircraft and, in truth, for all our citizens."[2]

It was Bölling's voice that the people of Germany woke up to only a few hours later, including Simone Wegener: "All my life I will never forget the morning of October 18, 1977. It was at 6:00 a.m. I heard it from the radio by my bed. It still gets to me when I think about it. The news bulletin included a list of the injured and dead, so to speak, from which it was clear that nothing had happened to my father."[3] Simone Wegener (today Simone Stewens) is one of the two daughters of the GSG 9 commander, at the time she was 21 years of age. Her younger sister Susanne was equally overwhelmed by the news: "We knew there was going to be a big operation. But for a long time we didn't know where they were, how tangible the planning was and the preparations for the storm. We only found out after the fact. I have to say that I was proud and also curious to hear what my father would say as an eyewitness, as someone who was right in the middle of the action."[4] For the 18-year-old student, the whole matter was first and foremost one thing: exciting.

With her mother, however, all well-established emotional dams had burst. As the wife of a high-ranking officer, she was always careful to maintain her composure and not to reveal her feelings, either in public or to her children. The night before the mission, she had gone for a walk with her older daughter to distract herself. "But our minds were elsewhere," she later confided to newspaper reporters. "I almost couldn't cope with myself and my nerves. This inner turmoil, this irritability."[5] Now she was sitting on the sofa in the living room, crying, in a mixture of relief and horror at the extreme situation her husband must have been in. "She knew that it was dangerous," says her daughter Susanne, "especially for my father, because he wasn't one of those people who send their men ahead and then stay under cover themselves."

Meanwhile, it was also known that a GSG 9 man had been injured during the operation. "I was sure that [it] must be Anselm who got shot," Gisela Weygold, who knew her husband well, said. Anselm, the leader of the 3rd Unit, was one of the wild ones with "The 9ers." Mrs. Wegold was relieved that "it quickly turned out that it was Werner Losert, and thank God nothing seriously bad happened to him, but it was quite exciting at first." The last she had heard from her husband was three days earlier, when she wanted to bring him fresh laundry and a piece of cake to the compound. The mission in Ankara had been called off and GSG 9 was back in Saint Augustin. "I enter the barracks, I hear helicopters, and I run into Dieter Tutter: 'What are you doing here?' he asks, and I say, 'Anselm called me.'—'Ah yes,' he says, 'he's up there,' and points to the helicopters taking off.—'So …?' But Dieter just shrugs, 'No idea.' And then we really didn't know anything at all. It is true that us women, we only got our information from TV. Nobody told us anything—well, rightly so. We probably wouldn't have been able to cope with that either. It was OK to do it that way, leaving us in the dark."

Nevertheless, worries remained, for days on end. The wives and girlfriends of "The 9ers" tried to support each other. Most of them had moved to Saint Augustin with their husbands when they had been accepted into GSG 9. They lived in the residential areas close to the compound with their young children, but without support from their families, who usually lived several hours away by car. While her husband chased after Flight LH-181 God knows where, Gisela Weygold invited other GSG 9 wives over for coffee and cake and joint daycare of the children, forcing themselves to keep busy. She firmly resolved not to let uncertainty get the better of her, while brushing off inquiries from family and friends. Gisela Weygold "always told my parents with all the conviction in my voice I could muster: 'Nothing will happen to them. No, don't listen to the news.' Of course, my heart was pounding as well, but only afterwards. In the situation you block that out. Only after the situation was resolved, I had a big sigh of relief. I could feel the weight fall off my shoulders."

Rescue and Suicide

As soon as news of the success in faraway Mogadishu hit the press agencies, the editors of the major newspapers in Hamburg, Cologne, Munich, and Berlin had stopped the presses. "At midnight, Bonn's supermen stormed the hostage jet," read the front pages the next morning, or "German secret force attacks—all hostages free!" as Germany's leading tabloid, *BILD*, headlined. Almost all the major news outlets printed hastily assembled special editions and extra pages. On the streets, in buses and subways, there was no other topic than the successful scoop. Waiting at traffic lights, drivers shouted the latest news to each other through lowered side windows. But more news rushed in, and the relief at the good tidings from Mogadishu lasted only a short time. During the morning it was announced that three of the Red Army

Faction prisoners in Stammheim had been found dead in their cells: Andreas Baader and Jan-Carl Raspe had shot themselves; Gudrun Ensslin had hanged herself from the bars of her cell window with a loudspeaker cable; Irmgard Möller's attempt to take her own life by stabbing herself in the chest with a bread knife had failed. She was hospitalized with serious injuries.

The discussion about the circumstances of the suicides quickly overshadowed the joy over the successful liberation. How was it possible that Germany's best-monitored prisoners could take their own lives unnoticed in the high-security wing of Stammheim Prison? How had they learned of the operation in Mogadishu immediately after it happened, in the middle of the night without radios, which they were not allowed to have? How had they been able to arrange collective suicides? How had Raspe and Baader obtained pistols? Was it actually suicide? Suicide under state supervision? Or even state murder? And finally, what did their sudden demise mean for the life of Hanns Martin Schleyer, who was still in the RAF's hands?

It was painfully clear to Schleyer's family that something was about to happen soon, something that could not be in their best interest. The weekend before, Jörg Schleyer's brother, Hanns-Eberhard, had failed with an injunction before the Federal Constitutional Court. With it, he wanted to force the government to comply with the RAF's demands and immediately exchange the incarcerated prisoners for his father. After the liberation of the *Landshut* hostages and the Stammheim suicides, all hope of saving his father's life was lost. Jörg Schleyer said, "We didn't waste a single thought on them releasing him just like that. We were convinced that it would end with an execution, we never considered anything else. Why should we? For six weeks you make such a fuss, you lose your three protagonists, and then you release Schleyer as a gesture of humanity? No. We were just waiting for the news to come in. My mother sat there paralyzed and was hard to talk to. Because she knew, of course, what this meant for my father."

Neither the freed hostages of the *Landshut* nor the GSG 9 men were aware of any of these developments in Germany. They were on their way back to Germany in two separate planes. The *Landshut* remained in Mogadishu. It was searched once again by the forensics team and photographed and would only be transferred to Germany sometime later. After the days-long hostage drama and the nighttime shootout, it was in no condition to fly and would probably have been an imposition for the freed passengers. For most of them, it was a traumatic experience to board an airplane again just a few hours after the end of their ordeal.

Many wished to fly in the same plane as their rescuers to say thank you. But although there would have been enough room for all of them in one aircraft, Commander Wegener assigned only a small squad for protection and a few paramedics for medical care. ("If anything had happened to them again, it would have been on us."[6]) The others went back in Wischnewski's Boeing. The GSG 9 commander wanted to avoid scenes of fraternization and embarrassment that might result from the exuberance of the moment; the GSG 9 forces were supposed to keep to themselves. In addition, Wegener wanted to discuss a few things with his unit leaders during the return flight that were not intended for outside ears. The rest of the troops were looking forward to the faces of their families, a warm shower, a proper meal, and a good night's sleep after the exertions of the past few days.

The aircraft with the returnees first landed in Frankfurt, where only the freed hostages were allowed to disembark. However, the two planes were parked right next to each other, so Dieter Fox was able to observe what was happening outside on the apron. It wasn't just the relatives of the *Landshut* passengers who were waiting there. Hordes of reporters and photographers overwhelmed the returnees, and the television cameras broadcast the arrival live. "We just said, 'Good heavens! Once we land in Cologne, we must make sure that we pack our stuff onto the buses, and quickly get to the compound.' Well, eventually we would arrive in Cologne-Bonn: It was even worse!"

When they rolled out in front of the terminal building barely an hour later, Werner Heimann wondered what all the fuss outside was about. "I look out the window and think, huh, is there a state visit scheduled here for today? The whole place was crowded, red carpet, marching band, hundreds of people. And we were taxiing toward it." Wegener instructed the pilot to find another spot to park the plane some quiet place away from the hustle and bustle, but the captain just shrugged and told him: Announcement from the Ministry of the Interior—they were instructed to park exactly here.

Wischnewski was the first one to get out. While he was greeted on the red carpet by Minister of the Interior Maihofer with a hug, a dispute about protocol issues broke out inside. A Border Guard officer had come in carrying a dress uniform for the commander. Wegener asked what he was supposed to do with it. Put it on, was the terse answer. That was too much for Wegener. "Forget it," he snapped at the officer. "What are you people thinking? My men are all still in the clothes they wore in the field, and so am I, so that's how I'm getting off the plane."—"That could mean trouble," the officer said meekly. "For you maybe, not for me."[7] However, it would also have been difficult to organize uniforms for the rest of the crew so quickly. Some of them, like Fox, had not brought a uniform at all, the uniforms of others were stowed in the plane's cargo hold. And outside, relatives and the press were waiting, along with the honor guard and music corps, the minister of the interior, and the "Gold Pheasants," as the Border Guard's top brass was known to the rank and file. It took quite a while before the front door of the plane opened again and the first GSG 9 men hesitantly stepped out. A correspondent commented on live television, "Tired out, some faces, it shows. The strain, the traces of a long night, the traces of an extreme effort of nerves and strength are written on people's faces."[8]

Out on the apron, Susanne Wegener waited for her father. She was amazed at the official buzz, "For the first time, I actually realized how important this mission was for the Federal Republic of Germany, how great the political relief, and under how much pressure everyone must have been." Not far from the Wegeners, Gisela Weygold was looking out for her husband. She had brought her seven-year-old daughter with her. "Cosima was standing in front of me, and I had put my hands on her shoulders." The two waited in tense anticipation for Papa Lemmy's face to appear. "And then she said, 'Mommy, what are you doing? You're hurting me!' My hands had clawed harder and harder into her shoulders. I was so excited that I didn't even notice."

But before Lemmy Weygold and his 3rd Unit appeared in the doorway, the men from the 1st Unit showed up. Jörg Probstmeier was one of the first to descend the gangway—and was embarrassed: "We were not prepared for this. We wanted to celebrate our success, but modestly, just amongst ourselves. We hadn't practiced for big, festive receptions. So we stepped down the stairs a little shy, we the 1st Unit. In contrast, Lemmy Weygold, the unit leader of the 3rd, ordered his boys: 'We're going out on the double.'" No hesitation there.

A few minutes later, finally, they were all lined up on the red carpet in front of the plane's wing, still in the civilian clothes they were wearing when they stormed an airplane barely 12 hours earlier, while the minister of the interior of the Federal Republic of Germany solemnly marched past the formation, accompanied by their commander in a leather jacket and running shoes. This unconventional sight defined the image of GSG 9 for a long time. The respective photos would appear on the evening news and be printed the next day in all the newspapers, not only in Germany. Wegener would find himself on the cover of *Time* magazine.

"We never expected that this would create such huge resonance," says Werner Heimann in retrospect. And neither he nor Jörg Probstmeier nor anybody else of the Mogadishu men had much use for the term "hero," which was now wafting through the headlines and editorial columns. "We didn't feel like heroes, but simply like police officers who had shown what they had trained for. We were no longer the world champions in training but had earned our own right to exist. We didn't expect any parades. There were no prideful sentiments of any such kind."

Modesty or not, when the "Deutschlandlied" sounded across the apron, some of them felt a pleasant shiver running down their spine, including Dieter Fox. "This was an uplifting moment for me. The fact that the national anthem was played for us few hobos who had been sent down there was something quite beautiful." The words of Minister of the Interior Maihofer did the rest:

> You have risked your life to save the lives of others. I think this sentence sums up everything you have done. Despite all the technical perfection you have acquired in years of hard training for such tasks, You have—and this is a small miracle—freed all passengers and all surviving members of the crew alive and healthy from the terrorists' grip. We have always wished for such a happy outcome to such a difficult undertaking, but we could hardly hope for it when we were faced with the difficult decision to order this operation to rescue the hostages, weighing

up all the risks and opportunities.... Last but not least, we also feared for the lives of each and every one of you during this dangerous mission. We were therefore overjoyed along with your relatives when we received the report that there was only one injury on the part of the men of GSG 9.... With your successful rescue operation, as I see it, you have set a lasting example that the terrorists eventually do not stand a chance if civilized nations stand together to defend them the way Somalia did with us in a difficult hour.... We are proud of you![9]

Then, finally, the families were allowed to join them. No one had deemed barriers or controls necessary. So as soon as the official reception was over, not only did wives, daughters, and sons flood onto the red carpet, representatives of the press also immediately besieged Fox and his comrades to ask them about their impressions and feelings. Some of the interviews were conducted while the men held their children in their arms for the first time. "That was something that should have been prevented, that wasn't good. I understand that the media wanted to have the fresh, unfiltered statements. But we were still too worked up with adrenalin and overwhelmed."

The rank and file were happy when the reporters finally let up. For the unit leaders and longest-serving SET leaders, however, the hype was not over just yet. In the airport building, the minister of the interior had arranged for a press conference. There, too, the mostly lower-ranking GSG 9 men like Werner Heimann received unaccustomed attention from the otherwise hierarchy-conscious BGS top brass: "When we came in casually dressed as we were, the higher ranks jumped up from their chairs and offered us their seats—we had never seen anything like it." When everyone had found their seats, Minister of the Interior Maihofer asked Wegener in front of the assembled press about the details and course of the operation. "Even ministers of the interior don't have to know everything," the commander replied sparsely. Whether the minister found this remark to be amusing or an affront is not known, but he joined the jovial laughter that rose in the hall at the blunt reply of GSG 9's commander. Werner Heimann, who was also asked how the mission had gone, was more jovial but hardly more exhaustive, "It was quite similar to an exercise, only better."

On the sidelines and somewhat lost, the officers of the 2nd Unit watched the hustle and bustle of the big event. They had marched up to the reception as GSG 9's honorary company. While the other units were underway chasing the *Landshut*, they had held the fort in Germany and continued to search unsuccessfully for Hanns Martin Schleyer. But no matter how hard they tried to convince themselves that this feat was an achievement of GSG 9 as a whole and thus their success as well, frustration at not having been present on the decisive mission was gnawing at them. Dieter Tutter was the leader of the honor formation: "It was difficult for me. It was similar to an athlete who keeps training and preparing all his life and then is not allowed to compete. Can you imagine what it means when you have signed up for such a special police force, going all in, with a full heart? You train your people, you have a unit that really stands out, magnificent people. And then there is a great success—and the other two units rise to be the heroes of Mogadishu! So we're lined up there as a company of honor, me in front. These are our comrades, and we don't begrudge them all the trimmings, not in the least. But Jesus, did it hurt!"

The Afternoon Off

After what felt like an eternity, the official program at Cologne Airport was finally over, the buses were loaded and on their way to Saint Augustin. But the short drive held another surprise in store. On the autobahn, countless oncoming cars greeted them honking and flashing their lights. And the street scene on arrival in the neighborhood reminded them of a mixture of World Cup fever, fairground and carnival. "I've never seen anything like it," Dieter Fox still shakes his head. "There were throngs of people waving from the rooftops of the buildings as we passed through—we didn't expect that. We waved back a little, but we were glad when we finally arrived at the barracks." There, the entrance hall was stuffed with flower bouquets, gift baskets and barrels of beer donated for the next GSG 9 party. There would be one for sure, but certainly not today, Dieter Fox said. "We were glad when we were among ourselves again, when we could take our wives and children in our arms, go home and get into the bathtub—or just sleep."

For others, sleeping was not an option. Some arranged for a couple of comrades and their families to dine in a fine restaurant as did Werner Heimann. "After all, they were generous enough to give us the afternoon off. They said, 'OK guys, have the rest of the day for yourselves, we'll see you back tomorrow at 10.' Special leave? No way! So we went home, full of euphoria of course." Susanne Wegener's father was exhilarated as well, despite sleep deprivation and extreme tension over the previous days: "When he returned, he was still completely flooded with adrenaline, even though the operation had been over for many hours by then. It wasn't like us sitting down together and him telling us from A to Z: now, that's how it went. He didn't report much at all at first. And what he reported did not come in a strict, coherent narrative, but in bits and pieces, always adding ideas and details that later came to his mind."

But also, there was no time for leisure and quiet reflection. GSG 9 was still on standby as the search for Hanns Martin Schleyer continued. He had been missing for more than six weeks. No one really felt like celebrating just yet. The joy about the successful operation in Mogadishu was overshadowed by the fact that despite the largest manhunt in German history, it had not yet been possible to find and free the kidnapped president of the German Employers' Association.

One day after GSG 9's triumphant return, on the afternoon of October 19, a woman's voice came over the phone at the Stuttgart office of the DPA news agency: "This is RAF. After 43 days, we have ended Hanns Martin Schleyer's miserable and corrupt existence. Herr Schmidt, who speculated on Schleyer's death in his power rationale from the beginning, can pick him up in Rue Charles Péguy in Mulhouse in a green Audi 100 with Bad Homburg license plates. For our pain and anger over the massacres in Mogadishu and Stammheim, his death is meaningless.... We will never forgive Schmidt and the imperialists who support him for the blood they have shed. The struggle has only begun. Freedom through armed anti-imperialist struggle!"[10]

What the Schleyer family had feared ever since they heard the news from Mogadishu and Stammheim now turned into devastating certainty. For them, the words of Federal President Walter Scheel at the state memorial service a week later would sound hollow: "We take a bow before the dead. We all know that we are in his debt. On behalf of all German citizens, I ask you, the relatives of Hanns Martin Schleyer, for forgiveness."[11]

GSG 9 chief Wegener attended the funeral. Afterward, he sought a conversation with Schleyer's son Hanns-Eberhard, who reacted bitterly.[*] Today, his brother Jörg Schleyer offers a much milder assessment of the decisions made by the German government: "They tried everything, just as we tried everything. We went all the way to the Bundesgerichtshof [Federal Constitutional Court], which I believe was legitimate. And the federal government naturally said: We can no longer allow ourselves to be blackmailed, we don't want a second Peter Lorenz[†] case. It was, as they say, a question of the weighing of values, and my father was the one who ... well, drew the short straw."

And GSG 9? Jörg Schleyer has been friends with Dieter Fox for several years. "I once told him: 'If you hadn't stormed the *Landshut*, my father could still be alive. I thought what you did was outstanding, getting 86 people out of that plane. That was certainly no walk in the park. But for my father, it was a death sentence.'"

---

[*] In later years, the relationship between the eldest Schleyer son and Wegener would ease.
[†] The conservative politician abducted in 1975 in Berlin. The federal government paid ransom for his release. In return, the freed prisoners immediately restarted their terrorist activities.

CHAPTER 12

Circus Wegener

The phone was ringing off the hook. In the commander's office, appointments kept flooding in. Conference with the minister of the interior at the ministry, reception with Helmut Schmidt at the Chancellery, press conference at the headquarters.... On day one after their return, Border Guard Group 9 was caught up in the general publicity maelstrom. "The perks of Mogadishu," one desk officer commented sarcastically. Rolf Tophoven eagerly took notes. Being a journalist by trade, he was also considered a leading anti-terrorism expert. His book *Fedayin—Guerilla ohne Grenzen* (*Fedayin—Guerrilla without Borders*)[1] was considered the gold standard in its analysis of Palestinian terror networks, appreciated by friend and foe. So naturally it was part of the library of the Red Army Faction prisoners in Stammheim Prison.* Tophoven had held a series of lectures about the subject at GSG 9 headquarters and had become intimate with the inner workings of the special intervention unit. He enjoyed the full trust of Wegener and GSG 9's leadership as well as virtually unlimited access to the premises.

"When Mogadishu was about to happen, I knew the night before that the guys were down there and that something was going on," Tophoven says. "I still remember the phone call with the leader of the 2nd Unit, Dieter Tutter, who had to stay behind, much to his chagrin. He was very cautious on the phone. But in the end Tutter said: 'Let's hope that everyone comes back safely.' It was clear to me then that the operation was imminent."[2] The next morning, his publisher rang up Tophoven. After the scoop in Africa, it was clear that he needed to write a book about Germany's new sensation. Titled *GSG 9—Kommando gegen Terrorismus*, it was to be published a few weeks later. For many years, the narrow volume, approved by GSG 9, would remain the only work in print to describe in some detail the special task force.

In the command office that morning, Adjutant Baum was visibly stressed with keeping the situation under control. "During the mission in Mogadishu we had more peace and quiet than now after our return," he complained to Tophoven while

---

* Contrary to the talk of "isolation torture," RAF prisoners enjoyed access to a variety of media, be it newspapers, weekly journals, or hundreds of political and historical books, as well as novels.

trying to get the next caller off his hands. He would have to get used to it. The media inquiries were not to end any time soon.

Outside headquarters, however, everyday life had already resumed, barely 24 hours after their return. Wegener had issued orders to restore operational readiness as quickly as possible, the simple reason being that the search for Hanns Martin Schleyer and his kidnappers was not yet over. "Now we have to dial everything back to zero,"[3] Dieter Fox told the journalist. This meant not only cleaning weapons and checking equipment, but also mentally processing what had happened in order to get back into operational mode.

As part of the obligatory debriefing, Wegener had instructed his unit and squad leaders to write mission reports, emphasizing that nothing should be glossed over. But apart from providing better insulation for the storm ladders so they wouldn't squeak when they were leant against the aircraft, Werner Heimann and his comrades could not think of much that could have been improved. "It all went extremely smoothly. Concerning the operational playbook, we all agreed that it couldn't have worked better."

Psychologically, of course, the mission would still have to be worked through. Luckily, traumatizing consequences did not occur, not even among the officers whose shots at the terrorists had been lethal. Commander Wegener alone is known to have killed at least one terrorist, as did at least one other "9er." According to Wegener's recollection, the man told him afterwards: "It was obvious that we had to shoot the hijacker. If we hadn't shot him, he would have shot hostages." Wegener justified himself in a similar way: "OK, I shot a man, but it happened to save the lives of others."[4] No officer seems to have suffered from any symptoms of post-traumatic stress disorder. This being said, it must be pointed out that in general at the time, it was not common in police units to put too much emphasis on this psychological aspect in the debriefing phase of operations.

Danger, however, lurked elsewhere in the form of simple routine. "Everyday life goes on as before. And GSG 9's everyday life is dull and stupid," said Dieter Fox. "Before Mogadishu, everyday life was exciting. But after something like this? Who wants to teach me anything about anything now? Staying grounded, that's the real difficulty." That required self-discipline and the constant reminder that they were no superheroes, but well-trained police officers who were preparing for new missions. Missions that would again be demanding and potentially dangerous. "Therefore, I need to meticulously process what I have experienced, keep my feet on the ground, not lose my marbles and stay the person I have been before. Yes, this was a highlight in my career which I have accomplished, and I am certainly allowed to be proud of it. But life in GSG 9 goes on." Most of them kept it together, but only most: "Some got carried away with their triumph and had great problems finding their stride again." In one case it even ended in suicide: a few years later, a retired GSG 9 officer shot himself with his service revolver. Fortunately, such an extreme consequence remained an isolated incident.

On that first "day after," journalist Tophoven did not detect any exuberance among the men. Or their commander, for that matter. "What happened in Mogadishu is in line with our general mission," Wegener dictated soberly for the benefit of the journalist's notebook. "We have carried it out in accordance with our training, and now we are continuing to work as before. Euphoria is not appropriate."[5] But keeping it real was not an easy task, as it turned out.

While the officers were preparing for their routine duty, Commander Wegener was called to the chancellor's office in Bonn for an unofficial appointment. Helmut Schmidt once again thanked the rescuers of the hostages (and thus the rescuers of his government). Then he announced that Wegener would be awarded the Bundesverdienstkreuz (Federal Cross of Merit), West Germany's highest medal of honor. Wegener inquired who else was to receive the award. "Well, just you," the chancellor answered somewhat puzzled. This did not sit well with Wegener. He insisted that either all men participating in the operation receive the award or none of them. "Are you insane?" the chancellor snapped at Wegener, more perplexed than irate: "We have never done anything like that before."

"This is certainly true," Wegener retorted. "But there has probably never been such a liberation operation in the Federal Republic of Germany, either."[6] Thus, Federal Germany's President Walter Scheel had to put his signature on more than five dozen certificates for the award ceremony the next day: 62 for the Mogadishu team of GSG 9, and five more for the *Landshut* crew, who also were awarded the medal. (Captain Jürgen Schumann received it posthumously.)

This happened a couple of days later and, of course, with the media's attendance. Yet again, Wegener was stressed. "This is worse than going on a mission," he hissed through clenched teeth when facing the renewed press hype and the glaring spotlights that had been set up for the international TV stations.[7] In the courtyard, the Border Guard had put armored vehicles on display for the 500 guests that had gathered in the chancellor's office to pay their respects: members of the crisis team, politicians of both government and opposition, delegations from Lufthansa, the Federal Criminal Police Office BKA, ministries and authorities. A dinner at the chancellor's mansion, the Palais Schaumburg, was to follow later—something Helmut Schmidt had never done before, either.

But first, Wegener received the Grand Cross of Merit of the Federal Republic of Germany, the unit leaders and SET leaders were awarded the Order of Merit First Class, and the squad members were presented with the Order of Merit with Ribbon. When Minister of the Interior Maihofer placed the medal around Wegener's neck, the commander stared at the red and gold cross in front of his chest for a while in disbelief. Looking up again, he lined up among his men for Chancellor Schmidt's speech of thanks:

> Come to the fore a bit, Herr Wegener, because I have been told that in my telegram of thanks, which reached you on board the plane on your return flight, I inadvertently indicated your rank as Senior Police Director. Dear Mr. Wegener, as far as the future is concerned, you will

remain in the position of Senior Police Director. You, Herr Senior Police Director, and your men have all set an example to our people that our Constitutional State is not helpless. You have also set an example of what community demands of all of us. Together you have set an example for the young people in this country, an example of what we all have to stand up for and for which some of us may be required to risk their own lives in an emergency. Thanks to your excellent training and equipment, and thanks to your courage, you brought the operation in Mogadishu to a happy end. It could have turned out differently.[8]

True enough! When the chancellor inquired in the subsequent conversation about Wegener's secret of success, the commander modestly replied: "I would like to quote a word from [Prussian King] Frederick the Great: 'A little bit *de la fortune* is required as well.'"

What are the Odds?

In Wegener's final report, there was no mention of any fortune. "The operation has clearly shown that the special training against hijackers carried out by GSG 9 has proven its worth." To which he was quick to add that "it needs to be intensified in the sense that it is made sure that aircraft of the Deutsche Lufthansa can be used for training and exercise purposes in the future as well." Weapons and equipment of GSG 9 have "fully proven their worth," apart from the man-stopping effect of the Magnum revolver, which Wegener was dissatisfied with. And with the failure of the radios, of course. Also, the protective clothing was not suitable for night-time use, and steel helmets proved unsuitable for use in an aircraft, which is why they were to be replaced by a single-colored visor cap for better recognition. (This suggestion never materialized.)

Otherwise, Wegener expressed his satisfaction with the cooperation between the Federal Criminal Police Office BKA, Lufthansa and GSG 9 and described the "non-interference of the representative of the political leadership on site" in the person of Minister of State Wischnewski as a prerequisite for the success of the mission in line with GSG 9's command system of Mission Tactics: "After the order was given, no tactical details were demanded of the tactical leader,"[9] i.e. himself.

What Wegener failed to mention, however, was the lucky star that was shining over the whole endeavor. Chancellor Schmidt later admitted that "at the time, a lot of good luck had brought success."[10] But when he wrote down this confession, many years after Mogadishu, Schmidt still did not know just how much good luck was involved in the operation. He had estimated the risk at 50:50 of the aircraft being blown up by the terrorists during the assault. GSG 9's Dieter Fox figures that the risk of it being blown up was significantly lower. But taking into account the at times hair-raising events and decisions made in the hours and days prior to the storm, he, too, believes that the overall chances of success of the mission were no higher than 50 percent. In the years that followed, he would discuss this question time and again with Wegener. The commander put his own estimate at 90 percent due to skill and only 10 percent to the kind of fortune that is with the one who is working hard for it. "He saw it from the vantage point of the commander," says Fox. But indeed, in view of all the factors that could have prevented success, the GSG 9 founder's view seems somewhat rosy. In the author's assessment, the outcome might have been very different:

- if Wegener had been denied the number of men he deemed necessary when ordered to take up pursuit at the outset of the skyjacking by Minister of the Interior Maihofer;
- if Wegener had not been allowed to keep following the *Landshut* after GSG 9 was ordered home after their detection in Ankara;
- if the Dubaians or Somalis had insisted on storming the plane themselves (Fox: "We could have taught the Somalis one or two tricks in the short amount of time available, but it would never have worked, because you need to really get a grip on the purpose of an exercise and of certain tactics, and this is nothing you can learn within a few hours.");
- if the guards at the airport checkpoint had not let Wegener, Baum and Fox pass;
- if the Somali officer had lost his nerve and actually sent in tanks; or
- if more than one GSG 9 man had come forward, reporting himself unfit to get on the plane.

And what about the raid itself? The flock of birds flying up on approach, the shadows cast by GSG 9 squads under the plane, the explosives planted on the plane doors—all these things could have caused the operation to fail at any time. Add the factors which would have not jeopardized the operation as such but could have tainted its happy outcome considerably, and the odds become even shakier: the loss of radio communication, the blocked right front door, the "lucky strike" in officer Losert's neck, the non-detonated grenade left in the cabin.

And what if it had actually gone wrong? What if there had been deaths amongst GSG 9 or the hostages? Veteran Fox is convinced today: "GSG 9 would have been disbanded that very night. There would have been no need for such a unit: They spent five years in preparation, expensive people, well equipped. The federal government spent a lot on infrastructure and posts and training and equipment, and after all these efforts such an operation goes wrong? Well, then they're useless." Gerhart Baum, who was appointed minister of the interior only a few months after Mogadishu, vigorously denies this. Under no circumstances would GSG 9 have been disbanded: "Never! Dear God, things like that can happen. People put their lives on the line. The need to have a GSG 9 would not have become superfluous as a result. Failure is always a possibility; of course there is a risk. But that wouldn't put GSG 9 in question as an institution."

Would it have been possible to uphold this stance if Schmidt's fear had come true? If instead of pictures of happily freed hostages, pictures of a burned-out *Landshut* had gone around the world, just like the pictures of the burned-out helicopters in Fürstenfeldbruck five years earlier? Luckily, no one in Bonn had to deal with such scenarios in 1977.

The German government received congratulations from all over the world. Israeli Prime Minister Menachem Begin and Foreign Minister Moshe Dayan sent telegrams to their German colleagues.[11] Turkish Prime Minister Süleyman Demirel expressed his admiration for the "determination and courage of the government of the Federal Republic of Germany and the men of the rescue mission." Spanish Prime Minister Adolfo Suárez marveled at the "calm and firm attitude" that also allowed the rescue of a group of Spanish citizens who were on board Flight LH-181; and US President Jimmy Carter assured his "friend Helmut" that the people of the United States shared his "admiration for what you have done."[12] Two American citizens had been passengers: a 44-year-old woman and her five-year-old son.

Terrorism's Defeat

On his visit to Bonn the day after Mogadishu, British Prime Minister Callaghan declared, "Bonn inflicts an important defeat on terrorism."[13] This reflected a widespread view. But was it true? Certainly, the liberation of the *Landshut* hostages was a major blow to the Red Army Faction and its international terrorist network and every single life saved was worth the effort. But how sustainable was what Wegener and his men had achieved? Was it more than a symbolic victory? Few journalists have spent their lives dealing with the RAF as intensively as Stefan Aust, former editor of weekly *Der Spiegel*. He concluded: "The immediate result of the news about the liberation of the hostages in Mogadishu led to the suicide of Baader, Ensslin and Jan-Carl Raspe. In this respect, the determined and successful deployment of GSG 9 had made it clear to the RAF cadres that their strategy had failed. Subsequently, the next generations of the RAF never again attempted to free RAF prisoners from their confinement by taking hostages."[14]

According to this view, GSG 9 set a deterrent example: The chances of successfully taking hostages seemed too low for the terrorists, the risk of failure too high. Karl-Heinz Dellwo was one of the RAF prisoners who were to be released by kidnapping Schleyer and seizing the *Landshut*. However, he denies that GSG 9 action in Mogadishu was the reason for the lack of further kidnappings of this kind: "I don't believe it was because of that. After the death of the Stammheim prisoners, the symbolic value of a liberation attempt was simply no longer a given."[15]

The likes of Dellwo considered themselves urban guerrillas in 1977 and he argues from that perspective. Dellwo states that in the long run, there are two realistic alternatives for an underground fighter in a revolutionary struggle: being killed or ending up in prison. The latter, however, was never considered a tolerable permanent state and final outcome; prison was not accepted to be "the invincible answer to the prevailing conditions." The liberation of prisoners was therefore understood as part of the revolutionary struggle. "And that is why it had a symbolic value that was connected with the prisoners in Stammheim. And this symbolic value was gone after 1977. After the failed attempt at the embassy in Stockholm [in 1975] and after 1977 it would have been completely apolitical to keep saying: We're going to liberate the prisoners. Because that would have meant that the group was really only interested in itself." It would have confirmed what critics had always accused the RAF of being: a mere "Liberate-the-guerilla guerilla."

Whatever the purposes and motivations, the fact remains that in the years to come the RAF was not the only terrorist group to keep their hands off both prisoner liberations and airplane hijackings. Internationally, too, air piracy declined significantly. Between 1968 and 1977 hardly a week went by without an airplane being hijacked somewhere in the world. After Mogadishu the number dropped by more than 30 percent through the 1980s and continued to fall in the course of the 1990s.[16] The expansion of security measures at airports and on airplanes undoubtedly played a significant role in this decline (e.g., baggage screening, security gates, etc.). But it was also clear that skyjackers and other terrorists had to think twice about risking a confrontation with GSG 9—or with other special intervention units which were often modeled after GSG 9 in an increasing number of countries.

Literally overnight, GSG 9 was counted among the best special police forces in the world, on par with the British SAS or the US Army Special Forces and Navy SEALs. Or with the Sajeret Matkal from Israel. The Israeli military attaché in Bonn and Ehud Barak were the first to congratulate Wegener on his success. For them, it came as no surprise. Three months before Mogadishu, journalist Rolf Tophoven had visited the Israeli border police for research and interviews with security experts. The then-commander of the Israeli border troops, Zvi Bar, was in charge of building up a border police force similar to GSG 9. During an exercise of the special unit YAMAM* in the Jordan Valley, Bar told Tophoven: "We consider GSG 9 to be one of the best counterterrorist units in the world in terms of their training concept, the mentality of the men, and the armament." When Tophoven replied that GSG 9 had not yet had a single really hot mission, Bar said, "Be sure, when the hour comes, they will do a brilliant job!"

Now the hour had come, the job was done, and the German special unit was world famous. The international press cheered. "Perfect debut for Bonn's counter-terror squad," the London *Times* headlined its full-page coverage. Paris's *France-Soir* gushed:

---

* YAMAM = Hebraic acronym for Centralized Special Unit. Counterterror Task Force of the Israeli Border Police established in 1974.

"Ah, that was a beautiful Sunday!" followed by an exclamation that sounded weird to German ears: "Our cause, our drama, our war ... our victory." Copenhagen's *Ekstra Bladet* commented: "The defeat of the terrorists has revived our belief that terrorism can be fought." In Nairobi, the *Standard* called on "Africa and the whole world to tip their hats." The *Daily Mail* dubbed GSG 9 "The Desert Foxes" in reference to WWII panzer General Rommel. And the *Evening News* headline simply demanded, "Rest of the world: please copy!"

In the *New York Times*, a commentator noted with satisfaction that in the fight against terrorism, it was not enough to be tough. Instead, West Germany had proven that it had everything it needed, which the commentator summed up as "tough, yes, but also prepared, flexible, smart." The German news magazine *Der Spiegel* mused that Germans could be "strong as well as human," which not only surprised foreign countries, 30 years after the end of World War II, but even the Germans themselves. It sent a different image of "the German" into the world, which up to this point had often been associated with the attribute "ugly."

"Never since the Germans were forcibly re-civilized have they been met with such a boisterous wave of understanding, solidarity and affection as in this October of '77," marveled *Der Spiegel* in its cover story "After Mogadishu: The Admired German": "Yes, the triumphalism of the ex-enemies and new friends of German efficiency, as pleasant as it might seem, almost had something embarrassing about it." Quite a few Germans rubbed their eyes in the face of such a wave of unexpected sympathy and felt somewhat abashed, like Jörg Probsmeier did on the red carpet during their reception at Cologne-Bonn Airport. German embassies were flooded with declarations of solidarity. The Washington mission alone reported 605 calls, most of them long-distance. In the United States, all the major television networks reported extensively on Germany's daring stroke. A violent assault, of all things, thus helped to project a civilized image of the Germans into the world.

On the other side of the Iron Curtain, the media remained comparatively silent, except of course for Karl-Eduard von Schnitzler, East Berlin's top propagandist. As was to be expected, he did not miss the opportunity to pour his buckets of dirt on the successful West German police force. On East Germany's television show *The Black Channel* he described the Federal Border Guard as "aggressive on the outside, anti-democratic and terrorist on the inside," and added that "this elite force is fully in line with Adolf Hitler's former *Leibstandarte* [bodyguard]."[17] Being insulted in this way by the infamous "Sudel-Ede" (Spatter Eddie) was something GSG 9 could confidently count as equivalent to being awarded a knighthood.

The successful liberation operation did not fail to have an effect on the national level either. The spontaneous cheers and support of "The 9ers" upon their return were not just an expression of relief at the rescue of 86 lives, any one of whom could have been oneself. It was a rare case of genuine patriotic sentiment from a country that still had issues with this kind of national pride. After the nationalistic

Armageddon that was the Third Reich, patriotism was not considered a civic virtue let alone duty, but rather looked upon with skepticism and suspicion and even frowned at by broad parts of the population. It smacked of revisionism, summoning the old, brown-shirted ghost. In the aftermath of the excessive Führer cult, most Germans were convinced that their nation had seen more than its fair share of violent escapades rooted in nationalism, more of an overdose, to be exact. Many people were instead eager to point out the young Federal Republic's many shortcomings and mistakes, often doing so with a certain masochistic, self-flagellant pleasure far beyond fair criticism of excessive patriotism (a national trait that in part exists to this day). Gustav Heinemann, third president of the Federal Republic, once famously answered the question whether or not he loved his country: "Oh, come on, I don't love states, I love my wife; that's it!"

Now, for once, was one of those few moments when people from all across the political spectrum were finally allowed to be proud of their country without any remorse. Beyond ideological convictions, the success of Mogadishu underscored the cohesion of the political and social system of the Federal Republic of Germany: government, opposition, parliament, provinces, state agencies, media, populace. There was a broad consensus with Helmut Schmidt's government, even reaching far into the radical left which had sympathized with the RAF for quite a long time.

Today, the operation is still regarded as a prime example of the resilience of German democracy, and those who had achieved it saw themselves suddenly in the center of attention. At a moment's notice, the world-champions-in-training had turned into globally sought-after heroes. International cooperation was nothing new for the task force; they had worked with the Israelis and the British since their inception. But until then it had mostly been a matter of the Germans profiting from the knowledge and technology of their partners. Now, however, requests were piling up from foreign governments eager to acquire such a unit themselves or to muscle up their existing regular forces for similar situations. By February 1978, no more than four months after Mogadishu, the respective department in the Ministry of the Interior had received "inquiries/requests from 33 countries on all continents requesting support in the fight against terrorism in the form of personal and/or material assistance from GSG 9."[18] Within a year, this figure would rise to more than 60 countries.

The Ministry of the Interior was happy and quick to promise cooperation to ever more foreign inquiries, often at the special request of the Foreign Ministry. Slowly but surely, GSG 9 thus turned into a handy instrument in the diplomatic toolbox of foreign relations. After the huge international approval, Foreign Minister Genscher showed considerable interest in passing his brainchild around to close allies, and also to use it as a prestigious advertising tool with less allied states when there was a national interest in doing so. A police counterterrorism unit looked far more innocuous than weapons or military aid, and was easier to justify at home. At the same time, agencies, ministries, and even GSG 9 itself did not always look too closely at who received support and what happened to it afterwards.

Sea Lions and Show Horses

But first, international guests flocked to Saint Augustin to marvel at Wegener's *"Wunderding"* (Wonder Thing), as a Brazilian major put it. The unit which had liberated an entire airliner packed with tourists without any casualties of its own became a spectacle. The military attaché of the Iranian embassy in Bonn made a pilgrimage to GSG 9 HQ, as did his South Korean counterpart, the director of the Turkish security authorities, as well as the police chief of Hong Kong, and Japanese security experts. Even a Soviet general had a look around. Whoever travelled to the West German capital for security talks also tried to get an appointment for a demonstration of the task force. In the months after Mogadishu, Fox, Heimann, and Probstmeier were kept busy showing off their skills again and again, often several times a week: shooting skills, hand-to-hand combat, abseiling from helicopters, presenting equipment and armaments. At times, they felt reminded of the sea lion show at the nearby Cologne Zoo. Unit leader Tutter, though, felt like a show horse in the ring: "We called ourselves 'Circus Wegener.' We were pissed off because we almost exclusively prepared for demonstrations all the time." This sentiment of becoming a fairground attraction seems to have been quite accurate. At the end of 1979, the Consulate General in Hong Kong asked the Foreign Office in Bonn to "support the application for invitation consideration to GSG 9 'International Circus' scheduled for early next year."[19]

With all the hype going on, the operational units were no longer able to pursue their training and further education projects. Regular duty was all but impossible. Just before Christmas 1977, two months after their return from the Horn of Africa, Wegener therefore sent an angry letter to the Ministry of the Interior. The occasion was the announced visit of two air force officers from the Netherlands. "The visits and requests for visits to GSG 9 have assumed an unmanageable scope," complained Wegener, adding that urgent matters important for maintaining operational readiness had therefore been put on hold. He maintained that GSG 9 of course endeavored to provide information and answer questions from qualified visitors, but would turn down all requests for visits from interested parties who did not meet the qualifications, i.e., who had nothing to do with the work of a special unit, but just felt like checking out what the Germans are capable of.

"Since Operation *Landshut*, there is the impression that the legitimate concerns of the unit continue to be ignored and that, after a spectacular operation, the unit is to be abused as a show troupe for the 'greater glory of others,'" complained the commander.[20] He did not mind securing international bonds, quite the opposite. But it was bonds with special (police) forces he was after, preferably the world's top ones, not nosy foreign officials with too much time on their hands. As it turned out, the interest was mutual, as he got to experience firsthand right after GSG 9's return from Mogadishu.

Weapons and Know-How for US Special Forces

Wegener had barely spent a few hours in bed at home when Adjutant Baum excitedly rang him up on the phone: "Herr Oberst, you are needed in Saint Augustin immediately!" Still sleep-deprived after the five-day marathon, the commander muttered: "What the hell is going on?"—"Sir, the Americans are here!"

A high-ranking US Army officer was waiting at GSG 9 headquarters, eager to meet Wegener and to initiate German-American cooperation.[21] Only a few weeks later, a Colonel Charles Beckwith came over to Germany on a reconnaissance mission to check out GSG 9, a task force that so far he had not reckoned with. Neither had the rest of the US military. Nor its lawmakers or government, for that matter.

Beckwith was not just anybody within the US Army. The Green Beret and Vietnam veteran was in the midst of creating a highly secretive new task force himself. To this end, he wanted to tap into GSG 9's skillset and freshly acquired operational experience. At that time there was no designation for his new unit, but soon it would become known by the name 1st Special Forces Operational Detachment-Delta, or Delta Force for short. And not much was really known beyond that name.

Up to this day, its existence has never been formally recognized by US authorities. But it is widely known that Beckwith modeled his new full-fledged counterterrorism unit after the British SAS. In the 1960s he was part of that force as an exchange officer, got acquainted with their counterterrorist and anti-guerilla tactics as well as with their motto "who dares wins," encouraging creativity and out-of-the-box thinking. This served as a natural role model when Beckwith designed Delta. But as it turned out, GSG 9 too had some impact in the way the new special force unit was formed, particularly in terms of its standard weaponry and—arguably more important—its command system. In the very beginning, moreover, it acted as an accelerator for Delta's inception, a kind of inadvertent midwife if you will.

The day after Wegener, Fox and 60 other GSG 9 men stormed the *Landshut*, "the shit just hit the fan" as Beckwith describes it in colorful terms. At the time, he was working at the Pentagon struggling to get the needed funding and personnel for his task force after years of meticulous planning and often frustrating lobbying. On this particular morning, "people began to talk about some place in Mogadishu. We looked it up. It was in Somalia," he wrote in his memoirs. "I knew there was a meeting going on in 'the tank' of the JCS [Joint Chiefs of Staff] and lots of people kept running back and forth." He was sitting in his office when someone rushed in, inquiring, "'What do you know about GSG 9? A lot of people are asking questions.'

I didn't know much. SAS, yes, but not that much about the West Germans. I thought they were a police unit and not military."[22]

Beckwith then, for the first time in his life, was ordered to General Bernard Rogers's office, the US Army's Chief of Staff. Rogers inquired about the brand-new flash bangs that had been used in the *Landshut* storm. Having served with the SAS, Beckwith knew their predecessors and that the British were specialized in their development. "When I finished, General Rogers told me of a note from the president [Jimmy Carter]. It had surfaced in the tank earlier that day and asked, 'Do we have the same capability as the West Germans?' Much discussion had ensued before it was decided we did not. One of the generals there had said, 'Well, I'm not going over to the White House and tell them we don't.'[23] General Rogers then informed the Chairman of the Joint Chiefs of Staff of his earlier decision to activate an elite unit whose mission was to combat terrorism."[24] This, certainly, gave Beckwith's new unit a kick start. After more than a decade banging the drum for it, more or less unheard by the upper echelons, he finally received the thumbs up from the top to go forward with Detachment Delta on this very day.

Eleven months later, Dieter Fox was sent from Saint Augustin to Fort Bragg, North Carolina, where headquarters of the new elite unit had been set up in a cleared-out army penitentiary. Fox and a GSG 9 explosives specialist were supposed to do some shooting and aircraft assault training with Delta's first generation of operators.* They were also invited to take part as advising observers in the selection process for new recruits and future operators. For two months in the autumn of 1978, Fox was thus able to witness firsthand the creation of Delta Force, even though the name was not yet officially established. "Their unit badge did exist [even though they were not yet allowed to display it], as did the mindset and the structure for the units, which were almost identical to GSG 9. The only thing missing was the official 'Go' from the government to take on missions."

Prior to his departure to Fort Bragg, Fox had the opportunity to personally meet with Colonel Beckwith at the US embassy in Bonn. To this day, he is full of praise for Delta Force's founding commander: "A great guy, they couldn't have wished for a better one. He was highly respected right up in the government; even some generals stood at attention when they met him. Being a highly decorated Vietnam veteran, he was simply an incredibly great guy as a soldier and a human, a far-sighted and tactically apt leader."

Beckwith in turn was visibly impressed by GSG 9's performance. Fox recalled that "he was particularly enthusiastic about our weapons." GSG 9 still used the old Heckler & Koch model P9 but just started carrying the newly developed HK P7 as well as the HK MP5 submachine gun, in both the standard, the MP5k (short) and

---

* The term *operator* instead of *operative* was chosen in the early days of Delta Force to set them apart from operatives of US agencies like the FBI or CIA.

the silenced MP5SD variant. Beckwith wanted all of them, Fox smirked: "When Wegener tried to sell him the long gun, though, our precision rifle PSG1, he backed off, claiming 'If I come back with the whole lot of them, my government will fire me. Acquiring this or that type of German weapon is one thing. But no American would approve of buying the entire arsenal. No way!'"

So when Fox went to Fort Bragg, he acted as a kind of sales intermediate for the German firearms industry, trying to convince the Americans of the quality of their latest technology. It did not take much convincing, though. He demonstrated the brand new semi-automatic HK P7 which had been developed for the West German police force after the Munich massacre in 1972. With its 9mm high-speed parabellum ammunition, the small, light and well-balanced pistol quickly turned out to be superior to its American counterparts. When put to the test in a comparative shooting at the 2nd Delta unit, it proved to be more precise and easier to handle than the rather clunky large-caliber revolvers in use by his US comrades. "They decided to use the P7 for covert operations in civilian settings, because they were ideal for carrying concealed under their jackets. The P7 was the perfect weapon for this purpose." The same went for the submachine gun MP5. It replaced the World War II M3, commonly called "grease gun," only keeping a few of the old ones for use as silenced weapons.[25] "But," added Fox, "it was with a heavy heart that the decision-makers said ok, we agree to use German weapons instead of our own American ones."

With respect to the scheduled tactical training in aircraft assault, the means were somewhat limited, since they did not have an aircraft or any models to practice on. Instead, the German visitors took part in a series of field and night exercises as well as two selection tests, one being the entrance examination for Special Forces. Fox was quite impressed by the demands and tasks to which the applicants were subjected, but not entirely in a positive sense: "It was tough, brutal, even inhumane. There was no comparison to what we did in GSG 9. They were military, of course, not police, so you always assume a war situation. They said we had World War II, Korea, Vietnam and whatnot. If our specialists have to go somewhere, they have to be able to do this and that. In other words, they were tested to the very limits of what a human was able to take. And if they passed they were heroically accepted. But if they made mistakes they were put on what they called the Rag Wagon and driven around in public for everyone to see their disgrace. I was told it was part of their tradition, no kidding."

Another part of their military tradition was their command system. In contrast to Wegener's Mission Tactics, the traditional idea of Command Tactics was still widely used which leaves the operative on the ground no wiggle room for changing their approach if circumstances change.

During a night helicopter exercise, Fox was able to witness firsthand what happens once this attitude is drilled deep enough into the mindset of a soldier. On the day before the exercise, they had checked out the supposed landing area. It turned out that it was plastered with tree stumps, the recently cut logs still lay scattered all over the forest floor. "It was a less-than-ideal site for jumping out of a helicopter at night in a supposed combat situation." Fox recalls the chopper pilot pointing out this obvious fact to the army captain he was supposed to drop there. "The pilot said: 'I'll take you a bit further down, there's a meadow.' But the captain said: 'No, I have orders to get down here.'—'No chance,' says the pilot, 'if you jump out here in the dark, you'll be sure to break your ankles on one of those tree trunks.'" A short discussion ensued about the shortest way to his destination and the risk of injuries, but finally the captain got his wish. He was hell-bent on fulfilling his orders by being dropped where he was supposed to be dropped. "So the pilot lets him jump out into the night. We fly on and when we get back to camp sometime later that day we hear: Captain Shoomaker has made it back, but with a broken leg. Complicated fracture, too. He later made it to general."

Sticking to orders. Some might hail this attitude as heroic. Fox prefers the term idiotic. "Not only does it contradict common sense, but potentially endangers whole missions, particularly if it is a special operation. The problem is not only that the individual man is not able to fulfill his mission. If he is the leader of a unit and taken out of the game he cannot lead. Beckwith recognized that." Drawing from his experience with the British SAS and having observed the modus operandi of GSG 9, Beckwith was determined to adopt Mission Tactics and adapt it to Delta Force's requirements. In meetings with Wegener and Fox, Beckwith told them: "We had so many casualties in Vietnam and I saw what happened when bad orders were given, through bad calculation, bad situation assessment, bad analysis. I want to get away from this rigid command system, because I know that when we get commands in that way, we can't do much with it within a special ops task force. So we can put Mission Tactics to good use."

Readers familiar with the history of US Special Forces might argue that unconventional thinking and personal initiative was always encouraged and even praised within these "irregular" units and that the German influence on Beckwith's view therefore seems exaggerated. However, those who served with Delta surely took note of his somewhat radical change in command attitude compared to the standard system. Eric Haney, who was among the first batch of Delta Force operators, described Beckwith's command style: "[He] laid down the law early on. Operators would develop their own tactics and operational methods. He had chosen us because we were all experienced fighters and no one needed to tell us how to go about our business. The men on the teams would determine the *how* of a mission, and Beckwith and his subordinate commanders would provide assets and coordination. But no one would ever *dictate* tactics to us or tell us how to risk our own lives."[26]

The new Mission Tactics went down well with the men operating under the rules of the new command system, recalls Fox: "The soldiers said: Man, that's it! Finally!

But the higher-ups in the Pentagon and elsewhere said: This is an American tactic. We've been using it for 300 years and we'll keep it up. And that's when Beckwith said: 'You might, but not me.' And he made himself many, many enemies because of the way he led: not by blindly following stupid old military thinking, but always wondering: 'How can I fully unleash my special unit's unique skills and capabilities when I send it into action?'"

Cooperation and exchange with Delta Force and other US units and agencies like the FBI's Hostage Rescue Team (HRT) and SEAL Team 6 turned out to be quite fruitful in the years and decades to come.* As did the cooperation with other "Premium Partners," as they are called in the internal GSG 9 terminology. These comprised more or less the classic Western European allies along the lines of the Iron Curtain, like France, UK, Spain, Netherlands, Austria, Australia, and of course Israel. In the days after the Mogadishu success, however, there were not only requests from these trustworthy nations with which West Germany entertained multiple economic, political and security ties. Dozens of requests for cooperation flooded in from countries whose human rights standards left much to be desired and/or were part of what was called the Communist Bloc under the leadership of the USSR. So, naturally the question soon arose: what to show and to whom?

---

* According to Robert Hemmerling, the current GSG 9 commander, one of only two plaques at the SEALs HQ in Norfolk commemorates the support of the German special intervention unit in setting up and training the unit in the early 1980s. The second plaque is dedicated to the support of an Israeli unit.

CHAPTER 13

Export Hit GSG 9

President Siad Barre was under pressure, big time. In the spring of 1977, the dictator had started a war with Somalia's neighbor, Ethiopia. But after initial successes, the attack had been repulsed, and Barre's great protector, the Soviet Union, was no longer supporting him but rather his opponent, the new socialist regime in Addis Ababa. Being a diehard socialist himself, Barre suddenly found himself deserted by his spiritual brothers and urgently in need of new partners. Lacking alternatives in the Eastern camp, he sought them in the West. Therefore, the Somali president did not waste any time when a chance showed up on the horizon.

On October 31, 1977, less than two weeks after he had allowed German police officers to carry out an aircraft assault on his territory, Barre sent a message to the West German government, channeled through its Chargé d'affaires Michael Libal. Somalia was asking "for military and political support against foreign interference in the Somali-Ethiopian conflict," Libal cabled home. Specifically, Barre requested weapons assistance and a security guarantee against an Ethiopian attack. "He justified the request by saying that Soviet interference with the aim of dominating the Horn of Africa also endangered the interests of the West, including the Federal Republic of Germany."[1]

Thus, Helmut Schmidt had to respond to Barre's wishes sooner than he would have cared to. The chancellor had given his word to the dictator, personally on the phone in a time of dire need. Now it was on him to make good on his word, particularly when it came to military and economic support. There was just one problem: Germany had long committed itself to the principle of non-proliferation of any kinds of weapons to regions of military tension. And the Horn of Africa was unquestionably a region of tension. So what to do? On the very day Barre's wish list arrived in Bonn, the cabinet approved an emergency aid program for Somalia: loans of 25 million Deutschmarks and another six million for technical assistance.

In a secret meeting with Somali ambassador Bokah a few days later, Schmidt again stressed that Bonn must not supply weapons "to crisis areas outside NATO" or provide security guarantees for countries outside the Atlantic alliance. He referred to the Federal Republic's long-term developmental aid projects, but then confided: "The federal government can ... also give financial support that can be used for defense purposes. However, such an agreement must remain strictly confidential."[2] Barre gladly accepted the offered support, especially since, as Ambassador Bokah pointed out to Minister of State Wischnewski a few days later, the Soviet Union had not supplied Somalia with any weapons since the hostage crisis in Mogadishu. But the dictator still had one more wish: an elite force of his own, modeled after Germany's GSG 9. Schmidt granted him that, too. It was to be the first of dozens of similar intergovernmental training and cooperation agreements with countries all over the world.

Thus, in September 1979, five instructors traveled from Saint Augustin to Mogadishu, where they were to train 50 Somali police officers for up to six months. According to an intergovernmental agreement, the program included weapons and firearms training, hand-to-hand combat, police operations and personal protection. The conditions were extremely unfavorable, though. The selection of recruits for the course was not based on aptitude, performance and motivation, but on completely different criteria, first and foremost membership in the president's clan. Barre only sent people he trusted, and they were by no means all members of the police but belonged to his bodyguard, the army or the Somali National Security Service (NSS), all of whom tended to look at each other with suspicion and even contempt.

At the beginning of January 1980, course leader Anselm Weygold telegraphed his third situation report to the ministry in Bonn: "Of 17 Somali instructors, I have had 2 relieved from the course. A further 3 to 4 replacements are planned for the next few days due to insufficient physical fitness and readiness. There are conflicts in the course between Som. instructors and course participants due to tribal affiliations, belonging to different organizations, Presidential Guard, army, etc.... Since there were hardly any instructors present on the 25th of December, most of whom were absent on flimsy grounds, I sent the course into recess for two days."[3] By the end of the first course three months later, Weygold was to dismiss a total of six course participants "for lack of suitability." His final report reveals the frustration that had built up over six months: "The level of training was completely inadequate compared to European standards. Particularly aggravating was the lack of understanding of technical contexts, the lack of any ability to think abstractly and the lack of personal drive on the part of the group leaders.... These far-reaching drive weaknesses running diagonally through the leadership levels of the Somali security sectors cast serious doubt on the continuation of the skills learned."[4]

Despite such concerns, the Somalis were treated to a second training course. At the end of 1980, Werner Heimann flew to the Horn of Africa with five other GSG 9 instructors: "We tried hard, we trained every day. But the people were simply not suitable to implement what they learned afterwards." In addition to the poor suitability of the participants, there was a lack of training equipment. The desired aircraft assault training suffered from a chronic lack of aircraft; not even ladders could be found. Weapons and practice ammunition remained similarly scarce. "In the absence of firearms, we gave them sticks as replacements. For the officers' pistols, they simply used their index finger, just like children do when they play cops and robbers."

The accommodations were comparatively luxurious, however: the Somalis had built a bungalow in the bush especially for the Germans, complete with a diesel generator to produce electricity. So the instructors were largely self-sufficient. They bought bread and rice at the market in Mogadishu, but otherwise mainly lived off what they hunted themselves, warthogs for the most part: "One guy in our team of six was brought up on a farm and knew how to wield a butcher's knife. Another one was a hunter and could also gut a wild boar." For Werner Heimann and his colleagues, the six months in Somalia thus became a "well-paid adventure vacation."

The training mission itself, on the other hand, proved to be a complete failure, as the summary of their commander at the "inspection and final review" stated bluntly: "The troops are not ready for deployment with this level of training.... Based on the results of this course and the fact that the attitude of the Somali services is not expected to change, it is intended not to conduct any further counterterrorism training in Somalia."[5] Consequently, GSG 9's mission was discontinued. Did Wegener's assessment of the situation contribute significantly to this decision? It seems more likely that the government considered its debt of gratitude to the Somali president to have been settled.

In retrospect, one must be grateful that the learning success of the Somali course participants remained rather modest. During the Somali civil war in the 1980s, dictator Barre came under increasing pressure before he was finally ousted in 1991. In 1988, the Somali army responded to uprisings in the north of the country with brutal repression, killing between 40,000 and 100,000 people and displacing hundreds of thousands more. For Werner Heimann, it is all but certain that officers whom he and his GSG 9 colleagues trained were involved in the massacres: "I assume that's what happened. But I don't have a bad conscience that it was perhaps me who trained these people. This training mandate was imposed on us by our government, and since it does not go against human rights to train people, you do the job. But after half a year, it was also pretty clear to us that Barre was far from having a trained GSG 9 at his disposal."

And what would have been the alternative? Should West Germany have evaded the dictator's wishes? Would it even have been able to? Less than a year after the liberation of the *Landshut*, Gerhart Baum was sworn in as minister of the interior. Soon after, he traveled to Mogadishu to thank the president once again for his decision to allow GSG 9 to operate on Somali territory, accompanied by Minister of State Wischnewski. "In situations like this, you need an ally, even if it's a dictator," he says without remorse. "The bad thing is that the dictator is gone at some point, and the country is worse off than ever before. That's hell."

From Special Force Midwife to Diplomatic Multi-Tool

The record of the events in Mogadishu made Somalia a special case in terms of international police cooperation, one that stood out from the many relationships with foreign nations and their special (police) forces. Cooperation with friendly states had existed since the founding days of GSG 9, but in the early years primarily with the Israelis and British. Commander Wegener attached great importance to international cooperation and was willing to go anywhere his troops could learn something. Conversely, he opened his unit to foreign guests early on. This was partly born from Wegener's conviction that you cannot fight international terrorism without international exchange.

The first visitor to Saint Augustin happened to be the Swiss Léon Borer, founder of the Einsatzgruppe Enzian (Gentian Task Force. Don't be fooled by the flowery name). This was in the beginning of 1973, at a time when GSG 9 was still a far cry from being ready for action. Borer took part in shooting and karate training, as well as in exercises for the "coup-de-main-type seizure of an object occupied by terrorists using helicopters and assault troops." He described his visit to GSG 9 in the subsequent field report as a "personal and professional highlight,"[6] and Commander Wegener later as his "master teacher."[7] Contacts between Germany and Switzerland were expanded in the following years, with training courses, study visits and lectures. In the summer of 1978, Borer's Enzian squad even asked GSG 9 for help in preparing for an aircraft assault in a hostage situation.

Similar excellent contacts existed with the Netherlands, whose special unit BSB* was built on the model of GSG 9, as was Austria's EKO† Cobra. The flow of information in such cases was never one-sided. The general attitude was that everybody could learn from everybody. Members of the newly formed Spanish anti-terrorist unit GEO,‡ for example, demonstrated for the Germans a technique for shooting—and scoring—with a submachine gun from the pillion seat of a motorcycle in hot pursuit while moving in demanding terrain. Instructor Heimann was enthusiastic, "Of course, we adopted it right away." After all, what resembled a harebrained James Bond-type stunt at first glance could actually ensure the survival of security personnel and their protectees.

The first American unit to train with GSG 9 was a secretive organization stationed in Germany, today known as Special Forces Detachment Berlin. Founded in 1956, their mission in case of a future war was to infiltrate East Germany. Their operatives were supposed to let the front roll over them and to secretly act behind Soviet lines in Berlin as well as in the countryside. They were to train and advise guerrilla forces, wreak havoc with the enemy wherever they could by whatever

---

* BSB (Brigade Speciale Beveiligingsopdrachten) = Special Security Missions Brigade.
† EKO (*Einsatzkommando*) = Task force.
‡ GEO (Grupo Especial de Operaciones) = Special Operations Group.

means necessary and create chaos and confusion in order to buy time for the Allied forces in Western Europe.

Starting in the mid-1970s, though, the Berlin Detachment was given an additional task. As James Stejskal details in his book *Special Forces Berlin*, the special ops directorate of the US Forces' European Command tasked the detachment with providing sniper teams as support for anti-hijacking operations of the Military Police at Berlin's airports in cases involving American aircraft. Before long, this task was extended to creating full-fledged counterterrorism capabilities, including aircraft storming and other hostage liberation situations. This required a lot of preparation and training for the necessary skills, more skills than cooperation partners like the FBI Counter Air Crimes and SWAT were able to provide at the time. So the detachment's leadership trained their eyes on Israeli counterterrorist units as well as on GSG 9.[8]

The first joint training session commenced in April 1977, six months before Mogadishu, when GSG 9 hosted nine members of Special Forces Berlin in Saint Augustin. The Americans seem to have been quite impressed with resources available to the German police unit as James Stejskal writes: "It looked like Porsche Designs was somehow involved with putting together their uniforms and equipment; if they weren't, Mercedes' Advanced Motor Group certainly was. GSG-9's patrol cars were Mercedes W123 sedans, modified with more horsepower, better brakes and complete with gun ports. Their weapons were straight out of Heckler & Koch's latest sales brochure: MP5 SMGs, P9S pistols and the G3 SG1 and PSG-1 sniper rifles. That said, the occasional Mauser 66 sniper rifle and Remington 870 shotgun were to be seen and a Smith & Wesson .357 magnum revolver was favored by the commander, Polizeidirektor (Colonel) Ulrich Wegener."[9]

The following days were packed with counterterrorism training 101: shooting, room-clearing exercises, assault tactics in theory and practice, breaching tactics for planes, trains and buses by all means possible including explosives and shotguns, handling of heavy Mercedes as well as lighter Ford Escorts on open roads, the German autobahn and in city environments. Apart from two trashed cars and a plastic bullet that accidentally ended up in the shooter's own leg, the course went more than satisfactorily and concluded with the participants receiving GSG 9 qualification badges from Commander Wegener.[10] More joint exercises were to follow and soon "[m]any of GSG-9's techniques, along with those of the SAS and the detachment's own were … fully integrated into unit training."[11] When it was time for the Berlin Detachment to prove their counterterrorism capabilities through an operational certification, GSG 9 was chosen to run a similar mission in parallel at the same time, but in a different location, a simulated aircraft hijacking (which to the detachment's surprise turned out to be a train hijacking). Both units passed their tests.[12]

Gradually, many of these cooperative projects and joint trainings were formalized and transferred into permanent structures. It was largely on the initiative of GSG 9 that the informal ATLAS alliance was founded in 2002, an association of special (police) forces from three dozen European countries along with some allies (the United States, Israel). Named after the mythical titan who carries the world on his shoulders, the alliance was intended to promote international cooperation in the fight against terrorism and organized crime.

The focus lies on exchange and friendly competition between the units, including at the Combat Team Conference (CTC).[13] Founded in 1983 at the instigation of Ulrich Wegener, it has been organized and hosted by GSG 9 to this day. However, the CTC has little in common with a conventional conference. It rather resembles a kind of police Olympics. Every four years, more than forty special units—military as well as police—from all over the world compete with each other over several days in Saint Augustin and the surrounding area (in 2024 won by the formerly mentioned Einsatzgruppe Enzian). Being the host, GSG 9 does not participate. However, every now and then a group of GSG 9 veterans does take part in the competition (and proudly report that they never come in last in the overall ranking).

In the aftermath of the Mogadishu campaign, however, no institution of the sort yet existed. Within a few weeks, GSG 9 was inundated with numerous inquiries from abroad. Requests for training assistance for existing or yet to be founded special units poured into the Ministry of the Interior from all over the world, some officially via embassies, others unofficially through direct contacts with GSG 9 via police intelligence agencies. The number of requests went through the roof and soon Commander Wegener began to block further requests so as not to let his GSG 9 degenerate entirely into a special unit for training special units.

The argument of excessive workload, however, often proved helpful to the ministerial bureaucracy as well, particularly when political considerations stood against cooperation. Quite a few countries were either stalled in this way or had their requests rejected outright. Sometimes it was for the simple reason that it was a country of the Eastern Bloc (e.g. Romania) or a frontline state in a war (Zambia). Sometimes cooperation simply promised no added political value, i.e., the countries were not considered important enough (Peru). In other cases, the drug mafia maintained close contacts within the government of the country concerned, right to the top echelons of the police and military (Colombia) or it was a matter of generally "problematic" countries (e.g. all of the Middle East) which had close contacts with Palestinian terrorist organizations, thus exactly with the parties they were actually supposed to fight (e.g. Syria). Moreover, there were those countries that were considered politically insignificant but, for whatever reason, it was not possible to simply turn them down. These were palmed off with a short visit to Saint Augustin for a couple of hours. Their police chiefs did not get to see the actual GSG 9, but they were allowed to marvel at the helicopter squadron that was based nearby, as well as the "BGS service dog system."

Nevertheless, many of the requests for training assistance that reached the Ministry of the Interior were granted—more often than not at the urging of the

Foreign Office if it served the actual or supposed political interests of the Federal Republic of Germany. GSG 9 founding father and sponsor Hans-Dietrich Genscher was in charge there after he had switched from minister of the interior to become minister of foreign affairs some years earlier.* He knew what he had with "his" unit. In September 1978, he wrote to Minister of the Interior Baum: "I would be grateful if you could take foreign policy considerations into account in your deliberations on the expansion program for strengthening internal security that was approved by the Cabinet. From my side, an expansion of GSG 9 personnel that provides for training opportunities abroad would be very welcome."[14]

From Australia to Zaire, GSG 9 instructors therefore trained members of foreign police and military units, either hosting them at courses in Saint Augustin or on site in the respective countries. A confidential table from the Ministry of the Interior from 1985 lists 61 nations with ties to GSG 9 since its inception, which adds up to roughly a third of all countries worldwide. But, of course, by no means were all relations made equal. The criteria by which approvals and denials were made were not always consistent, and they changed over time. For example, Saudi Arabia, being an adversary of Israel, was initially treated with restraint, but within a few years it developed into one of the most intensive cooperation partners, although neither the political situation nor its support for Palestinian terrorist organizations had changed significantly—not to mention its human rights record.

The Ministry of the Interior and the Foreign Office worked closely together in assessing foreign requests, judging according to their worthiness for cooperation as well as political expediency. In the coordination of international inquiries, the Foreign Ministry usually took on the role of the driving force in the interest of as many good relations with other states as possible, while the Ministry of the Interior tended to put on the brakes in view of the workload on GSG 9. This was necessary, too, because word quickly spread among the federal German agencies that the prospect of a training course with the "heroes of Mogadishu" was an excellent way to cultivate foreign contacts.

At informal meetings in international circles, representatives of the criminal police and intelligence services were eager to offer training assistance to their foreign counterparts—often without the knowledge of either GSG 9 or the ministry. Over the years, the unofficial wheeling and dealing took on such proportions that in 1984, Karl Heinz Amft, the inspector[†] of the Bundesgrenzschutz issued an internal memo to all the relevant offices in the Ministry of the Interior instructing them to "take note of and implement" the following: "In the future, the BfV, BKA, BND, etc. are to be informed that such mediations are undesirable. The requests are to

---

* He would remain in this post for exactly 18 years to the day, making him the longest-serving foreign minister in the history of Germany.
† Highest-ranking officer within the BGS.

be made through the designated channels. (German visitors abroad want to refrain from offering GSG 9 gifts)."[15] The phrase "want to refrain" was a polite term meant to be translated as "don't you dare!"

But even with GSG 9's own commander, the inspector did not always have an easy time. For as often as Wegener complained about imposed training courses without mutual benefit, the commander himself was happy to make promises for training assistance while bypassing the Ministry of the Interior if he believed it to be in the interest of his unit, much to the annoyance of his superior officer. When Wegener made direct arrangements for a training course with the Spanish unit GEO in 1983—again—the chief would not have it. Inspector Amft admonished Wegener to refer interested parties to the ministry in the future "without making any promises, agreeing on details or holding out the prospect." Having stated this firmly, he begrudgingly agreed to the envisaged visit of the GEO people "in consideration of the fundamentally desirable cooperation."[16]

A Fine-Tuned System

There were very clear differences in the scope of cooperation depending on the country. A three-tier system soon emerged, according to which foreign partners were granted access to GSG 9: visits, short courses, and in some cases full-fledged training regimens lasting weeks and even months.

Arrangements for the purpose of exchanging information were mostly short visits by police chiefs or individual officers for a few hours to a maximum of a few days. These included countries such as Argentina, Finland, and Jamaica. But by no means were all of them shown the full scope of GSG 9 skills. Sometimes the men simply refused to even demonstrate everything they could do. Says Dieter Tutter: "We said we wouldn't show certain techniques to the Chinese. When they came in they knew exactly what they wanted to see. But we didn't give them that." In most cases, though, Tutter and the others had little wiggle room in terms of the skills they chose to show and share.

The short training courses, in which a handful of participants were integrated into the ongoing training operations, usually lasted up to two weeks. This kept an additional workload for the instructors at bay. But the language barrier sometimes posed a problem, as did catering for participants from countries with markedly different customs and possibly diets. The full training courses lasted several months, sometimes accommodating dozens of participants. These included police and military units from friendly countries such as the Netherlands, Norway, New Zealand, Great Britain, and the United States, but also Egypt, Saudi Arabia, Thailand, Indonesia,[17] and Turkey—not all of which countries that have always had the best record in terms of democracy and the rule of law. This also goes for authoritarian Singapore.

In return for its support in establishing the Singapore Armed Forces Anti-Terror Team (SAF-ATT), there was a formal departmental agreement between the Singapore Ministry of Defense and the West German Ministry of the Interior. According to this agreement, from 1980 onward Singapore tolerated GSG 9 operations on its territory and granted it landing and residence rights in the event that it was necessary to carry out counterterrorism operations "in the geographic area of operations there." An internal paper states that Singapore allowed "full freedom of action on Singaporean soil in the event of terrorist violence in Southeast Asia directed against German interests and would provide personnel and material support in such a case."[18] The Federal Republic thus had a kind of police bridgehead in the Far East at its disposal. If an operation were to take place in the region, there would be no stray flights with almost empty fuel tanks in search of landing permission, as on the odyssey to Mogadishu.

This example illustrates one of the main political motives for intensive cooperation with so many countries: German security interests in the event of aircraft hijackings or other, comparable cases. Minister of the Interior Friedrich Zimmermann put it in a nutshell during a visit to GSG 9's headquarters in 1982: "The idea behind this is that it can be very useful for our national security interests, for example in the case of serious crimes affecting Germans abroad, if there is backup in foreign countries for necessary GSG 9 missions. The great cooperation shown by the government of Somalia at that time is by no means a matter of course among sovereign states."[19] Providing training for police or military forces by GSG 9 promoted the inclination to cooperate in a crisis. It also reduced friction if those among the respective police authorities had known each other personally beforehand and ideally had even trained with each other.

However, security aspects were not the only motive for the German government's great interest in supporting these training activities. In addition to supporting foreign relations and to taking advantage of the international reputation of such a showcase force, there were also hardcore economic interests. Saudi Arabia, as a case in point, was eager to spend quite a bit of money on German firearms, tanks and other armored vehicles, but due to strict weapons export regulations not all of these wishes could be fulfilled. To smoothen the waves, GSG 9 police training programs were offered as compensation for the requests the Arabians had been denied. And in at least one case GSG 9 served as a substitute when German weaponsmith Thyssen Rheinstahl GmbH was not able to provide the promised driving instructors for a delivery of 98 armored police vehicles. To avoid provoking the wrath of the Arabs and spoiling lucrative bonds, Commander Wegener agreed to send his GSG 9 instructors to give driving lessons under the desert sun. In this way, GSG 9 became a multi-use tool in the diplomatic toolbox of 1980s West Germany. Officially, of course, the purpose of such training was always the promotion of democratic structures and constitutional attitudes, particularly when dealing with nations not on par with Western standards.

The latter point is still cited as the main justification for police assistance in general and for special counterterrorist training in the style of GSG 9. Even today, many a "9er" passionately argues that the training programs succeeded in providing precisely this kind of example. Friedrich Eichele, former commander, for example, led many of these training missions in the 1980s and 1990s. "Of course, we had visitors here from states that you would turn your nose up at today."[20] He recalls endless heated discussions with their foreign comrades until way after the end of their shift—all very friendly, as he stresses.

"We introduced them to a different approach than what they were used to. You know, it's quite simple: If there is a bad boy who needs to be neutralized, the easiest way is to shoot him down from a distance. It is much more time-consuming but in line with the constitution to arrest this person unharmed, since then you have to use your brains and devise a smart plan. Above all, you must have a guideline with regard to the rule of law. We tried very hard to get this across. This was certainly not harmful for the Federal Republic of Germany, nor was it harmful for the cause of human rights."

CHAPTER 14

Beyond the Legend

As the heavy gates close behind the car, Markus Müller[1] points to a leveled wasteland on the left: "That's where our new headquarters is going to be built." It is supposed to be ready for occupancy in 2029. The old building from the 1970s lurks barely 90 meters behind the field. We turn right into a parking lot in front of the shooting and training center, which is also to be rebuilt within the next 10 years, larger and to the latest standards.

As we get out of the car, a deafening bang sounds from behind the hall, and white smoke rises. On closer inspection, we find instructors with a training unit, wearing earmuffs. They are demonstrating the destructive effect of IEDs (Improvised Explosive Devices), explains Müller, a press spokesman of the GSG 9 command office as he hands earmuffs to the visitor. Another IED is set off. "For practice, you need to experience the effect of these devices firsthand. Just another day at the office," grins Müller, collecting the protection gear and leading the way inside the building.

The facility has been in operation since 1985. Roughly 400,000–500,000 rounds of ammunition are fired here every year, almost exclusively by GSG 9 operatives, apart from the occasions when friendly units stay here for joint exercises, which happens every other month or so. Their wood-mounted unit plates and brass plaques are plastered all over the walls of the entrance hallway, right next to a display case containing Commander Wegener's dress uniform from the year of Mogadishu, 1977.

A strange rubber smell hangs in the air. It emanates from the wall panels that act as bullet traps, explains the head of the shooting center, who happily agrees to give a tour of the facility. In addition to a 25-yard standard shooting range, it includes a shooting "cinema," in which so-called intuitive shooting is practiced interactively via video projection, as well as what is called "the studio." It contains special rooms with movable walls, tables, beds and cupboards, ideal for simulating the penetration of apartments of different sizes and floor plans or for advancing techniques in stairwells. There are even two variants of the latter: one stairwell in which the landings are arranged at right angles in the classic way, the other in a spiral shape. "In terms of tactics, it makes a substantial difference," remarks Markus Müller. He himself was drilled in here countless times during his years as an active operational officer, always being observed by training staff in the control rooms on the upper floor of the facility. Müller points upwards to the light shafts: "Abseiling into the rooms from the roof is also possible."

Then it's on to the heart of the facility: a 30-meter-long hall, large enough to house the full-size fuselage of a passenger plane. One of these rests here on heavy hydraulic stilts. Not a real fuselage, though, but a wooden mock-up. Only the doors at the front, the rear and the hatches above the wings are metal. Since the mid-1980s, the operational units have been practicing here what once made them a legend: storming an aircraft. An aluminum ladder reaches from the ground floor up to a height of a good nine meters. This is how high the specialists would have to climb to reach the doors of a jumbo jet in real life. To simulate smaller aircraft types, the hydraulic rams supporting the fuselage can be lowered to the appropriate level.

Inside, the interior looks like a normal passenger plane, except for the missing ceiling which has been left out for observation purposes. Also, the entire aircraft is made of plywood, including seating, toilets and luggage compartments. "This full-size model is quite unique in the world," states the head of the shooting tactics center proudly as we climb aboard. The partitions are speckled with red, blue and green spots. "FX ammunition," explains the manager. "We shoot different colored bullets here to be able to discern who hit what and where." In addition to the paint marks, there are also small holes in the walls, left by 9mm bullets from the officers' service pistols. At times, live ammunition is also fired during exercises. The big advantage of the wood design is that it eliminates the risk of ricochets, which can never be ruled out with metal. The projectiles simply get stuck in the wood. Once the panels are perforated all over, they can easily be replaced. In real airplanes, such exercises with live ammunition would hardly be possible. Airlines are typically not too happy about bullet holes in their seats and windows.

Even today, though, GSG 9 still practices on real aircraft as well. There, the specialists can practice silent penetration "on the living object," but only in dry runs without actually firing their weapons. In contrast, on the full-scale model here in the hall they can use their weapons without their mistakes leading to fatal consequences. "And people are supposed to make mistakes," says the head of the training center. "We intentionally drive them to make mistakes in order to learn from them. We use light and sound effects to create situations in which we systematically strain the men beyond their limits. We do this so that they don't reach their limits in real operations." The aircraft dummy is ideal for this kind of exercise.

However, there will be no large-scale model like this in the planned new shooting range. Instead, there will be rooms where different types of operational areas can be technically simulated, be it aircraft, trains, buses etc. Tests with computer simulations, VR glasses, and augmented reality simulations have been underway for some time.

"It takes some getting used to at first, but after five minutes you're completely immersed in the situation." Thus, the need for such full-size physical models will soon become obsolete.

GSG 9 is undergoing a transformation. The wooden aircraft fuselage is just one symptom of this, as is the construction of the new home base. In the ever-changing world of terrorist threats, social change, technological development, and digitalization, the counterterror unit must try to keep pace—or even better, stay one step ahead. Is the force sufficiently equipped for this in its sixth decade of existence? What has become of the motley crew that Wegener once gathered around him, and where is it heading?

For one, the special task force is to move closer to the capital. The federal government moved from Bonn to Berlin almost three decades ago, and so did the Ministry of the Interior, the parent authority of the unit. But above all, so did a large number of potential targets for terrorist attacks: parliament, ministries, state agencies, foreign diplomats, and embassies—in short, all major parts of the governmental machinery are now located in Germany's not-so-new capital. In recent years, the tactics of terrorist attacks have also changed dramatically. Special intervention units need to be on the scene much faster than they did just a few years ago.

As usual, the Ministry of the Interior does not disclose figures on how many officers are involved in this extension and regrouping of GSG 9 "for tactical reasons," but the late founding commander, Wegener, spoke of 400 men in total back in the 2010s. If, according to official figures, the strength of the unit is to increase by a third, the 120-strong contingent of the early years is likely to have grown to between 530 and 550 by now. But is that really necessary? There are numerous, well-equipped special task forces in the federal states, namely the SEKs and MEKs. In terms of training and education, they see themselves on par with GSG 9. The unit from Saint Augustin has special skills, for example in the maritime sector, in bus and rail operations and, of course, in hostage rescues in airplanes. But is it necessary to maintain a separate federal force of this size for such rare operational contingencies?

The Federal Police answer this question with a clear and unequivocal yes, even though the total number of operations in this special field since Mogadishu amounts to one (resolving a hostage situation which involved a bus taken by some escaped prisoners in the 1990s), at least among those that have come to public attention. GSG 9 is still considered a valuable asset and there has never really been any discussion about it on the political level. Not publicly, in any case. The recent expansion toward Berlin was inconspicuously waved through the parliamentary committees in 2017, and none of the parties represented in the Bundestag has ever publicly questioned the size of the force, let alone its fundamental right to exist—even after a disastrous operation in 1993 when the arrest of two top RAF members turned into a Wild West-style shootout in an East German train station, leaving one of the terrorists dead on the platform as well as a GSG 9 operative.

At the time, the ensuing investigations and public debates pushed the German state into a serious crisis, resulting in the resignation of the minister of the interior and the sacking of the *Generalbundesanwalt* (or attorney general) as well as the vice president of the BKA and several other high-ranking public servants. In the press, there was the occasional call for the liquidation of GSG 9, but it was never seriously considered on the political level. GSG 9 still enjoys the full backing of the Government as well as the opposition. Conversely, no one complains about a lack of funding or staffing for GSG 9 from within the force. In contrast to the early days, the unit is held in high regard within the Federal Police, which is also reflected by the fact that both the president and, since 2023, the deputy president of the department responsible for Germany's specialized units are former GSG 9 men.

The Head of the Agency

The president of Federal Police Directorate 11 (BPol-11) welcomes the visitor to the functionally furnished office at the new headquarters of the agency. The red brick building from the pre-WWI era is located in the middle of Berlin on Schöneberger Ufer, not far from the government district. Olaf Lindner, tall, with dark, short-cropped hair, sticks to the matter-of-fact attitude he is known for during the interview. Only when it comes to the merits of the unit he commanded for a decade does he bestow nothing but the highest praise: the "spearhead of the German fight against terrorism," which "rightly enjoys a worldwide reputation"; the "Champions League of special units" and the like are the terms he chooses.

But legend or not, GSG 9 is just one of several units within the Federal Police Directorate that Lindner has to look after. There is the aviation group and the special defusing service group, the personal protection unit for missions abroad (mostly in German embassies), and there are the technicians of the operations and investigation support group as well as the special protection task force in air traffic (aka sky marshals). "GSG 9 certainly has a special portfolio of tasks," Lindner explains. "However, they are modest and reliable enough to know how to deal with this prominent position." Lindner speaks of GSG 9 as an "element of our team of teams," in which various capabilities for combating terrorism and violent organized crime are combined. Concerning the establishment of a branch office in Berlin, he is certain that "it will make GSG 9 more crisis-proof. It can react much more quickly to incidents that are not located in the west of Germany, but in the East and particularly in the capital."

So is everything just hunky dory? Not quite. The president of Police Directorate 11 is concerned about recruitment for the next generation of the federal counterterrorism unit. Since Wegener's time, there has been a recruitment issue, and over the five decades of its existence it has only marginally improved. The gap between open posts and successful applicants has narrowed in recent years, but it will probably never be completely closed, sighs Lindner. He shares these concerns with special task forces all over the world. This conundrum is not due to the number of applicants, it never has been. But the numbers of those who pass the recruitment test remain low; in addition, there are positions needing to be filled in the future, especially in Berlin. "On the other hand, in part it's our own fault, because we do not deviate from our strict requirements. We want to continue to offer the quality rightfully expected from us. So less is more, in this case."

The Chief Instructor

Frank Farnholdt[2] knows the complaints only too well. The "Head of Training and Further Education" joined GSG 9 in 1985 and has since seen several generations of operatives come and go. The selection process is far more demanding today, he concedes, and he is not entirely sure whether he would still pass it himself. They have a rule of thumb for the recruit assessment within GSG 9, the "rule of thirds" as it is called: out of 100 applicants, a good 30 pass the entrance test. Of this third, some subsequently fail the medical examination. By the end of the training phase, around 10 remain, i.e. another third. "In this year's training course we started with no more than twenty people. Currently, there are 16 of them left, and a few more will probably be sorted out."

That's hardly enough to fill the ranks. But this is not about just getting the ranks filled with anyone, says Farnholdt; it is about finding the right young people with the right attitude and spirit. "We don't want the go-getter who wants to join GSG 9 perhaps to boost his ego." However, the current crop of candidates is a completely different generation from when he started out, says the chief instructor, lamenting a general lack of endurance and capacity to suffer: "This has nothing to do with enduring pain, but simply with stretching beyond the comfort zone: 'Typically, I would lie down for a sleep now. But I can stay awake for once. Typically, I wouldn't go running because it's too hot outside. But I'm doing it anyway.' It's a lot of little things, but these little things are exactly what we need here. It's difficult for us these days, because this generation has grown up in a sheltered environment. We do notice a sense of entitlement. At times I would like to see the spirit of the past, especially when it comes to working with a little dose of idealism and not keeping the attitude of 'I need this, I need that. There is a little tear in my uniform trousers, I need new ones.' The old guys were of the type that when their uniform trousers were ripped they would simply jump into their own blue jeans and ask where they need to go."

However, it is not just those with the right spirit that are in high demand; it is also thinkers: "Unfortunately, the capacity to suffer in the way I've just described, in combination with the adequate brain capacity, is simply not well represented. There are studies that show that perhaps three percent of the population have the appropriate skills to fill this mold."

The Operative

Sebastian Pries[3] is one of the "three percent." On the outside he fits the cliché image of a GSG 9 officer: six foot two, well-muscled, short dark hair, well-groomed full beard, friendly and relaxed demeanor. The 32-year-old joined GSG 9 from the Federal Police in Bavaria after learning about the counterterrorism unit via internet forums and YouTube videos. The challenge appealed to him: the mix of physical and intellectual requirements, plus collaboration in a highly specialized team mastering demanding tasks. An additional factor, of course, was the little perks that come along with the job: parachuting, diving, fast roping from a helicopter.

However, there was a lot of respect for the GSG 9 legend at first: "If you do your research on the internet, it comes across as very heroic: all these great guys who accomplish great things and can basically do anything. But then, when you meet them, you realize that they're normal people who put their trousers on one leg at a time. The first time I was here for the assessment test, I saw people coming out of the main building. They were all dressed like normal people and I thought: I could go out for a beer with this guy; he could be a buddy."

Sebastian Pries went into the selection process with great trepidation, he says. He found it to be very demanding, but fair and doable, even for a non-superman. After 10 months of basic and special training, he has been working as an operative in an operational unit since 2019.

Currently, GSG 9 is focusing on organized crime in the biker gang, smuggling, and clan scenes: arresting potential offenders, enforcing arrest warrants when resistance is likely, or securing so-called search and seizure operations to ensure that their colleagues from the Criminal Investigation Department can do their job safely. Are these routine operations, then? "In my experience, there are no routine operations. Each one is considered in an individual manner, both in terms of the legal requirements and the particular situation in which it is happening." The half-serious term "deployment as training" that sometimes comes up in conversations should therefore be taken with a pinch of salt, Pries says. "We do train for much more complex scenarios. But such comparatively simple operations are by no means regarded as exercises. We don't say: This is not as an important operation so let's try something new. We always go for the best possible and safest course of action."

But naturally, during such relatively low-stakes missions only a fraction of their skills and abilities are called upon, skills that they have trained and perfected for years on end. Yes, he admits, the thought of one big Mogadishu-type mission looms in the back of their minds, but "when I talk to my colleagues, it's not all about 'The big mission has to come and that's the only reason I'm here.' We once had someone in our unit who was very keen on it. But at some point he drew the line and left, because he said it wasn't likely to happen. So I think it's a middle ground: We're not out on having a big mission. But there is a certain tension."

One day, he is sure, such a major mission will come anyway. The big question is what form it will take.

Until the turn of the millennium, special police forces mainly had to deal with comparatively static situations in which political or financial demands were made and there was some kind of negotiation taking place. That left them with time for bringing forces in and positioning them strategically, time for conducting reconnaissance and drawing up rescue plans. But what happens if there is nothing to negotiate? If there are no demands? If the terrorist has no interest in preserving their own life and not only acquiesce in their own death, but make it part or even the objective of their attack? As is the case with Islamist terrorists or people running amok? The advance warning times for bringing in the emergency services have shrunk drastically, at times to zero, as happened in the fatal Islamic terrorist attack on the Christmas market in Berlin in 2016 or the attack on Munich's Olympic shopping center in the same year. The more dynamically the situation unfolds, the less time there is to think through every option in detail.

The Unit Leader

"We feel the pressure because it's naturally unpleasant when decisions have to be made quickly," admits Matthias Conradi,[4] though he is quick to add: "Of course, we've trained for these situations a thousand times and acquired the skills we need." Since 2003, the 44-year-old family man has worked his way up from "trainee," as the newcomers are half-jokingly called here, to the position of instructor, squad leader and deputy unit leader. He has been in charge of the 1st Operational Unit since 2016. During this time, he has witnessed firsthand how much GSG 9's scope of operations and resources have changed, the key factor being time.

The task force has tried to adapt to this by reducing planning depth when preparing for each operation. Not everything is detailed down to the last minutiae in advance, and flexibility is required even more than before. It works somewhat like Lego, a modular system, ad hoc putting together the right combination of building blocks for the situation, these blocks being the available skills, tactics, weaponry and equipment. Since every minute counts, the ready-packed deployment bags of each operational unit on duty now always wait in the transport vehicles.

Meanwhile, the available equipment has expanded considerably, not only compared to the early days but even to 10 or 15 years ago. Technology has developed immensely: mobile internet, miniaturization of surveillance technology, the sheer number of possible communication channels which has exploded since the turn of the millennium. So, too, has the number of possible reconnaissance tools available to unit leaders like Matthias Conradi. "We used to talk about using a camera as a possible reconnaissance tool, but today we also talk about drones or robots."

There have also been massive technical upgrades in the way access is carried out, for example when entering homes. Again, this is a matter of digitalization and the modern networks that come with it. Conradi is reluctant to reveal exactly what can be achieved with this kind of technology—tactical reasons, of course. But it does not take a great deal of imagination to picture what something like this could look like. Webcams in the house could be tapped remotely; access to the home could be gained by decrypting digital keys stored on smart cards like the ones for hotel rooms; as a diversionary measure, automatic shutters could be raised and lowered via the cracked smart home app right before breaking in. Such speculation is naturally not confirmed by GSG 9. But "the technology we have gained in recent years is immense compared to what we had in the past. And it is becoming more and more specialized, which means that people have needed to acquire much more knowledge about these things in recent years," Conradi states. For this reason, specialization within the special unit has also increased. Each SET now has its own technician who is responsible for gaining access or defusing IEDs. In addition, in each SET an operator serves as a trained reconnaissance specialist, another one as paramedic.

However, the individual teams do not operate in a vacuum. They never did, but today the complexity of the operational situations is much greater than it was only a few years ago, especially due to so-called chaining measures, in which one operation merges into the next. "There are many forces involved that have to work in parallel with us. And the personnel for such an operation have grown accordingly. These are far more complex scenarios today compared to even when I started."

In this new environment, Mathias Conradi describes GSG 9 as a kind of service provider. At times, this sounds more like crisis consulting for start-up companies than a badass assault team: "We always strive to offer a customized solution for our clients to bring the operation to a successful conclusion. That's how we see ourselves."

Despite all the changes, some prejudices remain. "Many people still think that GSG 9 will come in and smash everything to pieces." Even half a century after its inception, the myth of GSG 9 as a shark squad persists, even among some requesting authorities within other police forces: "The image that haunts many people's minds is of lone fighters whose only tool is brute force. This can sometimes be the case if the situation requires it, but we offer many options, and afterwards the respective police commander for the operation is usually grateful for our advice. Everyone I've worked with in recent years has told me: 'I didn't think you'd act like this.' And people have adjusted their image of us accordingly," Conradi says.

All their new tech notwithstanding, the basic tactics have not changed since the founding days of GSG 9. What has changed, however, is the type of perpetrator: "When we are dealing with an Islamic terrorist, we have to be aware that he will probably fight to the death. Because, according to his world view, he wants to die as a martyr. If we know that the other person is under the influence of drugs, then it is relatively difficult to assess their reactions, or the bomber who is aiming for 'suicide by cop.' We have to be prepared to prevent exactly that." And "The 9ers" have to adjust their strategies and tactics accordingly.

In order to do this, however, GSG 9 must first be deployed. The threshold for this is the "reasonable assumption" that the target is in possession of firearms and ready to use them. According to the self-image of GSG 9 operatives, the trick is to plan the operation in such a way that the use of firearms is not needed. One of the means to achieve this: Intimidation by way of massive overpowering, which leaves the other party with as few options for action as possible, the clear message being: Don't even think about it! "We try to gain control as quickly as possible," Conradi confirms. "We act very firmly and consistently in order to show our opponent that there is no chance of success for him. This is also reflected in our choice of resources. If we are in a small apartment, for example, we usually use handguns. But if we know that people are armed with Kalashnikovs, then we don't need to consider pistols, we will go in with assault rifles." The actual use of their weapons remains the last resort for the protection of bystanders, hostages, and for personal protection. This is confirmed by the low number of operations involving the use of firearms: officially eight instances in 50 years. The binding principle of proportionality in the choice of means to stop a perpetrator still applies. This distinguishes it from a military unit.

Is this principle always observed? Of course, as everyone here says, unit leader Conradi replies with a mixture of annoyance and demonstrative incomprehension present in his handling of such a question. Nevertheless, it is hardly verifiable, because apart from the very forces involved, barely anyone can provide information about what exactly happens when the action begins, right? Well, not quite.

The Doctor

Renate Bohnen is responsible for the unit's general practitioners and company doctors, but her primary field of expertise is operational medicine. Bohnen—short gray haircut, round rimless glasses, pithy appearance—joined the Federal Border Guard in 2004 through a job advertisement in a German medical journal. GSG 9 was looking for *"ein Arzt"* (a doctor), which in the German language indicates a male person and which back then was perfectly normal in a job description. Bohnen applied anyway and beat three men in the selection process. Since then, as medical director of a team of 20, she has been in charge of the police medical service within the otherwise "male brotherhood, GSG 9."

In her function as operational medicine physician, she operates close enough to where the action is. This means that she doesn't wait for a situation to have been resolved and to be given the all clear before she gets going, as is the case in classic emergency medicine: "We have to get involved as soon as the shooting begins, otherwise it's maybe too late for the person lying there." The question of who the person lying there is doesn't matter, according to Bohnen. It could be a police officer, a bystander or even a hostage-taker: "I'm a doctor. We have taken a vow to help everyone, regardless of religion, race or crimes he may or may not have committed." If there are several injured people at the same time, they are treated according to the urgency and severity of the injury: "That's a medical decision. If the hostage-taker has an injury that will be lethal if it is not treated immediately, and our operative only suffers from a broken leg? Then the hostage-taker is treated first, of course."

In order to be able to provide help and first aid in the danger zone during operations, Bohnen had to undergo intense police training. For self-protection, she practiced martial arts, and learned how to handle weapons and ballistic protective equipment such as bulletproof vests and helmets, etc. "That's a fundamental part of it. It's the only way I can accompany the men on missions without becoming a burden to them or putting myself at risk."

Accordingly, the type of medical care is fundamentally different to what she was used to before. In the civilian sector, more than two-thirds of all deployments are internal emergencies: heart attacks, strokes, derailed blood sugar levels, circulatory collapses. With GSG 9, however, Bohnen mainly deals with stabs, cuts, gunshots, and explosion injuries. "When I started here, I had no idea about gunshot wounds. You sometimes get the odd stabbing wound in the emergency room. But I had never seen a gunshot wound before. And suddenly that was my main topic."

There are also glass splinter injuries caused by breaking through windows, and injuries from scuffles during arrests—lacerations, bruises, sprains, the odd broken nose or cut eyebrow, which may result from perpetrators violently resisting their arrest. But in Bohnen's experience, these situations have never gotten out of hand. "From what I've seen so far, I can only say that proportionality of means is the top priority, and the other person would have every chance of ending it without injury. But sometimes it is simply due to the dynamics of the case that aggression on the part of the opponent leads to injuries."

But what about the use of firearms? The operatives always aim at the periphery of the body, at arms, legs, never the chest or head, Bohnen insists. "The only thing that might happen is injuries from ricochets. Then the chest or head can be hit. But I've never experienced a targeted shot to any of these areas." This applies to GSG 9 as well as the SEKs of the provinces. For Bohnen, the most extreme example in this regard was the deployment of the SEK at Cologne Central Station in 2018. Her team had been called there to provide medical support. A man had taken a hostage in a pharmacy and could not be convinced to give up. Renate Bohnen treated the man immediately after the SEK hit. She counted a total of 11 bullet wounds, all in the periphery, none near vital organs. "Eleven holes where they didn't belong anatomically—that was impressive. The man survived." A medical miracle? Good luck? "Good work, I would say," claims Bohnen.

The way police officers deal with suspects in arrest situations sometimes makes the headlines, even below the level of such extreme situations. In 2020, the death of African American George Floyd sparked global outrage and mass protests across the United States. Cell phone images taken by bystanders showed a US police officer kneeling on the neck of Floyd for several minutes until he suffocated while being pinned to the ground in restraints. His gasping words "I can't breathe" turned into a global mantra against police violence. The officer was sentenced to 22 years in prison in the first instance. It was certainly the most spectacular documented case of police violence in recent decades.

But in Germany, too, there are regular reports of violent assaults on people in police custody, even lethal in some cases. So, how about during the robust operations of GSG 9? The operatives cannot exactly afford being squeamish if they have to reckon with being shot at. Has anyone perhaps handled a situation more violently than necessary, perhaps even when the actual crisis is over? Bohnen vigorously shakes her head: "That doesn't happen here; quite the opposite. If someone is pushed down to put them in restraints, great care is taken to ensure that they are put back on their feet immediately and that they can breathe properly. People are given very strict instructions and training on what it means to kneel on someone or push someone down, and what danger this entails. The top priority is to use as little force as possible, only what is really absolutely necessary."

The Commander (2014–2023)

"We think in police terms," confirms Jérôme Fuchs. "This means that we always aim to avoid any collateral damage and carry out a precise operation." Fuchs has a military background. After graduating from high school in 1990, he initially joined the Bundeswehr mountain troops. Two years later, he transferred to the federal crime agency BKA, and finally to GSG 9, where he rose to become unit leader of the maritime unit and was seconded to the FBI's Hostage Rescue Team (HRT). In 2014, at the age of 44, he finally took over as commander of the unit. Apart from his uniform, Fuchs exudes nothing military about him. He acts in a demonstratively relaxed way in his dealings with his colleagues, addressing them with the casual "Du" on a first name basis, which is still rather uncommon in a German work environment. Also, there are no rank insignia to be found on his epaulettes. The only indication that Fuchs is the boss is the number "1" attached to his sleeve with Velcro.

Even today, GSG 9 still has a reputation for having retained some of its paramilitary roots. Former SEK officers report with amusement how, just a few years ago, GSG 9 operatives reported for duty with a snappy salute, a habit which is frowned upon within regular German police. But even though he still has his people train internationally with special military units and compete in police competitions against the SAS, Navy SEALs, and Israel's Sayeret Matkal, Commander Fuchs does not see his GSG 9 as the cavalry of the modern fight against crime and terrorism as it is sometimes described. The concept of the cavalry is outdated anyway. He prefers the image of professional firefighters, "although this comparison only carries so far. GSG 9 can't be on site throughout Germany within a few minutes like the fire departments can." But in order to deal with modern challenges in the fight against terrorism, it needs to become more like a fire department, or rather some kind of central firefighter training and instruction institution to bring the local departments up to speed.

As described above, lead times for attacks have been dramatically reduced in recent years. It's been accepted that there just isn't enough time to wait for the cavalry to arrive and sort it out. This altered scenario not only calls for a different tactical approach, but also a different, decentralized deployment strategy. Fuchs sees the solution for the conundrum in knowledge transfer, especially to security forces outside GSG 9: "We have passed on significant parts of our know-how to those emergency services who are first on the scene in the event of a terrorist attack. In doing so, I believe we have made a significant contribution to improving the overall response capability of the Federal Police."

Following the attacks in 2015, particularly after the attack on the French satirical magazine *Charlie Hebdo* in Paris, a new unit was established, the Federal Police's Beweissicherungs- und Festnahmeeinheit Plus.* They are spread across five locations throughout Germany with fifty operatives each. In terrorist threat situations they are tasked with "tying up the attackers, protecting bystanders, treating the injured and evacuating them from the danger zone." Acting as a kind of localized "GSG 9 Light," they are supposed to either bridge the time needed to bring in special intervention units such as the SEKs of the provinces and GSG 9 or, if necessary, take action on their own if there is not enough time to wait.

According to Fuchs, it is crucial to intensively practice the complex interaction of all forces and units involved in high threat-level situations, starting with individual patrols at train stations or airports, moving on to the deployment of hundreds of riot police, the BFE+ and finally GSG 9. All of these elements need to be tactically integrated: "Until recently, we had never practiced anything in this complexity and depth, and of course there was intensive discussion and evaluation of these exercises. Where are starting points for improvement?"

The same principle applies to interaction with the SEKs of the provinces, says Fuchs, as well as to international networking, especially through the ATLAS network, which brings together 38 special units from the EU and allies such as the United States and Israel. As an example, Fuchs refers to the operations in Munich in 2016, when Austria's EKO Cobra supported the German security forces during the rampage at the Olympic shopping center, as well as at the G20 summit in Hamburg. In May 2021, ATLAS members from three countries supported Belgian forces in the search for a heavily armed right-wing extremist and former soldier who had entrenched

---

* Beweissicherungs- und Festnahmeeinheit Plus (BFE+) = Evidence Preservation and Arrest Unit Plus.

himself in a forest. According to investigators, he had equipped himself with rocket launchers and machine guns and is said to have planned attacks on mosques and government buildings. The Belgians would not have been able on their own to muster sufficient forces for the large-scale search operation in the 12,000-hectare national park.

However, a full-scale ATLAS operation including special ops units from multiple countries has not yet taken place. Whether it ever will is primarily a political question. Will foreign nations be allowed to operate on one's home territory? "That's not our decision to make," says Fuchs. "But we as a unit want to be prepared for it. And we're working hard on that." The basic idea behind these efforts has not changed since the days of Wegener, the founding commander, half a century ago: fighting international terrorism requires international cooperation.

No one here has any doubt that the need for a large-scale international operation will arise at some point. Be it tomorrow, next week, or in five years' time. Perhaps less spectacular than Mogadishu and less public, too, though no less demanding and no less important—and always fraught with the risk of complete and utter failure, no matter how meticulously they prepare. In the 2010s and early 2020s it appeared for a while that the international security situation might have eased a little. The COVID-19 pandemic caused a period of relative calm. But recent events in the Middle East and its reverberations throughout the world indicate that this calm might have been deceptive. For Fuchs, the comparison between GSG 9 and a fire department is therefore an obvious one. The fire department is trained to fight major fires, and even if their operations over long periods of time consist mainly of pumping water out of flooded cellars or picking cats out of trees, nobody would think of closing down the fire department just because there hasn't been a huge fire for a few years. Fuchs is convinced that the time will come when GSG 9 is needed again. Being the fire department for fighting crime and terrorism, they must be prepared and equipped for any contingency. "Because we are the final line. After us will be no one."

APPENDIX A

Thinking the Unthinkable

Commander Robert Hemmerling Talks GSG 9's Past, Present, and Future

Colonel Robert Hemmerling has been a member of GSG 9 for almost two decades. In this time, he has held various positions in the organization. Born in 1979, he began his police career at the age of 18, when he gained employment with the Bremen city police in 1996. In 2005, he applied for and was accepted into GSG 9. After completing basic and special training, Hemmerling became an operative for special assignments in GSG 9's 2nd Operational Unit which specializes in maritime operations. He went on to serve first as SET leader and later as deputy unit leader. From 2018–2020, he completed the master's degree program for higher police service at the German Police University before returning to "The 9ers," when he took on the role of head of operations, gaining responsibility for the operational units, for training, and further training, and later became deputy commander. In October 2023, he was eventually inaugurated as GSG 9's eighth commander of the Federal Police.

The interview takes place in early summer 2024, in the spacious but soberly furnished office of the GSG 9 commander, the same office his seven predecessors occupied in its Saint Augustin headquarters. The German tricolor next to the unit's green flag is the only insignia to give this place a somewhat ceremonial touch. The spare interior design reflects GSG 9's no-nonsense work ethics: They are here because they have a job to do. This job, it seems, has become even more demanding in recent years. And Hemmerling seems well aware of this fact.

Commander Hemmerling, these are turbulent times. You have been leading GSG 9 since October 2023, just after the terrorist attack in Israel happened. How did the first months of your tenure go?

I have taken over a well-established unit with highly motivated employees, comrades, and of course I have also been familiar with the tasks and challenges of the unit for several years now. And yes, the stakes have remained consistently high in recent months. Accordingly, this requires a high level of flexibility and commitment from the staff here and, of course, from myself.

There were plans for an official ceremony for the day you took over command from your predecessor Jérôme Fuchs, the official handover of the baton, so to speak. Numerous national and international guests had been invited from all over the world. But in the end, all of this did not materialize. Only a few days prior to the event, you sent out cancellation letters. Why?

We had picked October 18 for this event, a historic date for GSG 9 [the anniversary of the storming of the *Landshut* in Mogadishu] and, as you say, we had prepared it in the same way it should be done in our community, that if you have many international and national contacts, you will of course invite guests too. But then October 7 happened [the day when Israel was rocked to its core by the terrorist Hamas attacks] which really, really affected us all. We maintain very close ties with Israel and a longtime partnership with the Israeli special unit YAMAM. This unit was heavily challenged on October 7 and 8, heavily involved in action, they achieved superhuman things there. They fought heroically and saved many lives, but also lost lives of their own. So we were even more emotionally affected than the general public in Germany. Many members of GSG 9 have been to Israel more than once, so there is a close bond with the people of Israel. Consequently, with the events going on down there, we didn't feel like celebrating and we thought it was appropriate to scale things down.

You described the close ties with Israel. How did they come about? And how are they today?

Well, our birth is very closely linked to the history of terror against Israel and Israeli citizens in Munich 1972. Historically, I find it really remarkable that Ulrich Wegener, our first commander, traveled to Israel in the aftermath of the Munich massacre and received support there in setting up GSG 9 despite what just had happened here. In doing so, Israel made a huge contribution to German and European security at the time. This is the historic background, which in the course of many years developed into a tight partnership and even many a friendship. And today, the Israeli Special Forces are a premium partner for GSG 9. Why? Because it is a very innovative, very goal-oriented and adaptable special unit. Worldwide, it is one of the special forces with the most extensive field of experience. For us, this cooperation comes with many advantages. GSG 9 is a very well-connected specialist unit with a worldwide network. We do not operate under the same pressure as YAMAM and therefore have more opportunities to innovate in certain fields, more opportunities to carry things further. So, this is a very productive win-win situation for both of us.

How does this exchange work in real life? When you say innovative, is it about equipment, combat techniques, deployment techniques? What kind of exchange is taking place? I assume reciprocal visits and courses play a role?

Yes, absolutely. All of it is based on trust which only grows bit by bit. Such open cooperation, as we are lucky to have, takes place in the area of technical innovation and development, regular exchange of ideas about new developments in technology, in armament, but also in tactics, for example experiences on October 7 and 8. These are things that we can learn a great deal from and implement accordingly.

What were the immediate consequences of the October 7 massacre for GSG 9 beyond the knowledge transfer that you have just mentioned? Was there an impact on your work here in Germany?

It did have an impact on us as a special police force. On the one hand, it affected us on a human emotional level. I've just described how tight the connections are. If you imagine that we had recently undertaken joint exercises with some of the comrades injured or killed in the terrorist attacks there in October '23, that some of them were also friends, then it inevitably had an impact on the people here in the unit. And it was clear to us from the very first second when we found out what happened that we wanted to support them. And we did, by offering moral support, of course, but also technical logistical support.

What kind of technical support?

I'll give you two examples. After two days under really strong fire on October 7 and 8, there was a lack of medical equipment. Blood plasma was an issue. We put together a lot of stuff here to support them logistically. Also, operations like these, of course, will have not only physical but also emotional consequences. So there is also a need for aftercare, psychosocial aftercare. And we were able to help there too.

Did this mean you went down there with a contingent for the support?

The psychosocial aftercare took place here.

So, YAMAM members were brought to Germany to be treated here?

That's right.

You said these events impacted GSG 9 beyond the immediate support. What were the lessons learned?

One must state that this terrorist attack opened up a new dimension in terms of armament as well as the course of action of the perpetrators. And we certainly drew conclusions from this.

In what way? Hamas are carrying out their attacks in Israel. GSG 9 mainly operates in Germany. It's a very different situation here. In how far was it instructive for you learning about how Hamas operates, particularly in these gruesome attacks?

On a fundamental level, this is an issue with which we at GSG 9 are confronted in many other areas as well. I would call it "Anticipation Strategy," which is simply learning from forms of terrorist attacks which have not yet happened here in Germany, but certainly have happened abroad, not only in Israel. Because it is our task at GSG 9 to think the unthinkable. And accordingly, we must consider that certain devices or certain tactics may be used here at some point as well. It's our job to prepare for such scenarios.

So that means that the terrorist tactics we had to observe in Israel could threaten us at some point?

I wouldn't want to do a deep analysis right now. But as I said, it is our task and our approach to learn from terrorist attacks that have not yet happened here in Germany but do happen abroad and, of course, to find answers to those threats. Whether they take place here or not is another question. But our job is to prepare for it.

And of course, it's a great advantage to have a tight international network to this end. You have called Israel a premium partner for GSG 9. Which other premium partners do you maintain close relationships with?

In the USA our premium partners are the FBI Hostage Rescue Team, in particular with SEAL Team-6 and in parts also with Delta Force. These are really, very close partners with whom we have built a close relationship of trust over the years, with whom we meet regularly in workshops, in tactical joint exercises and with whom we are in constant exchange of experience about the latest developments. The same goes for the British SAS and SBS and the French GIGN.*

When you say exchange workshops, what does that look like? A couple of dozen GSG 9 operatives or leaders fly over to the United States for a couple of weeks and vice versa?

Exactly. The workshops are of the most diverse type, starting with operational units that go to tactical workshops with specific topics. It's about abseiling techniques, it's about the use of dogs, it's about the use of reconnaissance technology. Then there are the support units, i.e. our EOD (Explosive Ordnance Disposal) and our Beacher Cell,† who share operational experience or even the latest charges to open specific doors that are new to the market. So it's the most diverse form of this type of exchange you can imagine.

---

* GIGN (Groupe d'intervention de la Gendarmerie nationale or National Gendarmerie Intervention Group) = Elite police tactical unit of the French National Gendarmerie.
† Specialists in creating access with or without explosives.

APPENDIX A • 213

Including the leadership level?

Including the leadership level. The last time I was with HRT and SEAL Team-6 was just a couple of months ago.

One can always learn a lot of things from each other, of course, but the situation here in Germany is quite different. What are the challenges that you must face now, considering the changing circumstances that have arisen in recent years?

First of all, the analysis of the security situation takes place at the BKA,* and the evaluation at the Federal Police headquarters as well as in the BMI. As commander, I am not entitled to evaluate this in detail. But what I can say is that we as GSG 9 are affected by all the possible situation developments that are currently being discussed. This is, of course, the terrorist threat in Germany and in Europe. That is organized crime and these are hybrid threat scenarios that can develop from the war in Ukraine. We are right in the center of it.

If you compare this situation now with the situation four or five years ago—let's say before the COVID-19 pandemic—what has changed? And how does GSG 9 need to adapt to these changing situations and threat situations?

Throughout its history, GSG 9 needed to change and adapt to the changing challenges of the time over and over again. Always, the main success criteria were the ability to learn, to adapt and people who were willing and able to do something beyond the ordinary. But the requirements have fundamentally changed over the last few years. For example, the wave of terror that we had to witness in Europe back in 2015, in Paris and Brussels. It was all about deploying forces more quickly, so we adapted our concepts back then. There were certain things that we might not have shared before [with other forces] like certain tactics or technologies. We decided to broadly spread them out to our BFE+ in order to get them up to speed for the task. We have defined common standards with the SEKs of the Bundesländer to take account of this new ad hoc terrorist threat and to quickly advance our expertise.

Do you consider this knowledge transfer complete or is it an ongoing process? Of course, the situation is continuing to develop. And there are always new people joining the police force and they need to be trained. So is GSG 9 becoming something of a train-the-trainer force?

We consider ourselves a spearhead which can and must hand down know-how to others. For us at GSG 9, it is a constant challenge that the requirements of deployment are changing and that means that we must constantly adapt in technical areas, in tactics, but also in the organizational structure.

---

* BKA (Bundeskriminalamt) = Federal Criminal Police Office.

Let's take a look back at the history, the beginnings of GSG 9 in the 1970s. You mentioned the Olympic massacre. GSG 9 was founded in the aftermath, comprising three units with 117 men at first. What has changed since then, how have the challenges shifted? And how is GSG 9 doing today compared to those humble beginnings?

Perhaps first, what has remained the same? Back then, we had to break new ground in building GSG 9. Today, we must continue to find new answers to new challenges. So that has stayed the same. The same is true for the ability to learn and adapt, that has remained the same. It has remained the same that even today we depend on people who are prepared to get particularly involved and want to and can do something special. Of course, a whole lot of technology has changed since the 1970s. Much has changed in tactics, in our organizational structure. You mentioned the size of GSG 9 back then, this manpower has grown and accordingly, our areas of support have increased because the level of mechanization has increased. This means that now we really need experts in various fields, for example in the IT sector. These are people who don't necessarily be the fastest runner in the operational unit or be good at pull-ups, but who have a completely different skill set so that we can adequately manage the technology we have today. This need certainly has increased. Otherwise, we had the last organizational change here not so long ago. In September 2023, we restructured the operational units. We now have not four, but three operational units.* We now have snipers in every operational unit, which is also a consequence of the fact that we are spread over two locations.

So, with three operational units you return to the original structure of the early years? The three operational units were expanded to four units in the 1980s and now you are going back to your roots?

Yes, absolutely. But like today, the structure was the result of an assessment of the security situation back then. After all, we always have to look at the environment in which we are acting. Back then, we had a niche ability in the field of sharp shooting. Later we decided that we need to aggregate this capability, so that our snipers could exercise better together. In the meantime, the German Länder [provinces] with their SEKs caught up well in this field. And today we are deployed at two locations, one in Berlin, one here in Saint Augustin, and we need to be able to deploy our snipers with all our forces at a moment's notice.

We've now talked about structure and techniques and things like that. Has there also been a change in the way you deal with the people within GSG 9? Has there been a

---

* The reduction from four to three operational units has led to the use of unconventional nomenclature: The 1st Unit has been dissolved, leaving the 2nd and 3rd units located in Saint Augustin and the newly established 4th Unit in Berlin.

change in the mentality of people compared to the olden days? And what does that mean for your management approach and the way of leading?

Once again, what has remained the same? First off, the principle of leadership from the front has remained the same. When I joined GSG 9, it took me a while to understand what that actually means. Because sometimes there are situations when you have to tactically lead from behind, in particular, when you have to operate within several operation scenarios at once. As a leader, I always have to ask myself: where is the best place for me to assure the greatest impact or influence? And it may very well be that it is not right at the front line. Because leadership from the front also means something else. And that is the principle of leading by trust, meaning trust in the forces at the front line and trust that they will make the decisions that are necessary. And finally, leadership from the front also means I'm visible, I'm approachable, I take a stand, I don't mumble anything away. Our founding commander embodied this principle from the very beginning, at least that's how I see it in retrospect. And that is also an important aspect that is still valid today. And then the aspect of breaking new ground. Openness to other cultures, cooperation on equal footing with others are key aspects that have remained and which still shape GSG 9 today. So yes, I would say that a lot has remained of the values that we had in the early days.

Still, what has changed? During my interviews for this book, I spoke to some people who very openly talked about a change in the mentality of younger people applying for GSG 9. They told me that you have to deal with them differently and talk to them differently and motivate them differently. And they also come from a different educational background, social background, etc.

So we are part of society and the general social developments which, of course, catch up with us. From my experience I can say that today we need to explain more. Why? Conveying meaning. It is no longer good enough to just say get in line and do as I say, but you have to invest a little more in meaningful processes. That is the task of leadership. But it is doable. It is a generational issue. But then again, when I was a rookie here at GSG 9 some 20 years ago, I was invited to a farewell party for an old comrade and, boy, did they make me listen to all these complaints about "the young generation!" So much for that. I think every new generation is confronted with this to some extent. And on the other hand, we've seen it in social contexts such as the great floods in West Germany in 2021. We could see how young people volunteered to help in the affected regions. They wanted to do something meaningful. This is where you can get them hooked. You can get them on board if you explain to them that it makes sense what we're doing here. Yes, it's a process, but you have to go through it. And I think we're on a good track with the new generation.

Recently, GSG 9 gave itself a new so-called "Statement of Values." This happened under your predecessor, Commander Fuchs. Why was that necessary?

It started around 2020. Back then, being already in a leadership position, I was actively involved in it. And I wouldn't say that it was absolutely necessary or something we just needed to do. But it was something that was coming from within the unit for several reasons. There was the 50-year mark of our inception coming up. Also, we had just set up the new location in Berlin. So after many years at one headquarters, we were now spread out over two locations. The topic of generations within GSG 9 we've just mentioned plays into it as well. And against this backdrop, there was a strong desire coming from within the force saying: "Let's write up our core values that unite us and which we want to form our bonds in the future, perhaps for the next 50 years." And in the end, this has become a compass of values. We could not have foreseen that at the beginning. In retrospect, I would also say that one particularly valuable thing about this was the process, the way we got there. Simply by asking ourselves "Who are we?," "Who do we want to be?" We worked on this in workshops over a year and a half and included each and every person within the unit. At the end of this process, this value compass came out with seven core values that are important to us as GSG 9. And, above all, a definition of each of these values: Camaraderie is the backbone of GSG 9. What does comradeship mean to us? It means that individual and personal interests are second to the larger goal of the community. It means that we can always rely on the support of our people, even after we clock out. That is one such example.

Which are the core elements? You mentioned seven, but if you had to choose, would comradeship be the core element that makes up the self-image of GSG 9?

Comradeship is not an element, it is the backbone, if you will. There is the element of trust. We have trust in each other. I have trust in the men who are doing the job at the front. There is the topic of appreciation. We appreciate each other, we respect each other. That is a value for us. Respect for one's comrade but also respect for our fellow citizens. These are the core elements.

For a manager, trust is always a double-edged sword, often being associated with blind trust. Is trust difficult for you personally, or is that something that comes easy to you?

It's an absolute necessity. I don't really have much of a choice. Of course, I have to question myself again and again, too. And of course, you have to talk about this topic again and again. Where do I perhaps need to take a closer look? I do take a closer look, of course, but not in terms of a control measure, but as part of my ongoing [self-]education. I must not lose sight of what people are experiencing at the front and refresh these images from time to time, which of course grow older with me after a while and are not as present anymore. But the bottom line is that during an operation, I'm not the first man at the door and I can't help but trust.

Let's talk about leadership. You've mentioned your founding commander, Ulrich Wegener. You've put a lot of emphasis on the continuities. Still, what do you do differently to Ulrich Wegener, this dominant, highly revered father figure who seems to be always hovering over GSG 9?

I for my part, I always try to make a realistic assessment. And as I said just now, yes, he really followed a very, very good approach. He was very successful in setting up GSG 9 and took the right path. But of course, he was able to go down that path because the conditions were different back then than the ones we have today. There is no other way to say that. Today, the direct line to the minister of the interior [which Wegener entertained] would no longer be possible in the same way. As a result, he had all the access he needed in order to set up GSG 9. Overall, we have a bureaucracy problem in Germany. And that, of course, slows us down in certain respects. And that can, of course, slow down a unit like GSG 9.

When I read the files about the inception of GSG 9, the speed at which it all happened once the political decision was made was baffling. Within weeks GSG 9 was set up. Are you sometimes jealous of those times back then?

I think that has something to do with the post-Munich crisis. In such a case something like this is possible. It is still possible today, I think. But things just look different in everyday life. And, of course, a special unit such as GSG 9 depends on the fact that they can make quick, flexible decisions and, of course, have hierarchies that are as flat as possible.

Did you actually get to know Commander Wegener?

Yes. I joined the force in 2005, and he passed away in 2017. And he was always a very frequent guest at GSG 9. He had really close ties with the unit.

How did you perceive him? How did he come across?

He was still an impressive person. In fact, I remember him very, very fondly. I think it was 2016 when [former Minister of the Interior] Klaus Kinkel and Ulrich Wegener were together here in our vehicle hangar and the entire unit sat in circles around them. And they talked about the early days of GSG 9. It was about relations with Hans-Dietrich Genscher. Kinkel had been his office manager back then and that's how they knew each other from these early days, the founding period of GSG 9. I can't even remember for how long, but it was really a very, very nice moment for the entire force, as the two men there talked about the old days.

What did you learn from Wegener? The concept of leadership from the front? Is that the main lesson from his leadership style?

That is an essential aspect. Leadership from the front, but in the sense as I have just described it, also not only in a tactical sense, but also: being at the forefront. Take the heat, don't mumble anything away, be clear. And the second thing is openness to other nations, other partners. That is also something which may set us apart from others. Looking at it against the backdrop of the story in 1972, it's a remarkable achievement that Wegener managed to get support in Israel. It was of course far-sighted by the Israelis, but also by Wegener. As a unit we keep trying to infuse this openness into other collaborations today. And as a commander I aim to implement that as well.

So here comes the question again: What do you do differently today than Wegener back then? Are there things you can no longer do today that were possible then?

Well, [it's] difficult. It's hard to say. It's mainly the direct access, including access to the political level. It's just different today. And apart from that, it's difficult for me to say now, because I've never experienced him in day-to-day management. Certainly, like the GSG 9 as a whole, he certainly had his strengths and also his weaknesses.

In Mogadishu, Ulrich Wegener was not the first one to enter the aircraft, but he did go in there with his men. If I heard this correctly, this caused many military and police leaders to shake their heads in disbelief and disapproval. What do you think of it? Can you imagine something like that for yourself or is it out of the question?

Personally, it is difficult for me to make a verdict on this, because the whole thing was a highly exceptional situation. There is an airplane in parking position some distance away. There are explosives, there are armed perpetrators, the hostages are doused with alcohol. This is a highly dangerous situation. And, of course, the leader's tactical position is typically somewhat remote at a vantage point where he can get a good overview. But in such an exceptional situation, there are of course also psychological aspects. And then I can very well imagine that it's quite different if you say, "Ok guys, there is the aircraft, off you go," or if you say, "There's the aircraft, follow me!" It certainly makes a difference. And that's why I can imagine that in the situation it makes sense, and it was the right move.

The veterans who took part in the storming of the Landshut told me in unison: "It was unbelievable moral support for us, knowing that yes, he not only talks the talk, but walks the walk and he is with us right out there."

Exactly that. It is also this aspect of leadership that simply involves carrying the risk in order to simply signal to your men: Hey, I have confidence in this mission, we're in this together.

You made your way to GSG 9 about 20 years ago. You were with the state police before. Why did you apply for GSG 9? What was your motivation?

I was with the state police in an Evidence Preservation and Arrest Unit [BFE]. Some of my friends applied to SEK back then. I was always interested in it but then decided to move up to senior service. Of course, I heard from my friends what it was like at the SEK and I also heard about the first contacts they had made with GSG 9. And I was excited. I was excited about their international ties, I was excited about the options GSG 9 offers in terms of the technical and tactical side of things: helicopters, specialization in different fields, skydiving, scuba diving. That was very appealing to me and that's why I actually decided to do it when I was still studying for my higher police career. I told myself, that's what you do first, you go for it full thrust and if that doesn't work out, you can still join the SEK.

What did you know about GSG 9 before you joined them? You were already working in the same field. But were you familiar with GSG 9's history and their importance for German history back in the 1970s, particularly due to Mogadishu?

I've always been interested in history. So, yes, I was somewhat familiar with it, and it was also part of what tempted me to become part of this unit. What I knew, though, was only what the available literature and occasional reports were writing about it, which was not that much. There was only one book on the market back then, and that was it.* Today, there is much more information available, in much greater detail, a lot of which was added by your book, *GSG 9—Ein deutscher Mythos*. Of course, I know this unit much better now than I did back then. I know our strengths; I know our weaknesses. And the subject of modern myths is, of course, an interesting one. But mythos doesn't accomplish operations, so we need to be on the top of our game every day and give our best. And that's maybe the difference between today and the olden days with its history and perhaps the myth associated with it. Today, it's all a bit more down to earth. It's simply a matter of showing high performance and delivering high performance every single day.

If we once again look at the history of GSG 9, what does Mogadishu mean for the unit almost half a century on? In 2027, it will be 50 years since Mogadishu—a long time. Many generations of "9ers" have made their careers in these decades. So what significance does this operation have for the force after all that time?

So it is, of course, still a very important mission and what it's telling us today is the very reason for the existence of GSG 9. It was born out of a crisis, the 1972 Olympic Games. It had its first major test during the crisis of the German Autumn

---

* The book Commander Hemmerling is referring to is Rolf Tophoven's *GSG 9: Kommando gegen Terrorismus*.

of 1977. And that's when Germany depended on a functioning special unit, that's why it was set up, and that's still the case today. Having said this, we are today bound by daily routine, making our contribution to the general security situation with one mission every week on average. We are committed to this and for us it is important, too, since we keep learning from those missions. But our job as GSG 9 can and must be to think the unthinkable. Thinking the unthinkable and preparing for it. Because as the saying goes, after us will be no one.

One mission per week on average, that means around 50 assignments a year. That has been the case for the last couple of decades. Has it also become more intense?

That is a good question. This really needs to be analyzed in greater depth. What I can say is that the workload has definitely increased in recent years. Not necessarily the pure number of missions, which is also persistently high. But above all, more of the missions require us to coordinate with several other police forces in support of the Länder in large structural operations.

... structural meaning in this case?

Comprehensive structures on the perpetrator's side. Organized crime, for example, operates within comprehensive structures. We call them large structural operations. And when we take action in such a structural operation, this means that we target and search multiple objects at the same time or make multiple arrests at the same time. In these cases, there is a need for a larger number of special forces, of course, particularly if it targets an organization that is also armed.

So you are talking about those operations you read about in the news: "Today, in the early morning hours, there were tightly coordinated police raids taking place in several cities in North Rhine-Westphalia, Hesse, and Berlin."?

Exactly. Recently, we had a number of those dealing with smuggling rings, in the first place.

We have looked at GSG 9's history, now let's take a glimpse at the future. How well is GSG 9 prepared for what's to come? What developments are ahead of you?

I think we're well prepared. We are a well-established force, and we can really look positively into the future. We will continue to change organizationally in the future, from our point of view, this is a necessity. We are looking into creating a new GSG 9 location in the north of Germany on the coast and have identified possible sites, decision currently pending. But the political decision has been made and we are now on track moving forward with it. We believe it necessary to strengthen our ability to intervene quickly on the North and Baltic Seas, so, prospectively, we consider a location in the North quite useful in the future.

When you say prospectively, what is the timescale?

This is an ongoing development. It is difficult for me to give you a timescale. I can tell you, though, that we are currently living in incredibly difficult times for a project like this. The state budget situation is very tight and, accordingly, this is an issue that must be considered at several levels.

So we're not talking about months, but obviously years. Probably similar to GSG 9's location in Berlin, which was in the pipeline for a really long time before actually being put into action.

That's right. So, a location like that, you don't build overnight. Of course, you have to start with that at some point. A timetable has been drawn up, with command and operational resources being moved first, followed by parts of the support forces until the operational forces are finally deployed. As I said, we think it makes sense. But when that decision is finally made and even after it's made, it will still take years.

You put the emphasis on both the North and the Baltic Seas. Considering the current international threat situation, I would rather put my money on the Baltic Sea. What is your rationale behind it?

The idea of actually covering both. So you have to choose a location somewhere then, presumably, that is geo-strategically located in such a way that it can secure short intervention times on both seas.

What is the motivation behind it when you say you think it's necessary? What are the particular threats you see there? I mean, the elephant in the room is Russia, isn't it?

As I said, we are not the ones to cover the analysis of the general security situation. But I also said that of course all areas of the security situation that are being discussed today are something we deal with. And that covers the elephant in the room as well as the hybrid-threat scenarios that come with it. In order to do this, we actually need the ability to intervene quickly on water. These can be threats of all kinds, as we have had in the past.

In terms of hybrid security threats, cybersecurity is a keyword and an ever expanding one at that. Is this an area that is still expanding with GSG 9 as well?

Absolutely. Particularly for our own safety, of course, we are talking about hardened systems security against eavesdropping. This is a very, very important issue right now. GSG 9 is primarily not responsible for fighting cybercrime. Of course, if cybercrime becomes analog at some point, if you want to get your hands on a perpetrator group, for example, that is active in this or that area then we will be called in. But as far as investigations in this field are concerned, that is what other services are doing.

The latest technology emerging in this area is AI, of course. Does that matter to you? Are there any fields of application you have identified and looked into?

Absolutely. That is the same as with all future topics. They also affect us to some extent. Recently, I went to the final exercise of our mission reconnaissance officers at GSG 9, which is a long-running course they have to take before they take up this task in the operational units. And this final exercise was really complex, very well designed and then well executed. It included a set of drones hovering high above the target object, a building in this case. These drones were linked to remote-controlled robots inside the target object. The officer in charge from our intelligence department, who is responsible for drone technology, told me: "What you see up there is currently state-of-the-art technology. It's what everybody wants to have right now. But in a few months, the successor model will be released. And it will be capable of doing twice as much. This is where you can see the speed of development right now. And that is a huge challenge, of course, to keep up with it or even get a bit ahead of it. And that applies to us and that applies to the opposite side. In other words, AI will provide us with opportunities and risks as it does for what we call the "police counterpart."

But do you have sufficient funding to keep pace with technological development? Earlier, you mentioned the tight budget situation.

As GSG 9, we still have the privilege that our superior authority really understands that we also serve as a development engine, that is, we drive forward developments from which others benefit. So this is not our problem right now. One general challenge will be attracting specialists in this field of expertise. We are affected by this in the same way as the general labor market and it will reach us with vengeance. And as a state agency, we must also question whether our current processes are working in an ever faster moving environment with an ongoing battle for the brightest minds. In my opinion, we're still a bit behind, a bit too slow, and inflexible.

So, what you would do is shout out to the people: apply to GSG 9 if you are an IT expert and are cyber trained?

Absolutely. There is definitely a call for professionals in this field who want to do something meaningful, who want to get involved. They are always very welcome here.

But they would still have to pass the entrance exam for GSG 9?

That's the downside. Of course, they also have to go through a test procedure and need to meet certain physiological as well as psychological characteristics that we demand. But since these people bring a very special skill set to the table, these exams are different from the ones for our operational units. We are taking a phased approach here.

But certain requirements still exist?

Absolutely. But it's also a very exciting, interesting field of work.

In 2022, GSG 9 celebrated its 50th anniversary. Can you picture GSG 9 in 50 years from now?

Oh yes, I can very well imagine that. I believe there will always be a need in the area of internal and external security and therefore a special intervention unit that will still exist in 50 years from now. I couldn't predict today what it will look like, everything is developing at an incredible pace. But what will still be essential 50 years from now [is] the ability to learn, adaptability, and people who want to get involved above average and use their special skills for good ends.

Addendum

In early 2025, the pivotal, historic turn in the strategic focus of the current US administration and the resulting tensions between the United States and its European partners have challenged the trans-Atlantic cooperation on all kinds of security-related questions, be it in the field of the military or the police. In the process of preparing this book for publication, I took the opportunity to ask Commander Hemmerling about the future of US–German cooperation. This was his answer:

Cooperation with our American partners remains stable and I am not currently aware of any significant changes. To be honest, I don't expect the Americans to turn their backs on us in principle. Just like its American partners, GSG 9 operates at a tactical and operational level and of course, we are dependent on decisions at the political and strategic level. At the moment, these are certainly more difficult to predict.

However, a well-functioning international network is a key success factor for special forces worldwide—even for the most capable of them. For smaller units, this aspect is all the more crucial. While the Americans can act more autonomously in many respects, a close international network remains important for them as well. Against this background, I see no reason to assume a fundamental reorientation or a withdrawal from the proven collaboration. We have had a GSG 9 liaison officer at the FBI for many years. They have already assured us that they want to maintain our close partnership.

APPENDIX B

East Germany's "GSG 9"

To East Germany's security service there was no doubt about it, GSG 9 presented "another instrument of power in the repressive state apparatus" of the FRG, intended for "use against democrats and dissidents, those affected by occupational bans and communists."[1] In 1978, a report on the West German counterterrorist task force by the Stasi stated, "In addition to the need for countering terrorism and to protect the political and economic representatives of the state monopolist system and the system itself, the creation of GSG 9 must be considered an expression of the effort to expand the state apparatus in order to further strengthen its reactionary power and to liquidate achievements that were won by democratic forces under the conditions favorable to them after 1945."[2]

Since the inception of GSG 9 in 1972, the communist GDR's secret service held this "militarized repressive organ of the FRG,"[3] under tight observation, producing reports on the strength, equipment, armament, and training of GSG 9, providing press reviews on operations and foreign contacts, compiling dossiers and photo spreads on Commander Wegener and his successors, as well as information on identified officers and their lifestyle, and in at least one case, on amorous contacts with a "female person" from the GDR. The Stasi intercepted telephone calls and even had an informant in the unit itself.

In 1981, a Border Guard officer told a member of the MfS details about the "service regime in the operations center of GSG 9" and about its technical equipment such as telephones and radios.[4] Was the officer aware of the fact that his counterpart worked for MfS? The information on duty hours, shift changes, patrols, and field inspections he related is quite detailed. It does not seem plausible that they were picked up from a talkative "9er" over a beer at the bar. The BGS officials were always urged to be cautious with information about GSG 9, particularly during the Cold War. The informant likely knew who would be the final recipient of the information. However, this does not seem to have resulted in extensive cooperation; at least no further reports from this informant can be found in the Berlin Stasi archives.

The GDR's secret service showed considerable interest in the West German special intervention unit. But in this case, learning from the West meant learning to win, even if no one would have openly admitted it. After all, the official picture was quite different. In April 1980, the military magazine *Der Kämpfer* (*The Fighter*) published an article about the promotion of Ulrich Wegener from commander of the "secret service-directed elite force" GSG 9 to the head of the superior BGS department with the title "Mortal enemies of the people at the levers of power in the FRG." The general gist was that Wegener was an anti-communist militarist, who had once betrayed and cowardly fled the communist East Germany. At the 1972 Olympic Games, Wegener and his shady backers had used the Palestinian terrorist act as an ingenious pretext for setting up the repressive instrument GSG 9, the article claimed: "[i]t was relatively easy for the founders and supporters of this killer group to suggest to the public that they were only responsible for 'fighting terrorists, hostage-takers and armed violent criminals.' In truth, this militarily and martially styled group … is the core of a future 'Bonn intervention force,' which, following the American model, has to operate wherever the interests of FRG imperialism demand."

An article in the magazine *Visier* (*Visor*) a few years later sounded the same horn. About the "true mission" of GSG 9 it stated, "In reality, however, it was all about the formation of a highly trained military commando force from the very beginning, equipped with modern special technology. Intended for subversive combat and provocations, it was to be deployed both in border areas and in foreign countries."

It probably would have been no small surprise to the authors of such articles to learn that at the time of their writing the GDR had long since had its own counterterrorist unit at its disposal. A unit, moreover, that was inspired by the West German model, of all things. Its name: Diensteinheit IX.[*] "GSG 9 was our inspiration," confirms retired police director Ulrich Tauchel, once head of the Rostock branch of the GDR special intervention unit.[5] In contrast to its Western counterpart, Diensteinheit IX remained unknown until the fall of the Berlin Wall in 1989. Its existence was kept under wraps, even to the point of self-denial. The head of the Berlin headquarters at the time stated at an internal seminar, "If someone asks me whether there is such a unit in the GDR, then I say: 'No, we don't have anything like that.'" Of course, he had to say that since terrorism and violent crime did not exist in the self-described "workers' and peasants' paradise," at least officially it did not. There were police crime statistics, to be sure. But these were exclusively internal to the authorities and never published. Only isolated cases, if any, appeared in the official law enforcement statistics of the GDR public prosecutor's office. The logic that followed from this was clear: no cases, therefore no need for a special intervention unit. But the course of time did not adhere to official doctrine. The GDR leadership knew this, too.

---

[*] Diensteinheit IX = Department IX. East Germany's version of a counterterrorism police task force, modeled after GSG 9.

With Lada and Kalashnikovs

When terror struck Munich in 1972, the people of East Germany were as shocked as their compatriots in the West. The GDR television studio in the Olympic village was located directly opposite the Israeli accommodations, and the whole episode there received live coverage. The consternation over the bloody result was immense, and the East German leadership feared that something similar might soon happen in their own domain. The Central Committee of the SED* looked with trepidation to the World Youth Games in East Berlin. Tens of thousands of participants from all over the world were expected in the year following the Olympics.

In Berlin, 24-year-old riot policeman Erich Fabian was hastily given the task of instructing a small group of young Volkspolizei officers in counterterrorism. After six weeks of hard training, they went into action: "Of course, this was new territory for us. Many things would have been illusory to accomplish, but I think we could have solved simple tasks with the boys. We were all amateurs, and I didn't have much support in setting things up."[6] But things remained calm during the World Youth Games, and their skills were not put to the test.

Afterward, however, Fabian was appointed commanding officer of the newly established Department IX. The official founding order was issued in July 1974 by GDR minister of the interior and chief of the Volkspolizei, Colonel General Friedrich Dickel:

> To ensure effective prevention and defense against acts of violence,
> I GIVE THE ORDER:
> 1. With effect from November 1, 1974, Department IX offices are to be formed within the main criminal investigation department and the criminal investigation department of the district authorities of the German People's Police in Rostock, Schwerin, Potsdam, Magdeburg, Erfurt, Leipzig and Karl-Marx-Stadt.
>
> ...
>
> 3. The selection of cadres is to be completed by October 31, 1974, and only those officers are to be selected and confirmed who have demonstrated a high degree of political reliability in their previous work, and who have distinguished themselves through a high degree of alertness and discretion, exemplary work and training results, as well as a high degree of commitment. They need to be physically and mentally strong.[7]

It is noteworthy that this order was not only classified as secret, but that knowledge of its exact content was only made available to the highest police authorities in the GDR. The second level of command did not learn much more than the mere fact that such a unit did exist and that they were expected to cooperate with Department IX in the future. The strikingly similar naming of the secret unit to its West German

---

* SED (Sozialistische Einheitspartei Deutschlands) = Socialist Unity Party. Unchallenged ruling party throughout the history of the GDR from 1946 to 1989.

counterpart is probably due to coincidence. "The Roman numeral IX was still free in the GDR's organizational nomenclature," Fabian smiles. However, "when the parallel to the name GSG 9 was noticed, the person responsible for it probably didn't have much of a career ahead."

Erich Fabian headed the department in the Potsdam district not far from Berlin and was tasked with developing a concept for the new anti-terrorist unit. But in terms of theoretical and practical knowledge there was not much to fall back on. For one, there were no contacts with foreign units in the GDR, like the ones Wegener in the West was able to take advantage of. Exchanges with Eastern European task forces—with Poles, Czechs, Russians? Unthinkable! Even if there had been any such units at all. Which there weren't. Even within the same police jurisdictions, tactical knowledge was jealously guarded, as was typical in the notoriously distrustful executive branches of the GDR.

Literature on the subject was also rare. It basically consisted of a few confiscated magazines and books from the West handed to Fabian on the sly by an East German Border Guard friend, and a few military booklets and training films from the Soviets. That was it. At least Fabian was allowed to travel to Leipzig and do research in the Deutsche Bücherei (East Germany's national library): "It contained all literature that was published in Germany, and I was able to look at a few books about shooting training and hand-to-hand combat. There was no karate in our country, and no literature about it. And for shooting there were only the police regulations. That was stationary shooting according to regulations but not intended for operational shooting. We had to self-teach in order to acquire the experience to do this."

All the more eagerly, Fabian studied the reports on the strength, technology, operations and "training actions" of GSG 9, regularly supplied and updated by "scouts," as the foreign spies of the Stasi were officially called in Eastern Germany. Fabian was allowed to read them, of course always beginning with a prologue similar to the one quoted earlier, in which the enemy task force and its commander were reviled as instruments of West German imperialism. "I was fed this kind of stuff all the time. But for us, Wegener was a secret role model." So they pushed aside the ideological trash talk and looked for what was useful to them in GSG 9's structure, training and tactics, like combat shooting, or the set up for storming an occupied object.

Fabian began in 1973 with four recruits, but soon there were 30. The prospective counterterrorism fighter was to be between 25 and 39 years old, have unlimited physical and mental resilience, and have graduated from a technical or officer training school. There was no way to apply for the job, because officially the new unit did not exist. Instead, candidates from the Volkspolizei were transferred to Diensteinheit IX by "personnel order."

In a lonely patch of forest near the appropriately named hamlet of Verlorenwasser (Lostwater) in Brandenburg, the Stasi had a training camp set up, complete with classrooms for tactical instruction, barracks, firing ranges, and ruins for urban combat simulations. Fabian and his men were sent there to practice close combat, long-range reconnaissance, and hostage rescue. And they did, up to their limit of performance, "every day anew." They also practiced how to storm aircraft, at first in a wooden mock-up, later in a decommissioned Tupolev Tu-134 from the Soviet state airline Aeroflot. So naturally, they were fascinated when news coverage came in of the hostage rescue in Mogadishu in 1977. "We eagerly pounced on everything we could get our hands on to be able to understand and recreate that, at least a bit," Fabian recalls. "It was huge! We would have been able to liberate a small aircraft, but such a whopper would not have been possible for us."

Fabian's unit initially ran into issues similar to those faced by its role model in the West: the equipment and weapons they needed for their missions were almost non-existent. So they built their own from what was available and tried to enhance what they got. Their equipment resembled that of Western SEKs: bulletproof helmets, breathing masks, heavy protective vests—all of it Soviet-built, of course. "The first ones we had were Russian models. They were just as cumbersome and heavy as those of GSG 9. And when we walked, the metal parts rattled against each other, making you believe a knight in armor was approaching."

Diensteinheit IX was also motorized, with Ladas—not exactly on a par with GSG 9's heavy Mercedes Sedans, but still upscale by Eastern standards. Many colleagues even envied Fabian and his men, calling them "Lada troop," because on the autobahn they could sometimes get up to 100 miles per hour. Helicopters were also available if necessary.

Shooting was mainly done with Soviet-made weapons, but in the 1980s they managed to get their hands on pistols, submachine guns, and even precision rifles from West Germany, courtesy of Heckler & Koch. These were obtained from the shady business of the top GDR foreign currency procurer Alexander Shalck-Golodkovsky (who later came to unwanted fame for his deals with then-Bavarian Prime Minister Franz-Josef Strauss, causing huge political outrage when the scandal finally surfaced after the fall of the Berlin wall). In the beginning, though, Fabian had to take what was available, and that wasn't all that much. He proudly reports that they were able to convert the standard Kalashnikov AK-47 assault rifle into a precision rifle, complete with a self-developed silencer and riflescope, so that a good sniper was able to hit a target the size of a one-mark coin at a distance of 100 meters.

In the course of the 1970s, additional locations were set up in GDR district capitals: in Rostock, Schwerin, Magdeburg, Leipzig, Erfurt, Karl-Marx-Stadt,* Dresden, and Potsdam, each with five to seven officers, in addition to the staff office in the Berlin police headquarters with a couple of task forces of 15 men each. Later, the units were expanded to one or two dozen each, for a total of about 200 men, distributed throughout the GDR. Given the fact that the GDR's population was no

---

* After 1989, Karl-Marx-Stadt was redesignated to its old name, Chemnitz.

more than a quarter of the population of West Germany, the special intervention force was quite considerable in size.

The individual regions worked largely autonomously and could be requested by the criminal police of the respective district. From 1976, Ulrich Tauchel headed Diensteinheit IX in the city of Rostock on the coast of the Baltic Sea. He, too, had the reports on GSG 9 at his disposal and took his cue from them. "Above all, we adopted a lot from their training program. Whether it was the tactical training or sports. Basically, the training program of Diensteinheit IX corresponded to what was done in GSG 9."

Deserters and Decoys

The GDR counterterrorism units never had the opportunity to conduct an operation of comparable proportions as Mogadishu. "GSG 9-East" secured party congresses, festivals of the communist youth organization, FDJ,* and state visits, such as that of West Germany's Chancellor Schmidt in 1981. They secured the annual Leipzig Trade Fair on a regular basis, and in 1986 the crash site of a Tu-134 at the airport in East Berlin. In the search for a serial rapist, two gracefully built colleagues of Fabian's served as decoys: they were dressed up in wigs and women's clothes, styled by make-up artists from the nearby film studios in Potsdam. They were then sent out for several weeks on patrol at night on a lonely country road near Potsdam while their colleagues waited behind bushes and in roadside ditches for the perpetrator to show up. (He was finally identified and arrested using conventional criminology.)

The public was not allowed to know anything about all this, because, as mentioned, such violent crimes only occurred in the decadent West, not in the GDR. Neither did hostage-taking. Unofficially, though, Ulrich Tauchel received orders from the minister of the interior to inspect high-risk objects and obtain essential documents such as site plans and architectural drawings. He checked out savings banks, the regional branch of the state bank, the district leadership buildings of the state party SED, and district council buildings. However, such reconnaissance missions remained the exception.

Instead, one of the main tasks of Diensteinheit IX was to recapture deserters from the Soviet Army stationed on the soil of GDR. On average, they had to sortie once a week to arrest Russians who were very homesick but also very armed and bring them back to their garrisons. Tauchel's unit was called for such missions on a regular basis: "In GDR, there was this huge fear of Soviet soldiers fleeing to the West. But most of them just wanted to go home."

Being arrested by Diensteinheit IX was a stroke of luck for the fugitives: "If we caught them, at least they had a fair chance of a trial." The Russians were said to

---

* FDJ (Freie Deutsche Jugend) = Free German Youth. Junior staff organization of East Germany's SED party.

be far less squeamish and did not care too much for due process. Getting caught for desertion was synonymous with being locked away indefinitely in labor camps, beaten to death, or even receiving an instant death penalty without a formal trial. The escaped soldiers were all too aware of this—which rendered the operations quite delicate for the East German police officers. More than once they looked down the barrel of Kalashnikovs as they searched for the deserters in empty buildings or in the basements of housing estates.

Most of the time the deserters were quickly persuaded to give up, but sometimes they needed the impetus of tear gas. Once commando leader Fabian fired warning shots into a floor and ceiling in quick succession as a persuasive measure. "When two Russians ran away in Jüterbog, they shot at us. We had to shoot back then." Fortunately, nobody sustained life-threatening injuries in that instance, and there were never any fatalities, not in his nor in any of the other districts where his comrades had to deal with tracking down deserted soldiers, or perhaps with the odd bomb threat (which reliably turned out to be unfounded).

When, in the fall of 1989, civil protests signaled the end of the GDR, Diensteinheit IX in Potsdam was ordered to deploy against demonstrators. The group refused to move out. "We don't do that," Fabian told his superiors. If there had been violent riots, they would have fought them without a question, the former commander said. "But not against placards, slogans and peaceful demonstrators—although I'm sure some expected us to."

Tauchel and his Rostock team reacted the same way. "Well, of course, we were sitting in the central office armed and ready for action when the demonstrations happened. And we said: 'If there is any form of violence or if people are at risk, we will have to take action. But not if what happens falls under the law of rightful assembly.'" It is not hard to imagine the amount of bloodshed that could have resulted if they had obeyed their orders.

Thus, in due course, several of the Diensteinheit IX departments would become regional task forces of the once so much despised "imperialist West German oppression regime." Following the fall of communism, Diensteinheit IX in Potsdam was transformed into the Brandenburg SEK in 1990. The same happened with other district groups. In 1991, Ulrich Tauchel was promoted as the first commander of the SEK in Mecklenburg-Western Pomerania. After a review by the Commissioner for Stasi Records, most GDR police officers were transferred to the new, now Federal Republic, police units. The authorities concluded that the counterterrorist force had not committed any civil rights violations during the time of their deployment in the GDR.

Things could have turned out quite differently. Erich Fabian knows that his unit could have been misused exactly like the "militarized repressive organ" that the Stasi had scornfully designated its West German counterpart, GSG 9: "We were an instrument of power, and we were lucky to not be exploited."

Endnotes

Chapter 1

1. Interviews with Dieter Tutter in 2007 and 2020. All of the following quotations, paraphrases, and descriptions of Dieter Tutter are taken from these interviews.
2. Ulrich Wegener and Ulrike Zander, *GSG 9—Stärker als der Terror*, hg. von Harald Biermann (Berlin Münster: LIT, 2017), p. 36. Wegener passed away in 2017. Unless noted otherwise, all quotations of Ulrich Wegener are taken from this autobiographical book.
3. Interview with Jörg Schleyer in 2020. All following quotations, paraphrases, and descriptions of Jörg Schleyer are taken from this interview.
4. Unless otherwise stated, the remainder of the account of the events on that day follows Simon Reeve, *Ein Tag im September: die Geschichte des Geiseldramas bei den Olympischen Spielen in München 1972* (München: Heyne, 2006); Wegener and Zander, *GSG 9—Stärker als der Terror*; as well as Matthias Dahlke, *Der Anschlag auf Olympia '72. Die politischen Reaktionen auf den internationalen Terrorismus in Deutschland* (München: Peter Lang GmbH, Internationaler Verlag der Wissenschaften, 2006), pp. 57–75; the latter refers primarily to official documents and interrogation records.
5. List of demands Munich hostage-taking 1972, State Archives Munich, Police Headquarters Munich 1358, sheet 154; Reeve, *One Day in September*, p. 35, reports—like most accounts—a total of 234 prisoners as well as two Germans, Ulrike Meinhof and Andreas Baader. On the original list, which is kept in the Bavarian Main State Archives, there are only 130 names mentioned and that of Ulrike Meinhof.
6. Matthias Dahlke, *Demokratischer Staat und transnationaler Terrorismus: Drei Wege zur Unnachgiebigkeit in Westeuropa 1972–1975* (München, 2011), p. 63.
7. Hans-Dietrich Genscher, *Erinnerungen* (München: Goldmann, 1997), p. 152.
8. Ibid., p. 155.
9. As recently disclosed documents from the Berlin *Stasi* Archives reveal, East German journalists were able to observe from their posts opposite the Israeli accommodation that at least seven terrorists were involved. However, they did not pass on their information to the security authorities. Sven Felix Kellerhoff, *Anschlag auf Olympia: Was 1972 in München wirklich geschah* (Darmstadt, 2022), p. 66.
10. Wegener and Zander, *GSG 9—Stärker als der Terror*, p. 37
11. Hans-Dietrich Genscher, *Erinnerungen*, p. 151.
12. Policeman August Schöffel in Uli Weidenbach, *München '72—Die Dokumentation* (television documentary, Köln: Broadview TV, 2012).
13. Genscher, *Erinnerungen*, p. 157.
14. Quoted from Uli Weidenbach, *München '72—Die Dokumentation* (television documentary, 2012).

Chapter 2

1. Interview with Jörg Probstmeier, 2021. All quotations, paraphrases, and descriptions of Jörg Probstmeier are taken from this interview.
2. *Der Spiegel* 38/1972 (Hamburg: September 11, 1972) p. 20.
3. Ibid.
4. Cf. Eva Oberlosekamp, *Codename TREVI: Terrorismusbekämpfung und die Anfänge einer europäischen Innenpolitik in den 1970er Jahren, Quellen und Darstellungen zur Zeitgeschichte 111* (Boston/Berlin: Walter de Gruyter, 2017), pp. 11–13. Oberlosekamp points out that the largest share of attacks worldwide is in the United States and Latin America, but another focus lay on Western Europe.
5. Cf. Simon Reeve, *Ein Tag im September: die Geschichte des Geiseldramas bei den Olympischen Spielen in München 1972* (München: Heyne, 2006), p. 67.
6. Cf. Eli Karmon, *Coalitions between Terrorist Organizations: Revolutionaries, Nationalists, and Islamists* (Leiden; Boston: Martinus Nijhoff, 2005), pp. 68–71.
7. Genscher, *Erinnerungen*, p. 147.
8. Interview with Hans-Dietrich Genscher in 2007.
9. BArch B 106 /91147, Bd. 1–2.
10. Ibid.
11. Cf. Dahlke, *Demokratischer Staat und transnationaler Terrorismus*, p. 102. The mention of Zagreb refers to the hijacking of a Lufthansa plane to Zagreb in October 1977 in order to ransom the surviving Munich bombers. See the following chapter.
12. Reinhard Scholzen and Kerstin Froese, *GSG 9: Innenansichten eines Spezialverbandes des Bundesgrenzschutzes*, Spezialausg (Stuttgart: Motorbuch-Verl, 2007), p. 9.
13. Scholzen and Froese, *GSG 9*, pp. 8–9.
14. Wegener and Zander, *GSG 9—Stärker als der Terror*, p. 40.
15. Scholzen and Froese, *GSG 9*, p. 9.
16. Ibid.
17. BArch B 106/91147, Bd. 1–2.
18. Genscher, *Erinnerungen*, p. 138.
19. Hans-Dieter Heumann, *Hans-Dietrich Genscher. Die Biographie* (Paderborn, 2011), p. 138.
20. Genscher, *Erinnerungen*, p. 162.
21. Ibid., p. 163.
22. Interview with the author for a radio documentary in 2007.
23. "Scharfschützen nur als Ultima Ratio," in: *Deutsches Allgemeines Sonntagsblatt* vom 24.9.1972. Kuhlmann's tough stance may be explained by the police union's traditional policy of demanding and promoting a civilian and non-authoritarian police force that was on eye level with the people. The establishment of a special unit in the paramilitary-organized BGS, which was equipped with weapons of war, seemed to run counter to this policy and Kuhlmann considered BGS officers not actual policemen. However, at the time of the cited newspaper interview, the long-standing union leader found himself already somewhat isolated with this position. During the 1970s, the police union's attitude toward the BGS shifted considerably to a more accepting stance.
24. BArch B106/88880.
25. Ibid.
26. BArch B 106/91147, Vol. 1–2.
27. BArch B106/88880.
28. BArch B 106/91147, Vol. 1–2.

ENDNOTES • 235

Chapter 3

1. Experts sometimes doubt that the BGS was indeed a paramilitary organization. The legal scholar Marc Wagner, for one, argues that there were no military regulations for the BGS in the event of war and that the use of weapons was restricted to self-defense. If this was the case, however, the question arises as to what purpose the BGS had machine guns, grenade launchers, and armor-piercing weapons at its disposal. Also, the law enforcement officers legally had military combatant status until 1994. With regard to organization, hierarchy, equipment, and armament, a strong military component can hardly be denied. Cf. Marc Wagner, "Von der 'Repolizeilitarisierung' zum Reformreigen—60 Jahre Bundespolizei," in *Die Polizei. Fachzeitschrift für die öffentliche Sicherheit mit Beiträgen aus der Deutschen Hochschule der Polizei*, No. 102. Jahrgang. Heft 4, April 2011: pp. 97–106, p. 100.
2. Quoted from Wagner, "Von der 'Repolizeilitarisierung' zum Reformreigen—60 Jahre Bundespolizei," p. 99.
3. Wagner, "Von der 'Repolizeilitarisierung' zum Reformreigen—60 Jahre Bundespolizei," p. 98.
4. Ulrich Wegener and Ulrike Zander, *GSG 9—Stärker als der Terror*, p. 4.
5. Wegener and Zander, *GSG 9—Stärker als der Terror*, pp. 6–8. Beyond such self-testimonies, Ulrich Wegener's biography has not yet been researched in any detail. Therefore, the following account is based on little more than this information and on descriptions of his companions, in the knowledge that these are for the most part difficult to verify.
6. Genscher, *Erinnerungen*, p. 161.
7. Ibid.
8. Wegener and Zander, *GSG 9—Stärker als der Terror*, p. 42.
9. Cf. Wolfgang Kraushaar, "Elf Tage im Februar," *Die Welt*, September 22, 2012, pp. 8–9.
10. Wegener and Zander, *GSG 9—Stärker als der Terror*, p. 43.
11. Yael Greenfeter, "Israel in Shock as Munich Killers Freed This week in Haaretz: 1972," *Ha'aretz*, November 4, 2010, https://www.haaretz.com/1.5134761.
12. Eva Oberloskamp, "Das Olympia-Attentat 1972: Politische Lernprozesse im Umgang mit dem transnationalen Terrorismus," in: *Vierteljahrshefte für Zeitgeschichte*, vol. 60, no. 3, 2012, pp. 321–52, https://doi.org/10.1524/vfzg.2012.0018; "PA/AA, B 1, Bd. 509," letter from the Federal German Embassy, Tel Aviv, November 21, 1972, Lufthansa incident, here: Final report, p. 334.
13. Wegener and Zander, *GSG 9—Stärker als der Terror*, pp. 43–44.
14. Interview with Reuven Caspy in 2020. All following quotations, paraphrases, and descriptions of Reuven Caspy are taken from this interview.
15. Wegener and Zander, *GSG 9—Stärker als der Terror*, pp. 44–45.
16. Ibid., p. 44.
17. Ibid., p. 45.
18. Ibid., p. 46.
19. BArch B 106/115427, Vol. 1–2, o. J., Bundesarchiv Koblenz.

Chapter 4

1. BArch B 106/91147, Vol. 1–2.
2. Interviews with Dieter Fox in 2019, 2020, and 2024. Unless otherwise noted, all the following quotes, paraphrases, and descriptions of Dieter Fox are taken from these interviews.
3. Reinhard Scholzen, *BGS: Geschichte der Bundespolizei* (Stuttgart: Motorbuch Verlag, 2007), p. 173.

4. BArch B 106/91147, Vol. 1–2.
5. Ibid.
6. Ulrich Wegener and Ulrike Zander, *GSG 9–Stärker als der Terror*, p. 50.
7. The necessity of this development may be seen from the fact that it was only after a fatal accident during an abseiling exercise from a helicopter that the responsible authorities approved this development in 1980, although a GSG 9 technician's proposal for such a system had been on the table for a long time and Wegener had previously vehemently pointed out the dangers of the existing system after several accidents with casualties. Cf. BArch B 106/387060, Vol. 1—"Erprobung von Abseilgeräten für die GSG 9 technische Ausstattung," o. J., Koblenz, Bundesarchiv. See also the following chapter.
8. Wegener and Zander, *GSG 9—Stärker als der Terror*, p. 53.
9. Carlos Marighella, *Handbuch des Stadtguerillero*, 1969, https://www.nadir.org/nadir/initiativ/rev_linke/rli/handbuch.html.
10. Rolf Tophoven, "Nachruf Ulrich K. Wegener," *Consulting Plus* (blog), accessed January 4, 2021, https://www.consulting-plus.de/allgemein/nachruf-ulrich-k-wegener/.
11. Wegener and Zander, *GSG 9—Stärker als der Terror*, p. 51.
12. Ibid., p. 56.
13. Dieter Schenk, *BKA-Polizeihilfe für Folterregime* (Bonn: Dietz, 2008). Dieter Fox: "I have known Klaus Blätte since 1972 and also his opinion on various operational tactics. Nevertheless, I can hardly imagine that he should have expressed something like this in this form."

Chapter 5

1. BArch B 106/91147, Vol. 1–2, o. J., Koblenz, Bundesarchiv.
2. Interview with Werner Heimann in 2020. All following quotations, paraphrases, and descriptions are taken from this interview.
3. These problems encountered by the early GSG 9 are strikingly similar to the obstacles other founders of special ops forces had to face. Commander Charlie Beckwith, for one, reports not only his quarrels with the hierarchy and administration of the US Army when planning for Delta Force, but also fierce resistance from commanders of Ranger units who prevented their top men from applying to the new counterterror unit. Cf. Charlie Beckwith, *Delta Force*, pp. 148–59.
4. Wegener and Zander, *GSG 9—Stärker als der Terror*, pp. 49–50.
5. Ibid., p. 56.
6. Concept for the establishment and deployment of a Federal Border Guard unit for special police operations of 19.9.1972, BArch B106 / 88880.
7. Wegener and Zander, *GSG 9—Stärker als der Terror*, p. 55.
8. Interview with Günter Weber in 2020. All following quotations, paraphrases, and descriptions are taken from this interview.
9. Wegener and Zander, *GSG 9—Stärker als der Terror*, p. 53.
10. Ibid., pp. 53–54.
11. Ibid., p. 48.
12. Ibid.
13. BArch B 106/371618, o. J., Koblenz, Bundesarchiv.
14. Wegener and Zander, *GSG 9—Stärker als der Terror*, p. 48.
15. BArch B106 / 88880. Ranger training: named after the military unit US Rangers, which at the time was considered a role-model for GSG 9, along with the Israeli counterterrorist units.
16. Cf. reports of Department BGS II 1 on equipment and training status from June to September 1973. BArch B 106/91147, Vol. 3, o. J., Koblenz, Bundesarchiv.

17. Cf. BArch B 106/387060, Vol. 1—*Erprobung von Abseilgeräten für die GSG 9 technische Ausstattung*, o. J., Koblenz, Bundesarchiv, sheets 126–30.
18. BArch B 106/387060, Vol. 1—*Erprobung von Abseilgeräten für die GSG 9 technische Ausstattung*.

Chapter 6

1. BArch B 106/371856, Vol. 1–4—*Einsätze der GSG 9 zur Unterstützung des Bundeskriminalamtes 1970–1996*, o. J., Koblenz, Bundesarchiv, sheet 404.
2. Cf. BArch B 106/115427, Vol. 1–2, o. J., Bundesarchiv Koblenz.
3. BArch B 106/115427, Vol. 1–2.
4. Ibid.
5. Today, Köln-Bonn International Airport.
6. Wegener and Zander, *GSG 9—Stärker als der Terror*, p. 59.
7. Ibid.
8. BArch B 106/91147, Vol. 1–2, o. J., Koblenz, Bundesarchiv.
9. Cf. BArch B106 / 88880, o. J., Koblenz, Bundesarchiv Koblenz.
10. BArch B106 / 88880.
11. Interview with Walter Schmitz in 2021. All following quotations, paraphrases, and descriptions of Schmitz are taken from this interview.
12. "Befehl und Gehorsam—das geht nicht mehr," *Der Spiegel*, No. 6, February 4, 1973, https://www.spiegel.de/politik/befehl-und-gehorsam-das-geht-nicht-mehr-a-b0365297-0002-0001-0000-000042675539?context=issue.
13. Wegener and Zander, *GSG 9—Stärker als der Terror*, p. 57.

Chapter 7

1. Interview with Jörg Schleyer, 2020. All following quotes, paraphrases, and descriptions of Jörg Schleyer are taken from this interview.
2. Quoted from Peters, *Hundert Tage: die RAF-Chronik 1977*, original edition (München: Knaur, 2017), p. 320.
3. Peters, *Hundert Tage: die RAF-Chronik 1977*, p. 322.
4. Interviews with Gerhart Baum in 2020 and 2021. All following quotations, paraphrases, and descriptions of Gerhart Baum are taken from these conversations.
5. Karl-Heinz Dellwo, Tina Petersen, and Christoph Twickel, *Das Projektil sind wir: der Aufbruch einer Generation, die RAF und die Kritik der Waffen* (Hamburg: Edition Nautilus, 2007), pp. 100–3.
6. Kraushaar, *Die blinden Flecken der RAF* (Bonn, 2018), p. 132.
7. Helmut Schmidt, *Außer Dienst: eine Bilanz*, 8th ed. (München: Pantheon-Verl, 2010), p. 170.

Chapter 8

1. Quoted from Lutz Hachmeister, *Schleyer: eine deutsche Geschichte* (München: C.H. Beck, 2004), p. 328.
2. Quoted from Butz Peters, *Hundert Tage: die RAF-Chronik 1977*, p. 158.
3. Quoted from Stefan Aust, *Der Baader Meinhof Komplex*, p. 653.
4. Wegener and Zander, *GSG 9—Stärker als der Terror*, p. 76.
5. For almost half a century, there has been intensive debate and speculation among contemporary historians what happened to this particular telex. Recently discovered documents suggest the

possibility that the East German "*Stasi*" State Security had something to do with its disappearance. According to research by two journalists, Erftstadt was a hotspot for agent activities of GDR's secret service in West Germany during the Cold War, since it was close to Cologne as well as to West Germany's capital of Bonn. In the high-rise building where the RAF hid Schleyer, of all places, the *Stasi* had rented out two apartments, which it used as a hiding place for important undercover agents. However, there is no solid evidence that the *Stasi* allowed the notorious telex to disappear in order to protect its agents. Cf. Georg Bönisch and Sven Röbel, *Fernschreiben 827 Der Fall Schleyer, die RAF und die Stasi* (Köln: Greven-Verlag, 2021).

6. Herrmann Höcherl, "Bericht über die Untersuchung von Fahndungspannen im Mord- und Entführungsfall Schleyer," Bundestagsdrucksache (Bonn: Bundestag, June 7, 1978), p. 24.
7. Aust, *Der Baader Meinhof Komplex*, p. 692.
8. Ibid., p. 693.
9. Ibid., p. 697.
10. Ibid., p. 699.
11. Wegener and Zander, *GSG 9—Stärker als der Terror*, p. 77.
12. Hermann and Koch, *Entscheidung in Mogadischu: Die 50 Tage nach Schleyers Entführung. Dokumente, Bilder, Zeugen* (Hamburg: Gruner & Jahr, 1977), pp. 59–60.
13. Wegener and Zander, *GSG 9—Stärker als der Terror*, pp. 77–78.
14. Hans-Jürgen Wischnewski, *Mit Leidenschaft und Augenmass. In Mogadischu und anderswo. Politische Memoiren* (München: Goldmann, 1991), pp. 215–16.
15. Ibid., p. 214.
16. Wischnewski, *Mit Leidenschaft und Augenmass*, p. 217.

Chapter 9

1. Kai Hermann and Peter Koch, *Entscheidung in Mogadischu*, p. 120.
2. Wegener and Zander, *GSG 9—Stärker als der Terror*, p. 79.
3. Amit Das Gupta u. a., *Akten zur Auswärtigen Politik der Bundesrepublik Deutschland: 1977* (München: R. Oldenbourg Verlag, 2008). DOK 299, pp. 1436–38.
4. Hans-Jürgen Wischnewski, *Mit Leidenschaft und Augenmass: In Mogadischu und anderswo. Politische Memoiren*, p. 218.
5. Wischnewski, *Mit Leidenschaft und Augenmass*, p. 218.
6. "Lufthansa Hijacking and Follow-up, Pt. A," October 26, 1977, The National Archives of the UK.
7. Wegener and Zander, *GSG 9—Stärker als der Terror*, p. 80.
8. Wischnewski, *Mit Leidenschaft und Augenmass*, p. 219.
9. "FCO 76/1760 Lufthansa hijacking and follow-up, pt. A—Telegram Dubai 160712Z (Armitage) to FCO," October 16, 1977, The National Archives of the UK.
10. Wegener and Zander, *GSG 9—Stärker als der Terror*, p. 80.
11. Telephone conversation of Chancellor Schmidt with President Sheikh Zayed Bin Sultan al-Nahayan on October 16, 1977, in: Das Gupta u. a., *Akten zur Auswärtigen Politik der Bundesrepublik Deutschland: 1977*. Doc 291, pp. 1399–1402, here p. 1401.
12. Wegener and Zander, *GSG 9—Stärker als der Terror*, p. 81.
13. Hermann and Koch, *Entscheidung in Mogadischu*, p. 147.
14. Cf. "Telegram Bonn 131930Z (Bullard) to Nicosia and C.B.F.C.—Hijacking of Lufthansa Flights in the Middle East—FCO 8/2838," o. J., The National Archives of the UK.
15. Conversation between Chancellor Schmidt and Somali Ambassador Bokah on October 17, 1977, in: Das Gupta u. a., *Akten zur Auswärtigen Politik der Bundesrepublik Deutschland: 1977*. Doc 292, pp. 1402–3. It is not entirely clear whether Schmidt was actually unaware of the true

nationality of the kidnappers or whether he was being insincere with the ambassador in order to make it easier for the Somali government to decide on a liberation operation.
16. Telephone conversation between Chancellor Schmidt and Prime Minister Callaghan on October 16, 1977, Das Gupta u. a., *Akten zur Auswärtigen Politik der Bundesrepublik Deutschland: 1977.* Doc 289, pp. 1395–97.
17. Wegener and Zander, *GSG 9—Stärker als der Terror*, pp. 82–83.
18. Tim Geiger, "Die 'Landshut' in Mogadischu—Das außenpolitische Krisenmanagement der Bundesregierung angesichts der terroristischen Herausforderung 1977," *Vierteljahreshefte für Zeitgeschichte*, No. 3/2009 (2009): 413–56, p. 442.
19. Chancellor Schmidt's conversation with Somali Ambassador Bokah on October 17, 1977, in: Das Gupta u. a., *Akten zur Auswärtigen Politik der Bundesrepublik Deutschland: 1977*, Doc 292, pp. 1402–3.
20. Wegener and Zander, *GSG 9—Stärker als der Terror*, p. 84.
21. Chancellor Schmidt telephone conversation with Minister of State Wischnewski, z. Z. Mogadischu on October 17, 1977, in: Das Gupta u. a., *Akten zur Auswärtigen Politik der Bundesrepublik Deutschland: 1977.* doc 293, pp. 1404–8, here p. 1407.
22. Wischnewski, *Mit Leidenschaft und Augenmass*, pp. 223–24.
23. Wegener and Zander, *GSG 9—Stärker als der Terror*, p. 85.
24. Hermann and Koch, *Entscheidung in Mogadischu*, p. 169.
25. Henry Tanner, "GERMAN TROOPS FREE HOSTAGES ON HIJACKED PLANE IN SOMALIA; FOUR TERRORISTS KILLED IN RAID," *New York Times*, October 18, 1977.
26. Hermann and Koch, *Entscheidung in Mogadischu*, p. 177.
27. Ibid., pp. 178–79.
28. Wischnewski, *Mit Leidenschaft und Augenmass*, p. 225.
29. There also might have been support from other state leaders. A memorandum of the Swiss government indicates that US President Jimmy Carter urged Somali President Barre to support the German liberation efforts. However, the respective message is not to be found within the published records of the Office of the Historian at the US Department of State. Source: Swiss Federal Archives, Diplomatic Documents Switzerland (Dodis), dodis.ch/50252.
30. Aust, *Der Baader Meinhof Komplex*, p. 822.
31. Sven Felix Kellerhoff, "Anruf aus dem Kanzleramt. 'Seid Ihr verrückt?,'" *Die Welt*, April 2, 2016, https://www.welt.de/politik/deutschland/article153888091/Anruf-aus-dem-Kanzleramt-Seid-Ihr-verrueckt.html.
32. Aust, *Der Baader Meinhof Komplex*, p. 822.
33. Wischnewski, *Mit Leidenschaft und Augenmass*, p. 226.

Chapter 10

1. Ulrich Wegener, BArch B 106/201999—Einsatz 'Landshut' der GSG 9—Einsatzbericht, o. J., Koblenz, Bundesarchiv, sheets 18–27. All following quotes from Wegener's mission report are taken from this source.
2. Wegener and Zander, *GSG 9—Stärker als der Terror*, p. 87.
3. Ibid., p. 89.
4. Ibid.
5. Ibid., p. 94.
6. Helmut Schmidt, *Außer Dienst: eine Bilanz*, p. 171.
7. Kai Hermann und Peter Koch, *Entscheidung in Mogadischu*, p. 185.
8. Wegener and Zander, *GSG 9—Stärker als der Terror*, p. 88.

9. Hans-Jürgen Wischnewski, *Mit Leidenschaft und Augenmass*, p. 229.
10. Wegener and Zander, *GSG 9—Stärker als der Terror*, p. 87.
11. Aust, *Der Baader Meinhof Komplex*, pp. 826–27.
12. Interview with Jürgen Vietor in 2019. Unless otherwise noted, all following quotes, paraphrases, and descriptions of Jürgen Vietor are taken from this interview.
13. Hermann and Koch, *Entscheidung in Mogadischu*, Annex VIII.
14. Wegener and Zander, *GSG 9—Stärker als der Terror*, p. 93.
15. Wischnewski, *Mit Leidenschaft und Augenmass*, p. 417.
16. Wegener and Zander, *GSG 9—Stärker als der Terror*, p. 94.
17. Ibid., p. 95.
18. Quoted from Butz Peters, *Hundert Tage: die RAF–Chronik 1977*, pp. 245–46.
19. Wischnewski, *Mit Leidenschaft und Augenmass*, p. 230.
20. "Barry Davies. SAS Soldier Who Took Part in a Daring Assault on a Hijacked German Aircraft in Somalia and Wrote Accounts of the Special Forces," *The Times*, April 26, 2016, p. 54.
21. "BEFREIUNG DER 'LANDSHUT': 'Ich war überzeugt, dass es laufen würde,'" *Die Welt online*, October 13, 2007, https://www.welt.de/politik/article1260097/Ich-war-ueberzeugt-dass-es-laufen-wuerde.html.
22. Barry Davies, *Fire Magic: Hijack at Mogadishu* (London: Bloomsbury, 1994), p. 111.
23. Ibid., dust jacket description.
24. Ibid., pp. 142–43.
25. Ibid., p. 144.

Chapter 11

1. Breaking news on Deutschlandfunk, October 18, 1977.
2. ARD *Tagesschau* of October 18, 1977.
3. Wegener and Zander, *GSG 9—Stärker als der Terror*, pp. 96–97.
4. Interview with Susanne Wegener in 2020. All following quotes, paraphrases, and descriptions of Susanne Wegener are taken from this interview.
5. Margret Kämpf / Klaus Schmitz, "Sie weiß um die Gefahren seines Berufs—Alle gratulieren Frau Wegener," in: Kölner Stadt-Anzeiger, October 19, 1977.
6. Wegener and Zander, *GSG 9—Stärker als der Terror*, p. 95.
7. Ibid., p. 96.
8. Live broadcast on ARD national television from October 18, 1977.
9. Quoted from Hans-Jürgen Wischnewski, *Mit Leidenschaft und Augenmass*, pp. 233–34.
10. Peters, *1977: RAF gegen Bundesrepublik*, pp. 422–23.
11. Wischnewski, *Mit Leidenschaft und Augenmass*, p. 237.

Chapter 12

1. Rolf Tophoven, *Fedayin, Guerilla ohne Grenzen: Geschichte, soziale Struktur u. polit. Ziele d. palästinens. Widerstandsorganisationen; die israel. Konter-Guerilla* (Frankfurt am Main: Bernard und Graefe, 1974).
2. Interviews with Rolf Tophoven in 2020. All following quotations, paraphrases, and mentions of Rolf Tophoven are taken from these conversations.
3. Rolf Tophoven, *GSG 9: Kommando gegen Terrorismus* (Koblenz; Bonn: Wehr und Wissen, 1977), p. 74.

4. Wegener and Zander, *GSG 9—Stärker als der Terror*, p. 102.
5. Ibid., p. 74.
6. Ibid., p. 97.
7. Almut Hauenschild, "Die verlegenen Helden von Mogadischu," *Die Welt*, October 21, 1977.
8. BArch B 136/34853—Reden und Interviews des BK Schmidt; Ansprache des Bundeskanzlers gegenüber der Gruppe GSG 9 sowie anderen an der Rettungsaktion in Mogadischu Beteiligten im Bundeskanzleramt am 20. Okt. 1977, o. J., Koblenz, Bundesarchiv.
9. Ulrich Wegener, BArch B 106/201999—Einsatz 'Landshut' der GSG 9—Einsatzbericht, o. J., Koblenz, Bundesarchiv, sheet 27.
10. Helmut Schmidt, *Außer Dienst: eine Bilanz*, p. 171.
11. Cf. Michael Kniepe, "Broadcast 'Put Lives in Danger,'" *The Times*, October 19, 1977, p. 8.
12. "Bulletin Nr. 104/S.949: Glückwünsche des Auslands zur Rettung der Geiseln" (Presse- und Informationsamt der Bundesregierung, October 20, 1977), p. 949.
13. Quoted from Karrin Hanshew, *Terror and democracy in West Germany* (Cambridge: Cambridge University Press, 2012), p. 229.
14. Wegener and Zander, *GSG 9—Stärker als der Terror*, p. 97.
15. Interview with Karl-Heinz Dellwo in 2020. All following quotations, paraphrases, and descriptions taken from this interview.
16. Cf. Kent N Gourdin, *A Profile of the Global Airline Industry*, 2016, https://public.ebookcentral.proquest.com/ choice/publicfullrecord.aspx?p=4189524.
17. Tim Geiger, "Die 'Landshut' in Mogadischu—Das außenpolitische Krisenmanagement der Bundesregierung angesichts der terroristischen Herausforderung 1977," *Vierteljahreshefte für Zeitgeschichte*, No. 3/2009 (2009): pp. 413–56, p. 447.
18. BArch B 106/371728—Terrorismusbekämpfung.- Unterstützungs- und Ausbildungsersuchen ausländischer Staaten an die GSG 9, o. J., Koblenz, Bundesarchiv, sheet 86.
19. BArch B 106 / 371727, o. J., Koblenz, Bundesarchiv.
20. Ibid.
21. Cf. Wegener and Zander, *GSG 9—Stärker als der Terror*, p. 101.
22. Charlie A. Beckwith and Donald Knox, *Delta Force: A Memoir by the Founder of the U.S. Military's Most Secretive Special-Operations Unit* (Old Saybrook, CT: Tantor Media, 2014), pp. 128–29.
23. This statement was most certainly made in good faith albeit it not being entirely accurate. Beginning in 1974, the US military started building up counterterror capabilities. However, these were set up in Europe and not widely communicated within the US military. In fact, it was kept so secretive that even inside the Pentagon only few people were familiar with it. Cf. James Stejskal: *Special Forces Berlin, 1956–1990*, pp. 96ff.
24. Beckwith and Knox, *Delta Force*, p. 129.
25. Cf. Eric L. Haney, *Inside Delta Force: The Story of America's Elite Counterterrorist Unit*, Dell mass market ed. (New York: Dell, 2003), p. 116.
26. Haney, *Inside Delta Force*, pp. 154–55.

Chapter 13

1. Drahtbericht No. 181; Referat 320, quoted in Institut für Zeitgeschichte (Hrsg.), *Akten zur Auswärtigen Politik derBundesrepublik Deutschland: 1977*, p. 1514, footnote 3.
2. *Akten zur Auswärtigen Politik der Bundesrepublik Deutschland: 1977*, p. 1514, document 315, conversation between Federal Chancellor Schmidt and Somali Ambassador Bokah on November 3, 1977, secret.
3. BArch B 106 / 371726, sheet 11.

4. Ibid., sheet 29–37.
5. Ibid., sheet 271–272.
6. BArch B 106 / 371618.
7. Cf. Gregor Wenda, "Internationalität ist unschätzbar," in: Öffentliche Sicherheit, H. 5-6 / 20, pp. 40–45. Perhaps for this reason, in his confidential final report of 1973, he describes his impressions of the follow-up of operations involving the use of firearms quite impartially, a procedure that—at least from today's point of view—seems curious to questionable: "If a perpetrator is shot, taking immediate care of the shooter(s) by a high-ranking personality is of the utmost importance (praise, congratulations, the prospect of a promotion, instilling alcohol, etc.) so that the shooter is not overcome by feelings of guilt." BArchB 106 / 371618. The "instilling of alcohol" as a recommended measure after the use of firearms is denied emphatically by the veterans interviewed for this book.
8. Cf. James Stejskal, *Special Forces Berlin*, pp. 96–98.
9. Ibid., p. 111.
10. Cf. Ibid., p. 113.
11. Ibid., p. 148.
12. Ibid., p. 144.
13. Originally *Combat Team Competition*.
14. BArch B 106 / 371728, sheet 65.
15. Cf. BArch B 106 / 371673.
16. Ibid.
17. In 1981, two Indonesian army officers were trained at Saint Augustin for six months, one being Prabowo Subianto, the current president of Indonesia (as of 2025).
18. Cf. BArch B 106 / 371673.
19. BArch B136 / 45549, sheet 136.
20. Interview with Friedrich Eichele in 2020.

Chapter 14

1. Name changed due to security precautions.
2. Name changed due to security precautions.
3. Name changed due to security precautions.
4. Name changed due to security precautions.

Appendix A

1. BArch, MfS, Abt. BCD, No. 3433, Stasi-Unterlagen-Archiv, Bundesarchiv, sheet 005.
2. Ibid.
3. BArch, MfS, ZAIG, No. 11657, BStU Berlin, Bundesarchiv, sheet 005.
4. BArch MfS, HA XXII, 1041/3, BStU Berlin, Bundesarchiv, sheet 0021–0023.
5. Interview with Ulrich Tauchel in 2021. All quotations, paraphrases, and descriptions of Ulrich Tauchel following are taken from this interview.
6. Interview with Erich Fabian in 2021. All quotations, paraphrases, and descriptions of Erich Fabian following are taken from this interview.
7. "Befehl Nr. 002/74 des Ministers des Innern und Chef der Deutschen Volkspolizei über die Erhöhung der Wirksamkeit der Maßnahmen zur Vorbeugung und Abwehr von Gewaltakten vom 10. Juli 1974, BArch DO 1/58765," July 10, 1974, Stasi-Unterlagen-Archiv, Bundesarchiv.

Bibliography

Primary Sources

Interviews

Baum, Gerhart (1932–2025), federal minister of the interior from 1978–1982.
Bohnen, Renate, police officer, head of Operational Emergency Medicine GSG 9.
Caspy, Reuven, founder, Israeli counterterror unit.
Conradi, Matthias, police officer, GSG 9 operative, currently (2025) leader 1st Operational Unit (name altered for reasons of personal protection).
Dellwo, Karl-Heinz, former Red Army Faction terrorist, served an 18-year sentence for his involvement in the occupation of the German embassy in Stockholm in 1975, released from prison in 1995. Lives and works in Hamburg as filmmaker, publisher, and innkeeper.
Eichele, Friedrich, GSG 9 commander 1997–2005. Retired.
Fabian, Erich, police officer of the GDR, founder of Diensteinheit IX, the East German counterpart of GSG 9 and commander of their Potsdam branch. Retired.
Farnholdt, Frank, police officer, GSG 9 operative since 1985, currently (2024) in charge of GSG 9's assessment and training department (name altered for reasons of personal protection).
Fox, Dieter, police officer GSG 9 operative from 1972–1986, call sign "Odin." Retired.
Fuchs, Jérôme, GSG 9 commander 2014–2023, at time of writing deputy president of Bundespolizeidirektion 11 (or Federal Police Department 11), GSG 9's parent agency.
Genscher, Hans-Dietrich (1927–2016), federal minister of the interior from 1969–1974, federal minister of the exterior from 1974–1992. This interview was conducted in 2007.
Heimann, Werner, police officer, GSG 9 operative from 1973–1987, call sign "Murmel." Retired.
Lindner, Olaf, GSG 9 commander 2005–2014, currently (2025) president of Bundespolizeidirektion 11 (or Federal Police Department 11).
Pries, Sebastian, police officer, currently (2025) GSG 9 operative (name altered for reasons of personal protection).
Probstmeier, Jörg, police officer, GSG 9 operative from 1975–1990, call sign "Yeti." Retired.
Schleyer, Jörg, son of Hanns Martin Schleyer, whose abduction by RAF terrorists lead to the events culminating in the liberation of Lufthansa Flight LH-181.
Schmitz, Walter, police officer, co-founder of SEK Cologne and Düsseldorf. Retired.
Tauchel, Ulrich, police officer of the GDR, commander of Diensteinheit IX, department Rostock, later commander of SEK Brandenburg. Retired.
Tophoven, Rolf, journalist and book author, expert on (counter) terrorism.
Tutter, Dieter, police officer, GSG 9 operative from 1972–1982, call sign "Ede." Leader of the 2nd Operational Unit. Retired.
Tutter-Weygold, Gisela, first marriage with GSG 9 operative Anselm Weygold, second marriage with Dieter Tutter.
Vietor, Jürgen, co-pilot of Lufthansa aircraft Boeing 737 *Landshut* (Flight LH-181). Retired.

Weber, Günter, director of Institut für Konfliktforschung und Krisenberatung, München.
Wegener, Susanne, daughter of GSG 9 Commander Ulrich Wegener.

Archives

Bayerisches Hauptstaatsarchiv München.
Bundesarchiv Koblenz (BArch B106 = Bundesinnenministerium; BArch B136 = Bundeskanzleramt).
Diplomatic Documents of Switzerland (Dodis), dodis.ch, Bern.
National Archives of the UK, Kew.
Stasi-Unterlagen-Archiv Berlin (BArch MfS).
Privatarchiv Frank Kawelovski, Mülheim / Ruhr.
Privatarchiv Philipp Meyer, Neuwied.

Secondary Sources

Sources which this book has used from magazines, newspapers, and online publications, as well as television and radio programs, are listed in the endnotes.

Books and Academic Articles

Aust, Stefan. *Der Baader Meinhof Komplex*, 3rd ed., Hamburg, 2008.
Beckwith, Charlie A. and Donald Knox. *Delta Force, A Memoir by the Founder of the U.S. Military's Most Secretive Special-Operations Unit*. Old Saybrook, CT: Tantor Media, 2014.
Biess, Frank. *Republik der Angst: Eine andere Geschichte der Bundesrepublik*. Reinbek: Rowohlt Buchverlag, 2019.
Bönisch, Georg and Sven Röbel. *Fernschreiben 827: Der Fall Schleyer, die RAF und die Stasi*. Köln: Greven, 2021.
Dahlke, Matthias. *Demokratischer Staat und transnationaler Terrorismus. Drei Wege zur Unnachgiebigkeit in Westeuropa 1972–1975*. München: Oldenbourg Wissenschaftsverlag, 2011.
Dahlke, Matthias. "Der blinde Fleck. Transnationaler und nationaler Terrorismus auf dem Weg zum 'Deutschen Herbst,'" in *Zeitgeschichte-online*, May 2007.
Davies, Barry. *Fire Magic: Hijack at Mogadishu*. Bloomsbury Publishing: London, 1994.
Dellwo, Karl-Heinz, Tina Petersen, and Christoph Twickel. *Das Projektil sind wir. Der Aufbruch einer Generation, die RAF und die Kritik der Waffen*. Hamburg: Nautilus, 2007.
Geiger, Tim. "Die 'Landshut' in Mogadischu: Das außenpolitische Krisenmanagement der Bundesregierung angesichts der terroristischen Herausforderung 1977," in: *Vierteljahreshefte für Zeitgeschichte* 57 (2009), 3, S. 413–56.
Genscher, Hans-Dietrich. *Erinnerungen*. München: Goldmann, 1997.
Hachmeister, Lutz. *Schleyer: Eine deutsche Geschichte*. München: C. H. Beck, 2004.
Hanshew, Karrin. *Terror and Democracy in West Germany*. Cambridge: Cambridge University Press, 2012.
Hermann, Kai and Peter Koch, *Entscheidung in Mogadischu: Die 50 Tage nach Schleyers Entführung. Dokumente, Bilder, Zeugen*. Hamburg: Gruner und Jahr, 1977.
Heumann, Hans-Dieter. *Hans-Dietrich Genscher. Die Biographie*. Paderborn: Brill Schöningh, 2011.
Hoffmann, Martin. *Rote Armee Fraktion. Texte und Materialien zur Geschichte der RAF*. Berlin, 1997.
Institut für Zeitgeschichte (Hrsg.). *Akten zur Auswärtigen Politik der Bundesrepublik Deutschland: 1977*. München, 2008.
Karmon, Ely. *Coalitions between Terrorist Organizations: Revolutionaries, Nationalists, and Islamists*. Boston: Leiden University, 2005.

Kellerhoff, Sven Felix. *Anschlag auf Olympia. Was 1972 in München wirklich geschah*. Darmstadt: Theiss in Herder, 2022.
Kraushaar, Wolfgang. "Der nicht erklarte Ausnahmezustand. Staatliches Handeln wahrend des so genannten Deutschen Herbstes," in: *Bundeszentrale für Politische Bildung, Die Geschichte der RAF*, Online-Dossier August 20, 2007, https://www.bpb.de/themen/linksextremismus/geschichte-der-raf/49296/der-nicht-erklaerte-ausnahmezustand/ (accessed March 23, 2022).
Kraushaar, Wolfgang. *Die blinden Flecken der RAF*. Bonn: Klett-Cotta, 2018.
Marighella, Carlos. *Handbuch des Stadtguerillero*. n.p.: Anares, n.d.
Müll, Diana and Christine Bode. *Mogadischu. Die Entführung der 'Landshut' und meine dramatische Befreiung*, 2nd ed. München: Riva, 2018.
Oberloskamp, Eva. *Codename TREVI. Terrorismusbekämpfung und die Anfänge einer europäischen Innenpolitik in den 1970er Jahren*. Berlin: De Gruyter Oldenbourg, 2017.
Oberloskamp, Eva. "*Das Olympia-Attentat 1972: Politische Lernprozesse im Umgang mit dem transnationalen Terrorismus*" in *Vierteljahreshefte für Zeitgeschichte* 60 (2012), 3, S. 321–52.
Peters, Butz. *1977: RAF gegen Bundesrepublik*. München: Droemer HC, 2017.
Peters, Butz. *Hundert Tage: Die RAF-Chronik 1977*. München: Knaur TB, 2017.
Reeve, Simon. *Ein Tag im September. Die Geschichte des Geiseldramas bei den Olympischen Spielen in München 1972*. München: Heyne, 2006. (Published in English as *One Day in September*, New York: Arcade, 2000.)
Schenk, Dieter. *BKA-Polizeihilfe für Folterregime*. Bonn: Dietz, J. H. W., Nachf, 2008.
Schmidt, Helmut. *Außer Dienst. Eine Bilanz*. 8th ed., München: Pantheon, 2010.
Schmidt-Eenboom, Erich and Ulrich Stoll. *Die Partisanen der NATO. Stay-Behind-Organisationen in Deutschland 1946–1991*. 2nd ed., Berlin: Ch. Links Verlag, 2016.
Schneider, Werner. *Die Olympischen Spiele 1972*. Gütersloh: Bertelsmann, 1972.
Stejskal, James. *Special Forces Berlin: Clandestine Cold War Operations of the US Army's Elite, 1956–1990*. Philadelphia; Oxford: Casemate Publishers, 2017.
Tophoven, Rolf. *Fedayin: Guerilla ohne Grenzen. Geschichte, soziale Struktur und politische Ziele der palästinensischen Widerstandsorganisationen; die israelische Konter-Guerilla*. Frankfurt am Main, Bernhard&Graefe, Mchn., 1974.
Tophoven, Rolf. *GSG 9: Kommando gegen Terrorismus*. Bonn: Wehr und Wissen, 1977.
Wegener, Ulrich and Ulrike Zander. *GSG 9—Stärker als der Terror*, Berlin; Münster: LIT Verlag, 2017.
Wischnewski, Hans-Jürgen. *Mit Leidenschaft und Augenmaß: In Mogadischu und anderswo. Politische Memoiren*. München: C. Bertelsmann, 1991.

Index

Adenauer, Chancellor Konrad, 33–36
aircraft
    Bell UH-1D Huey, 73, 111
    Boeing 707, 9, 126, 128, 134, 136–37, 151–52
    Boeing 727, 12, 77, 111, 117–18,
    Boeing 737, 77–78, 109–10, 113, 119, 122, 130, 143, 146, 154
    helicopter, 6, 12–15, 17, 24, 28, 47, 49, 65, 69, 70, 73, 78, 106, 111, 118, 161, 174, 178, 181–82, 188, 190, 200, 219, 229. *See also* Bell UH-1D Huey, Puma transport helicopter
    Landshut, x, xii, 10, 78–79, 109, 113, 115–17, 119, 121–29, 131–34, 135–38, 141–47, 149, 151, 153, 155, 157, 162–63, 165, 167, 171, 173, 178–80, 187, 210, 218. *See also* Lufthansa
    Puma transport helicopter, 111
Allied Forces, 90, 189
Al Maktum, Sheikh Mohammed Bin Rashid, 121
Amft, Inspector BGS Karl Heinz, 191–92
Ankara, 115–18, 161, 173
APO (Außerparlamentarische Opposition), 91
Arafat, Yasser, 4. *See also* Fatah
arson, 18, 37, 89
ATLAS, 189, 206–7
Auftragstaktik, 41, 62, 102
Austria, 25, 183, 188, 206

Baader-Meinhof, 6, 96
Baader, Andreas, 6, 19, 93–94, 98, 109, 162, 174
Bad Kleinen, xiii
Baltic Sea, 99, 220–21, 230
Barak, Task Force Commander Ehud, 9–10, 15, 38–40, 175
Barre, President Siad, 128, 130–32, 152, 185–87

Baum, Frieder Peter, 30, 45, 117, 121–22, 125–26, 130, 135–36, 169, 173, 179
Baum, Federal Minister of the Interior Gerhart, 92, 95, 104, 173, 187, 191
Bavaria, 2, 4, 7, 10, 14, 20–21, 27, 35, 46, 69, 74, 81–82, 106, 109, 200, 229
Beckwith, Colonel Charles, 179–82
Befehlstaktik, 40, 62
Beirut, 19, 76, 113, 117, 148
Belfast, 75
Berlin, x, 1, 20–21, 27, 29, 33–35, 37, 51, 81, 89, 127, 161, 167, 176, 188–89, 197–99, 201, 214, 216, 220–21, 225–30. *See also* fall of the Berlin Wall
Bewegung 2. Juni (June 2 Movement), 2, 89, 93, 97
BfV (Bundesamt für Verfassungsschutz), 25, 26, 191
BGS (Bundesgrenzschutz), ix, xii, 1, 4, 23–30, 31–36, 44–45, 47–49, 57, 59, 63, 67–69, 73, 75, 81, 91, 93, 106, 135, 165, 190–91, 225–26. *See also* Federal Border Guard
BKA (Bundeskriminalamt), 2, 24, 25–26, 50, 55, 74, 87, 91–93, 100–8, 111–12, 117, 139, 160, 171–72, 191, 198, 205, 213
blackmail, 77, 97, 112, 167
Black September terrorist group, 4, 19, 77
Blätte, Deputy Commander Klaus, 55, 66, 136, 141, 149, 151
BMI (Bundesministerium des Innern), 25, 83–84, 213
BMW, 50, 75
BND (Bundesnachrichtendienst), 9–10, 76, 117, 191
Bohnen, Renate, 203–5
Bölling, Government spokesman Klaus, 100, 133, 160
BOLO (Be on the Lookout), 81, 101

248 • INDEX

Bokah, Ambassador, 185–86
Bonn, x, xi, 4, 6–8, 20, 25–26, 29, 35, 37–38, 43, 58, 65, 70, 74, 76, 95, 100–1, 109, 112, 117–18, 115–16, 121, 127–29, 133–34, 136, 138, 150–51, 159–61, 163, 171, 174–76, 178, 180, 185, 197, 226. *See also* Cologne-Bonn Airport
Borer, Léon, 63, 188
Brandenburg, 228, 231
Brandenburgers, 52, 54
Brandt, Chancellor Willy, 4, 7, 12, 18, 20–22, 118
Brezhnev, Soviet leader Leonid, 74
British Empire Medal (BEM), 153, 155
Brussels, 19, 105, 213
Buback, federal prosecutor General Siegfried, 85, 87–88, 91, 97–98, 99
Bund, 51, 80, 83
Bundesarchiv, xii
Bundesland/Bundesländer, 20, 23, 27, 36, 73, 83, 213
Bundespolizei, ix, 27, 33, 51. *See also* GSG 9 der Bundespolizei (Grenzschutzgruppe 9)
Bundestag, 22–23, 27, 32, 47, 90, 95–96, 197
Bundeswehr (Federal Armed Forces), 23, 26, 31–33, 35, 46, 52, 66–67, 75, 205

Cairo, 11–12, 143, 145
Callaghan, Prime Minister James, 120, 125, 174
Carter, President Jimmy, 174, 180
Caspy, Reuven, 38–41, 54
Chancellery, 43, 74, 100, 120, 169
Charlie Hebdo, 206
Cobra, 25, 188, 206
Cold War, x, 3, 32, 225
Cologne (Köln), xii, 5, 26, 29, 98–108, 110–11, 115–18, 121, 127, 161, 163, 166, 178, 204. *See also* Cologne-Bonn Airport
Cologne-Bonn Airport, xii, 29, 83, 121, 166, 176
Combat Team Conference (CTC), 190
Command Tactics. *See* Befehlstaktik
communism, 32, 34, 52–53, 71, 126, 183, 225–26, 230–31
Conradi, Matthias, 201–3
Conference of Ministers of the Interior, 20, 21, 24, 28, 51, 81
Conollystraße 31, 4–8

counterterrorism, 9, 13, 16, 21, 24–25, 28, 36, 39–40, 45, 76, 110, 133, 175, 179, 187, 189, 193–94, 198, 200, 225–31
COVID-19, 207, 213
Crete, 119, 137
crime, 6, 14, 16, 22, 29, 38, 49, 53–54, 72, 74–75, 82, 91–92, 97, 99, 103–5, 189, 190, 193, 198, 200, 204–5, 207, 213, 220–21, 226, 230
cybercrime, xi, 221
Cyprus, 11, 115

Daimler, 3, 65, 87
Daume, President of the West German Olympic Committee Willi, 4
Davies, Sergeant Barry, 120–21, 153–58
Dellwo, Karl-Heinz, 94, 109, 174
Delta Force (US Army), 21, 25, 179–80, 182–83, 212
Deutscher Herbst, x, xiii, 85, 87. *See also* German Autumn
Deutschlandfunk, 159
Diensteinheit IX (Department IX), 226, 228–31
Dillmann, Gaby, 131, 148, 151, 156
Djibouti, 128–30, 132, 134
DM (Deutsche Mark), 23, 27, 44, 47, 50, 72, 92, 94, 104, 109, 117, 185
Dubai, 113, 117–18, 120–27, 143, 153–55, 173
Düsseldorf, 74, 83

Eastern Bloc, 33, 71, 128, 183, 190
East Germany, 34, 127, 176, 188, 225–30
Eichele, Commander Friedrich, 194
Einsatzgruppe Enzian, 188, 190
Eisenhower, General Dwight D., 33
EKO Cobra (Einsatzkommando Cobra), 188, 206
El Al, 37, 41, 77
Employers' Association, 87–88, 99–100, 106, 166
Ensslin, Gudrun, 19, 93, 109, 162, 174
Entebbe, 38, 79, 125, 128, 147
Enzian, 25, 63, 188, 190
Erftstadt, 104–6, 242
Ethiopia, 128–29, 132, 136, 185

Fabian, Erich, 227–31
fall of the Berlin Wall, 226, 229

Farnholdt, Frank, 199
Fatah, 4, 19, 77
FBI (Federal Bureau of Investigation), 26, 53, 63, 92, 180, 183, 189, 205, 212, 223
   Hostage Rescue Team (HRT), 183, 205, 212
FDJ (Freie Deutsche Jugend), 230
Fedayeen, 4
Federal Border Guard, xi, xii, 1, 2, 5, 11, 15, 17, 23, 25–29, 36, 43, 46–47, 63–64, 67, 84–85, 160, 176, 203. *See also* BGS (Bundesgrenzschutz)
Federal Police. *See* Bundespolizei
Federation of German Industries (BDI), 88
Filbinger, Prime Minister Hans, 81
Finland, 46, 192
Flight LH-181, 5, 20, 41, 79, 96, 109, 111–13, 115, 117, 119–20, 126–28, 133, 140, 158, 161, 174
Floyd, George, 205
Fort Bragg, 180–81
Fox, Dieter, 43–49, 52–55, 58, 61, 63, 68–70, 73–74, 77–78, 99, 102–10, 115–17, 121–30, 135–44, 147, 149, 152–58, 163–67, 170, 172–73, 176–82
Frankfurt, 6, 37, 74, 77, 87, 98, 109, 113, 118, 127, 132, 163
Frankfurter Allgemeine Zeitung (FAZ), 71
Frankfurter Rundschau, 21
Frederick the Great, 34, 172
Free Democrats (FDP), 22
Freiburg, 87
FRG (Federal Republic of Germany), 41, 124, 225–26
Fuchs, Commander Jérôme, x, xi, 205–7, 210, 216
Fürstenfeldbruck military airfield, 11–14, 17, 20, 41, 48, 50, 174

Genscher, Federal Minister of the Interior/Exterior Hans-Dietrich, 2, 4, 7–8, 10–16, 20–28, 31–37, 47–48, 71, 81–82, 91–93, 100, 110, 127–28, 160, 177, 191, 217
German Autumn, x, 85, 87, 94–98, 104, 219. *See also* Deutscher Herbst
Germany. *See* East Germany, West Germany
Gestapo (Geheime Staatspolizei), 26, 53
GdP (Gewerkschaft der Polizei), 27, 84

GDR (German Democratic Republic), 34–35, 127, 225–31
GIGN (Groupe d'intervention de la Gendarmerie nationale), 212
Grundgesetz, 10, 24, 90
Grützner, Hubertus, 24–25
GSG 9 der Bundespolizei (Grenzschutzgruppe 9),
   1st Operational Unit, 30, 45, 57, 201
   2nd Operational Unit, 57, 209
   3rd Operational Unit, 57
   4th Operational Unit, x, 57
   SET (*Spezialeinsatztrupp*/Special Operations Teams), x, 61, 64, 101–2, 108, 119, 138, 144–45, 156, 165, 171, 202, 209
guerrilla, 19, 52, 97, 169, 174, 188

Ha'aretz, 18
Hamas, 210–11. *See also* October 7 massacre
Haney, Eric, 182
Hassan, Abu. *See* Salameh, Ali Hassan
Heath, Prime Minister Edward, 22
Heckler & Koch, 48, 180, 189, 229
Heimann, Werner, 58, 63–67, 75, 79–80, 108, 110, 116, 119, 122, 137–38, 142–48, 152, 155 57, 163–66, 170, 178, 186–88
Hellmann, Klaus, 58
Hemmerling, Commander Robert, xi, 183, 209, 219, 223
Herold, Horst, 2, 26, 87, 91–92, 100–1, 103–5
Hesse, 27, 74, 81, 220
hijacker, x, 13, 43, 78, 98, 113, 115, 120–21, 124, 127–28, 131–32, 134, 153, 170, 172. *See also* skyjacking
Hitler, Adolf, 33–34, 53, 88, 90, 176
Hitlerjugend (Hitler Youth), 34
Holocaust, 1, 37, 53
Hong Kong, 178
human rights, 93, 183, 187, 191, 194

IDF (Israeli Defence Force), 37. *See also* ZAHAL
Indochina, 73
Indonesia, xi, 192
infrared night-vision device, 13, 48, 70
Irish Republican Army (IRA), 18–19, 75
Iron Curtain, 23, 26, 32, 58, 176, 183
Islam, 201–2
Israel, 1, 4, 11–13, 15, 17–19, 31–46, 53, 62, 76–77, 83, 118, 128, 133, 147, 154–55,

174, 177, 183, 188–91, 205, 209–12, 218, 227
Israeli Armed Forces, 36, 54
Israeli Border Police, 175. *See also* YAMAM
Issa, 7, 11–12, 14–15, 32
Italy, 18, 111

Japan, 19, 106, 178
JCS, Joint Chiefs of Staff, 179
Jeddah, 76, 127–28

karate, 64, 70, 188, 288
kidnap, 8, 12, 54, 87–89, 97–98, 100–12, 116, 119, 132–33, 140, 148, 151, 159–60, 166, 170, 174
Kiel, 21, 77, 88
Kinkel, Bureau Chief Klaus, 26, 128, 159, 217
Kripo (Kriminalpolizei), 50
Kuhlmann, 27–28, 79
Kuwait, 77, 113, 117

Lada, 227, 229
Länder, 20, 23, 26–28, 36, 51, 81–83, 85, 214, 220
Larnaka International Airport, 115
Lawrence, T. E. (aka Lawrence of Arabia), 52
Libal, Chargé d'affaires Michael, 131–32, 140, 145, 185
Lindner, Commander Olaf, 198–99
Lorenz, Peter, 89, 167
Lufthansa, x, xii, 10, 12–14, 20, 37, 41, 76–79, 109, 111, 113, 119, 121–22, 124–25, 127, 133, 138–39, 145, 151, 159–60, 171–72. *See also Landshut*
Lydd, 75

Mahler, Horst, 19
Mahmoud, Captain Martyr, 124–25, 128, 131–32, 143–45, 147
Majorca, 109, 113, 119
manhunt, 82, 85, 99–101, 103, 105–13, 166
Marighella, Carlos, 52
Maihofer, Minister of the Interior Werner, 88, 100–1, 109, 111, 139, 163–65, 171, 173
Meinhof, Ulrike, 5–6, 19, 53, 93–98
Meinungsforschungsinstitut Allensbach, 97
Meir, Prime Minister Golda, 6, 9, 38
MEK (*Mobiles Einsatzkommando*), xvii, 82–83, 85, 197

Mercedes, 47–48, 59, 65, 75, 99–100, 106, 110, 189, 229
Merk, Bavarian Minister of the Interior Bruno, 4, 7–8, 13
Middle East, 19, 36, 39, 118, 122, 190, 207
Ministry of the Interior, xiii, 24–25, 27–29, 31, 35, 59, 65, 70, 73–74, 76, 81–85, 90, 92, 111, 115, 117–18, 159, 163, 177–78, 190–93, 197
Mission Tactics. *See* Auftragstaktik
Mogadishu, xii, 20, 40–41, 77–80, 113, 128–34, 136, 138–40, 145, 148–50, 152, 154–55, 159–62, 164, 166–67, 169–79, 183, 186–93, 195–97, 200, 207, 210, 218–19, 229–30
Mohnhaupt, Brigitte, 93
Möller, Irmgard, 109, 162
Morrison, Major Alastair, 120–21, 153, 155, 158
Moscow, 54, 127
Müller, Markus, 195–96
Munich, 1–12, 15, 17–23, 28–30, 34, 36–44, 48, 60, 71, 74, 77, 81–82, 98, 125, 149, 161, 201, 206, 210, 217, 227
massacre, 17–23, 29, 38, 48, 50–51, 81, 83–84, 98, 125, 149, 181, 201, 227

NATO, 9, 33, 35, 119, 185
Nazi Party, 1, 17, 34, 37, 53, 71, 88, 90–91, 103. *See also* Hitler, Adolf, SS (Schutzstaffel), Third Reich
Netanyahu, Prime Minister Benjamin, 38
Netanyahu, Yonatan, 38, 79
Netherlands, xi, 105, 178, 183, 188, 192
Newrzella, Michael, xiii
Northern Ireland, 18, 75
North Rhine-Westphalia, 27, 51, 81–82, 85, 104, 220
Norway, 148, 192
Notstandsgesetze, 32, 89–90
NSDAP (Nationalsozialistische Deutsche Arbeiterpartei). *See* Nazi Party
Nuremberg, 78, 91

October 7 massacre, 210–11. *See also* Hamas
Office for the Protection of the Constitution. *See* BfV
Olympic. *See also* Munich massacre
Committee, 2–5

Games, 1–4, 6, 17, 19, 22, 27–28, 36–37, 50, 74, 76, 82, 98, 201, 219, 226–27
Village, 2–5, 10, 13–15, 17–18, 43, 74, 227
Operation *Feuerzauber*, 113, 135–53, 157
Operation *Sunshine*, 11
OTL (*Oberstleutnant*), 29

Palais Schaumburg, 74, 171
Palestinian, 4–15, 18–19, 22, 36–39, 76–77, 79, 118, 123, 125–26, 128, 169, 190–91, 226
Paris, 175, 206–7, 213
Pentagon, 179, 183
PFLP (Popular Front for the Liberation of Palestine), 18, 77, 109
PHW (Polizei-Hauptwachtmeister), 147
PLO (Palestine Liberation Organization), 128
Poland, 9
Polizeihauptinspektor, 32
Polizeihauptkommissar, 32
Polizeivollzugsbeamter (PVB), 57
Pompidou, President Georges, 22
Ponto, Jürgen, 85, 87–89, 91, 97–98, 99, 107
Potsdam, 34, 227–31
POW (prisoner of war), 34, 88
Pries, Sebastian, 200
prison, 5–6, 19, 34–35, 51, 74, 88, 93–98, 105, 109, 112–13, 115–16, 118, 128, 130–32, 140, 143–44, 148, 162, 167, 169, 174–75, 197, 205
Probstmeier, Jörg, 17, 70, 119, 137, 141–42, 155, 164, 178
PVB (*Polizeivollzugsbeamter*), 57

racism, 53
RAF (Rote Armee Fraktion), 5–6, 19–20, 74, 79, 85, 87–89, 93–98, 99–109, 111–13, 118, 125, 128, 144, 166, 169, 174–75, 177, 197
Rangers, 21, 23, 36, 64, 122–23, 130, 240
Rammelmayr, Georg, 50, 82
Raspe, Jan-Carl, 19, 109, 162, 174
Red Cross, 118–19
Reichsprogromnacht, 37
Reichswehr, 33
Revolutionäre Zellen (RZ), 79, 89, 93
Rhine, x, 27, 51, 67, 74, 81–85, 104, 105, 220
Rhineland-Palatinate, 81
Rogers, General Bernard, 180
Romania, 190

Rome, 77, 109, 111, 113, 131, 139
Rostock, 226–27, 230–31
Roter Morgen, 71
Ruhnau, State Secretary Heinz, 129, 150
Russia, 3, 34, 40, 54, 78, 83, 221, 228–31

SA (*Sturmabteilung*), 90
Saint Augustin, ix, x, xii, 28, 30, 43–44, 46, 57–58, 63, 65, 73, 75, 78, 83, 85, 100, 102, 110, 118, 120–21, 135, 159, 161, 166, 178–80, 186, 188–91, 197, 209, 214
Sajeret Matkal, 9–10, 36, 38–40, 175
Salameh, Ali Hassan (aka Abu Hassan), 19
Salewski, Wolfgang, 59, 131–32, 140, 143
SAS (Special Air Service, British Royal Army), 36, 120–22, 126, 146, 153–55, 158, 175, 179–80, 182, 189, 205, 212
Saudi Arabia, 127, 191–93
SBS (Special Boat Service, British Royal Navy), 122, 212
Scheel, Foreign Minister Walter, 4, 167, 171
Schleswig-Holstein, 51, 81
Schleyer, Hanns-Eberhard, 106, 111, 162, 167
Schleyer, Hanns Martin, 3, 6, 85, 87–88, 91, 96, 98, 99–113, 119, 151, 162, 165–67, 170, 174
Schleyer, Jörg, 3, 6, 87–88, 98, 106, 112, 162, 167
Schleyer, Waltrude, 3, 98
Schmidt, Chancellor Helmut, 95–98, 100, 117–18, 120–25, 129, 132–33, 139, 150–51, 167, 169, 171–72, 174, 177, 185–86, 230
Schnitzler, Karl-Eduard von, 166
Scholz, People, 138, 146, 152
Schreiber, Police Chief Manfred, 2, 4, 7, 11
Schröder, Federal Minister of the Interior Gerhard, 90
Schumann, Captain Jürgen, 109, 124–25, 127–28, 131, 137, 171
Schupo (*Schutzpolizist*), 49
SDS (Sozialistischer Deutscher Studentenbund), 91
SEAL Team-6 (US Navy), 183, 212–13
secret service, 34, 41, 76, 93, 225–26
SED (Sozialistische Einheitspartei Deutschlands), 34, 227, 230
SEK (*Spezialeinsatzkommando*), xviii, 82–84, 197, 204–5, 219, 231

Shah of Iran, 89–90
Siebengebirge, x, 65
Siegfried Line, 103
Singapore Armed Forces Anti-Terror Team (SAF-ATT), 193
Six-Day War, 9, 77
skyjacking, 41, 76–78, 111–13, 118, 126, 173, 175. *See also* hijacker
sniper, 9, 12–15, 17, 28, 48, 50, 64–65, 68, 72, 74, 82, 136, 141, 149, 155–56, 189, 214, 229
Soccer World Cup, 74, 76, 166
Social Democrats (SPD), 22, 90
SOKO (*Sonderkommission*), 103–5
Somalia, 10, 109, 128–29, 136, 165, 179, 185–88, 193
Somali Rangers, 130
Soviet Union, 3, 127–28, 183, 185–86. *See also* Russia
Special Intervention Unit, 11, 21, 24, 31, 36, 40, 45, 57, 61, 65, 75, 82–85, 169, 175, 183, 197, 206, 223, 225–26. *See also* GSG 9
Spiegel, Der, 18, 50, 81–82, 84, 174, 176
SS (*Schutzstaffel*), 53, 88, 91. *See also* Waffen-SS
Stammheim Prison, 94, 162, 169, 174
Stasi (Staatssicherheit), 34, 225, 228, 231
Stockholm, 74, 79, 89, 97, 104, 175
Strauß, CSU Franz-Josef, 4
Stuttgart, 65, 71, 74, 87, 98, 166
suicide, 13, 55, 161–62, 170, 174, 203
SWAT (Special Weapons and Tactics), 36, 63, 189
Sweden, 46. *See also* Stockholm
Switzerland, 25, 63, 75, 103, 188

Tauchel, Ulrich, 226, 230–31
Tel Aviv, 9–10, 19, 38, 133
television (TV), 3, 5–6, 9–11, 14, 43, 70, 98, 116, 118, 133, 145, 158, 161, 163, 171, 176, 227
Third Reich, 7, 17, 33, 37, 53, 88–89, 91, 177. *See also* Nazi
Tophoven, Rolf, 169, 171, 175, 219
"Toy Train," 25–26
Tröger, Mayor of Olympic village Walter, 4
Turkey, 115–16, 146, 192. *See also* Ankara
Tutter, Lieutenant Dieter, 1–2, 5, 11, 13, 15, 29–30, 44–49, 55, 58–59, 63, 66–70, 80, 83, 85, 110, 118–21, 159–61, 165, 169, 178, 192

Uganda, 38, 79
Uni-Center, 107–8, 110, 116, 127
United Arab Emirates (UAE), 118, 120–21, 123
United States, 3, 20, 25, 36, 174, 176, 190, 192, 205–6, 212, 223
USSR. *See* Soviet Union

Vietnam War, 73, 89
Vietor, Jürgen, 126, 128, 144, 147–49, 151, 156
Vogel, Minister of Justice Hans-Jochen, 4, 75, 100
Volkspolizei, 34, 227–28
Volkswagen, 47–48
von Lutzau, Rüdiger, 131
VS-NfD (Verschlusssache—nur für den Dienstgebrauch), 43

Warsaw Pact, 9
weaponry, xi, 13, 48, 179, 201. *See also* Heckler & Koch, SWAT
bazooka, 32
grenade, 4, 7, 11, 15, 32, 39, 111, 120–21, 146–48, 151, 153, 155–56, 173, 239
grenade launcher, 11, 32
HK P7, 180–81
IED (Improvised Explosive Device), 76, 195, 202
Kalashnikov, 14, 39, 53, 135, 203, 227, 229, 231
M3, "grease gun," 181
machine gun, 2, 8, 11, 13, 22, 32, 48, 50, 70–71, 74, 100, 105, 107, 111, 180–81, 188, 207, 229
Magnum revolver, 48, 172, 189
Makarov pistol, 148
MP (*Maschinenpistole*/submachine gun), 102, 181
pistol, x, 13, 48, 84, 148, 162, 181, 187, 189, 196, 203, 229
stun grenade, 120–21, 146, 153
tear gas, 231
TNT, 132, 151
Weber, Günter, 60–61
Wegener, Commander Ulrich, 2, 4, 7–16, 21–30, 31–43, 45–48, 51–55, 57–60, 62,

69–70, 77–79, 81, 83, 85, 91, 99–101, 104–11, 115–17, 120–23, 125–30, 132, 134–37, 144–51, 153–58, 160, 162–66, 169–82, 188–93, 195, 197–98, 207, 210, 217–18, 225–28
Wegener, Simone, 160
Wegener, Susanne, 160, 163, 166
Wehrmacht, 33, 35, 52–54
Western Alliance, 33
West German Foreign Intelligence Service. *See* BND (Bundesnachrichtendienst)
West Germany, 1–2, 18–19, 23, 26, 29, 32–33, 35, 70, 87–88, 94, 97, 127, 171, 176, 183, 187, 193, 215, 229–30
Weygold, Anselm, 161, 186
Weygold, Gisela, 161, 164
Weygold, Lemmy, 164

Wiesbaden, 26, 100
Wischnewski, Minister of State Hans-Jürgen, 100, 109, 112, 117–18, 120–34, 136, 138–40, 149–52, 162–63, 172, 186–87
World War I, 52, 55, 198
World War II, xii, 1, 11, 20, 36, 53–54, 62, 88, 91, 103, 176, 181
World Youth Games, 227

YAMAM, 41, 175, 210–11
Yemen, 97, 109, 113, 118, 125–27

Zagreb, 22, 37, 39
ZAHAL, 37. *See also* IDF (Israeli Defence Force)
Zamir, Intelligence Chief Zvi, 10, 13–14, 37
Zimmermann, Federal Minister of the Interior Friedrich, 193